THE CULTIVATED ORANGES AND LEMONS OF INDIA AND CEYLON

THE CULTIVATED ORANGES AND LEMONS OF INDIA AND CEYLON

ATLAS OF PLATES, WITH DESCRIPTIVE LETTER-PRESS

BY

E. BONAVIA, M.D.
BRIG. SURG. I.M.S.

GYAN

Published by

Gyan Publishing House
5, Ansari Road
Daryaganj, New Delhi-110002
Phone: 011-47034999, 9811692060
E-mail: books@gyanbooks.com

Distribution Network
gyanbooks.com
India, USA, Canada, UK, Australia, France

ISBN : 978-81-212-2257-0 (HB)

First Published, 1890

2nd Impression 2021

Printed at: Gyan Press, Delhi.

The Cultivated
Oranges and Lemons of India and Ceylon
Author: E. Bonavia

THE CULTIVATED

ORANGES AND LEMONS

OF

INDIA AND CEYLON.

ATLAS OF PLATES, WITH DESCRIPTIVE LETTER-PRESS.

BY

E. BONAVIA, M.D.

BRIG. SURG. I.M.S.

LONDON:

W. H. ALLEN & CO., 13 WATERLOO PLACE, PALL MALL. S.W.

1890.

CONTENTS.

1. Seville Group ... ... *From* PLATE I. *to* XVIII.
2. "Khatta" Orange Group ... ... ,, ,, XIX. ,, XXXIX.
3. Portugal or Malta Orange Group ... ... ,, ,, XL. ,, LVIII.
4. "Amilbêd" and Pummelo Group ... ... ,, ,, LIX. ,, XCII.
5. "Sŭntara" Orange Group ... ... ,, ,, XCIII. ,, CXVIa.
6. Mandarin and "Keonla" Group ... ... ,, ,, CXVII. ,, CXXVIII.
7. Jamíri Group ... ... ,, ,, CXXIX. ,, CXXXVIII.
8. "Turunj," "Madkankur," and "Bajoura" Group ... ... ,, ,, CXXXIX. ,, CLXXVII.
9. Lemons and Pummelo-Lemons Group ... ... ,, ,, CLXXVIII. ,, CCXXIV.
10. True Limes and "Lima" Group ... ... ,, ,, CCXXV. ,, CCXXXIII.
11. Miscellaneous Drawings ... ... ,, ,, CCXXXIV. ,, CCLIX.

PLATE I.

a and *b* are the Aurantium acidum, copied from Rumphius's Flora Amboyn. (Table 33, Vol. II.)

Miquel considers this Aurantium acidum of Rumphius identical with Citrus vulgaris of Risso. In my opinion it is a Séville orange.

c and *d* are the bitter orange of Hagkala, Ceylon. The surface was of a deep orange, foveolate and polished. The colour was vivid, approaching lobster red. It had a flattened mammilla round the apex, where there was a *soupçon* of roughness.

The pulp was orange, and the juice abundant; sour, and slightly bitter. The oil-glands of the rind small, centre solid; seeds white, when cut.

I consider this a Séville orange. The leaves were like those of other Sévilles, lanceolate with winged petiole, and distinctly aromatic.

ERRATA.

Plate 116A (explanation) third line.—For *a* read *c*, and for *c* read *a*.

Plate 209.—First Figure on the left is *a*, and *c* requires letter A near the dots.

Plate 129 (explanation) first line.—For "ventricose" read "verrucose."

Plate 234 (explanation) sixth line.—For "No. 53," read "No. 54."

NOTE.—The scale of inches in the Plates, mentioned in the Preface, has been omitted because the fruits have the sizes given in inches, although they are reduced from the natural size.

PLATE I.

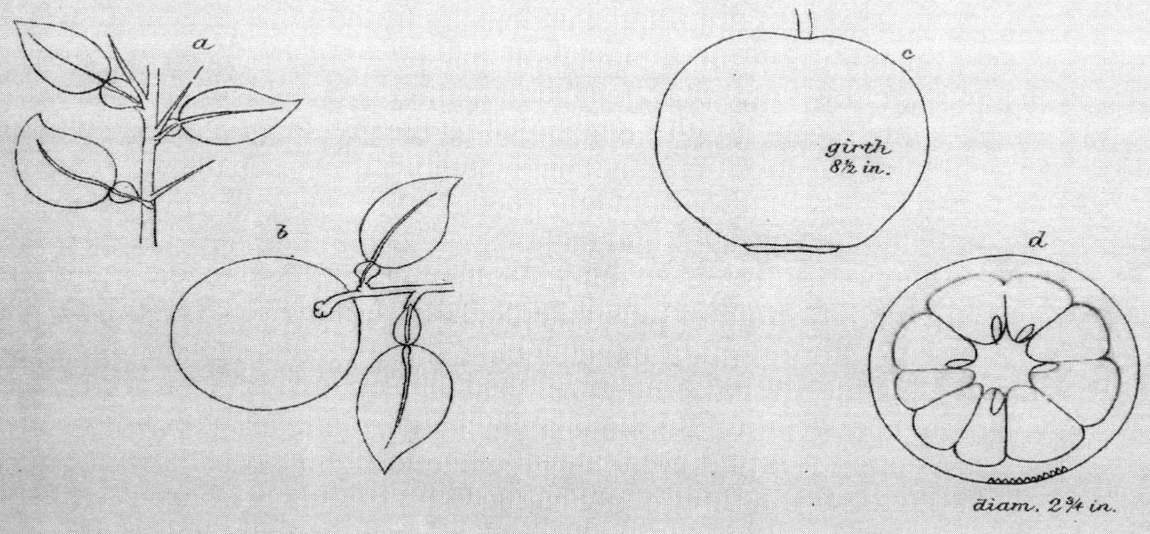

PLATE II.

The "Keep" of Nepal.

a and *b* show an unripe fruit of this Nepal citrus. I omitted to take full notes of this specimen, but if I remember rightly the juice was sour.

c is a rain leaf.

d and *e* spring leaves. All have the character of Séville orange leaves; but as I have not full notes, this citrus must be left as doubtful, with regard to its position in the citrus family.

PLATE II.

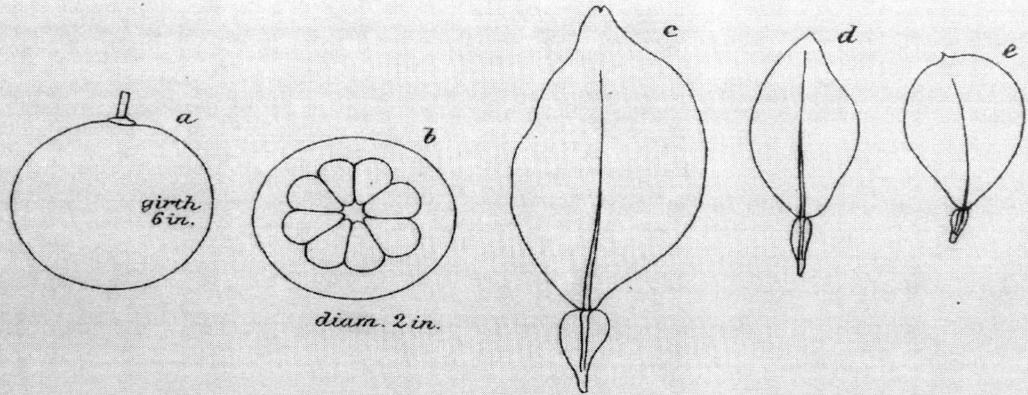

PLATE III.

A Séville Orange, which was received from Calcutta, under the name of "Gorá Lemboo."

a and *b* show the unripe fruit. The surface is chagrined with closely-set foveoli. It is not smooth; but nothing so rough as some other Sévilles. The oil-cells of the rind are of three sizes. The rind is very bitter and pungent, the pulp is pale, but with only an orange *tinge* (because unripe?), juice abundant and sour.

c and *d* are rain leaves; the former, at the point, has an outline of the mamilla of an ordinary lemon. This, however, may mean nothing.

e is a spring leaf. All the leaves are tough, like those of the Pummelo, and with a distinct Séville aroma. Their oil-cells are distinct, and of three sizes. I think it undoubtedly a *Séville* orange.

NOTE.—The vernacular name with which this came is probably wrong. Voigt's list of Calcutta citrus puts "Gora néboo," as one of the *limes* (see Appendix, No. 55).

PLATE III.

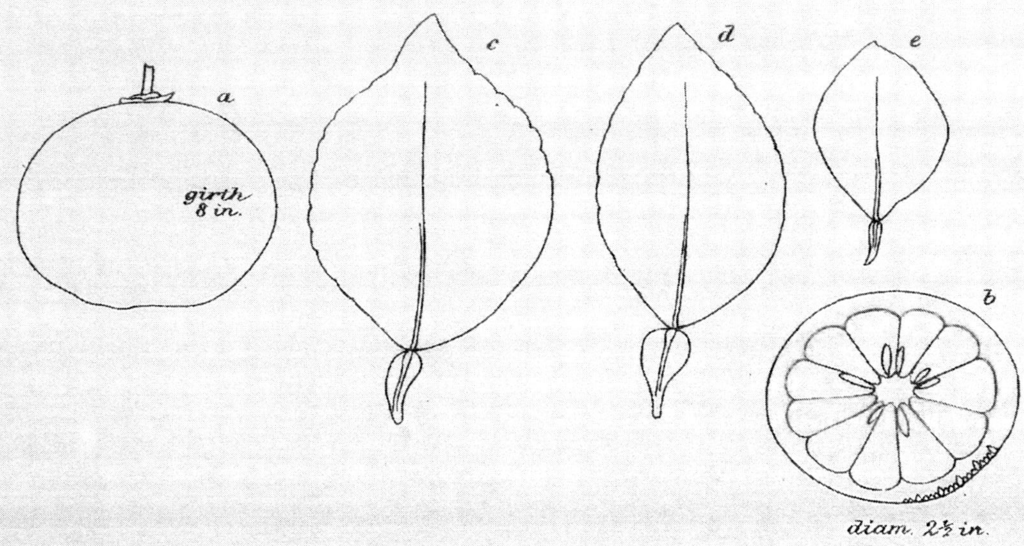

PLATE IV.

Séville orange, which came from Mooltan under the name of "Khattá" orange.

a and *b* show an outline and section of this orange. The surface was slightly chagrined, and covered with foveoli, which appeared like microscopic craters, probably because this specimen was rather dry. This orange was not rougher than a "Súntara" orange. The rind cells were distinct; the pulp pale orange, and the juice pleasantly sour.

c and *d* are rain leaves, and *e* and *f* probably spring leaves. All the leaves had a distinct Séville aroma, and the broad petiole wings point to the same Séville character. The leaf-blades were rather thin, like those of the "Khatta," and some leaves had narrow petiole wings, like those of the latter. Their oil-cells were of three sizes and distinct. I found no spines on the branches sent. The majority of the characters of this specimen were those of a *Séville*, and not of a "Khatta" orange.

PLATE IV.

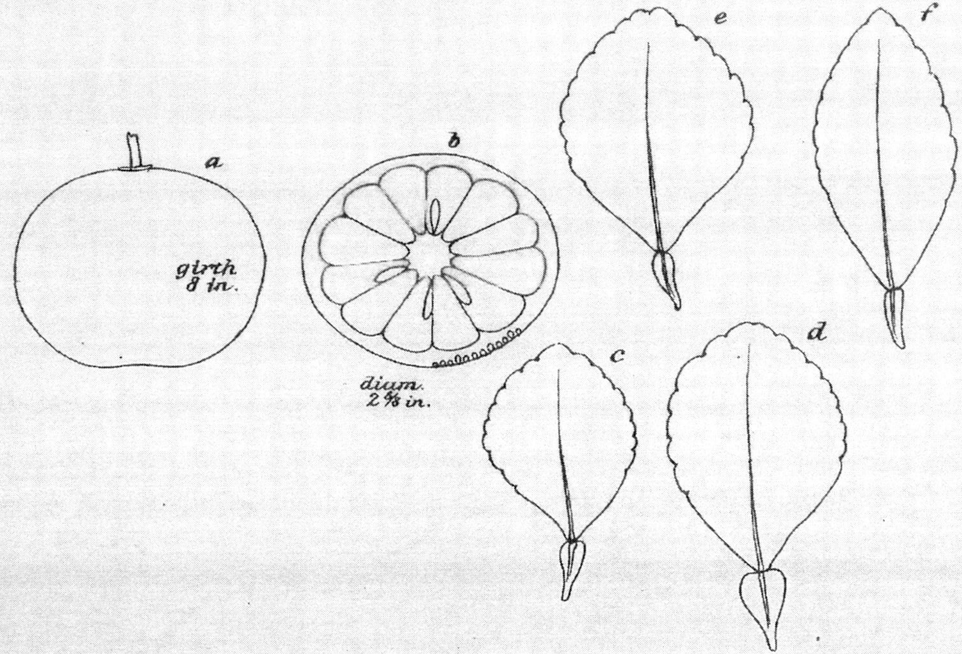

PLATE V.

The Lucknow Séville Orange, the *Nâranj* of the Lucknow *nurserymen.*

a and *b* are the outline and section of the *náranj* of Lucknow. The exterior is dark orange, quite smooth and *polished.* It resembles a cooking apple, or small musk melon. The pulp-vesicles are coarse, and of an orange-yellow colour. The juice is sour and bitter (?); the rind very aromatic and distinctly bitter. Possibly, I may have carelessly tasted the pulp, and may have got some of the *rind* bitter into my mouth, which may have become mixed up with the juice.

c and *d* are rain leaves, and *c* and *f* spring leaves, all with the characteristic scent of the Sévilles. It is strange that of all the Sévilles I have seen in India, this Lucknow variety is the only one which has the native name of *Náranj*, the Arabic synonym which Risso gives to the Séville Orange.

PLATE V.

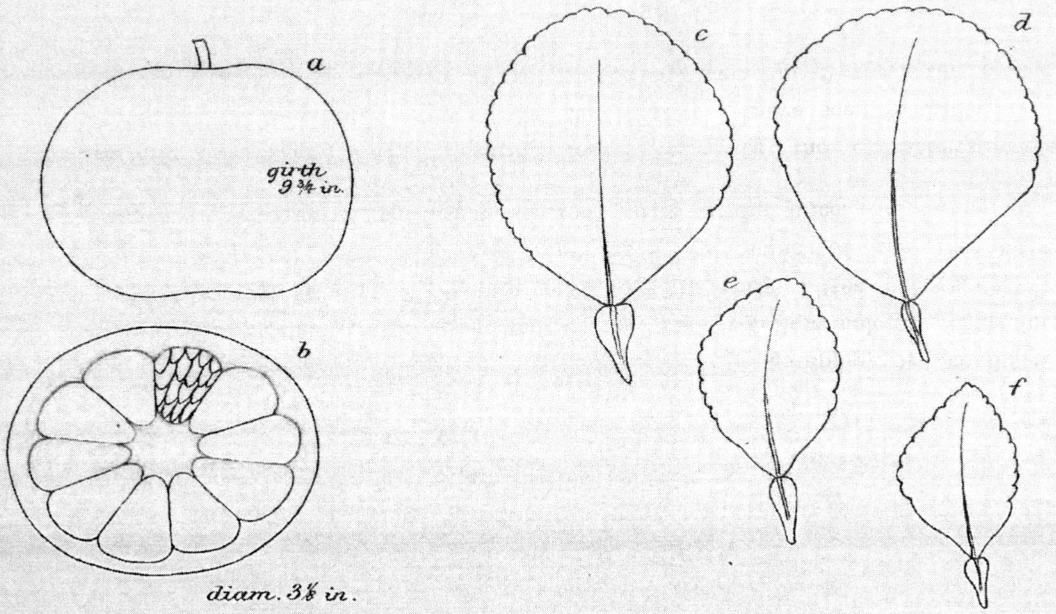

PLATE VI.

The Séville Orange of Kandy, and other parts of Ceylon, known there by the name of *Amool Dódan* (sour round orange).

a had a rather smooth surface, only pitted with shallow foveoli-cavities. Some other specimens were slightly warty in the apex half. The rind was aromatic and bitter.

b. The section shows in the rind curious pointed oil-cells, as if they were small juice vesicles. The pulp was pale orange, and the juice sour and slightly bitter.

c is a largely developed rain leaf.

d. A spring leaf; both had the characteristic aroma of the Sévilles, and had the leathery feel and polished surface of that variety.

NOTE.—In Ceylon I found enormous leaves of the citrus, which are probably due to the moisture and warmth of the climate.

PLATE VI.

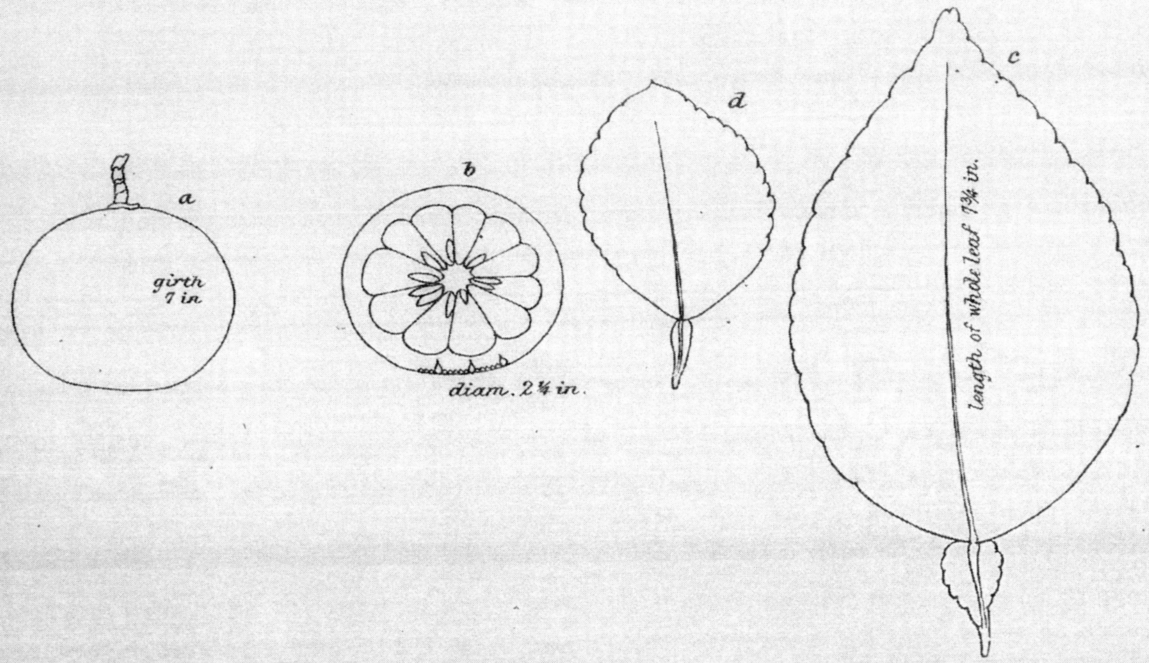

PLATE VII.

Other forms of the "*Amool Dódan*" of Ceylon.

a and *b* were of an orange colour, chagrined with numerous foveoli; slightly rough round the apex, and with an occasional wart round the base.

c is a decidedly lanceolate leaf, with fine serrations, and broad wings to its petiole. The rind of the fruit was aromatic, and the leaves had the distinct aroma of the Séville leaf.

d is the Séville orange of the English markets. Some have a rougher exterior. It is of a deep orange colour, closely and evenly foveolate all over, but otherwise this specimen was rather smooth; rind aromatic and very bitter, skin about a quarter of an inch thick; pulp acid, with only a *soupçon* of bitterness; seeds many. It is given for comparison.

PLATE VII.

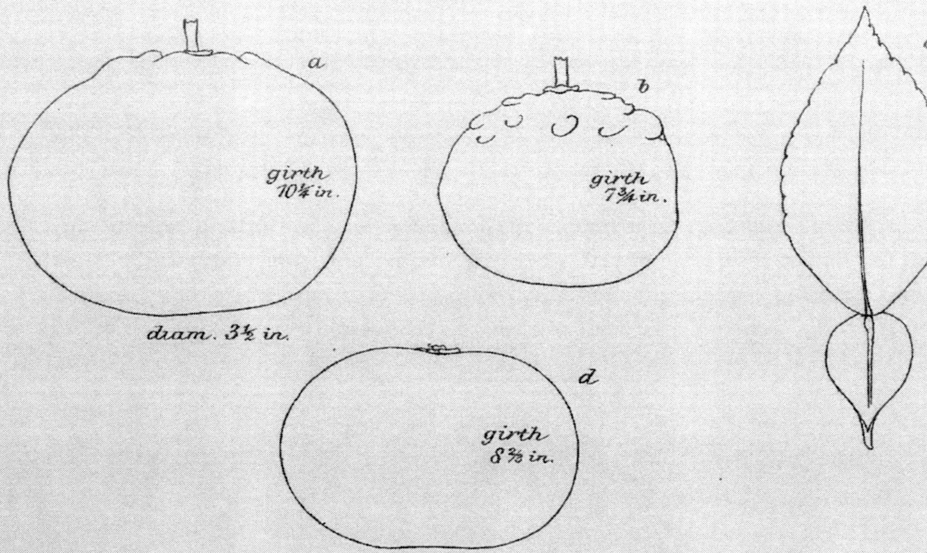

PLATE VIII.

a and *b* are copied from the monograph on the citrus by Risso and Poiteau, where it is called *Citrus bigaradia*; the "Bigaradier franc" of the French; the "Arancio forte" of the Italians, and the *nâranj* of the Arabs. The surface is minutely warty, like the Malta Séville of the Lucknow Horticultural Garden.

c and *d* are largely developed leaves taken from a young and spiny tree in Kandy. I did not see the fruit of this tree. The leaves resemble those of the Pummelo; the petiole wings, however, are not so large. They are leathery and polished, like those of a Séville tree, and their strong aromatic scent is also that of the Sévilles. The leaves are glabrous everywhere, excepting a few hairs on the unexpanded leaf-buds; a few of the leaves were round, and had only a margined petiole. They resemble Fig. *c* of Plate VI.

PLATE VIII.

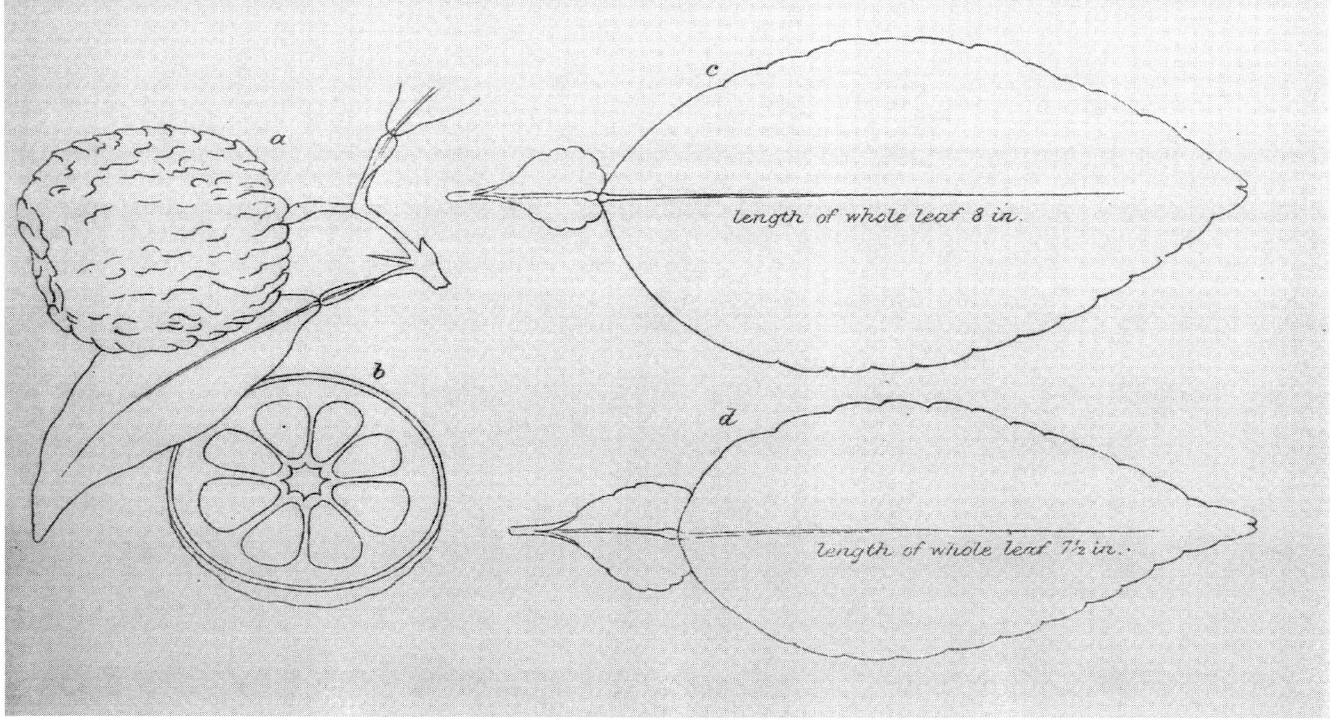

PLATE IX.

A Séville Orange from *Toolshipur*, Gonda, which was received under the name of *Jhambîri*!

a and *b*. Externally it was of an orange colour, rough, and slightly verrucose. The rind was very bitter and aromatic; the pulp pale orange and sour; the centre solid, and the seeds white, when cut.

c a rain leaf, and *d* a spring leaf; both tough and leathery, and sweet scented, like all Séville leaves.

NOTE.—For the true "Jhambiri" see Pl. CXXXI., and others.

PLATE IX.

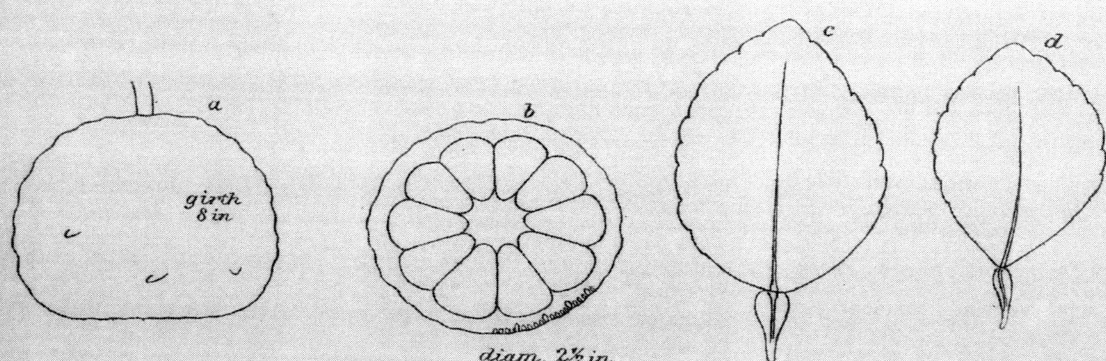

PLATE X.

A Séville Orange, which I obtained at Mangalore, under the name of *Kârna*, or *Kanchikái*. It is said to grow there, and also in Coorg and Mysore.

a and *b* were of an orange colour, rough and inclined to be warty round the apex. I was told these were small specimens, and that the fruit was often much larger; *b* was much smoother than *a*.

c is a section of *a*. The rind was very bitter; pulp pale orange, sour and slightly bitter, and many-seeded.

I did not see the leaves of this citrus; but I was told by a person who knows the *Kárna* of Mysore that it has a tough leaf, and is aromatic, with a large wing to its petiole.

PLATE X.

PLATE XI.

The Malta Séville Orange of the Lucknow Horticultural Garden, obtained from a bud of the stock on which an imported (in 1863) Malta orange-tree was grafted.

a. This specimen was unripe, of a *deep* green colour, having the outline of a round Malta orange, but chagrined and minutely warty all over, like the specimen taken from Risso (Plate VIII., Fig. *a*), or *Arancio forte* of the Italians.

b is a section of the same, with pale orange-yellow pulp, coarse vesicles, and sour juice with scarcely any bitter taste. The rind was very bitter, aromatic, and pungent; seeds numerous.

c and *d* are rain leaves, and *e*, *f*, *g*, and *h* spring leaves. All have the characteristic aromatic sweet scent of the Sévilles, which is a scent *sui generis*, and not found in other races of oranges. The Séville orange-tree is, in my opinion, recognizable by this scent alone. Mr. Ridley, in comparing the leaves of this and of the *nâranj* of the nursery-men, said he could see no difference between them, except that the *nâranj* had generally a less developed petiole wing.

PLATE XI.

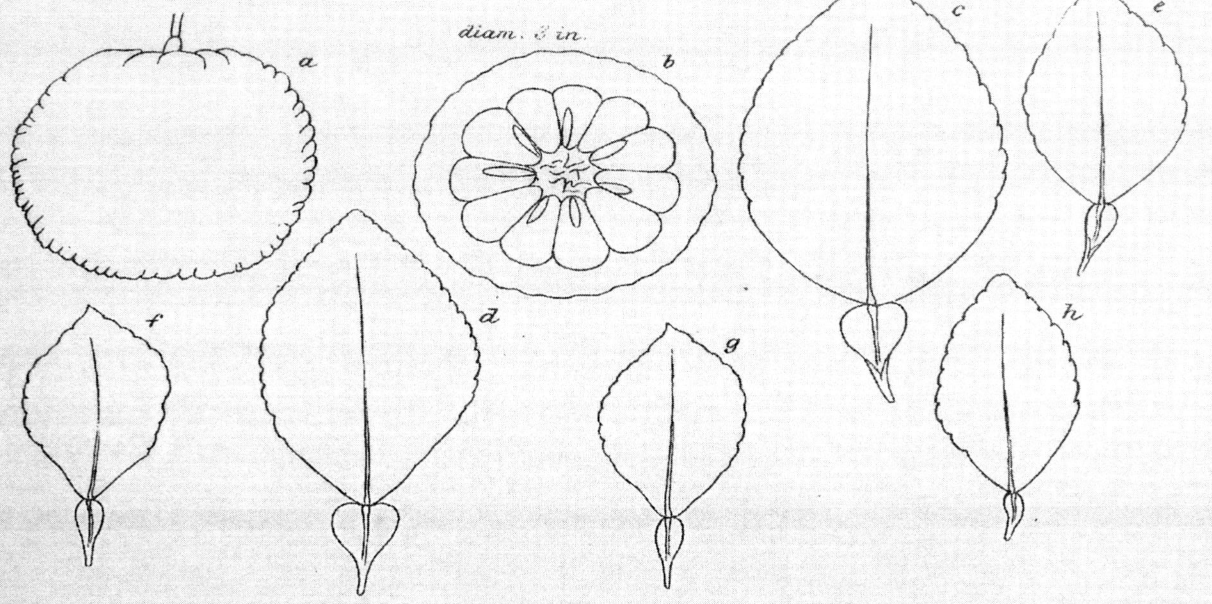

PLATE XII.

A large and ripe specimen of the Malta Séville Orange of the Lucknow Horticultural Garden.

a is sub-warty, rough, and of a deep orange colour, like that of the *Keonla* orange. It is closely foveolate all over.

b is the section of the same, showing the thick and very pithy skin. The rind is bitter, aromatic, and pungent, with a fine marmalade flavour. Some of these Sévilles have a rind so full of oil that simply *placing* one on paper stains it. The pulp is pale orange, and very sour, but not bitter; centre hollow.

c, *d*, and *e* are rain leaves, and *f*, *g*, and *h* spring leaves; *i* is the spine I found on the branch that came with the specimen. Some varieties of the Séville orange have hardly any spines, others have prominent ones.

NOTE.—Séville oranges have usually a large *solid* centre; this, however, had it hollow, with the central column isolated. (See Appendix, No. 62.)

PLATE XII.

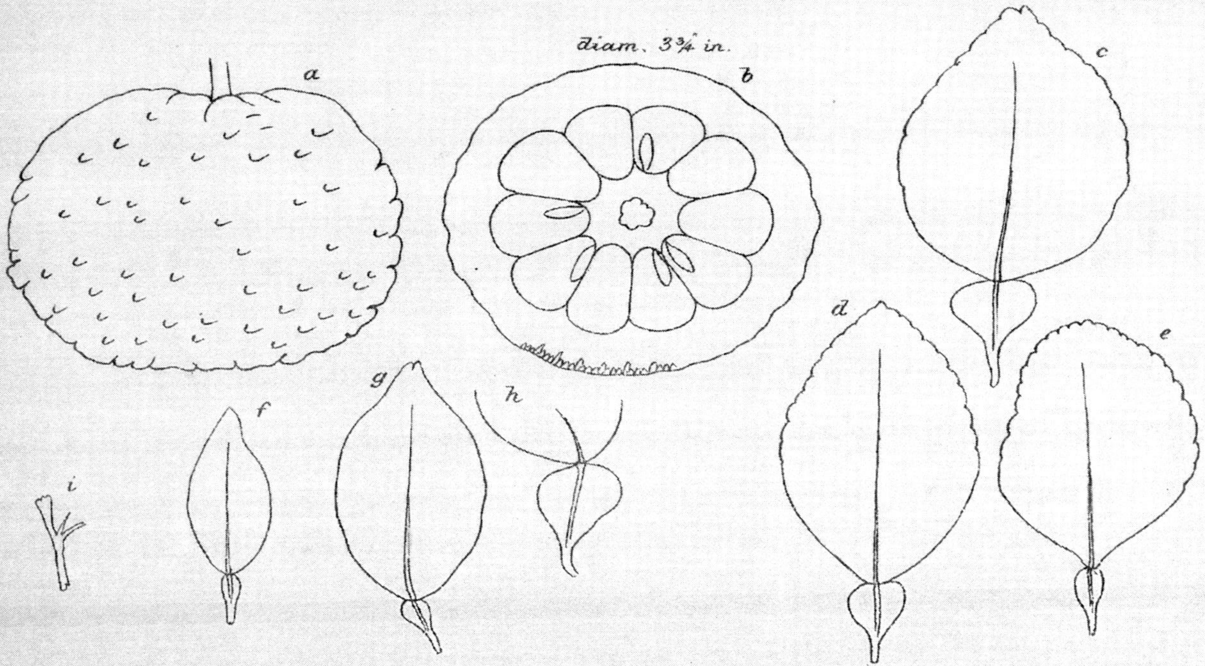

PLATE XIII.

A Séville Orange from Gonda, received under the name of *Sadâphal.* It is stated to flower and fruit there all the year round, and hence the name of "*Sadâphal.*"

a was of a pale orange; an unripe specimen was of a dark green, and more chagrined. It was slightly sub-warty round the apex, closely foveolate all over; rind bitter, aromatic, and pungent. Its skin was half an inch thick, with the pithy part sweetish. The bitter lies mainly in the *outer oily part.* Many of the Sévilles in India, if left too long on the tree, have their pulp dried up. Pulp of the unripe specimen was pale orange, and intensely sour, *not bitter;* some seeds were greenish, and others white, when cut.

b, a rain leaf, and *c* a spring leaf; both leathery and shiny, and with the usual sweet aroma of the Séville leaves.

Note.—For the true "*Sadâphal*" see Plate CCIX.

PLATE XIII.

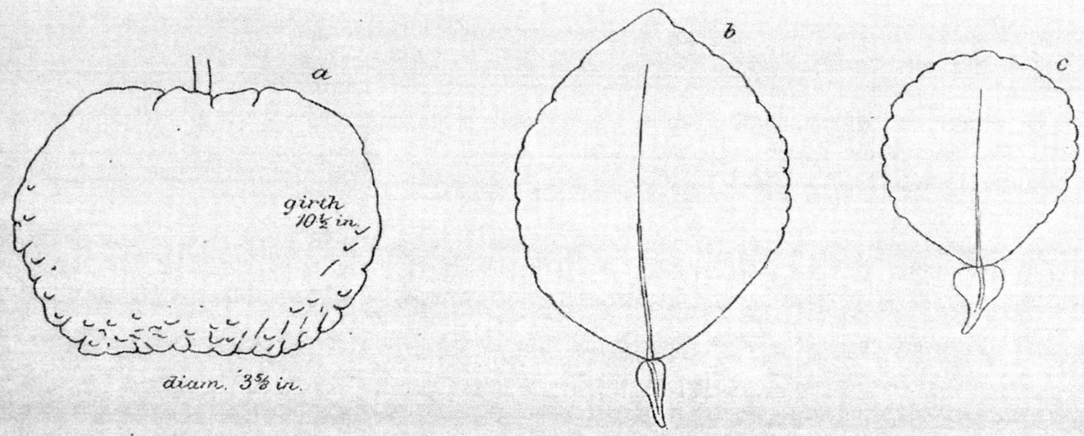

PLATE XIV.

A Séville orange from the Etawah Jail Garden. The origin of these Séville trees I have not been able to trace. I found them ticketed as *Punjab* Sévilles. I have called them Etawah Sévilles.

a. Orange colour, prominently chagrined all over.

b is a section of *a*; juice vesicles coarse, pale, and interspersed with orange yellow vesicles. An unripe specimen had pale orange pulp, and scanty juice, sour, and *slightly* bitter; the rind was very aromatic and oily. These Séville oranges, if left too long on the tree become quite juiceless.

c and *d* are well-developed rain leaves, with a highly polished surface. I have failed to find any spines on these Etawah Séville trees. The aroma of their leaves is *distinctly* that of other Sévilles.

PLATE XIV.

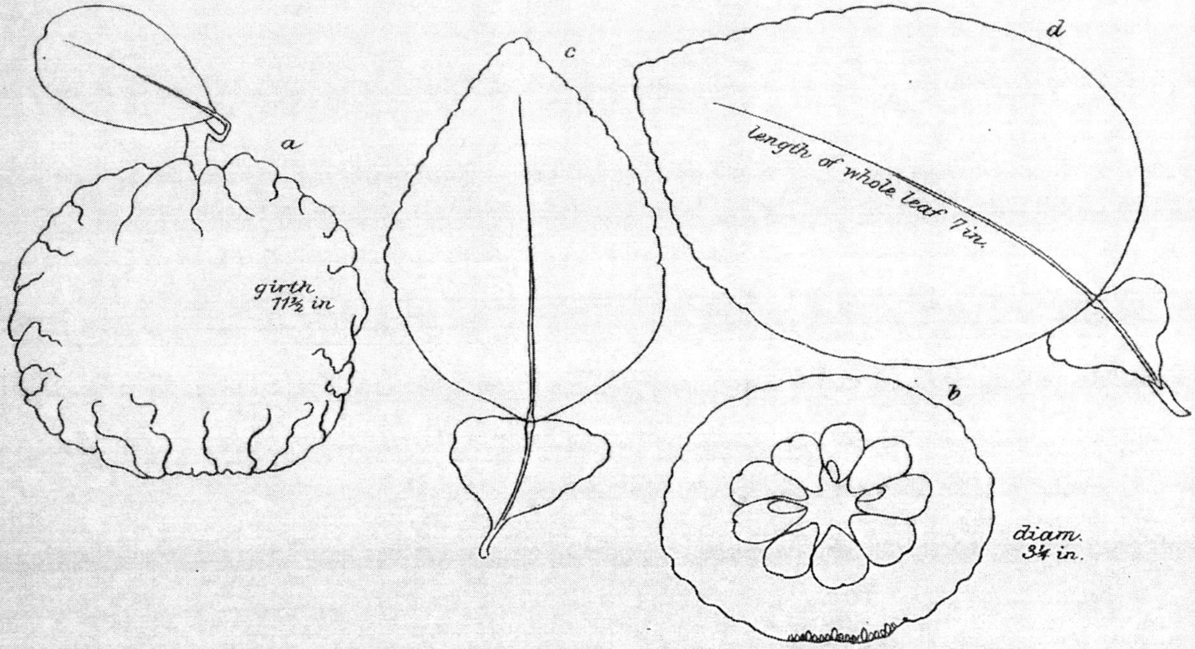

PLATE XV.

a is a *Dumrèz* form of Etawah Séville orange, more warty than those of the spring crop.

b, *c*, and *d* are leaves taken from the same tree; all broadly lanceolate, but one (*c*) has only a margined petiole.

e is another Séville orange of the English markets, given for comparison. It is of a *deep* orange colour, closely and evenly foveolate all over; but otherwise not very chagrined. Some specimens are slightly sub-warty; rind aromatic and very bitter; skin about a quarter of an inch thick; pulp acid, with only a *soupçon* of bitterness; many-seeded.

PLATE XV.

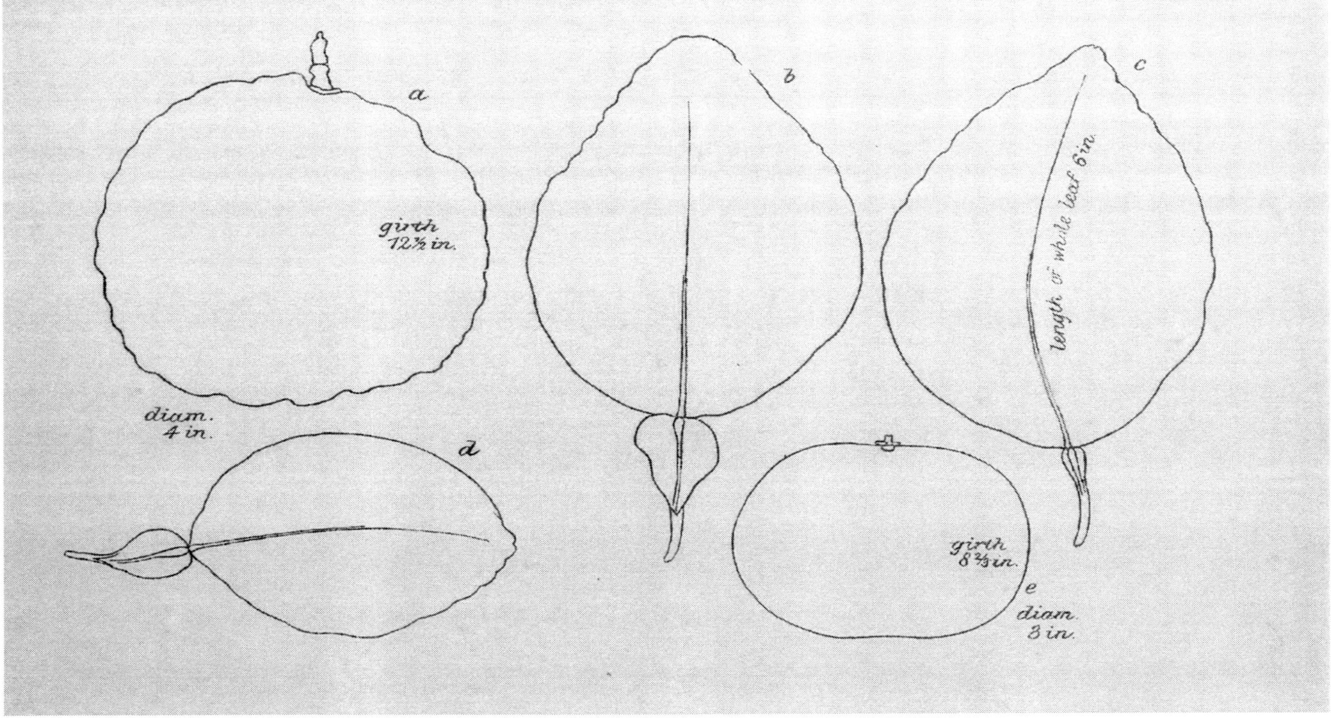

a
girth
12½ in.
diam.
4 in.
b
c
length of whole leaf 6 in.
d
girth
8⅔ in.
e
diam.
3 in.

PLATE XVI.

_a_, _b_, _c_, _d_, and _e_ are leaves taken from one and the same tree of the Etawah Séville orange. The well-developed leaf of this variety is either rounded, or broadly lanceolate. Some leaves have their petioles only margined; but the typical leaf has a broad-winged petiole.

_f_, _g_, _h_ are spring leaves, with margined petioles, and are not unlike those of the "_Súntara_" orange, except for their leatheriness and distinct Séville aroma.

PLATE XVI.

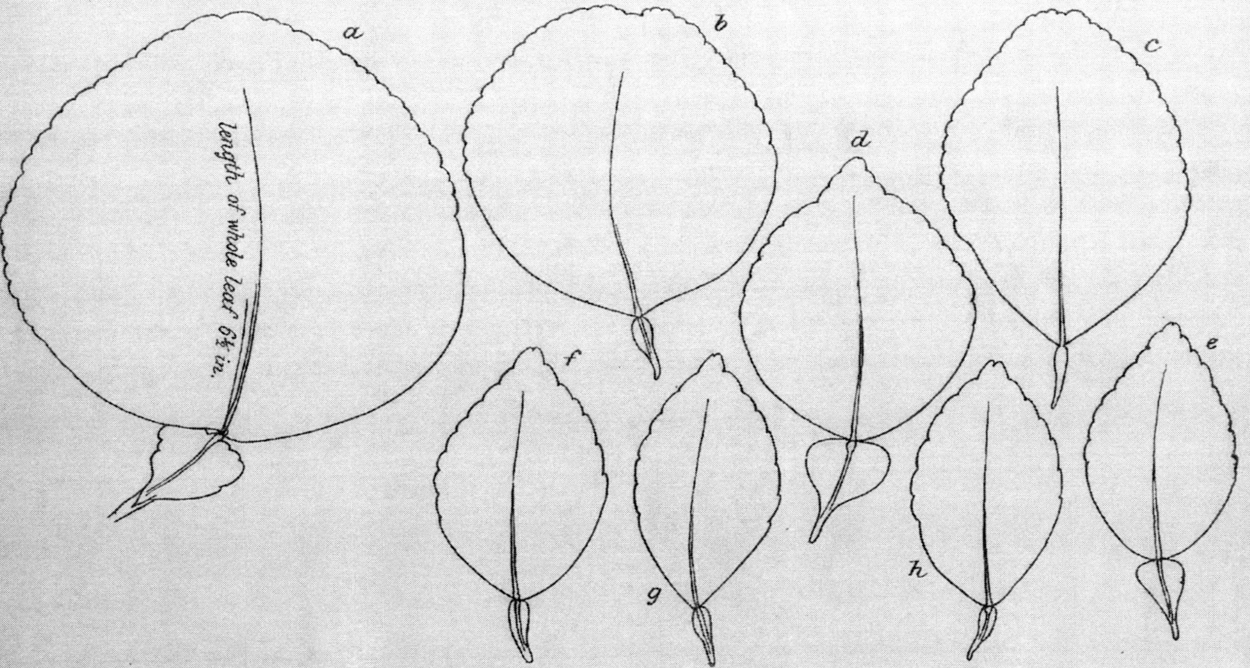

PLATE XVII.

These are citrus leaves sent to me by Mr. John Payne, from some forest near Devikulam, in South India. He says *a* and *b* were taken from a tree at the edge of the jungle, and therefore this particular tree, from seeing the light, was in a flourishing condition; while *c* and *d* were taken from trees in the middle of the jungle, and were therefore shaded by other trees, and less luxuriant. He said orange-trees of the thickness of a thick walking-stick were common in those jungles; they were growing in a wild state. All these leaves, although somewhat dry, had the characteristic scent of the *Séville orange leaf*, and their shape quite corresponds to that of the Ceylon Séville leaf. Dr. Trimen, in his *Systematic Catalogue of Plants Indigenous to or Growing Wild in Ceylon*, does not mention any kind of citrus.

PLATE XVII.

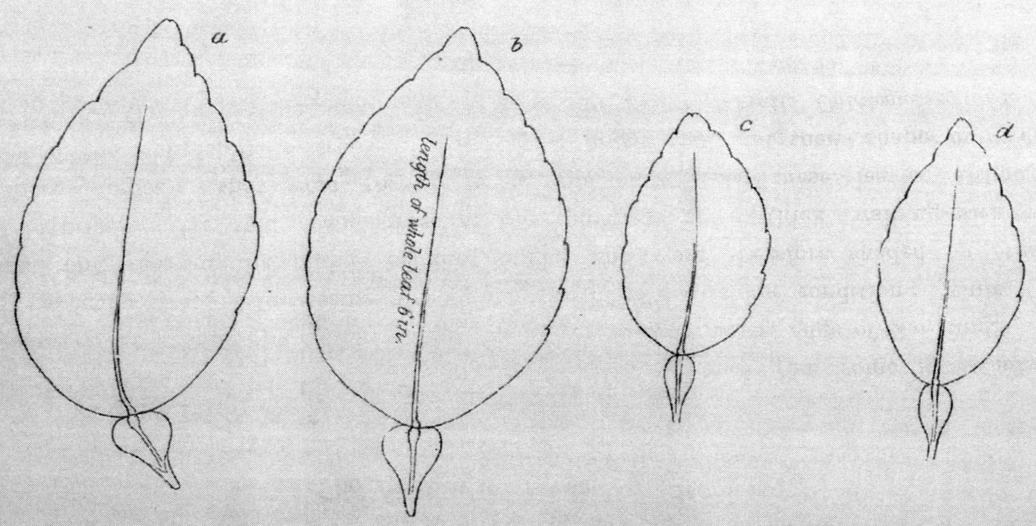

PLATE XVIII.

The "Nartun" of Tanjore.

a is a *Keonla* shaped orange, which I got in one of the Tanjore Gardens. They called it "Nartun." One man called it "Kamalà." Its shape is almost exactly that of the Poona *Keonla*. It is deep orange, foveolate, uneven, and warty round the apex. The latter is much depressed. The skin is thick, though rather loosely attached. The rind has the scent of *Laniana*; pulp pale orange-yellow; juice abundant, and of a pleasant sour taste, without any sweetness, although ripe (21 Dec.). Seeds are white when cut, though when young they are greenish.

b and *c* are its typical leaves, with large petiole wings.

d is an occasional leaf. The scent of the leaves is resinous and unpleasant, and their texture thick and leathery, like those of the Sévilles. (Col. Yule's *Glossary*, p. 490, says that in Tamul, *Narta marum* means the "wild orange tree.")

e and *f* is an oblate orange I bought in the Tanjore bazaar. They told me it was "Nartun." It was orange-yellow, and foveolate all over, otherwise it was fairly smooth; pulp pale orange and *sour*, with a hollow centre; vesicles coarse; skin thick, easily detached, but not loose; rind *very bitter*; pithy part spongy. As I did not see its leaves, I cannot say whether it was identical with *a* or not. I sowed the seeds of this "Nartun," and the leaves of the young seedlings gave the *distinctive* aroma of the Sévilles, so I have little doubt that it belongs to that group.

PLATE XVIII.

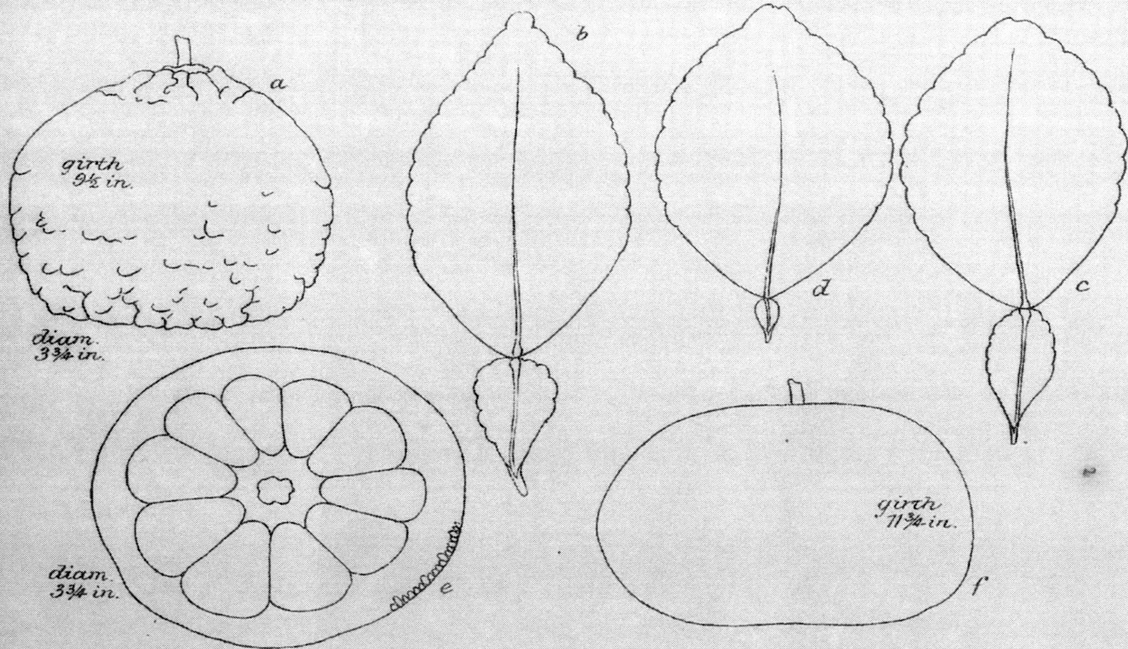

PLATE XIX.

Khatta orange from Jubbulpur (received under the name of *Attarra* lime).

a. Exterior not rougher than a Malta orange; although not very smooth it is not very rough. It is pitted with oil-glands. This specimen was unripe, and of a pale green.

b. The pulp is of a decided orange-yellow; juice abundant and very sour.

c, *d*, *e*, are rain-leaves.

f. Spring leaf.

g. The spine attached to the branch of the specimen.

NOTE.—For the Citrus called *Attarra*, see Plate CCX.

PLATE XIX.

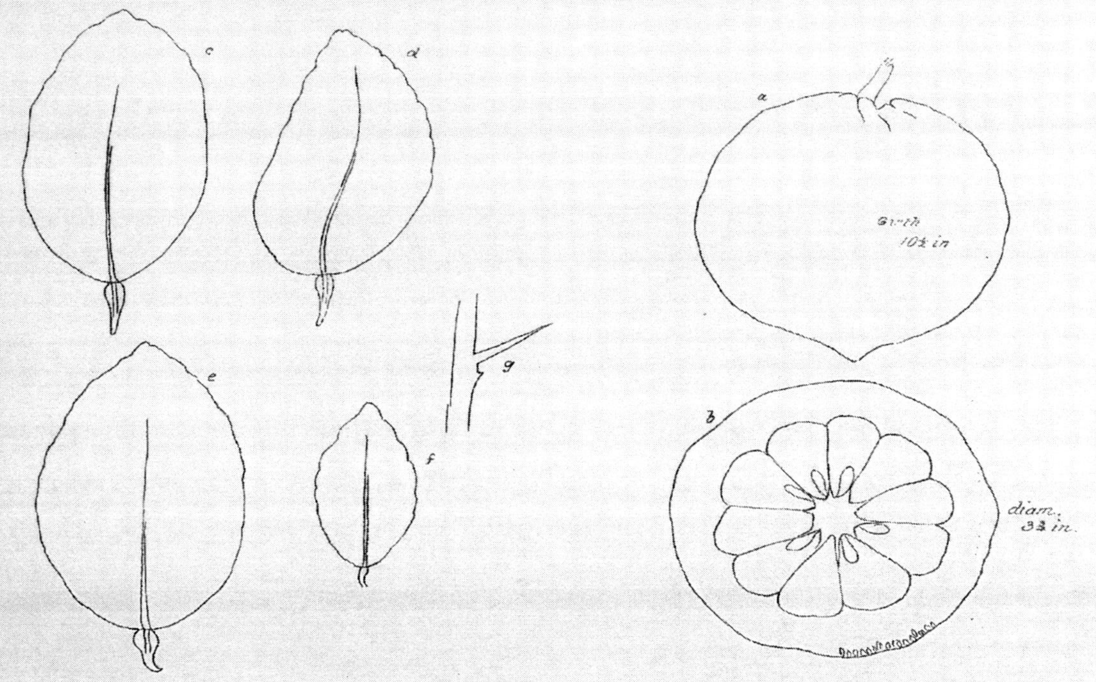

PLATE XX.

Khattá orange from Auraya, Etawah district.

a. Exterior smooth, though not polished, and foveolate with oil-glands. This specimen had no mammilla.

b. Pulp orange yellow with the taste of a very sour orange. The white or pithy part of the skin is very slightly sub-acid and spongy, like that of a pummelo.

c and *d* are rain-leaves.

e is a spring leaf.

f. A spine on the branch of the specimen.

PLATE XX.

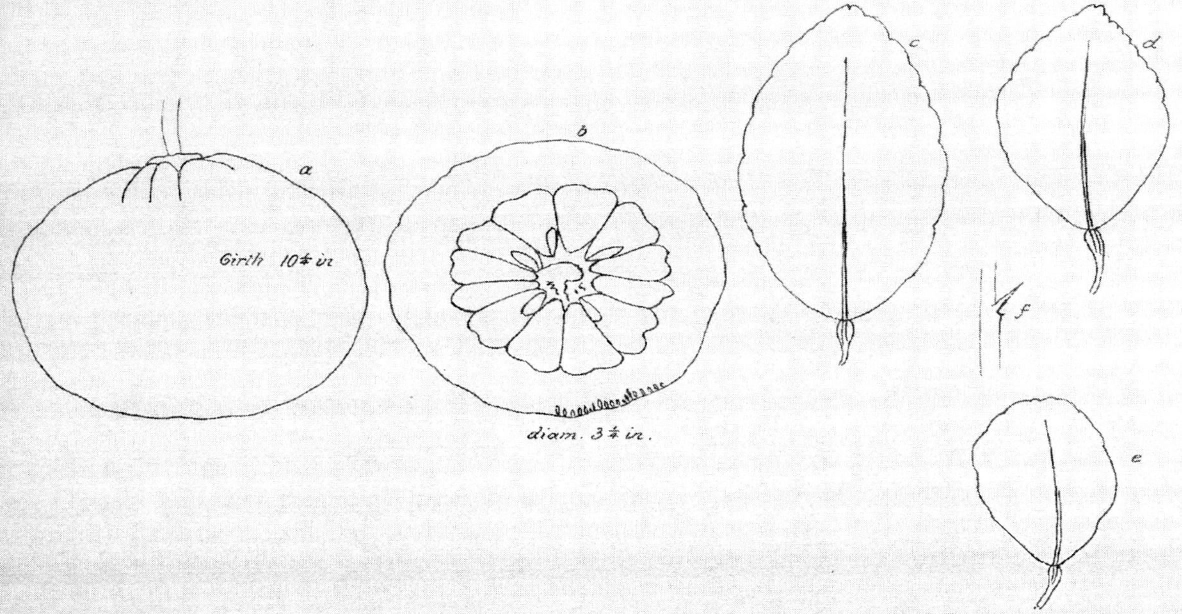

PLATE XXI.

Khattà orange from Messrs. Carew & Co.'s garden, Rosa, Shahjahanpur.

a. Exterior surface chagrined, soft and almost ripe. Between the larger foveoli are eminences covered with the smaller glands.

The section having nothing uncommon was not given. The pulp was pale orange, with abundant sour and *slightly* bitter taste. The skin was more than $\frac{1}{4}$ inch thick.

b is a rain leaf.

c and *d.* Spring leaves. The size of the leaves and the larger or smaller development of serrations or crenations is usually a matter of luxuriance, although some pummelos have hardly any.

e. It is a spine on the branch of the specimen.

PLATE XXI.

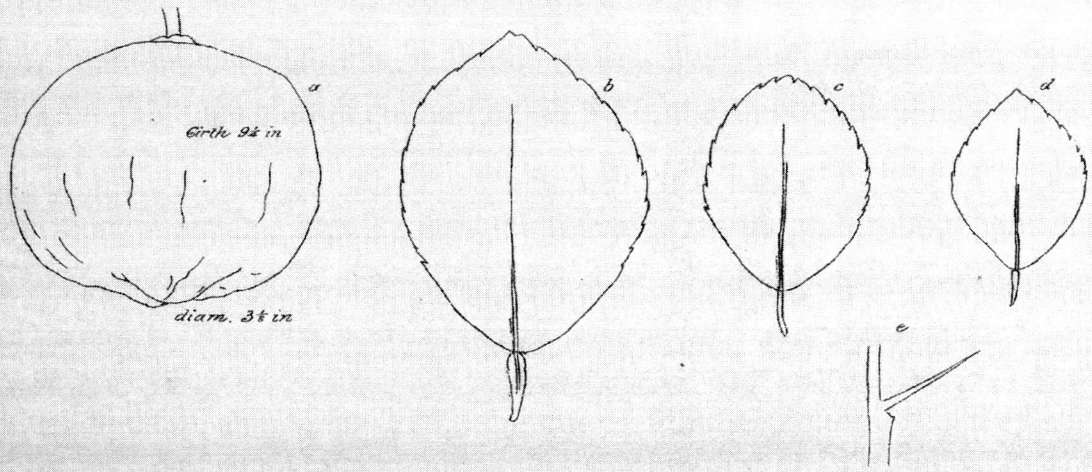

PLATE XXII.

Khattá orange from Calcutta (received under the name of *Sherbetee-lemboo*).

a is an unripe specimen, closely pitted with large and small foveoli. It is sub-warty and furrowed round the apex.

b. The oil-cells of the skin are of three sizes, and are bat-shaped. The pulp is pale orange and acid, with a *slightly* bitter juice.

c is a rain leaf.

d and *e.* Spring leaves.

f. A spine on the branch of the specimen.

Note.—No reliance can be placed on vernacular names for purposes of grouping. *Sherbetee nimboo* all over Upper India is given to the *mitha mimboo*, or sweet lemon.

PLATE XXII.

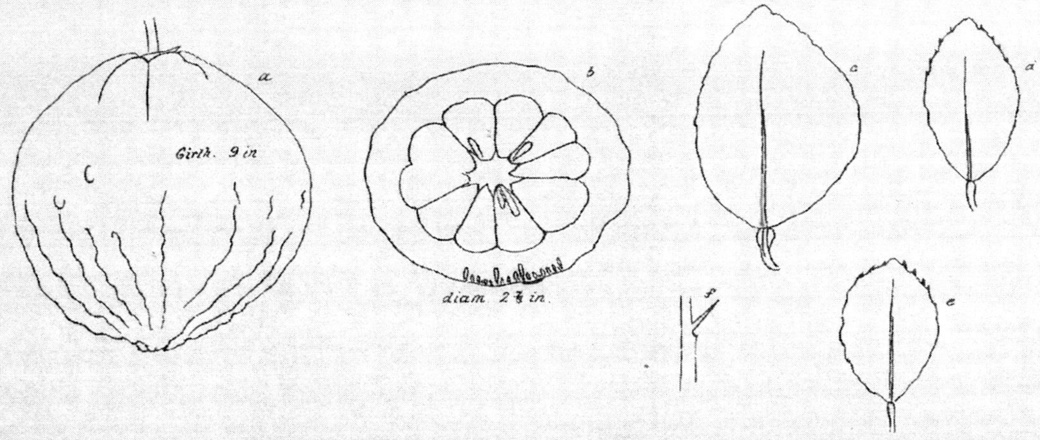

PLATE XXIII.

Khattá orange from Etawah. (Flowers purplish externally, axilliary, in twos and threes, with little scent.)

a. Ordinary form, with a pronounced mammilla. When ripe, of a rich maize-orange. Birds or other animals eat it, although sour. The exterior is rough and foveolate.

b. Pulp is of a pale orange-yellow, and, although sour, it has a flavour of orange (not lemon) pulp.

c. Exceptional, oblate form. Both forms are sometimes found on the same tree.

d. Well developed rain leaf.

e and *f.* Spring leaves.

g. Ordinary spine on the flowering branches.

PLATE XXIII.

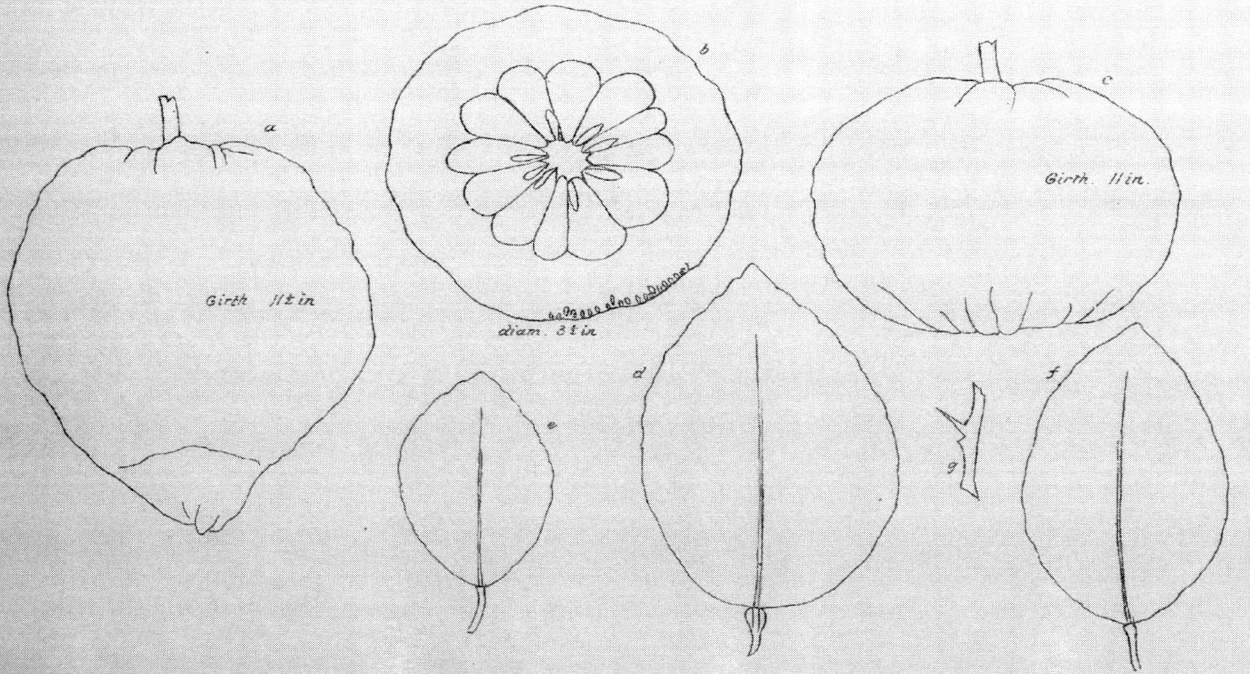

PLATE XXIV.

Leaves taken from a *Khattá* orange tree of Etawah.

a and *b*. Emarginate leaves.

c and *d*. Acuminate leaves.

e. Neither emarginate nor acuminate, with a rounded point. All are well-developed leaves.

f. Occasional spine met with on the *Khattá* orange tree.

PLATE XXIV.

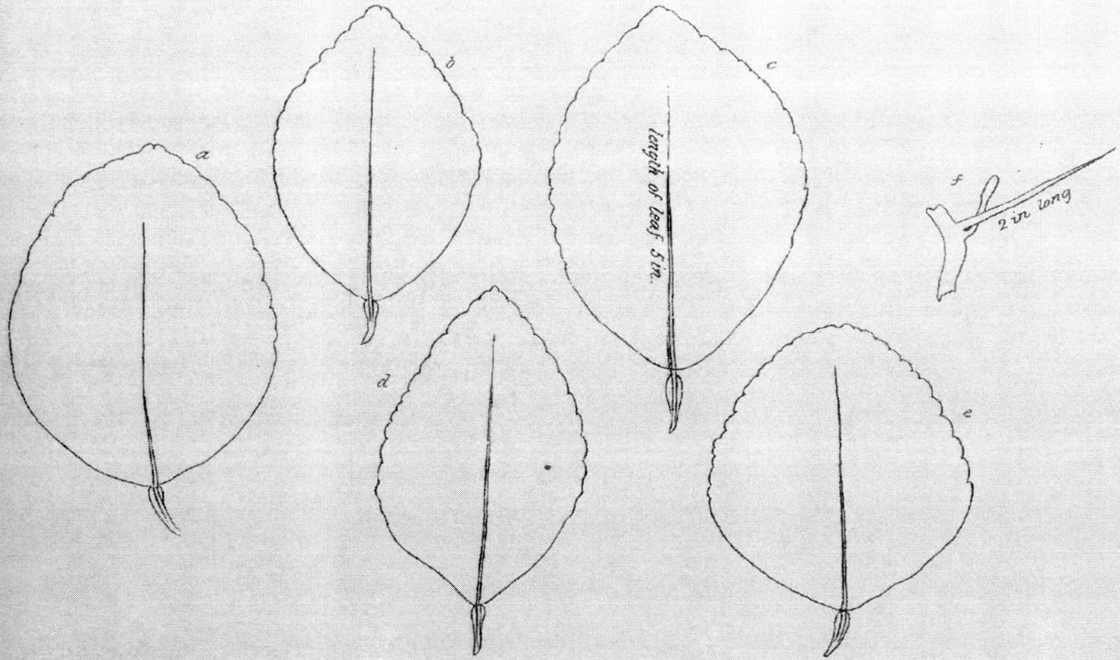

PLATE XXV.

Khattà oranges from Bholi, Etawah district (received under the name of *Kàrna*).

a. Form with flattened mammilla.

b. Form with prominent mammilla.

Both were hard and unripe (October). Externally they were not rough, but foveolate, with intermediate smaller oil-cells. The pulp of both was orange, with abundant sour and *slightly* bitter juice. Being unripe the skin was solid, and $\frac{1}{2}$ an inch thick. They had both large and small oil-cells in the rind, and the latter was not very aromatic. The sections having nothing uncommon are not given.

c. Ordinary spring leaf.

d. Very emarginate spring leaf.

Note.—This variety of citrus is sometimes called *Kàrna* (meaning bitter, according to Mr. Growse, B.C.S.), but more frequently *Khattà*.

PLATE XXV.

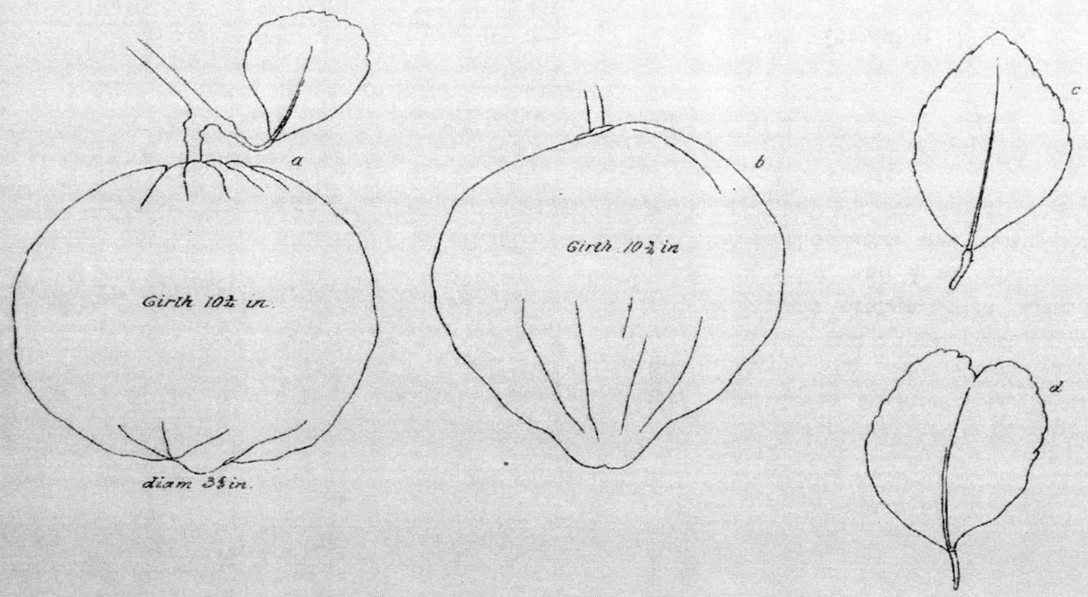

PLATE XXVI.

Khattà oranges from Saharanpur and Lucknow.

a. Came from Saharunpur, under the name of *Kàrna* lime. Its young unexpanded leaves were *pubescent*.

The exterior of the fruit was yellow-orange, rough, with large shallow foveoli. The skin was not easily detached. Pulp orange, juice abundant, and *only* sour; centre solid. Rind sweetish and aromatic, *not* bitter, and only slightly pungent. Pith sweetish and not spongy. Pulp carpels slightly emarginate in section.

From Bulrampur, Gonda, I received one much like this, under the name of *Kàrna nimboo*. It had a rougher and duller surface, and a hollow centre, and a paler orange pulp. Its girth was 14½ in., and its apex had a *slightly* projecting mammilla.

b is the same kind of orange from Lucknow. It is called there either *Khattà* or *Kàrna*. When ripe it is of a deep orange-yellow.

c and *d* are spring leaves of the Lucknow *Kàrna*. These leaves had only two sizes of oil-cells distinct. The third size was indistinct.

PLATE XXVI.

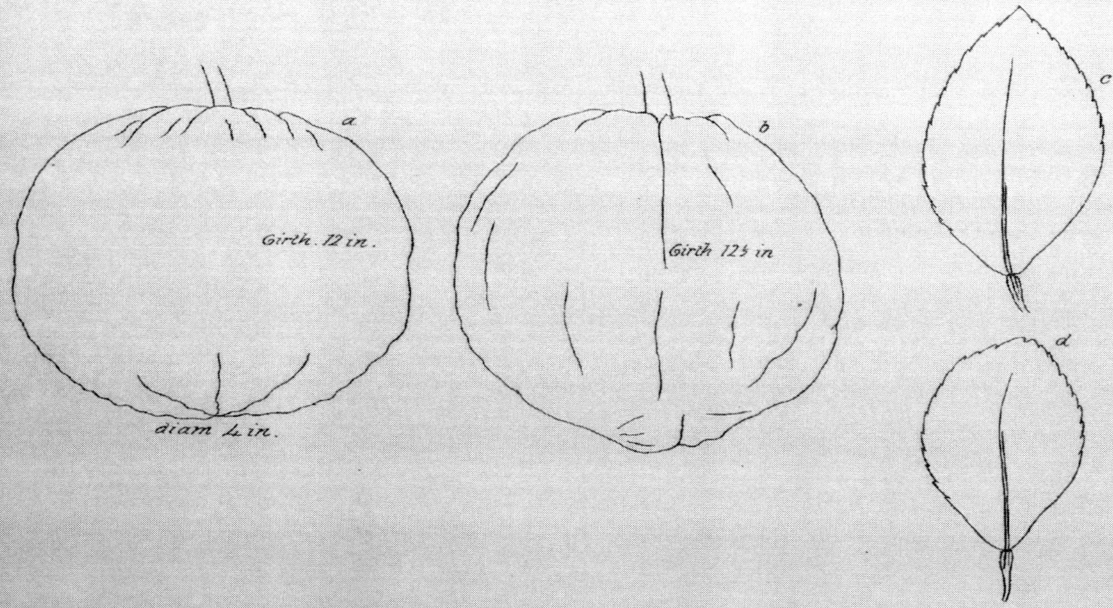

PLATE XXVII.

Two *Khattà* oranges, sent from Gonda by Major Buller; he stated they both came off the *same tree*.

a is the smooth form, of a maize-orange exterior, quite smooth, only foveolate. The pulp was pale orange, and the skin $\frac{1}{3}$ in. thick.

b is the warty form, with a maize-orange exterior. The front side was, as is shown, very warty; the hidden side was less warty; the mammilla at the apex was very prominent.

The pulp was pale orange, and the skin $\frac{3}{4}$ in. thick. The warts were covered with foveoli, as shown on the right side A.

Major Buller stated that had he not seen them both on the same tree he would not have believed it possible that both forms could have been borne by the same tree.

NOTE.—Can these two forms on one tree, dependent, as I think, on *difference of season*, throw any light on the origin of *Bizzaria*, and so called *trifacial* oranges? (*Vide* Appendix, No. 65.)

PLATE XXVII.

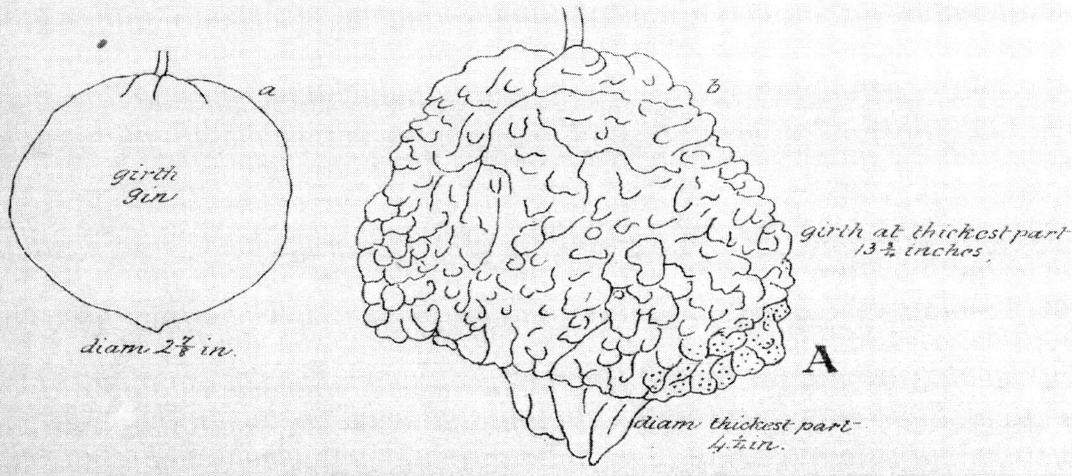

A

PLATE XXVIII.

Khattà orange from Khoorja, Bolundshuhr district.

a. This was a green and unripe specimen, with the general outline of a *Khattà*, but with the warty surface of a true citron.

b is a section of the above. The pulp was orange; the juice sour and slightly bitter. The rind had three sizes of oil-cells. The warts were covered with foveoli-depressions of the oil-cells, as in the preceding specimen.

c. A rain leaf.

d and *e.* Spring leaves. The spines I found on the branch were mere points.

This specimen floated very well in water.

NOTE.—At first I did not know what to make of this specimen, but when I saw the warty form on the same branch as the smooth form, the place of the Khoorja specimen became evident.

PLATE XXVIII.

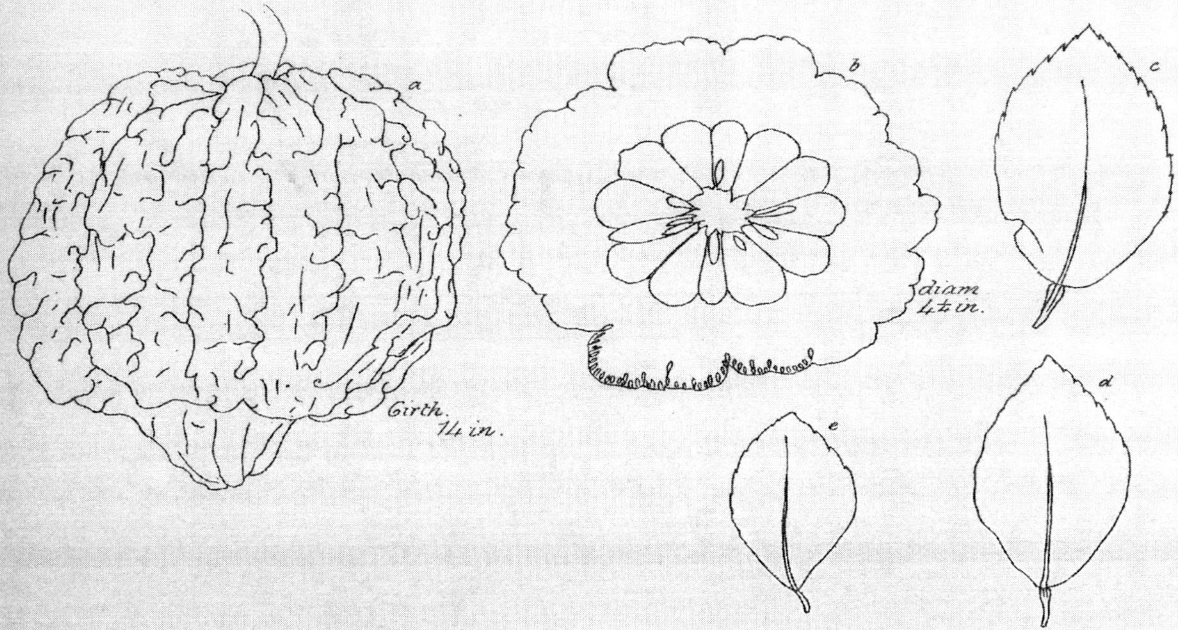

PLATE XXIX.

Two specimens of the *Khattà* orange, taken by myself from the *same branch* of a tree in the Benares Public Garden.

a. The warty form, which natives call *Dumrèz.* This after crop sets in the rains. This outline very inadequately indicates the extreme wartiness of this specimen. The large projecting warts were covered with foveoli depressions, as shown on the right side A. It was as warty as the wartiest citron proper, if not more.

b. This specimen was almost smooth, with only here and there an unevenness of the surface, as shown by the cross lines.

PLATE XXIX.

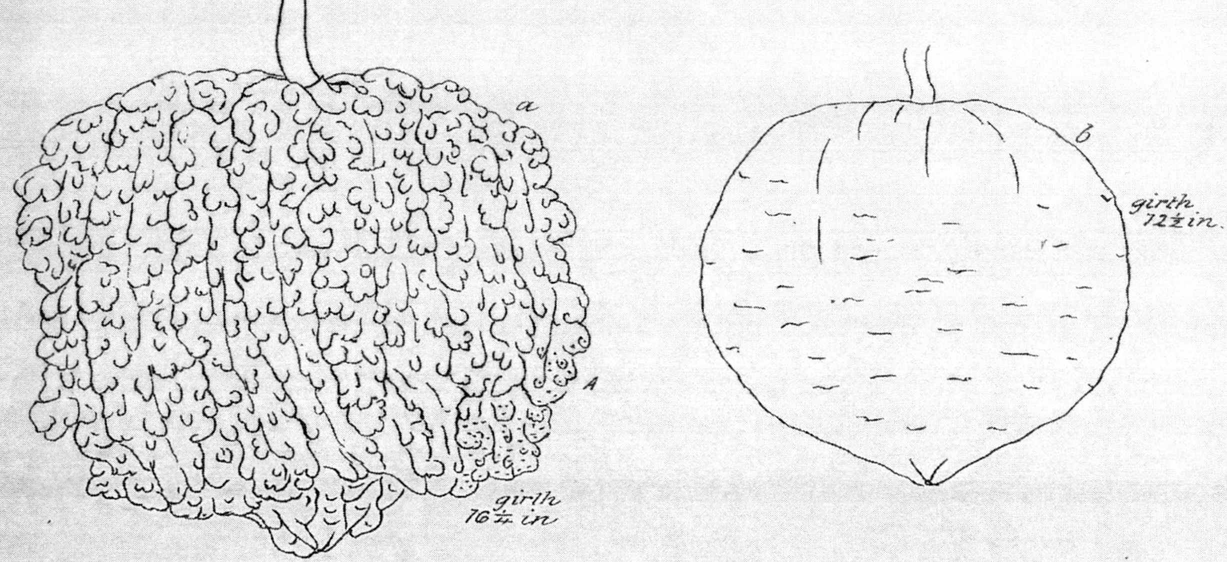

PLATE XXX.

Sections of the Benares warty and smooth *Khattá* oranges, shown on Plate XXIX.

a. This fruit was not ripe; the pulp was pale orange; the juice was scanty and sour; the seeds where white when cut; the pithy part of the skin was spongy and sweetish; and the centre was solid.

b. This fruit was ripe; the pulp pale orange and sour; the juice rather abundant; the seeds when cut where white; and the centre of the fruit solid.

PLATE XXX.

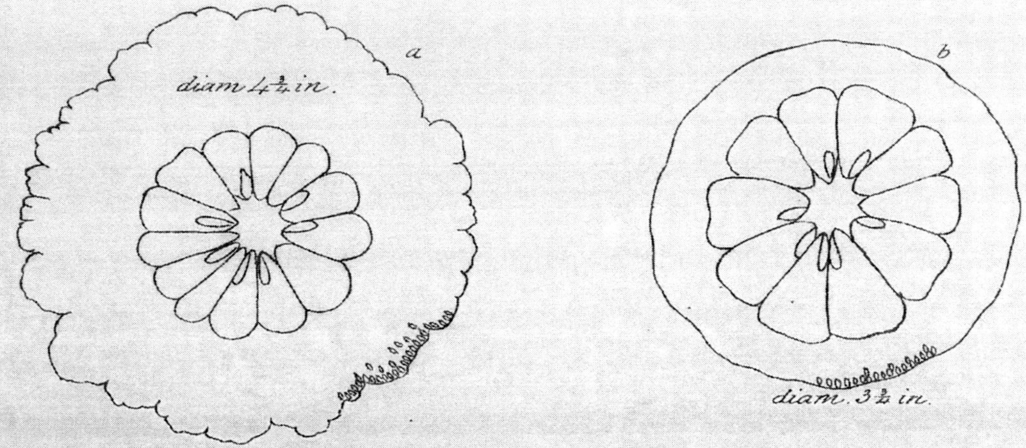

PLATE XXXI.

A specimen of the *Khattà* orange type. It came from Jubbulpur under the name of *Gulgul*.

a. An elongated warty orange; the warts were rather lumpy. Colour of a *Khattà* orange, that is of a maize-orange. It was spotted all over with oil-glands, and slightly furrowed longitudinally.

b. Section of the same. Pulp pale orange-yellow; juice abundant and very sour. White and pithy part of skin sweetish. Rind very aromatic, and resembles that of the Malta lemon.

c. Rain leaf.

d and *e.* Spring leaves.

f. A spine found on the branch, received with the fruit.

Whether this *Gulgul* be a *Dumrez* form of the *Khattà* orange, or whether the tree produces only this form, I do not know. (*Vide* next plate.)

PLATE XXXI.

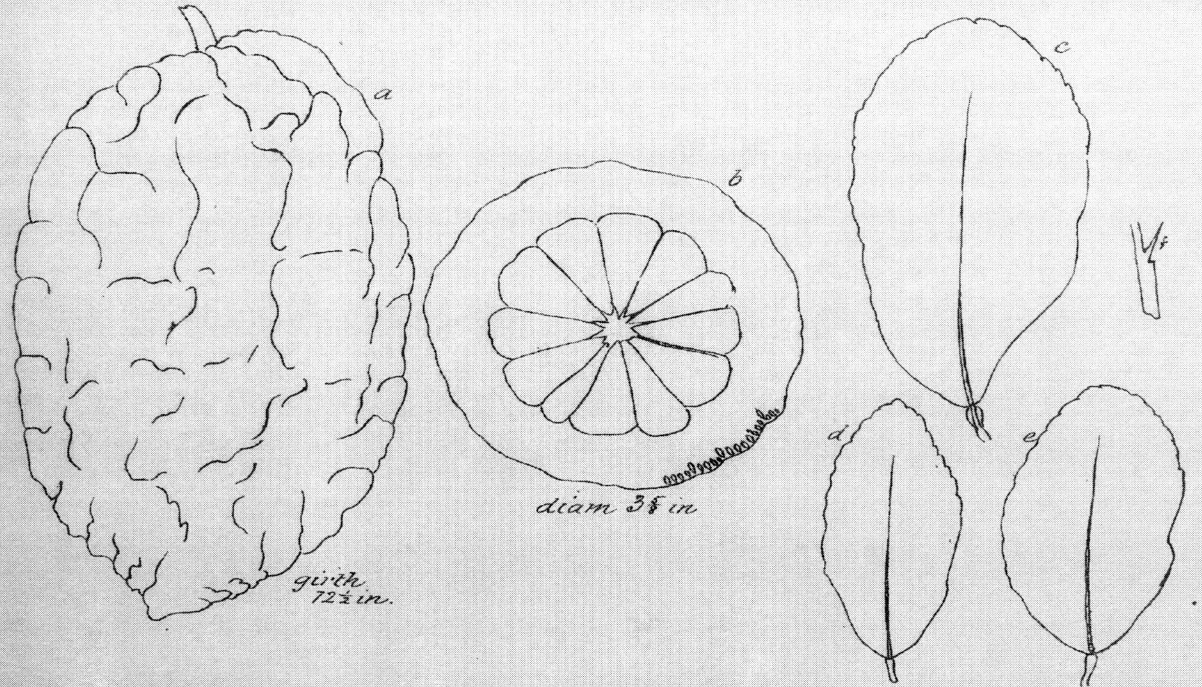

PLATE XXXII.

A specimen of the *Khattà* orange type, from Lahore. It was sent under the name of *Gulgul*, by Mr. H. G. Hein, Superintendent Horticultural Garden of Lahore.

It is sub-warty. The sound given by tapping it with the fingers is that given by a pummelo.

The exterior is of a *deep* lemon-yellow, with a polished surface. The surface is more shiny in the cavities of the oil-cells, which are as large as shown on the side A. Between the cells the surface is slightly raised. The rind has a fine aromatic scent.

PLATE XXXII.

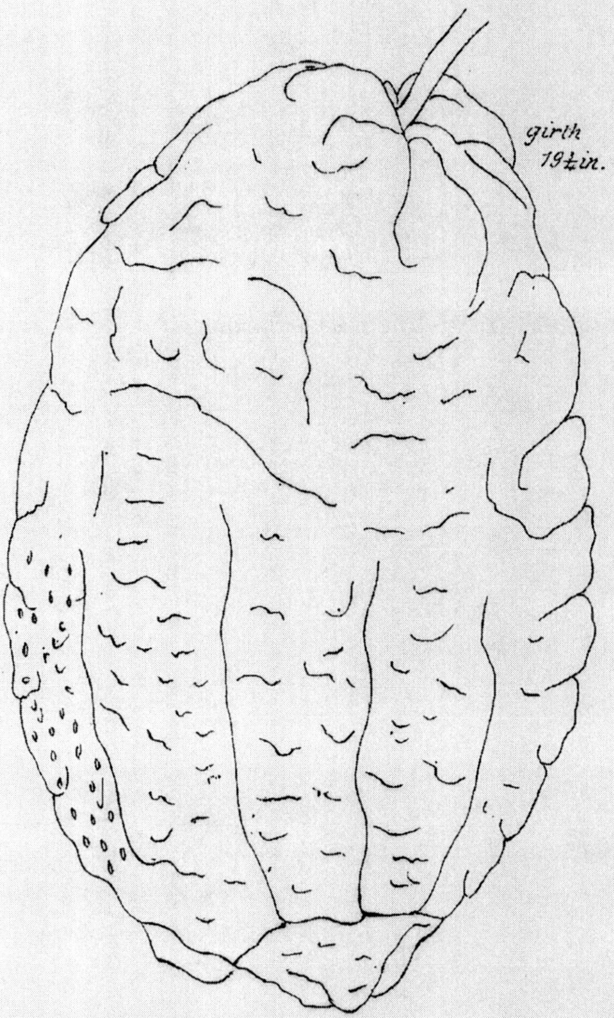

A

PLATE XXXIII.

A section of the Lahore *Gulgul*, given on Plate XXXII.

The oil-cells of the rind are large and distantly situated. The pith is snow white, very spongy, and sweetish, but nothing like the solid white and sweet skin of a true citron. The pulp is pale like that of a lemon, but just verging on the pale orange. The seeds are large and numerous, and cream white when cut. The juice is very abundant, and of a pure sharp acid flavour. The centre is hollow. The aroma of the rind strikes me as being more orangy than lemony. On account of its abundant acid juice this citrus appears a very desirable variety.

PLATE XXXIII.

Longest diam. 6½ in.

PLATE XXXIV.

Leaves of the Lahore *Gulgul*, shown on the foregoing Plates XXXII. and XXXIII.

a and *b* are well-developed rain leaves, showing the wings of the petioles more than usually developed; more crenate than serrate.

c and *d* are spring leaves, which come out with the spring flower crop, in February or March, more serrate than crenate. These are more like lemon leaves.

All have a faint scent, as is usual with *Khattà* orange leaves. The young leaves are *tomentose*, and even the old leaves have *tomentum* on the petioles, midrib, and angles between the leaflet, and wings of the petiole. The young stem is also *tomentose*.

e. A spine found on the branch that came with the specimen.

NOTE.—Tomentum, which has been considered the specific character of the pummelo shoots, appears characteristic of *most huge* citrus, of various types.

PLATE XXXIV.

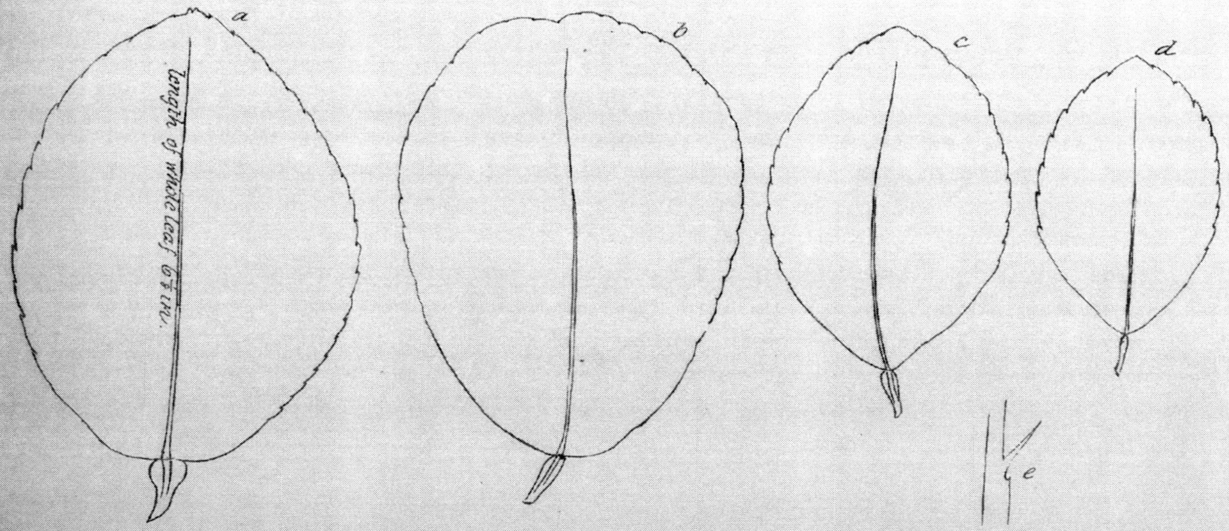

PLATE XXXV.

Specimen of the *Khattà* orange type, from Bulrampur, Gonda district. It was sent by Major Buller, under the name of *Kathairee nimboo*, or "Jack" citrus. It also goes by the name of *Rus-kankur*, and also *Beòra*. Externally it was lemon-colour. Probably it was not a fully-ripened specimen. The surface consisted of lumpy knobs. The mammilla was flattened. The oil-cells were large, transparent and distinct, as shown at *a*. Some were *convex*, and others *concave*. This specimen alone would be enough to disprove Risso's theory that acid pulp was found with *concave* rind cells, and sweet pulp with *convex* cells (*vide* Chapter on "Morphology"). The rind was fragrant, and the whole fruit floated very well in water. It should be noted that "Kunker," "Kanker," "Kankree," all mean "Kàkree," or its Sanskrit equivalent "Kàkkatee"—a sort of melon.

PLATE XXXV.

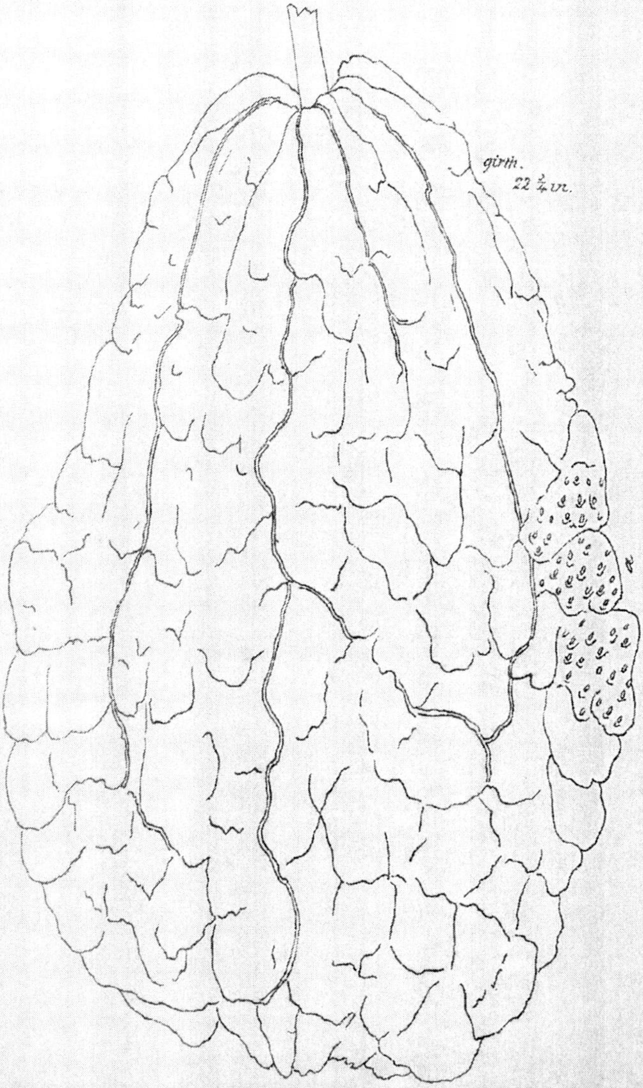

PLATE XXXVI.

Section of the Bulrampur *Kathairee nimboo.* The oil-cell portion of the skin is $\frac{1}{4}$-inch thick, and the cells are large and separate. The pithy part is snow-white, soft and spongy. It is said to be the only part of the fruit which is eaten. Pulp pale, like that of a lemon, with perhaps an imaginary tinge of the palest orange colour. Juice abundant, and very sour; seeds few; juice-vesicles arise also from the *sides* of the carpels; centre hollow. This is much like the *Gulgul* of Lahore.

Another specimen, also sent by Major Buller from Tulshipur, Gonda, was still larger than this. It had a girth of 24 inches; it was 10 inches long; and had a diameter of $7\frac{1}{2}$ inches. It was the largest I have seen. Its pulp was white, and it had *no seeds.*

PLATE XXXVI.

longest diam. 7½in.

PLATE XXXVII.

Leaves of the *Kathairee nimboo* of Bulrampur, in the "Tarai" at the foot of the Himalayas.

a and *b* are well-developed rain leaves, with the wings of the petioles sufficiently well developed.

c is a spring leaf, with the petiole only margined. The young shoots and young *calyces* are purple, and *pubescent*. The flower buds are purple. The leaves are rather lemon-scented. The midrib and petioles of the old leaves still retain some of the pubescence. Some of the leaves are serrated or crenated from the base, like those of the *Bajouras* and *Turunj*, or citron proper.

d is a spine found on the branch attached to the specimen.

PLATE XXXVII.

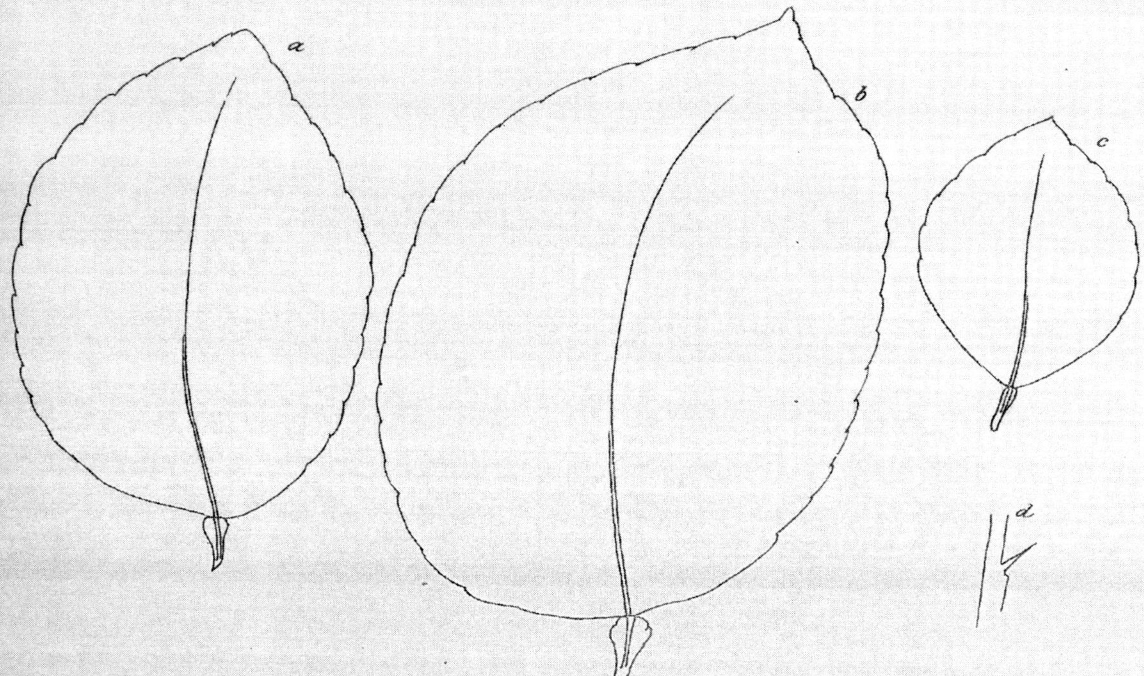

PLATE XXXVIII.

a and *b* are the *Karnphàl* of Almora sent by Mr. H. Harris. I suppose *Karnphàl* is a contraction of *Karnaphal*, or fruit of the *Karna*. The *Khattà* is sometimes called *Karna*. Externally it is orange-yellow; surface smooth and slightly foveolate, with a flattish mammilla at the base. It looks like a *Khattà* orange, and has the same aroma in the rind, without bitterness. The pithy part is yellowish-white; pulp transparent orange, sour, and juice abundant, without bitterness.

c and *d* are its typical leaves, which are similar to those of the common *Khattà* orange of the plains; a fully-developed rain leaf and a spring leaf.

Note.—This and the following specimen arrived after I had arranged the plates, and so I put them at the end of the group.

PLATE XXXVIII.

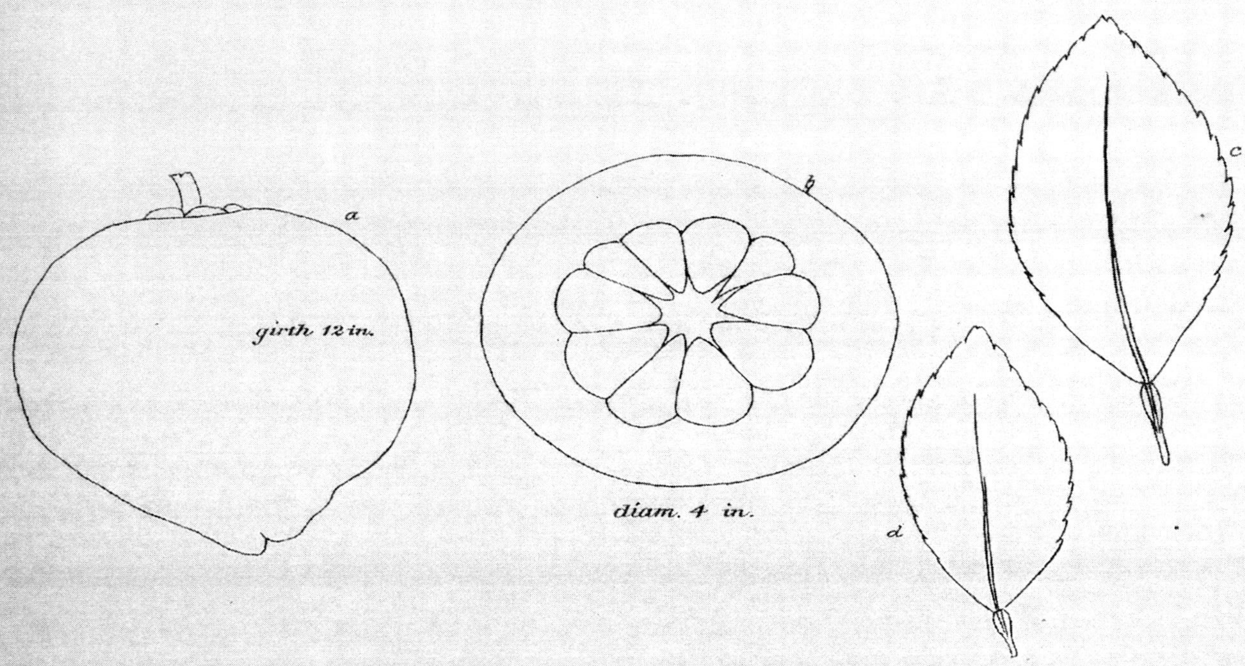

PLATE XXXIX.

a and *b* is the *Kathphàl* of Almora, sent by Mr. H. Harris. This name is probably a contraction of *Khattàphàl*, or fruit of the *Khattà* orange.

Externally it is maize-orange, with an uneven surface, studded with large and small pinholes. It looks much like a *Khattà* orange, and has the same aroma and taste in its rind. The pithy part is yellowish-white; the pulp is orange, and the juice sour and abundant.

c is a fully-developed rain leaf.

d, *e*, and *f* are spring leaves.

g is the spire that came with the specimen.

PLATE XXXIX.

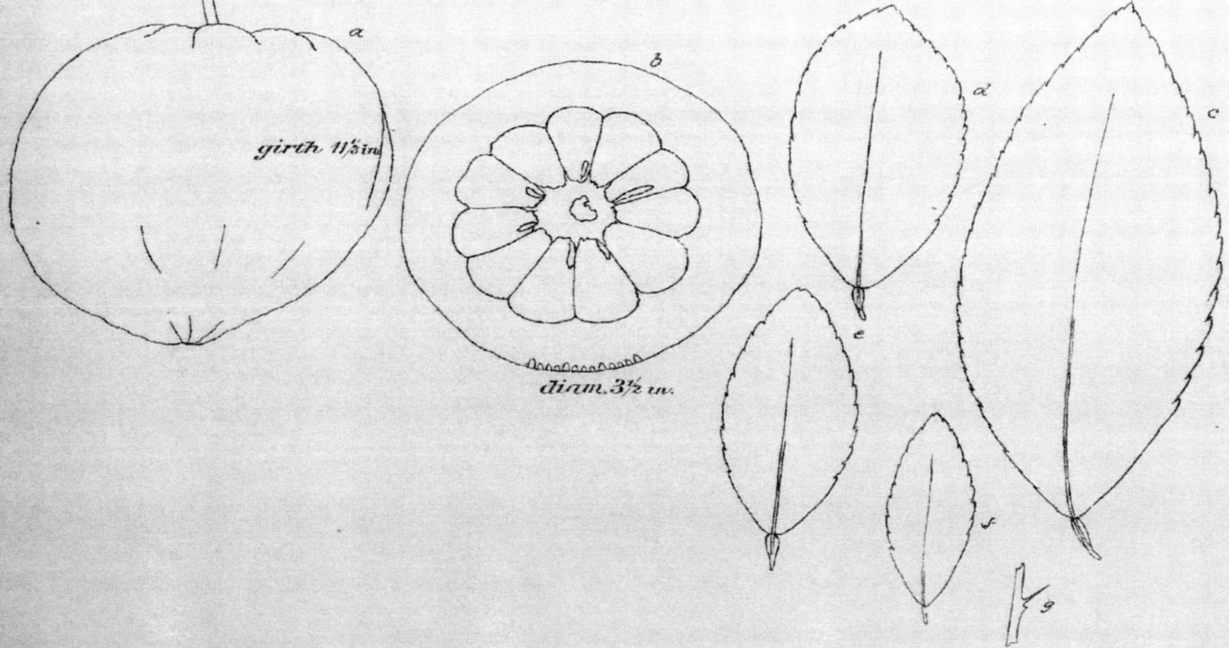

PLATE XL.

Four figures of Citrus aurantium, taken from Risso and Poiteau's monograph.

a is called "oranger à fruit conifère," with pale yellow pulp; half sweet and half acid, with a little bitterness. The authors say this variety is on the debatable ground between the oranges and lemons.

b is the "oranger à fruit pyriform." The pulp is orange-yellow in the centre, and blood-coloured towards the rind. It is very fine flavoured.

c is the "oranger à fruit toruleux," with the rind-carpels distinct.

d is the "oranger à fruit rugueux," commonly called "oranger des bois de St. Domingue."

Risso states that in St. Domingo this orange was used by preference in cases of *weakness after fever*.

It is not impossible that the Italians may have got the notion of "decoction of lemon" for fever, and weakness after fever, from the West India Islands.

PLATE XL.

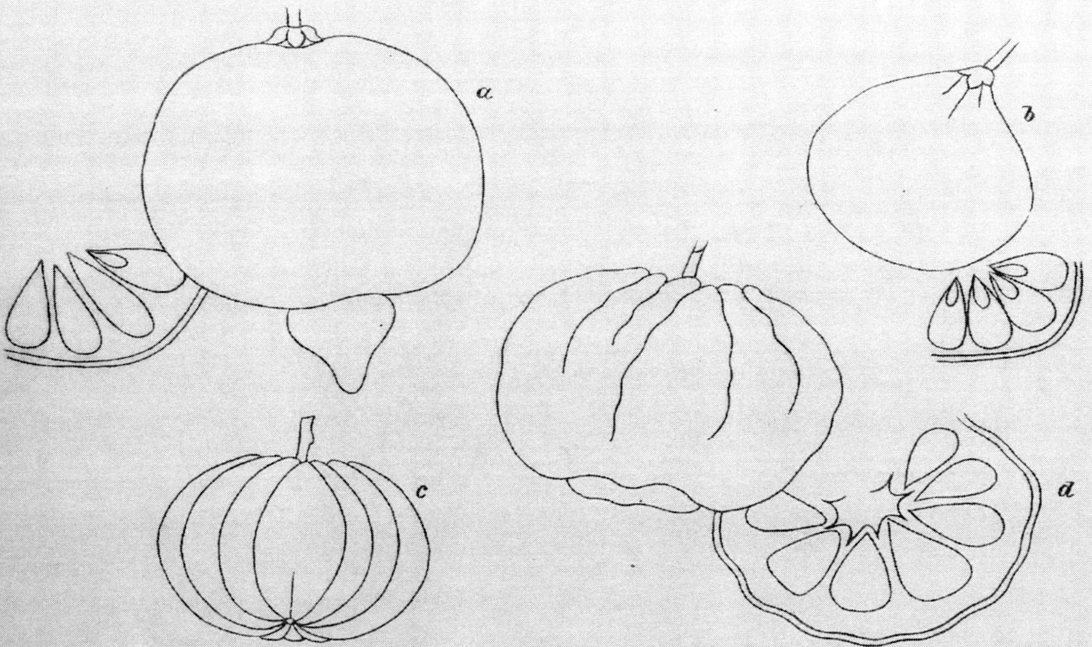

PLATE XLI.

Malta orange from Hagkala, Ceylon.

a and *b*. The exterior of this slightly unripe orange was greenish-yellow, with pale orange oil-glands of various sizes. Pulp pale orange, juice abundant and sour-sweet. Skin rather thick. A good kind of orange of the Malta type. Flowers white with five petals.

c and *d*. Rain leaves with the distinctive scent of the Malta orange leaf.

PLATE XLI.

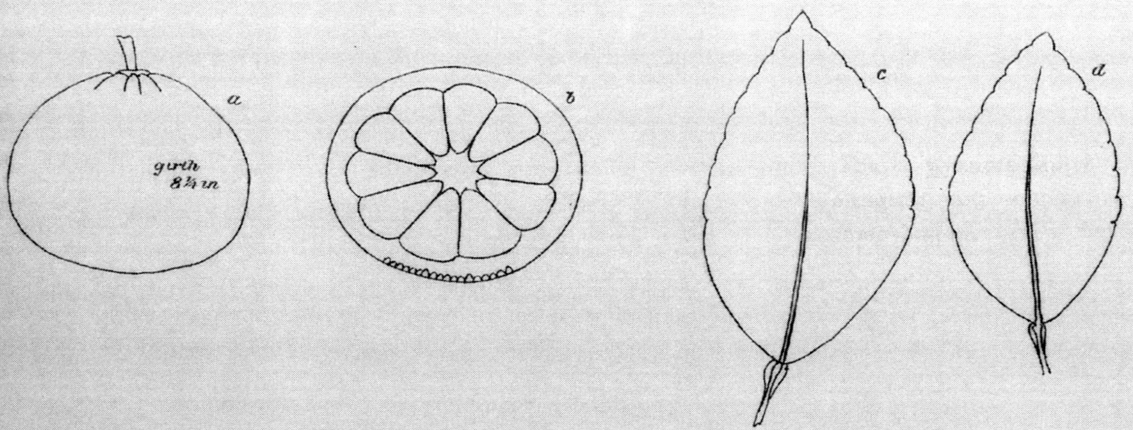

PLATE XLII.

Malta oranges from Colombo, Ceylon.

a and *c*. Exterior orange-yellow, pitted all over with shallow cavities; at the bottom of each there is a large oil-gland. The intermediate spaces are filled with miliary convexities, consisting of the smaller oil-glauds. *c* is the section of *a*. The skin is rather thick. The pulp is of a darker shade of orange than the Malta varieties of India. The centre is all but solid. It is many seeded; seeds white when cut.

b is another specimen, pitted like *a*, but the intermediate spaces are much smoother, and in places shiny. It is thinner skinned, more juicy, and finer flavoured than *a*. The natives of Ceylon call this either orange, or "Peni-dòdan," which means "sweet and round," while all the other oranges of the "Suntara" type they call by the name of "Mandarin." (None of these, however, is true Mandarin.) The Malta oranges of Kandy are like those of Colombo.

PLATE XLII.

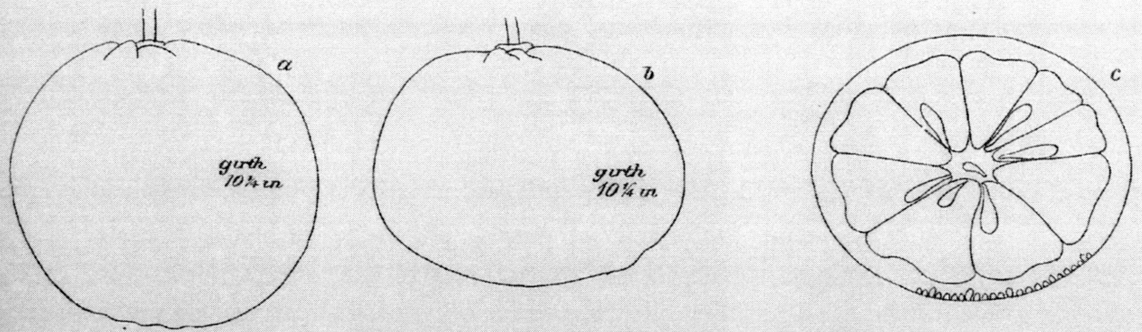

PLATE XLIII.

Oranges of the Malta type from Tanjore, South India.

a and *b* are the "Bàndir" orange of Tanjore, called by the English "sweet lime." It is of a yellowish-orange when ripe. It is generally smooth and pitted all over with large foveoli, the intermediate spaces having miliary convexities. The pulp is pale orange, juicy, and of a pleasant, sweet, and sub-acid flavour. The juice-vesicles are rather coarse, the centre hollow, and the seeds white when cut.

Another specimen had thinner skin, juice very abundant and sweet, with a distant *soupçon* of sub-acid. This is a very fine orange; can be cut across in halves and eaten with a spoon; well worth propagating and disseminating.

c and *d* is the so-called Spanish orange of Tanjore. It is yellow externally, slightly foveolate, and covered with miliary projections. The rind has a slight scent of Lantana. The pulp is darker than other Indian oranges of the same type, and deep orange; juice abundant, and *very* pleasant, sweet, and sub-acid; centre solid, and seeds white when cut. Both are distinctly of the Malta orange type.

PLATE XLIII.

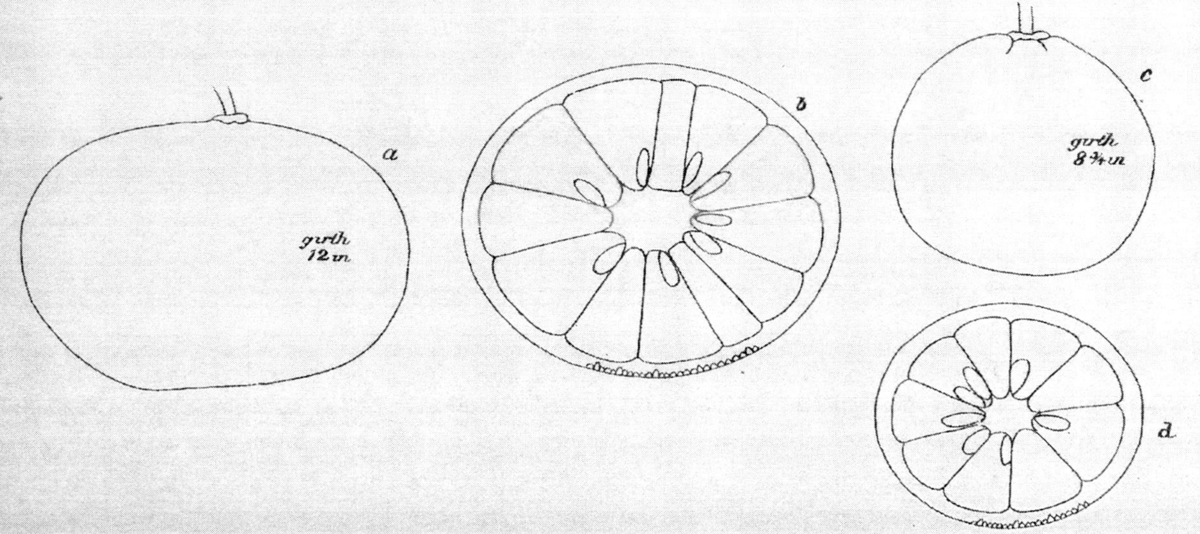

PLATE XLIV.

The "Mussèmbi" orange of Poona.

a and *c* are one orange. The characteristic feature of this variety of the Malta orange is that externally it has closely-set,. longitudinal furrows, running from base to apex, with a tendency to become subwarty in the larger specimens, like *f*. The exterior is orange-yellow, generally with an aureola round the apex, which is probably the remains of an extinct mammilla. The pulp is pale orange, juice abundant, with the distinctive flavour of the Malta orange; seeds white when cut; centre solid, as in *c*, or hollow, as in *e*.

b is a smoother specimen, and *d* has only a trace of furrows round the base. The smooth specimens have a much thinner skin; their juice-vesicles are finer, and their juice is more abundant. *e* is the section of *d*.

g is a rain leaf of the "Mussèmbi" orange of Poona. Natives of Poona say they can keep this orange on the tree for a year, without spoiling. It is supplied to the Bombay market, where I purchased *a* and *b*. It is a distinct and very desirable variety. One I got at Poona I kept from 25th December to 28th January. It remained fresh and juicy, and became more highly coloured round the apex.

PLATE XLIV.

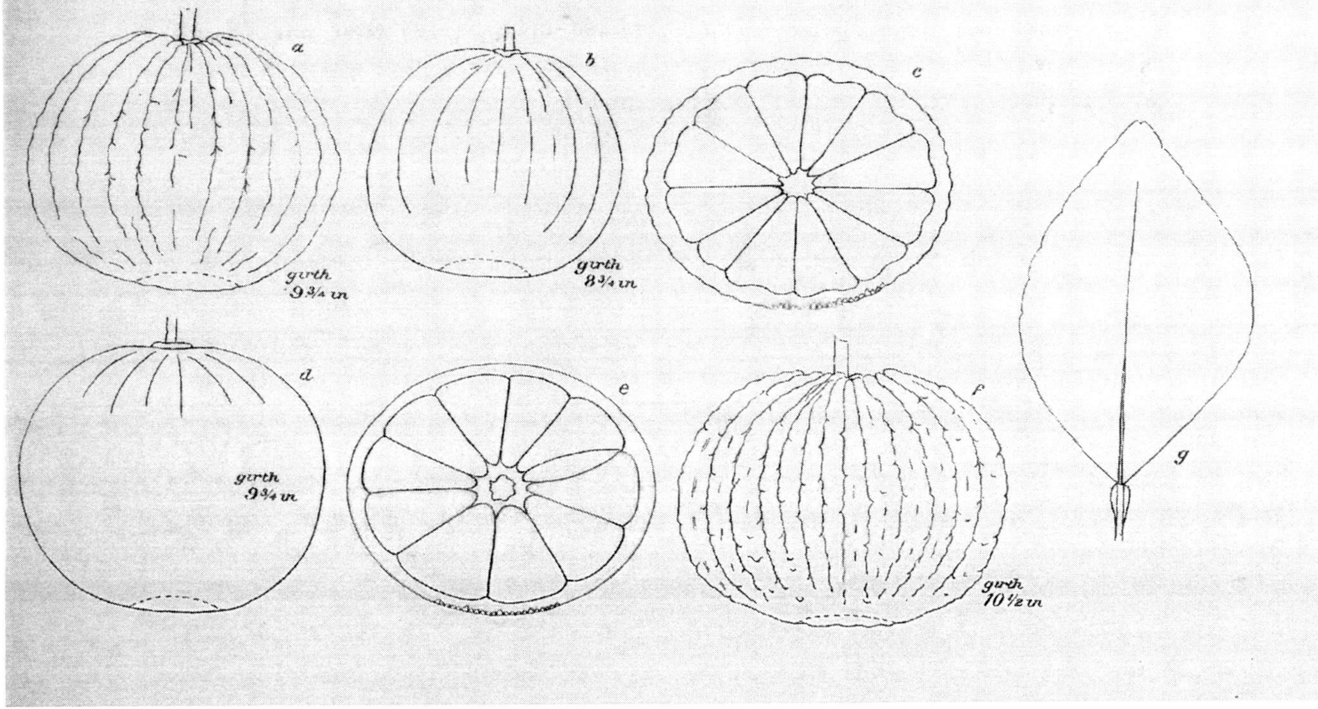

PLATE XLV.

The *true* "Mussèmbi" oranges of the Bombay market. These come from Zanzibar, and "Mussèmbi is evidently a corruption of *Mozambique*. It is also called *Malta orange* in Bombay.

Most of the specimens are ovoid or egg-oranges, like *a*, *b*, *c*, *g*, and *i*, but round forms like *d* are also found. They are orange-yellow, and foveolate all over. The skin is thin and some are seedless. When quite ripe they are very sweet. Those who know this orange in Zanzibar say it is much better than the Malta or Spanish orange, that is oranges of the same type grown in Malta and Spain.

d resembled the Sicily orange.

e is the section of *a*, *f* is the section of *b*, *g* and *i* were of a deep orange colour, *h* is the section of *g*. Both these had many seeds. In two others I found only three seeds, and *a* was seedless. In this variety the juice-vesicles were attached also a little way up the *sides* of the pulp carpels.

PLATE XLV.

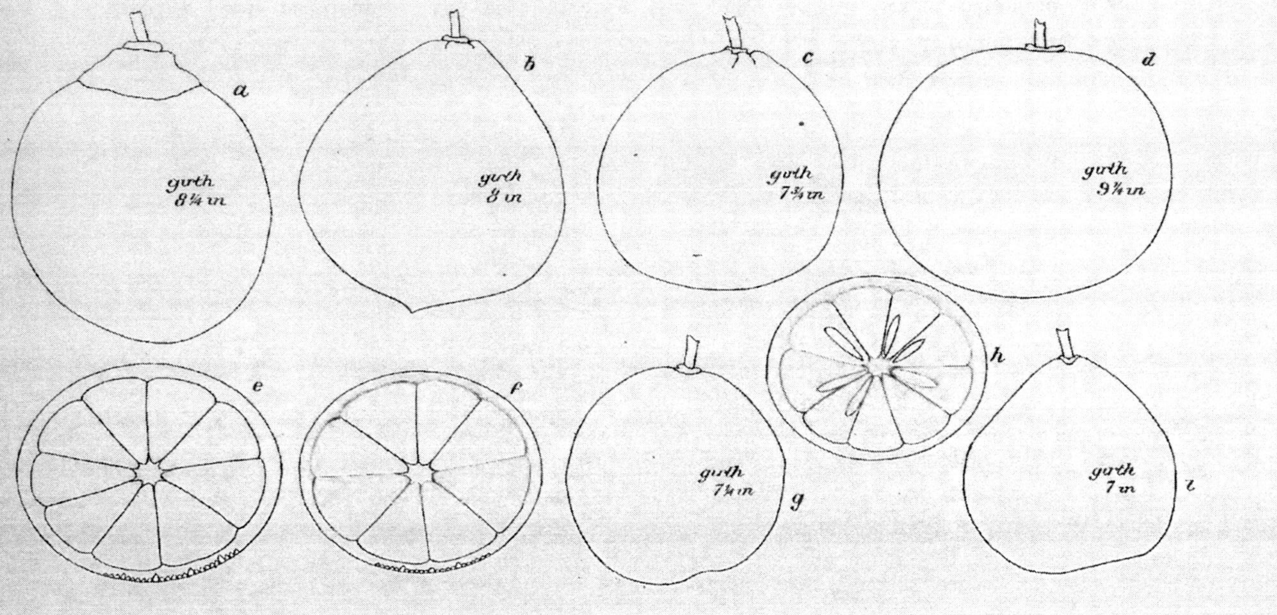

a
girth 8¼ in
b
girth 8 in
c
girth 7¾ in
d
girth 9¼ in
e
f
g
girth 7¼ in
h
i
girth 7 in

PLATE XLVI.

Other specimens of the Malta orange type.

a and *b* are called the Suez orange, by Mr. C. Nickels, of the Passewa factory, Jaunpore. He obtained the fruit in Suez, and from their seeds grew this specimen at his factory. I received it on the 30th January. It was of a bright orange colour, evidently *ripened on the tree*; smooth and only slightly foveolate. When cut the perfume of the fruit is distinctive, and that of the Malta orange type. Pulp of a deeper orange than others of this type grown in India, and as deep as that of the Zanzibar orange; juice abundant, and of a delicious, sweet, and sub-acid flavour. It is one of the best oranges of this type which I have tasted in India. The pithy part of the skin was of a yellowish-white; the rind only aromatic, scarcely bitter or pungent.

c is a rain leaf, well developed, and *d* a spring leaf.

e is an orange of this type which I obtained on the SS. *Chunda* (B. I. S. N. Co.), said to have been purchased at Madras about five or six weeks before. It had a thin skin, abundant sweet juice, and many seeds, with a solid centre. It was of the Malta type.

PLATE XLVI.

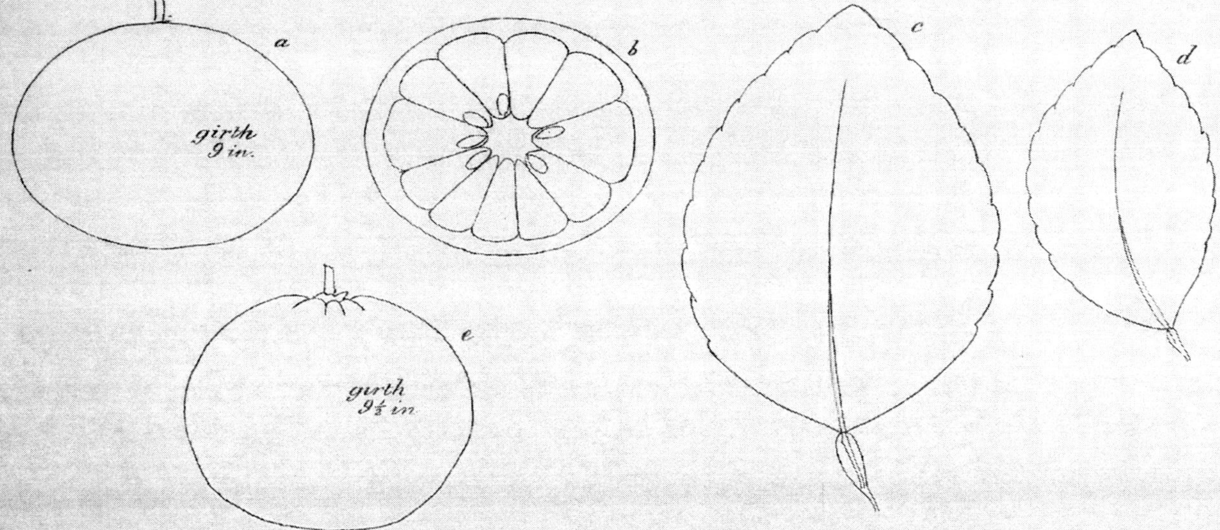

PLATE XLVII.

Malta egg-oranges from Etawah.

a and *c*. Exterior chagrined with foveoli, and intermediate miliary elevations. A larger specimen, of which *e* is a section, was more chagrined, and its pinholes more decided. It had not only deep foveoli, but other less deep foveoli between them, and between these again there were miliary convexities. The oil-cells of *c* and *e* are rather exaggerated to show clearly the three sizes of oil-cells, to which the foveoli and miliary eminences correspond.

b and *d* show a smaller and smoother egg-orange, with a thin skin, the foveoli being distinct only at the base and apex. The colour of the pulp of all is of a pale orange; abundant and sub-acid juice. These specimens had only from four to seven seeds. Usually the egg-orange in Europe is *seedless*, and corresponds to the *orange sans pépins* of Risso; but in India it is often full of seeds.

f and *g* are spring leaves; the latter shows the wing of the petiole continuous with the blade of the leaflet on one side. This is normal in some of the citrons, and occurs often in some pummelos. *h* and *i* are also spring leaves.

PLATE XLVII.

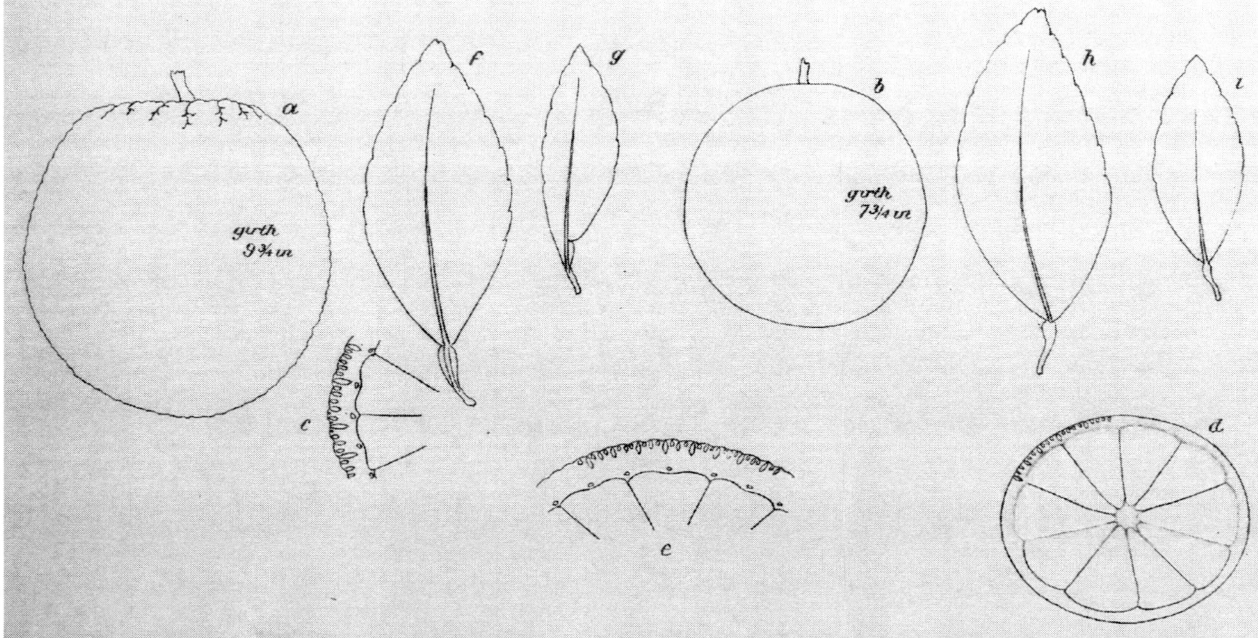

PLATE XLVIII.

Malta round orange, from Etawah (frequently but *wrongly* called Sylhet orange).

There is a notion among natives that this orange is better and more juicy when plucked in its green state in October. This notion may have arisen from some varieties becoming, either from quality of soil or want of cultivation, dry and juiceless if left too long on the tree.

a and *b*. A fully grown but unripe specimen, with foveoli close to each other. Surface chagrined, with the usual miliary eminences; pulp orange, juice very abundant, sweet and sub-acid. From each half of this orange I squeezed a full wine-glass of juice.

c and *d* are leaves taken from the same branch of the round orange.

e and *f* are leaves taken from the same branch of the egg-orange. Both show the small spine, which is rather characteristic of this type of orange.

PLATE XLVIII.

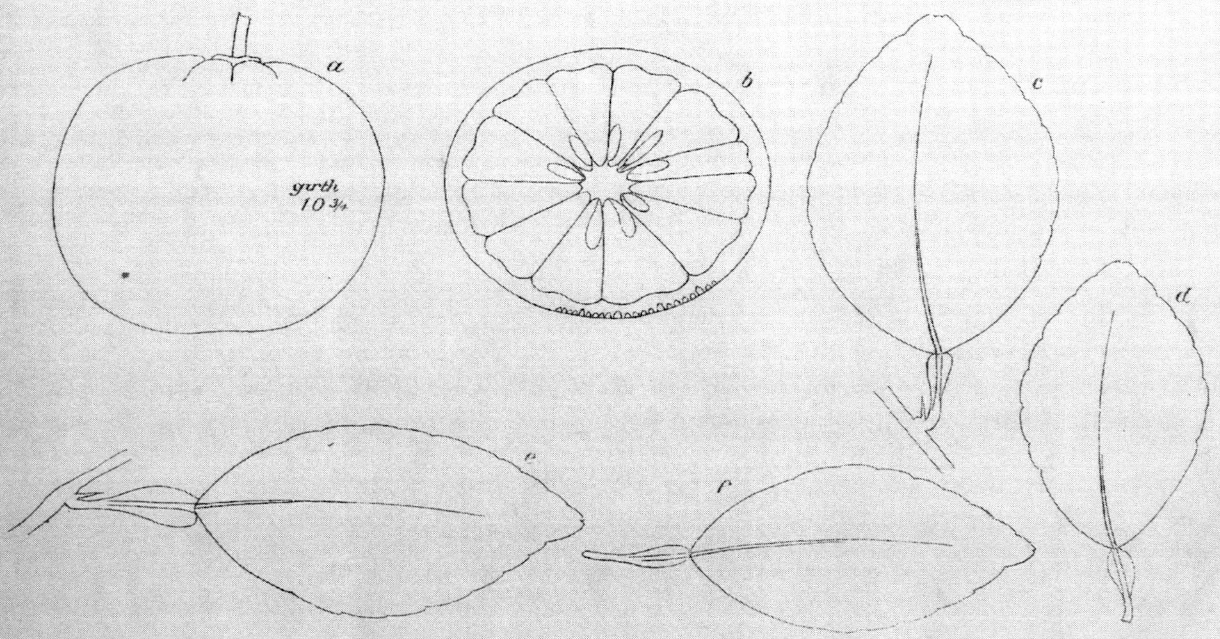

PLATE XLIX.

Another specimen of the Malta round orange.

a and *b*. Surface chagrined, pinholes rather close; surface covered with miliary oil-glands. In this specimen the juice-vesicles were developed also from the *sides* of the pulp carpels, as shown in *b* and *h*. Some of them were in an undeveloped state, much like the oil-cells of the rind; *i* shows them in a section of the side of *h*.

k shows some of the pedicelled juice-vesicles isolated and hanging down, the others having been removed to prevent confusion. In many of the large specimens of the Malta orange type the circumference part of the pulp carpels has an emargination as shown in *b* at *x*. This is common in pummelos.

c is a rain leaf; *d* and *e* very small spring leaves; and *f* is the small spine of this type of orange.

g shows little points on the under side of some of the leaves, as if caused by some insect.

PLATE XLIX.

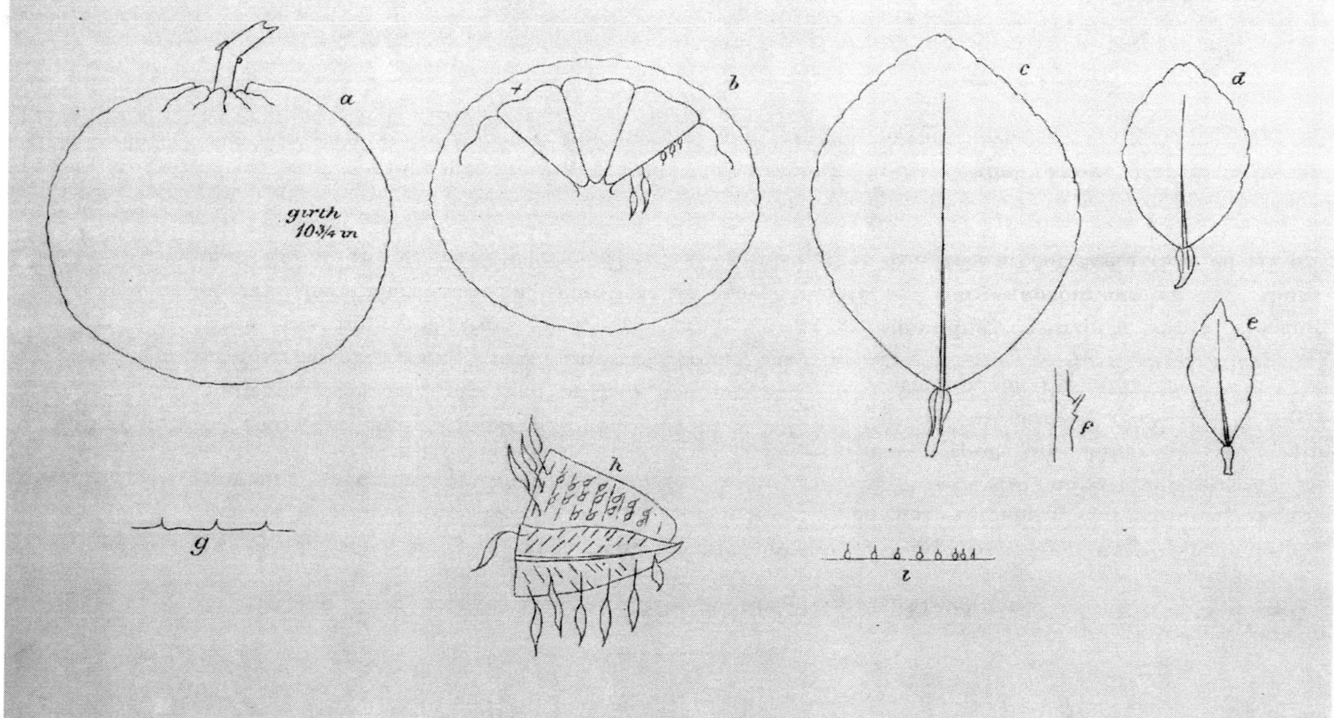

PLATE L.

Malta blood orange, from the Horticultural Garden, Lucknow.

a and *b* is a large, thick-skinned specimen, deeply foveolate, and coarsely chagrined. Pulp orange, streaked occasionally with blood colour; juice not abundant, and without much flavour; seeds white when cut.

c and *d* is a smoother and thinner skinned specimen, of an orange exterior, and only foveolate. Pulp pale orange, streaked with blood colour. The flavour of the Malta type of orange is *sui generis*, and different from the flavour of the *Suntara* orange type. This was imported from Malta in 1863; it never showed in Lucknow more blood colour than mere streaks, showing probably something was wanting either in the soil or mode of cultivation. It may be also that the trees sent were not of the full-blooded variety.

e is a rain leaf, and *f* and *g* are spring leaves. The scent of the Malta orange leaf is feeble, and different from that of the Séville, and of the *Suntara* type.

PLATE L.

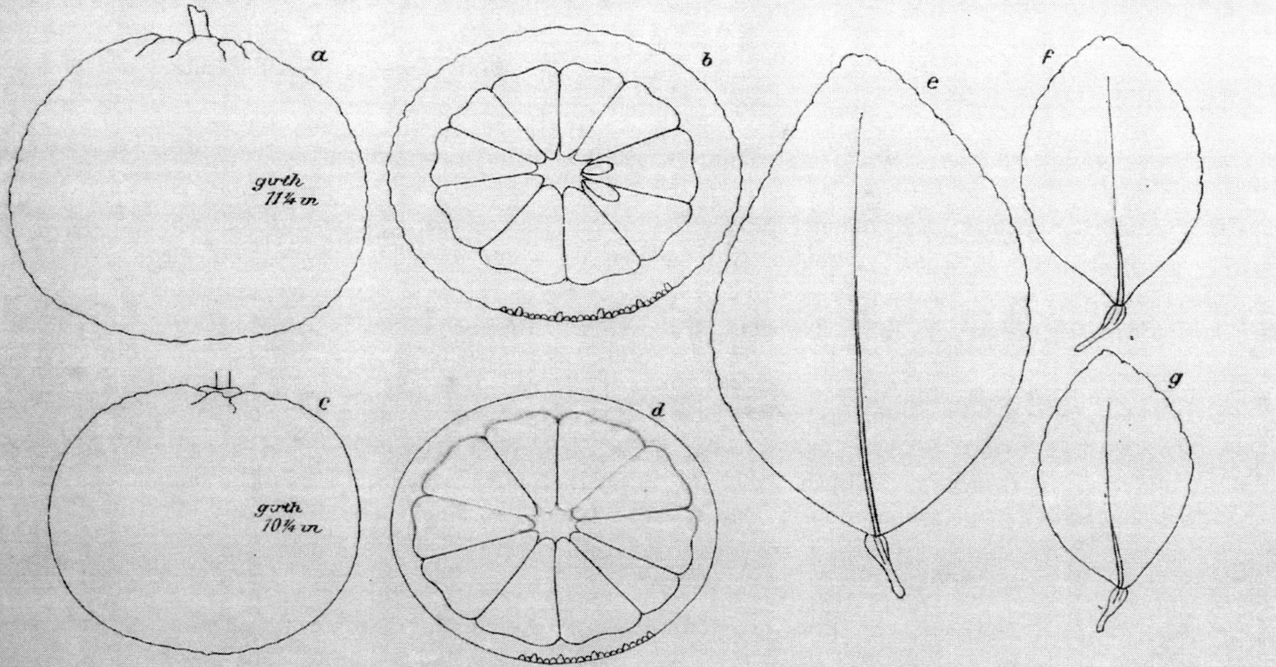

PLATE LI.

Blood oranges sent by Mr. Steel, Deputy Commissioner of Gujranwàla, Punjab. The original trees were imported from Malta by Colonel Clarke, D.C., between 1852 and 1856. Some specimens were from the *original* imported trees, still living; and some were from budded plants. The latter gave smaller fruit, but *as good* as the others.

a and *b*. Exterior of a bright orange; apex half smeared with a tinge of blood red; foveolate all over, with the intermediate spaces dotted with smaller oil-cells. All the specimens sent were more or less slightly oblong. *c* is the section of *b*. The oil-cells of the *rind* are small and of an orange colour, but now and again a few are found with a *blood colour*; pithy part of skin yellowish-white. Pulp of a uniform orange-claret colour throughout, and of a delicious sweetness and perfection of flavour, not a bit inferior to those grown in Malta. Seeds very few; centre almost solid.

d and *e* are spring leaves of this orange.

PLATE LI.

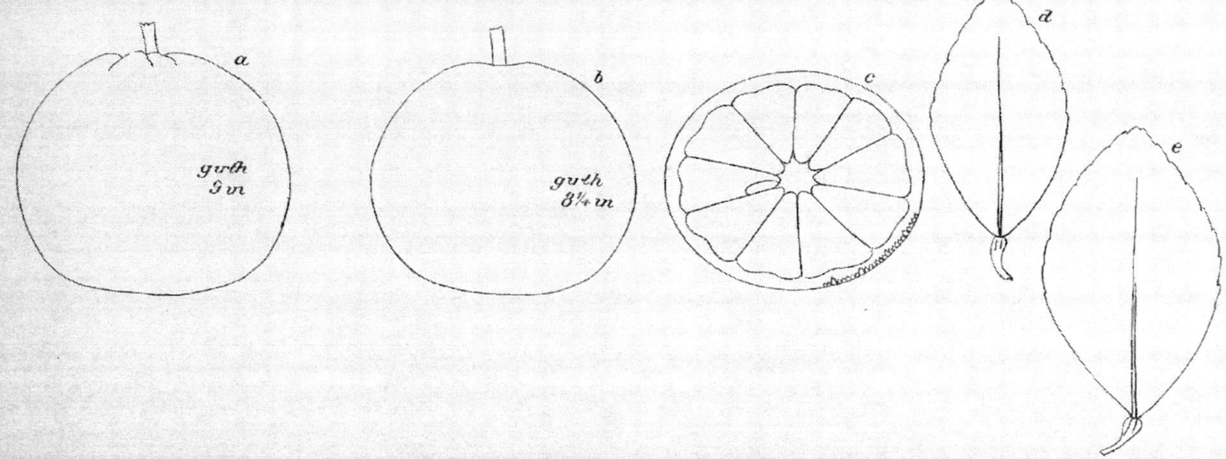

PLATE LII.

Blood orange sent by Mr. C. Nickels, of Jaunpore, N.W.P. The trees were imported by him from England in 1872.

a and *b*. Exterior deep orange, with a deeper blush on one side, and foveolate all over. Scent, when cut, distinctive and that of the Malta orange type. Pithy part of the skin yellowish-white; rind only aromatic, scarcely bitter or pungent. Pulp orange, deeper than that of others, excepting the Suez and Zanzibar orange. Here and there were streaks and little dabs of blood colour. Flavour delicious, with a slight mixture of sub-acid. Seeds white when cut.

c and *d* are probably rain leaves, showing rather well-developed petiole wings; the former has one half slightly undeveloped.

PLATE LII.

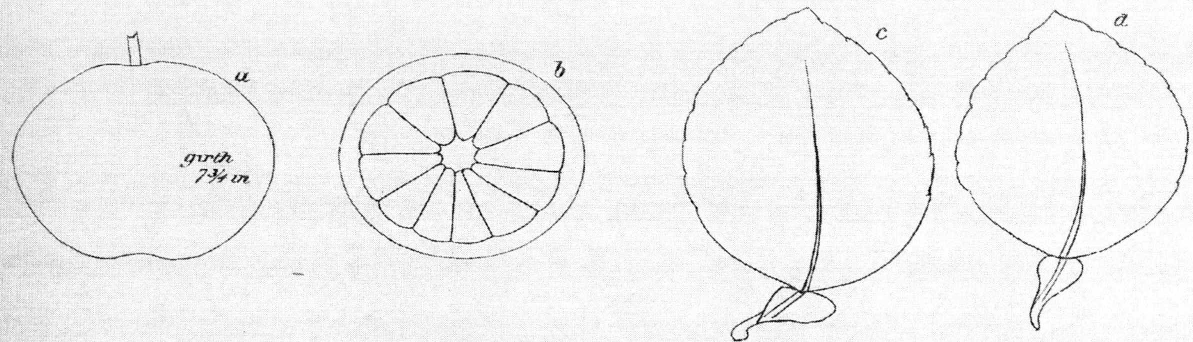

PLATE LIII.

a and *b* are leaves from a round Malta orange tree of Etawah; *b*, for size, shape, and thickness of blade resembled a pummelo leaf, the petiole being only margined, and not large winged, as is usual in pummelo leaves.

c and *d* are also leaves of a Malta orange tree, one having a winged petiole, the other a margined petiole.

PLATE LIII.

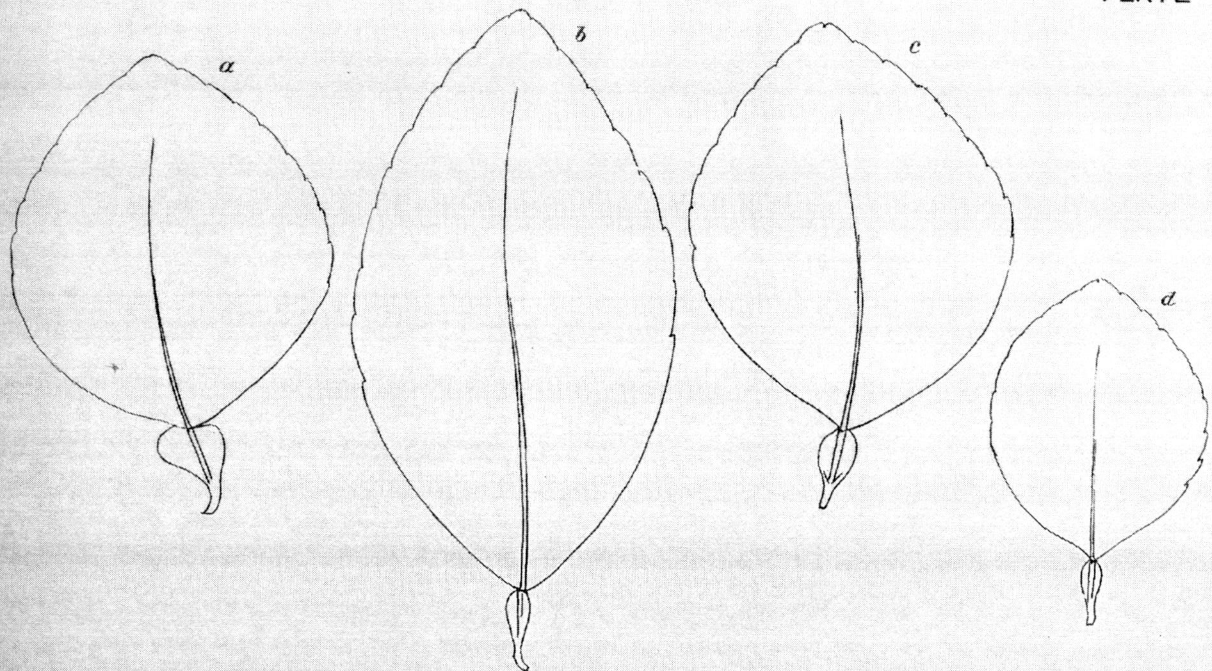

PLATE LIV.

a, *b*, and *c* are also leaves of the Malta orange tree of Etawah. Usually this variety has a stout petiole, only margined.

d and *e* are leaves of the true Sylhet orange, of the Suntara type. Usually their petioles are more slender than the former, and only margined, thinner and less polished; the minute oil-glands slightly project on the surface, giving them a somewhat chagrined appearance. These leaves are given for comparison. There is scarcely a citrus tree which has all its leaves at all times typical. On any tree one is sure to find some leaves which might be easily mistaken for the leaves of some other variety. The rain leaves usually differ much in development from the spring leaves.

PLATE LIV.

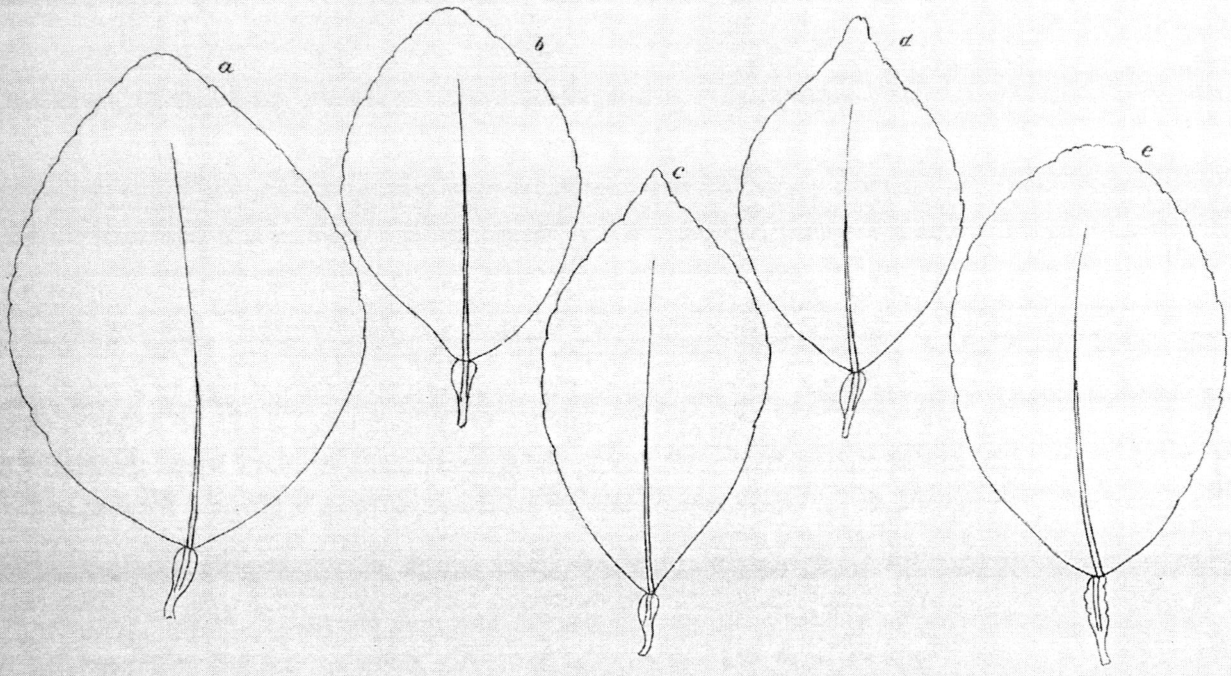

PLATE LV.

a, *b*, and *c* are leaves taken from the *same* tree of the Malta orange of Etawah. It will be seen how widely the petiole of *a* differs from the petiole of *c*. In reality, however, the typical petiole, that is like which most of the leaves on a tree are found, is that of *b*.

PLATE LV.

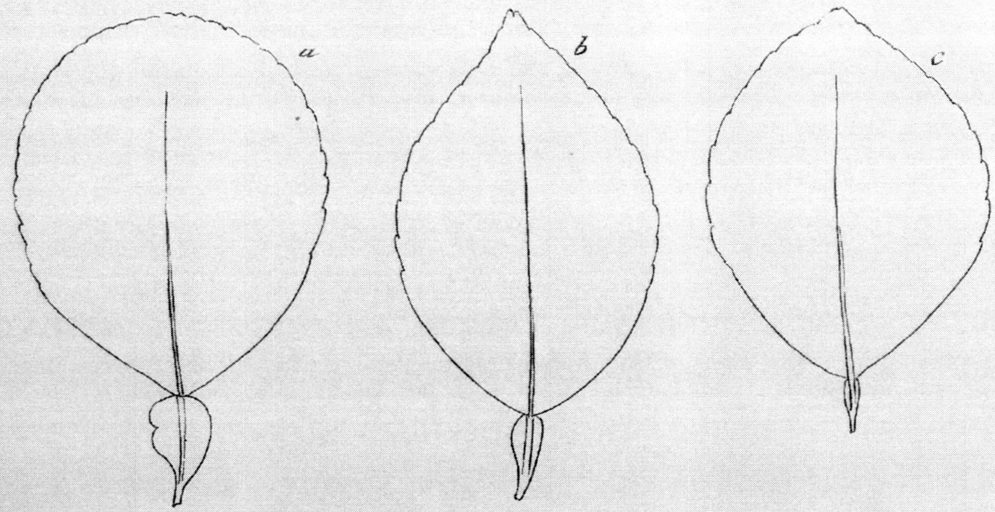

PLATE LVI.

This is the "Poonchee Jambole" (or small pummelo) of Kandy, Ceylon. Some call it "Amool-dòdan," or sour orange.

a, *b*, and *c*. When ripe the exterior is of a deep lemon-yellow, pitted all over with foveoli, the intermediate spaces being filled with smaller oil-cells. If it were orange coloured it might be easily taken for a thick-skinned Malta orange, although the skin can be separated more easily than in the latter. The exterior of *b* is a little coarser than *a*. *c* is the section of *a*. The pithy part of the skin has a lemon-yellow blush. The pulp is pale yellowish, like that of a lemon. The juice-vesicles are large, and the juice is abundant, and of a pleasant sub-acid flavour, without sweetness. The seeds are like those of the pummelo, large and rugose.

e and *d* are rain leaves, and *f* and *g* spring leaves. The majority have a decidedly winged petiole like *e* and *d*, but I found nothing to approach the large wings of a pummelo leaf. They had no special aroma, and their scent approached those of the Malta orange. On tapping the fruit with the fingers it gave the sound of a pummelo, on account of the thick, spongy skin. I saw a basket full of this citrus, and they *all* had the colour, average size, and shape of those given. I look upon it as a yellow variety of the *Malta orange*. The smaller of the spines *h* supports this view, as also the scent of the leaves.

PLATE LVI.

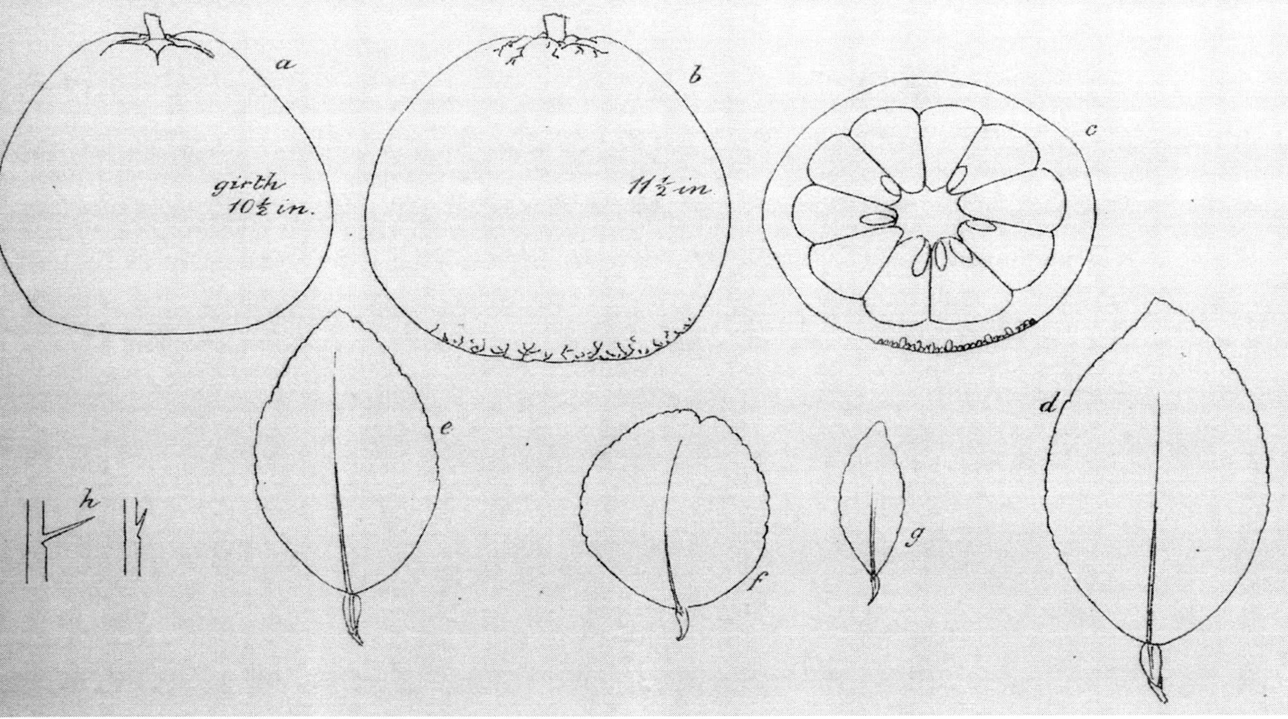

PLATE LVII.

Other leaves of the Malta orange trees of Etawah.

a and *b* are rain leaves, and *c* shows the tip and petiole of another leaf. All these three leaves were taken from the *same* tree.

d and *e* are rain leaves taken from another Malta orange tree.

NOTE.—All these forms of leaves, taken from the *same* tree, are given, in order to impress the reader with the necessity of making observations, not only on one tree, but on many, and under different circumstances. By only examining one leaf one might perhaps be impressed with a type of leaf of a *totally different variety*.

PLATE LVII.

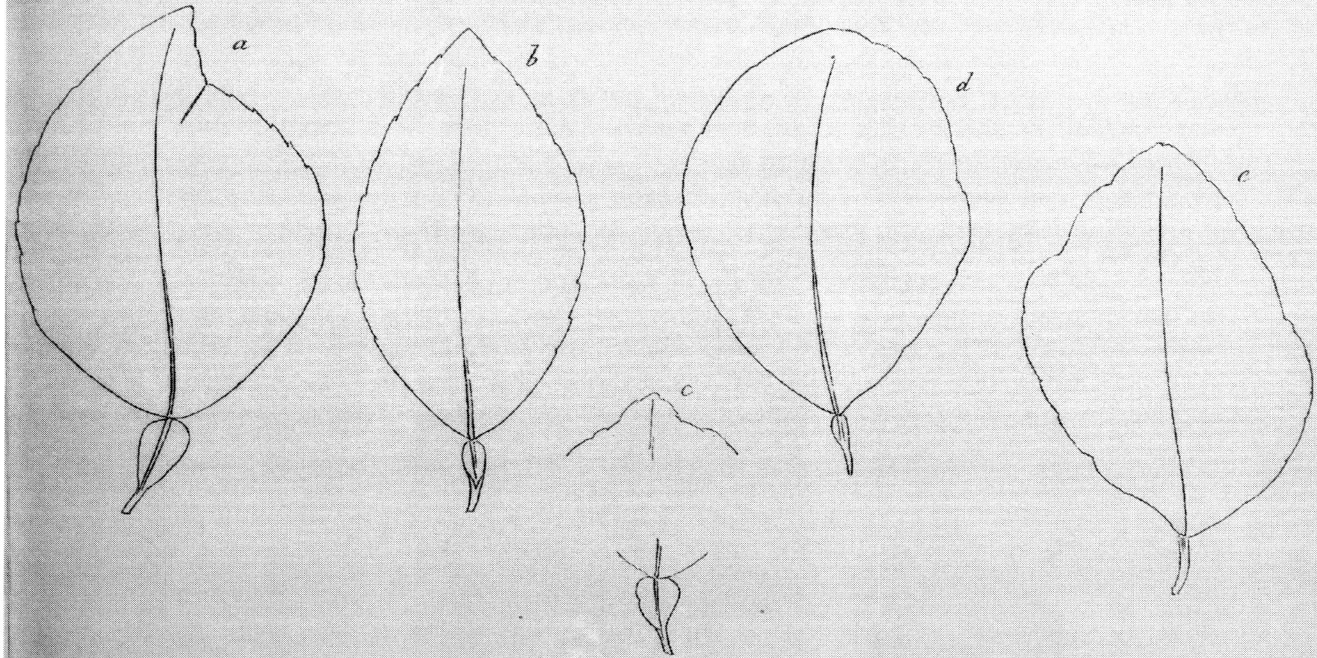

PLATE LVIII.

This plate shows oranges of the Malta or Portugal type purchased from shops in England. They are here given for purposes of comparison.

a is called the *Jaffa* orange. Some specimens are much larger. It is a large egg-orange, pitted all over with foveoli. It resembles the Malta egg-orange, but is larger.

b and *c* are what are called *Dènia* oranges. The skin is very closely adherent.

d and *e* I purchased under the name of *St. Michael's* oranges. *d* was orange-yellow, finely chagrined, and covered with shallow depressions and intermediate miliary projections; skin thin, and closely adherent; flavour fair, and seeds none. *d* was a flatter specimen with thickish skin, which had a sweetish aromatic taste, without any bitterness; pulp of a pleasant flavour and slightly sub-acid. I fancy many of the imported oranges are plucked a good deal before they are ripe. In my experience, unless an orange is well ripened on the tree, it never possesses the *right* flavour.

f is the *Florida* orange, quite ripe and very fresh (14th March). The exterior is orange, blushed with a sooty fine powder, which can be washed off, excepting from the foveoli. I have often observed this blackness on this type of orange; I do not know what it is. Skin rather thin, adherent; centre solid; seeds numerous, long, but many are imperfect; colour of pulp orange, and flavour very fine indeed; sweet, with a minimum of sub-acid.

PLATE LVIII.

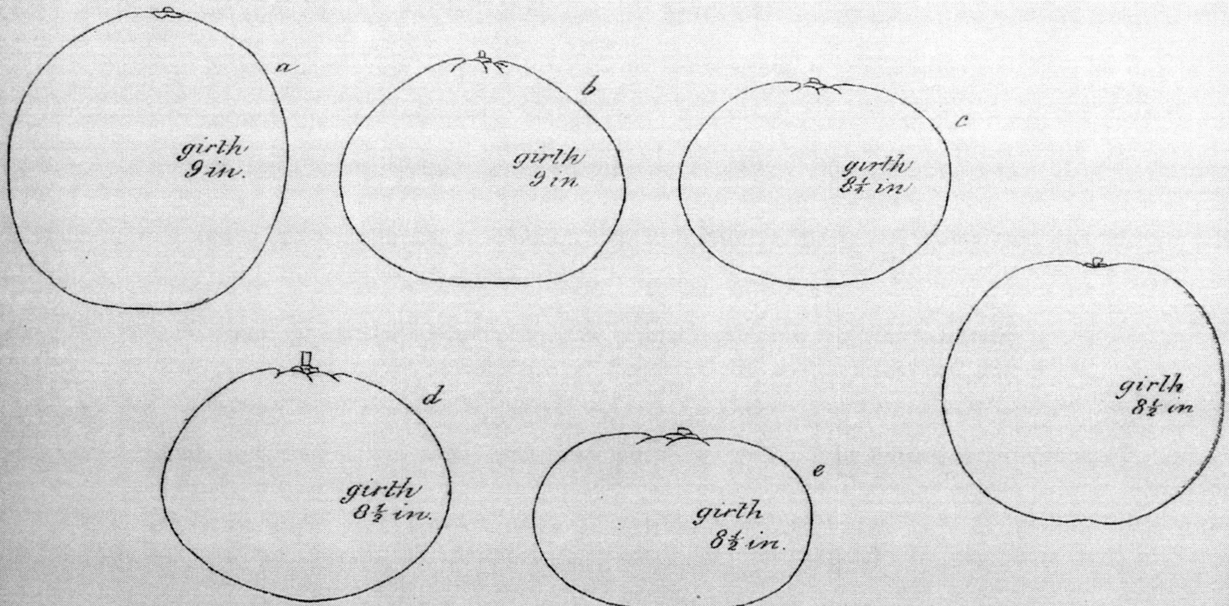
a
girth
9 in.
b
girth
9 in
c
girth
8¼ in
d
girth
8½ in.
e
girth
8½ in.
f
girth
8½ in

PLATE LIX.

The drawings of this plate are taken from the Flora amboyn. of Rumphius.

a and *b* are the Aurantium pompelmoes (Cassomba of the Malays), of Tab. xxiv. fig. 2, vol. ii. of Rumphius. If I have read him rightly, he says that fig. *B* denotes the natural shape (no spines in his drawing). He describes four kinds, one of which is irregular and tubercled. He says there are both red and white pulped pompelmoes.

Loureiro at p. 467, under the head of Citrus decumana, says: "Spinous, *glabrous*, petioles large, with cordate wings, pulp red or white, sweet or acid; very thick skin. A variety is *very sweet*, and with a white pulp and yellow exterior."

a shows a spineless branch, with *entire* leaves, of the Pummelo.

c and *d* are taken from Tab. xxxv. vol. ii. of Rumphius. They represent the Aurantium dulcis verrucosum, with a perfectly round fruit, *A* representing warts. The branch has crenate leaves, with small petiole wings, and small spines.

e represents a bunch of this fruit.

Miguel, in his Flor. Ind. Batav., places this Aurantium of Rumphius as "Citrus decumana, var. verrucosa" (?).

Note.—*c*, *d*, and *e* should, I think, have been placed with the *Portugal orange* group.

PLATE LIX.

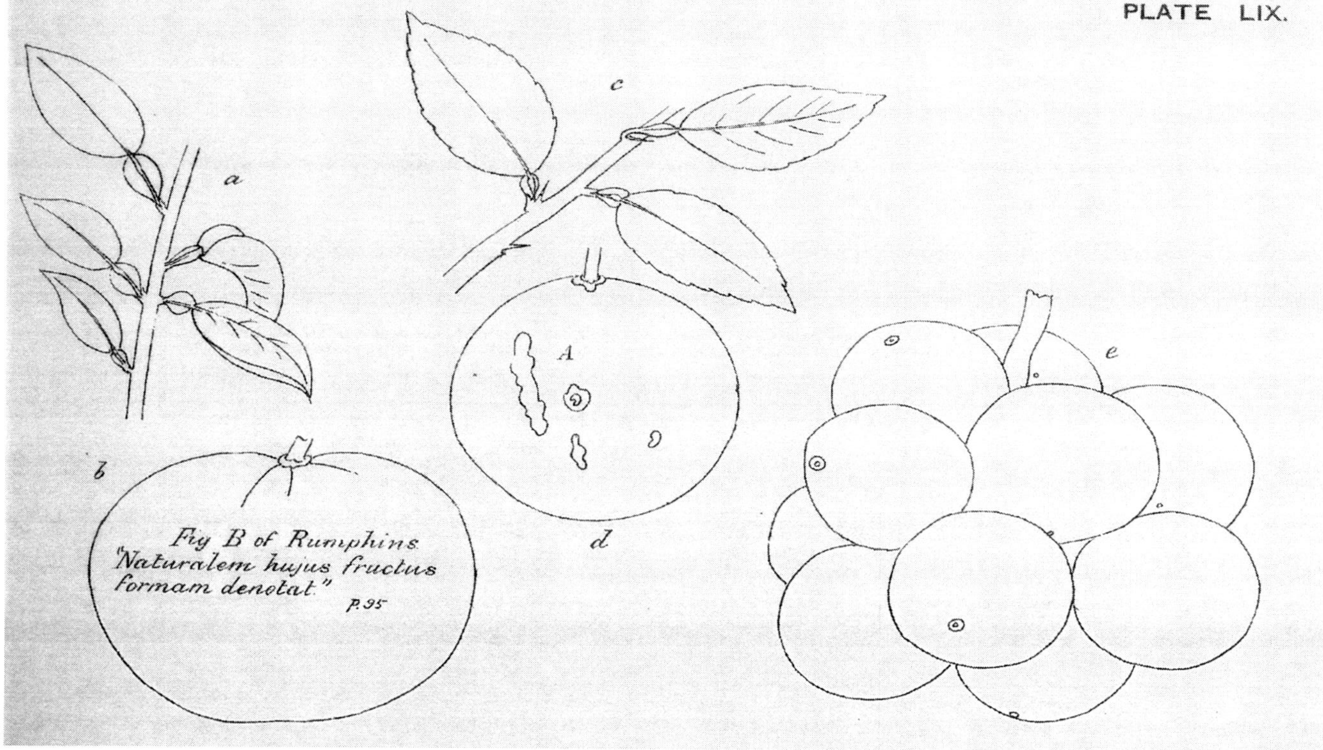
a
b
c
A
d
e
Fig B of Rumphins
"Naturalem hujus fructus
formam denotat."
P. 95

PLATE LX.

Is an *Amilbêd* from Rohilcund.

a and *b* show this *Amilbêd*; lemon-yellow externally; round the mammilla it is smooth; in other parts it is closely studded with miliary elevations. It was the only citrus which came with the above name, and which had a *mammilla*, somewhat like that of the *Khattá* orange. The pulp was pale orange, with abundant and sour juice. It is said it never sweetens. Some of the pulp carpels were open towards the centre of the fruit, which was hollow. It floated very well in water.

c and *d* are well-developed rain leaves; one with only a margined petiole, and the other with small wings to its petiole.

Note.—*Amilbêd* should properly be written *Ămălbêd*, *Ămăl* coming, it is said, from the Sanskrit word meaning *sour*.

PLATE LX.

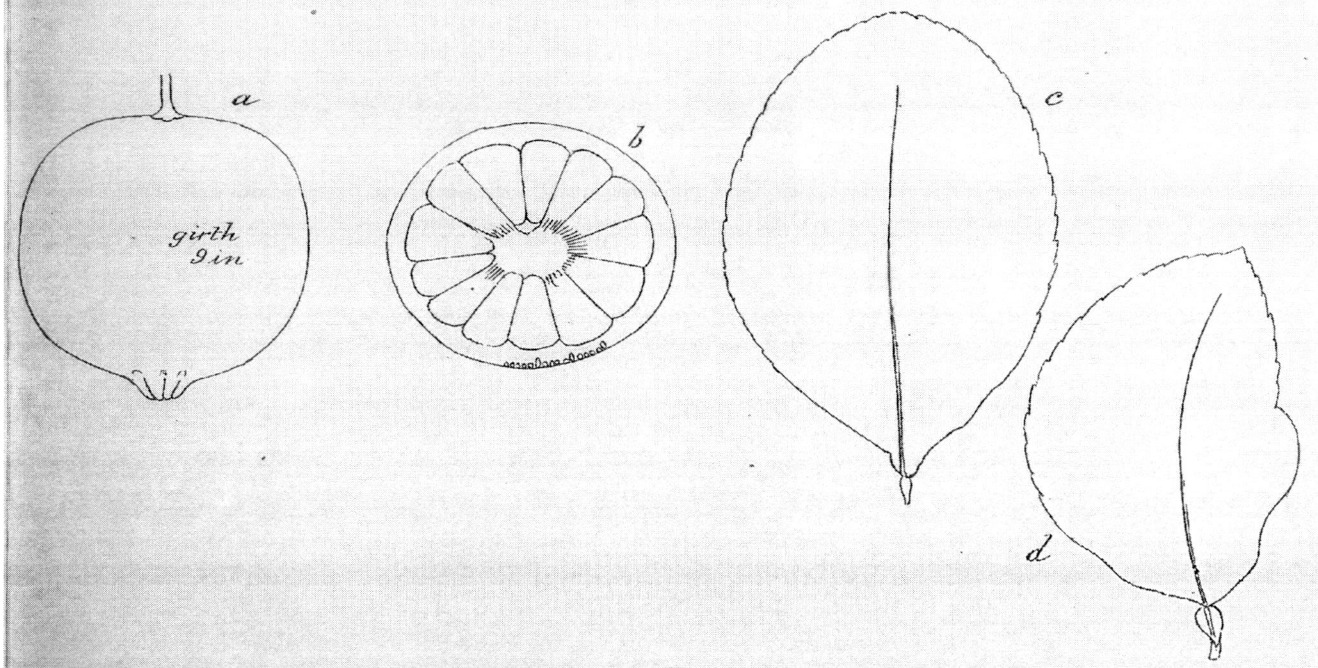

PLATE LXI.

An *Amilbêd* from Ajitmul, in the Etawah District (some call it *Amilbènt*).

a and *b* show this perfectly oblate specimen, with a perfectly polished surface, distantly pitted with oil-glands. When unripe it is light green, and pale yellow when ripe. The pulp is orange-yellow and sour; juice abundant. When I was examining this fruit, it struck me as on its way from an orange to a pummelo.

c is a well-developed rain leaf, and *d* and *e* spring leaves. In the section *b* there is a central column A, detached from the carpels, and only united to them by the surrounding threads.

PLATE LXI.

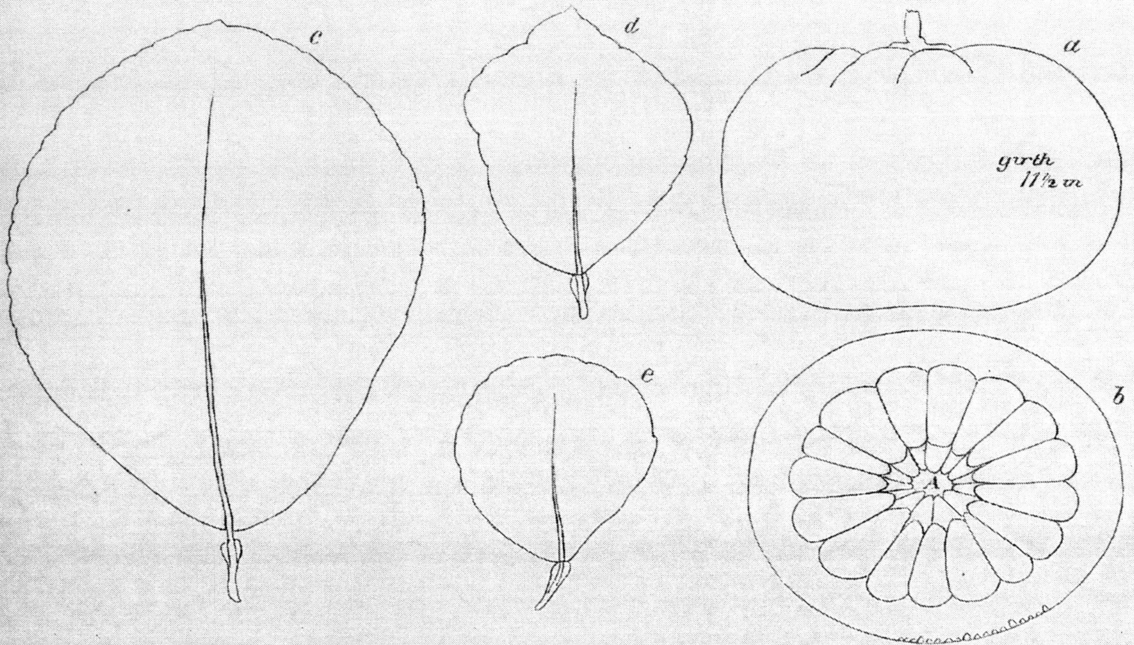

PLATE LXII.

Is the small *Amilbêd* of Lucknow.

a and *b* show this citrus with a *very slight* indication of a mammilla. When ripe it is light yellow, with a smooth and shiny surface, simply pitted with oil-glands. When unripe it is of a vivid green, and looks like a large roasting apple. The pulp is orange-yellow; juice abundant, and very acid. Some of the pulp carpels were open towards the centre, and two had an indentation, or emargination, on the circumference part, as shown by AA in the section.

c is a fully-developed rain leaf, and *d* a spring leaf; the former is more serrate than crenate, and the three sizes of its oil-cells are quite distinct.

PLATE LXII.

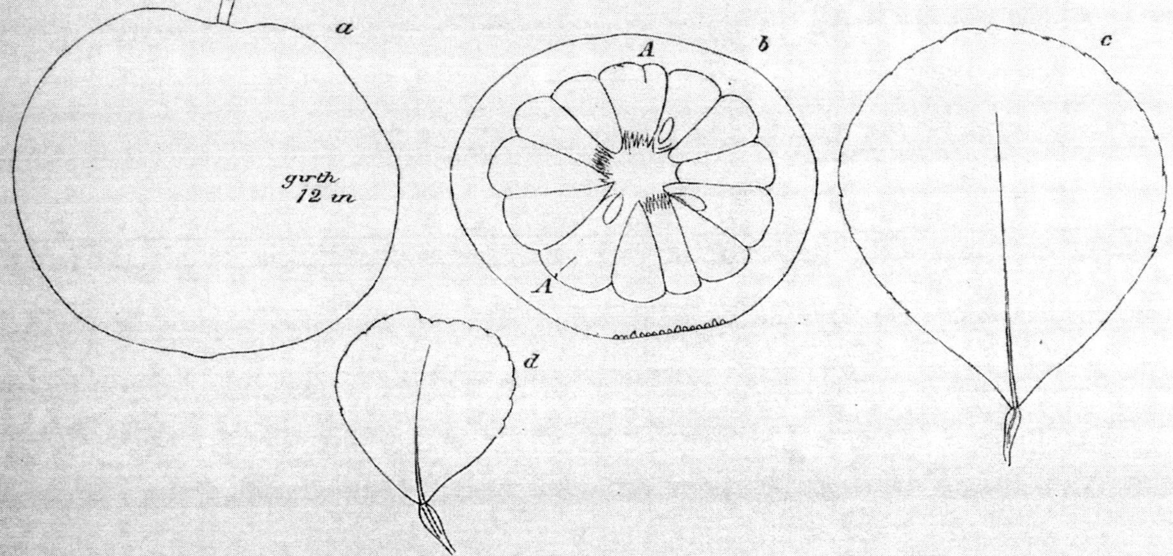

PLATE LXIII.

An *Amilbêd* from Bulrampur, Gonda.

a and *b* show this oblate citrus, with a deep lemon-coloured exterior, rather smooth and shiny, with distant foveoli, and smaller ones between them. The pulp is transparent and of a pale orange-yellow; juice abundant, and of a pure acid flavour. The seeds were small for the size of the fruit. The pulp carpels were open towards the centre, the latter being a large hollow space.

c shows a well-developed rain leaf with oil-cells of all sizes, quite distinct; and *d* a spring leaf.

e a small spine which came with the branch. The young unexpanded leaf-buds were quite *pubescent*. The leaves were slightly lemon scented.

b shows the central column A remaining adherent to only one carpel, and dragged to the one side.

PLATE LXIII.

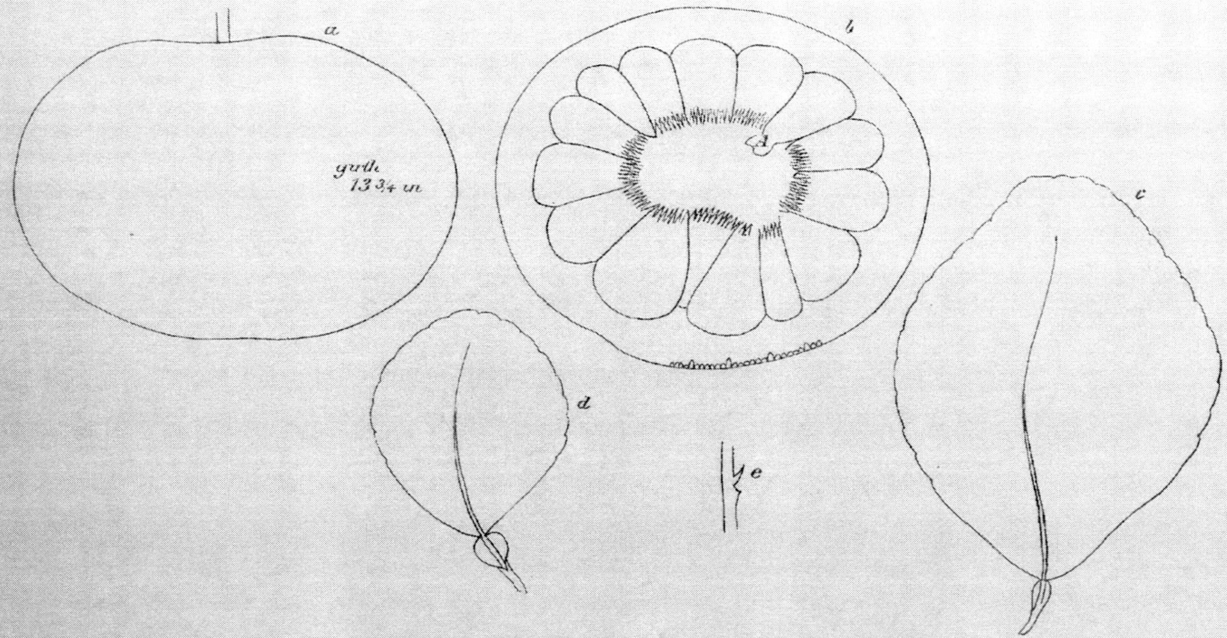

PLATE LXIV.

A pyriform *Amilbêd* from Rampur, Rohilcund.

a and *b* show its distinct pyriform outline, with smooth surface. It had slight foveoli, and the smooth intermediate spaces had indistinct transparent oil-cells. This *Amilbêd* was different from the foregoing. It had a *white* pulp, like that of a lemon, with scanty and very sour juice. It was unripe, which may account for the scantiness of its juice.

c and *d* are rain leaves; *e* is a spring leaf.

I found no spines on the branch sent.

PLATE LXIV.

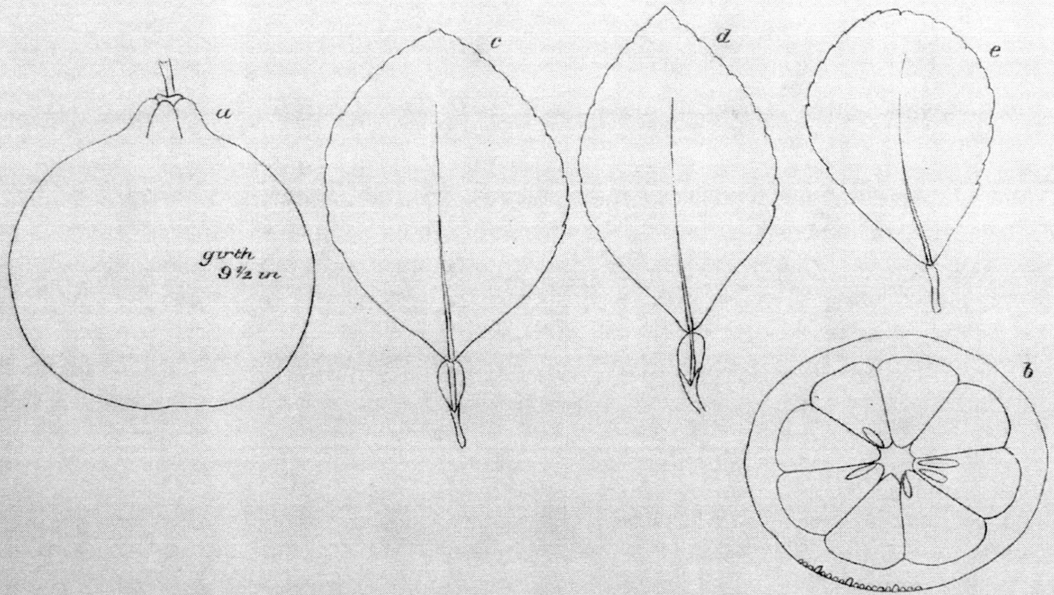

PLATE LXV.

Is an ovoid *Amilbêd* from Benares.

a and *b* show its outline and section. Externally it is not unlike a large *Gulgul* lemon, without its mammilla. It is lemon-yellow and smooth. Its pulp is pale, like that of a lemon. Its centre solid, and the circumference part of the pulp carpels has a distinct indentation or emargination. These indentations correspond to the midribs of the carpels. The juice is abundant and sour.

The leaves, which I have not seen, would probably decide whether this is an *Amilbêd*, or a *Gulgul* lemon.

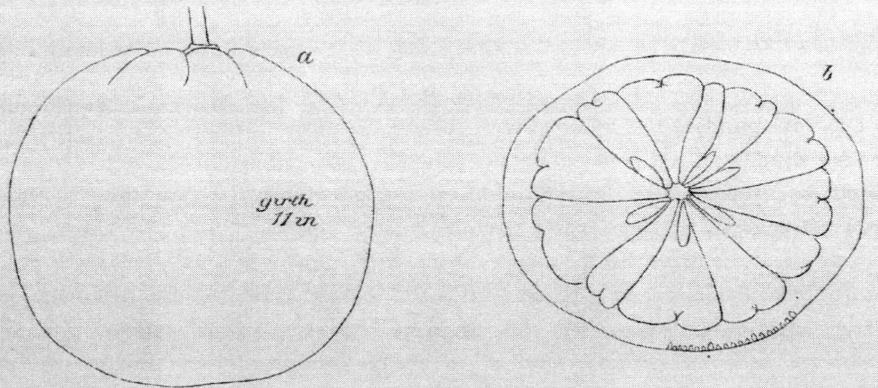
a
girth
11 in
b

PLATE LXVI.

Is a citrus, received from Messrs. Carew & Co., of Rosa, Shahjahanpur, under the name of *Chakôtra*, or Pummelo.

a and *b* show its outline and section. It is of a pale yellow, neither very smooth nor at all rough. It has slight foveoli, representing the openings of the large oil-cells, with intermediate small ones, which are not raised. In section these oil-cells of the rind have a curious appearance. The larger ones have a long neck and are shaped like battledores. They are not unlike small juice-vesicles. Each carpel, on its circumference side, had a little projection A, representing the main vessel of its midrib.

c and *d* are well-developed spring leaves, thin and quite different from Pummelo leaves. Pulp lemon-like, sour and bitter.

e, *f*, *g*, and *h* represent spring leaves.

The spines on the branches sent were mere feeble *points*. Taking all its characters into consideration, I believe this to be an *Amilbêd*, and not a "Chakôtra" proper.

PLATE LXVI.

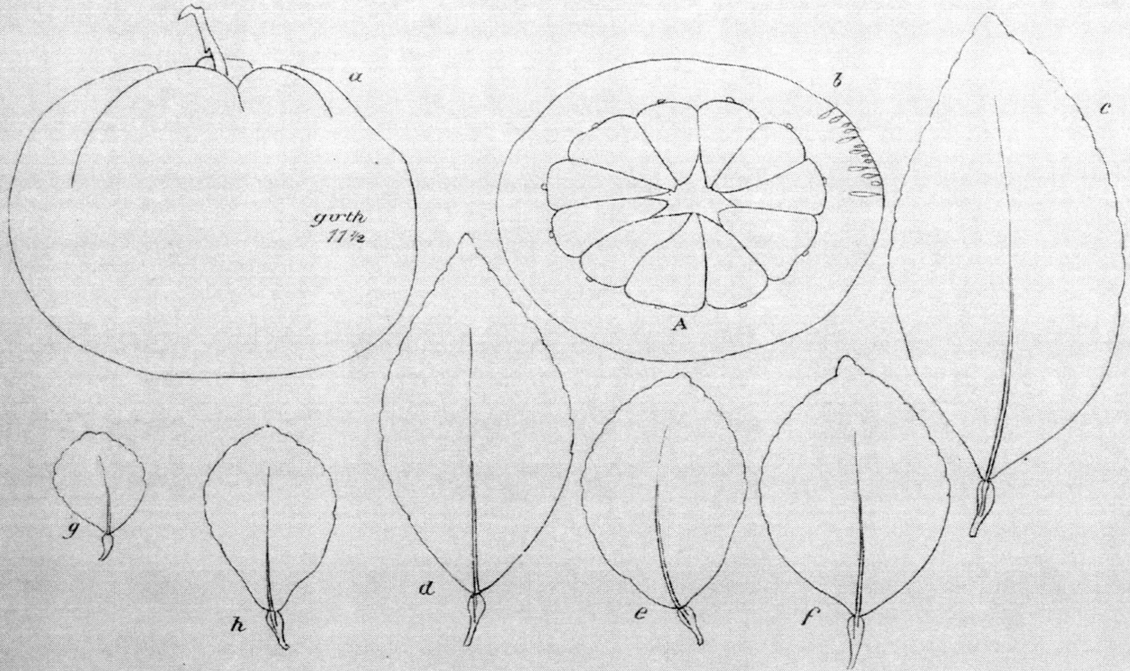

PLATE LXVII.

Amilbéd Kalàn, or large *Amilbêd* of Lucknow.

a shows its irregular outline. It is, when ripe, of a deeper yellow than the *Kaghzi nimboo* or lime. Its surface, beyond being undulating, is rather smooth; only pitted with oil-cell openings. The pulp is very pale, like that of a lemon. The juice-vesicles are coarse; the juice very abundant, and of a pure acid; seeds very numerous. This is a desirable variety, on account of its abundant and purely acid juice.

c is a rain leaf, thick and tough, reminding one of a pummelo leaf; *d* is a spring leaf. The oil-cells of the leaves, of three sizes, were distinct.

PLATE LXVII.

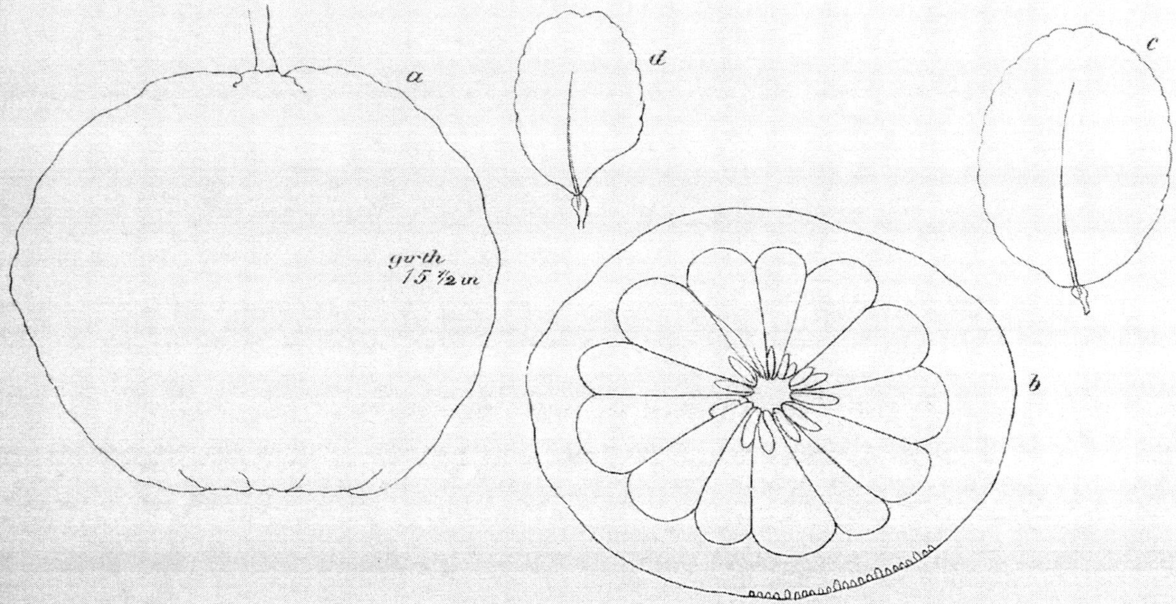

PLATE LXVIII.

The *Dèsi Kalamba* of Calcutta. (*Dèsi* means "belonging to India," in contradistinction to *Beläti*, or foreign.)

a and *b* show its outline and section. Its exterior was neither rough nor smooth. It had shallow and distant foveoli. The intermediate spaces were covered with convex cells, each having a minute earth-coloured scab or crust, as if caused by some insect. The pulp was pale, and pinkish at the circumference. The juice was abundant and sour, with a pleasant taste of pummelo, and a slight dash of bitterness.

c and *d* were papery leaves, unlike pummelo leaves.

e is the small spine found on the branches sent.

It appeared to me that this citrus was more like an *Amilbêd Kalan* than a pummelo proper.

Dèsi might either mean that it belonged to India, or it might be a contemptuous term, meaning an *inferior* article.

PLATE LXVIII.

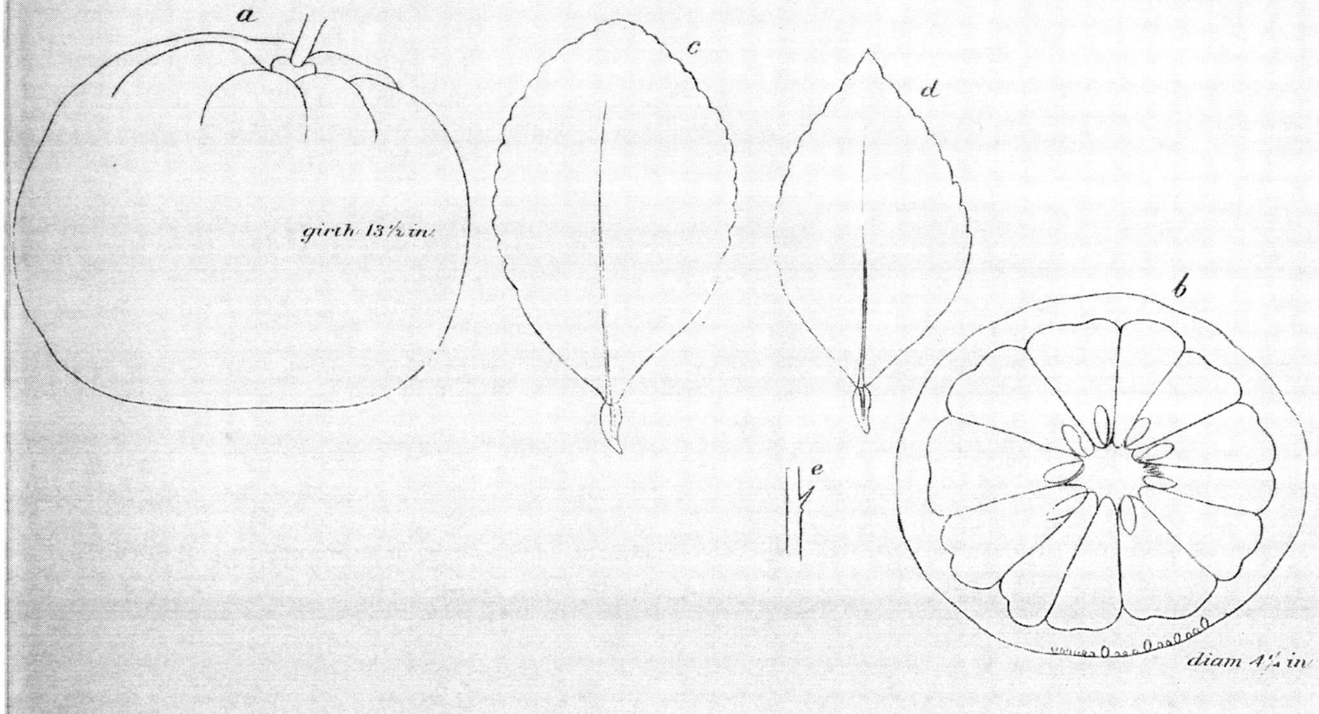

PLATE LXIX.

The *Keem* citron of the Saharunpur Botanic Garden.

a shows its undulating and sub-warty surface. Its exterior is lemon-yellow, with large lumpy folds round the base. The foveoli are large and shallow, with the interspaces bulging out. The apex mammilla is depressed and obliterated. Its former existence being only indicated by an aureola.

b shows the section and its thick skin. It had a very bitter rind; but very aromatic. The pithy part was soft and spongy; the pulp coarse, pale, with a faint tinge of pinkish orange; the juice abundant and very sour; the centre hollow. Many of the carpels were open towards the centre.

c is a well-developed leaf, with its petiole simply margined.

d, the spine found on the branch sent.

In my opinion this is a variety of *Amilbêd Kalàn*. Mr. Gollam says that its flowers are large and pure white; the young shoots are slightly downy. I do not know what *Keem* means, if I have read it rightly.

PLATE LXIX.

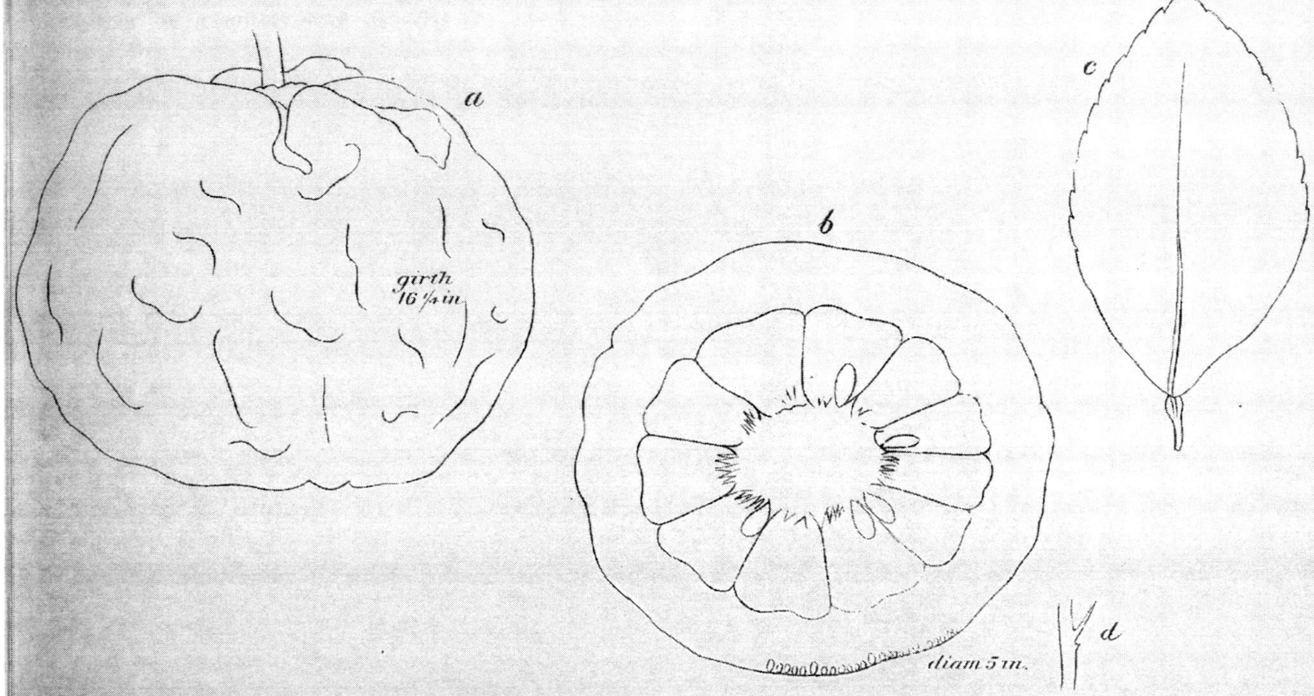

PLATE LXX.

Is a *Chakôtra* or pummelo sent from Gonda, and supposed to have come originally from Nepàl.

a shows its pyriform outline. Its exterior was lemon-yellow, with a tinge of red on one side. The oil-cells were slightly convex; there were no foveoli depressions. The skin was $\frac{1}{3}$ of an inch thick; the pulp pinkish. The pulp carpels irregular, and rather emarginate on their circumference side; the centre hollow.

b shows a well-developed leaf almost entire, and *very slightly* tomentose. The shape of the leaves, and absence of crenations are like the *Chakôtra* of Etawah, which has a large oblate fruit. This shaped fruit in Etawah is called *Mahtábi*.

All the foregoing specimens of citrus, which came under the name of *Amilbêd*, had only margined petioles. Here we have the large cordate wings of the pummelo proper.

PLATE LXX.

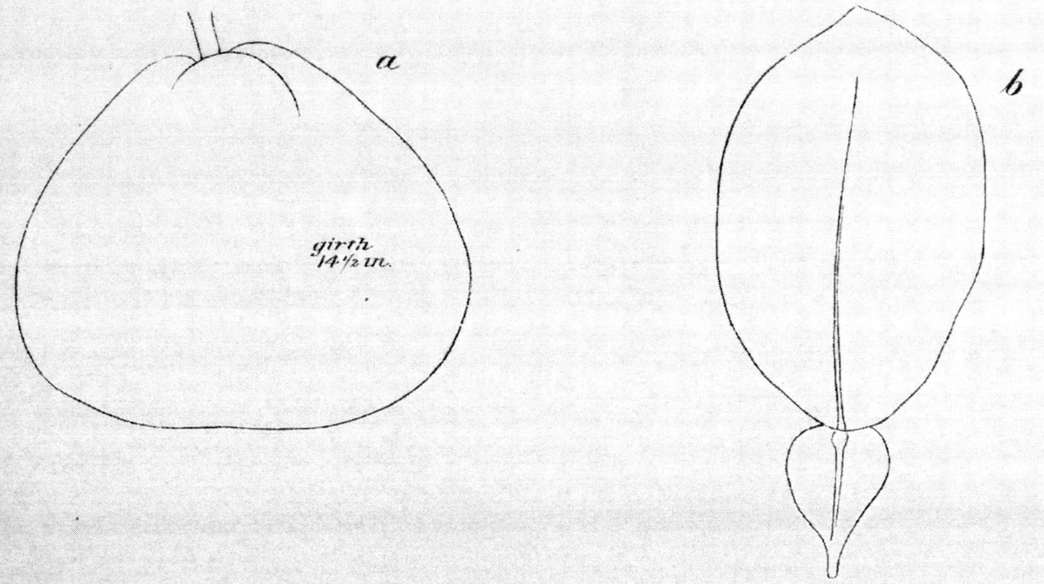

PLATE LXXI.

Is another *Chakôtra* from Gonda.

a shows its pyriform outline, almost an exact copy of the foregoing one on Plate LXX. Like it, it is lemon-yellow, with very slightly projecting oil-cells. Its skin was ½ an inch thick; its pulp pale towards the centre, and pinkish towards the circumference; centre, small and hollow; carpels regular, and not emarginate.

b shows a well-developed leaf, crenate, tomentose, and ovo-lanceolate.

I have given this plate to show that, although this fruit is almost indistinguishable from the preceding, the tree is of a different variety, with ovo-lanceolate, *crenate*, and *tomentose* leaves; while the foregoing has lanceolate, *entire*, and almost *glabrous* leaves. Besides, the pulp carpels of this are *not* emarginate, while those of the foregoing *are* slightly so.

PLATE LXXI.

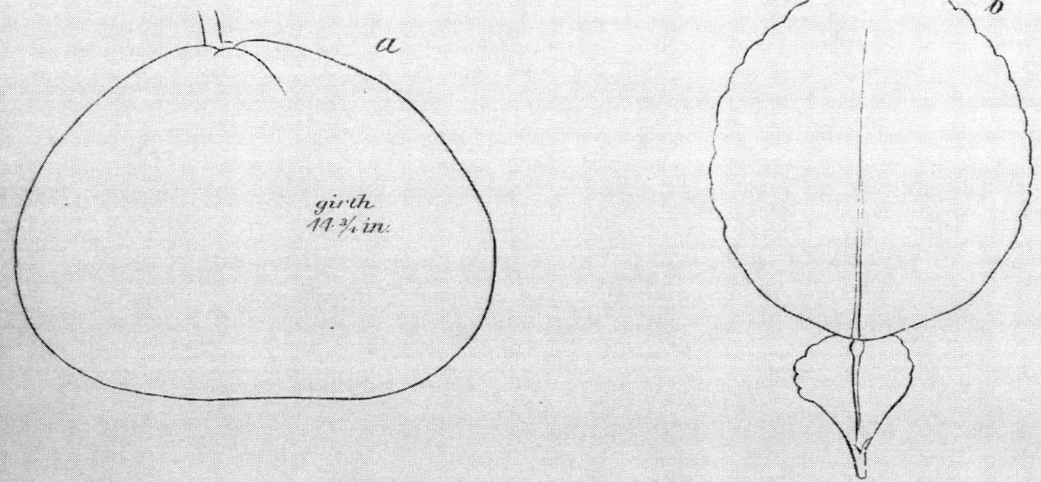

PLATE LXXII.

This is a pyriform pummelo, which I purchased at the Sohagpur station, G.I.P. Ry.

a and *b* show its outline and section. It was lemon-yellow, smooth, and tinged with red in many places. It was closely dotted all over with oil-cells of irregular shape and of various sizes. The centre was solid, with a ring of vessels as shown at A of section *b*. The pulp was red round the circumference, and pale towards the centre. It had many seeds. (Note the elongated centre, and see Chapter on "Morphology.")

c shows the disposition of the juice vesicles in the carpels, as shown in a cross section. They were short excepting towards the centre of the fruit. Many were like enlarged oil-cells; pear shaped. The attachments were not only on the circumference part of the carpel, *as is usual with many citrus*, but also on the sides, as far as B B. The vesicles projected into the middle of the carpel; but at B B they projected towards the centre of the fruit, and were much longer. Some of the juice-vesicles were pedicelled, but the majority were sessile. (*See* Appendix No. 62.)

NOTE.—The elongated centre A gives an impression of this fruit having originally come from the fusion of two ovaries. (*Vide* Plates CCXXIII. and CCXXIV.)

PLATE LXXII.

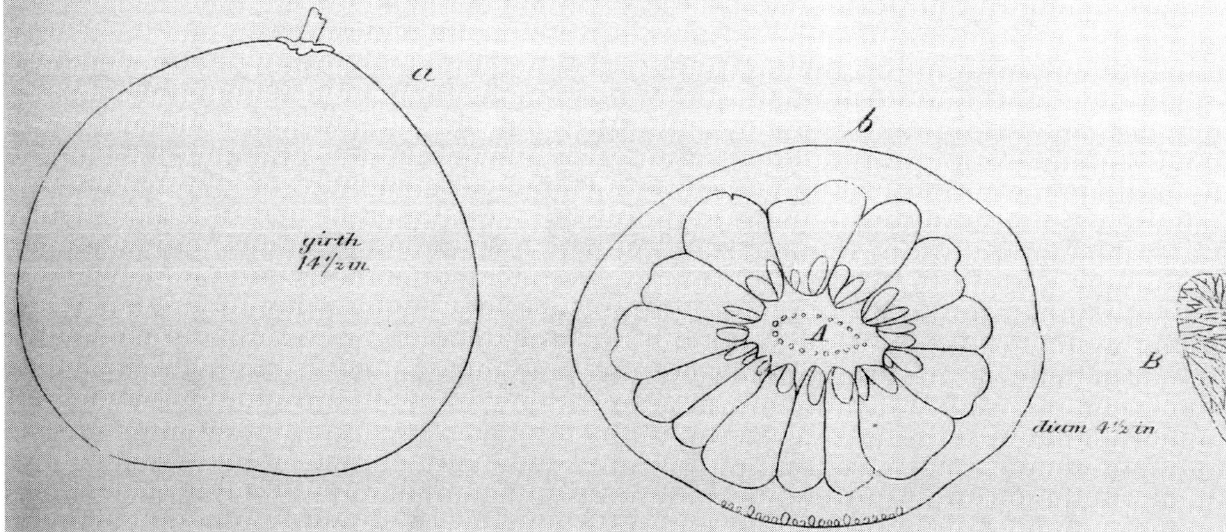

PLATE LXXIII.

a came from Bulrampur, Gonda, with the name of *Mahtâbi Chaôktra*. It is said that the fruit often weighs $1\frac{1}{2}$ seers, or 3 lbs. It is said to ripen in November, and also in March (I suppose the latter is the *Dumrèz* crop). It is lemon-yellow, with shallow green furrows round the base, indicated by the lines A A. Round the base the oil-cells are shallow *cavities*; elsewhere they are *convex* elevations. In its longitudinal furrows it resembles the *Mussèmbi* orange of Poona. The skin of this specimen was one inch thick; the pulp, of a pleasant sub-acid; in parts pinkish, in parts like a white pummelo; it was seedless.

c is a fully-developed leaf of *a*. It is crenate, and its scent is very faint. The young shoots are pubescent.

b is the *Chakôtra Ghâgus* of Bulrampur, said to be *sweet*. It was not sweet, but sub-acid, and in every way like the bigger one *a*. The young shoots were also pubescent. I saw no difference between these two, although they bore different names. Another variety, called *Chakaya Chakôtra*, and said to be *sweet*, was also sub-acid, like most pummelos.

PLATE LXXIII.

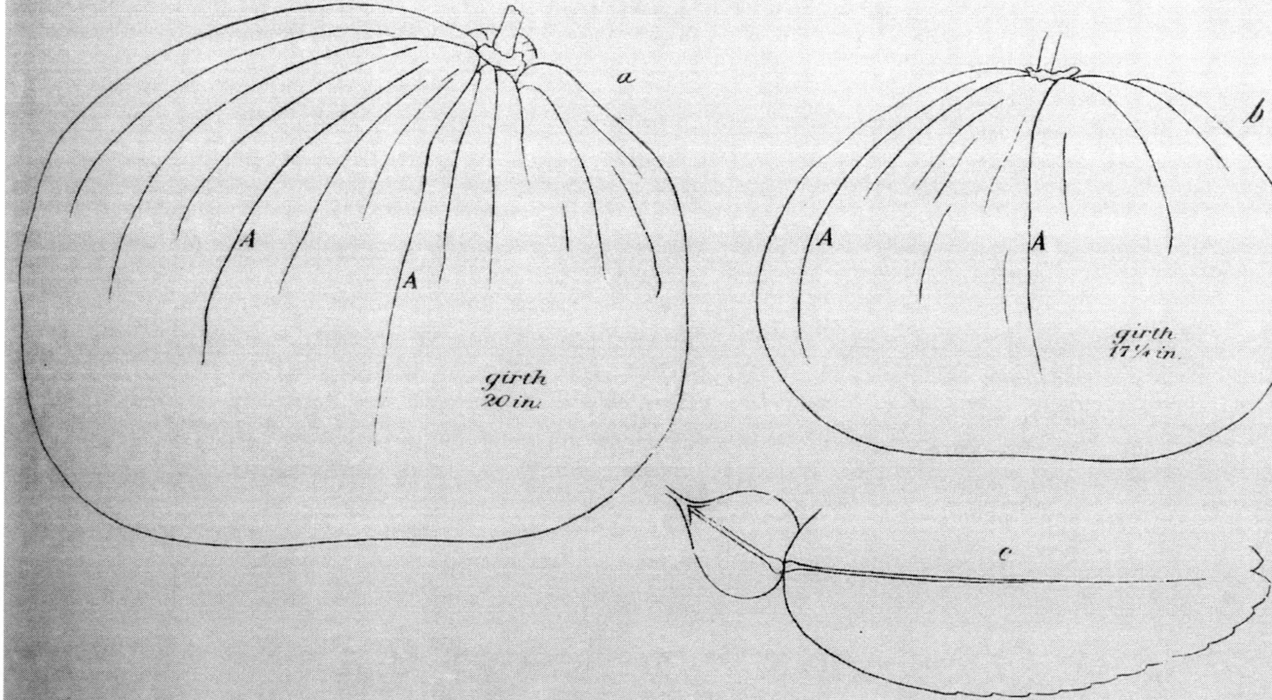

PLATE LXXIV.

A "Chakôtra" from Bulrampur, Gonda, said to be uncommon.

a and *b* are the outline and section of this pummelo. It was of a lemon-yellow. The surface was covered with foveoli, at distances of $\frac{1}{3}$ of an inch. The intermediate spaces had both *convex* and *plane* oil-cells. The convex ones were polished, the others not so. The pulp was pale and greenish, with a very light pinkish tinge on the B side. The skin was thicker on the B side than on the A side, probably from better development, as is shown also by the larger pulp carpels. The juice was abundant, and of a pleasant sub-acid ; and it had *no seeds*.

c is a rain leaf, and *d* a spring leaf. The spring leaves were either entire or crenate. The spines were mere points.

Besides being seedless, I could see nothing uncommon about this pummelo. If *c* represents a fully-developed rain leaf, which I doubt, this variety may have smaller leaves, with smaller petiole wings, than is usual.

PLATE LXXIV.

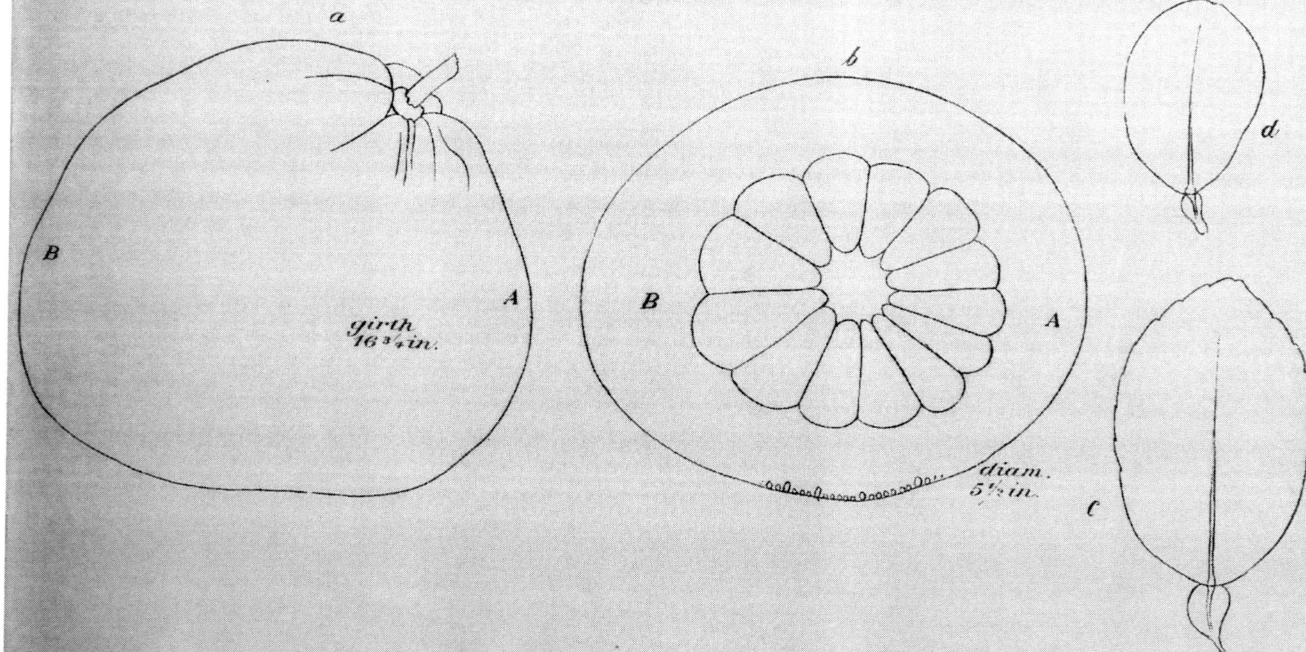

PLATE LXXV.

This is the *Jambòle*, or *Jamboo Nárun*, of Ceylon.

a and *b* show the outline and section of this ovoid pummelo; the wavy outline indicates the projections of the oil-cells of three sizes, the disposition of which is shown at A. The exterior is pale yellow, covered all over with only *convex* oil-cells of three sizes. There are no depressions. The convexities are easily squashed with the nail. The scent of their essential oil is peculiar. The pulp is transparent yellowish white, with the faintest tint of pink towards the centre. The juice-cells are large, and the juice of a nice sub-acid and aromatic flavour, without any bitterness. It is many-seeded. The seeds, when cut, are white. The oil-cells of the rind are globular and quite distinct. The pithy part of the skin is spongy, and, as in some other pummelos, bitter.

PLATE LXXV.

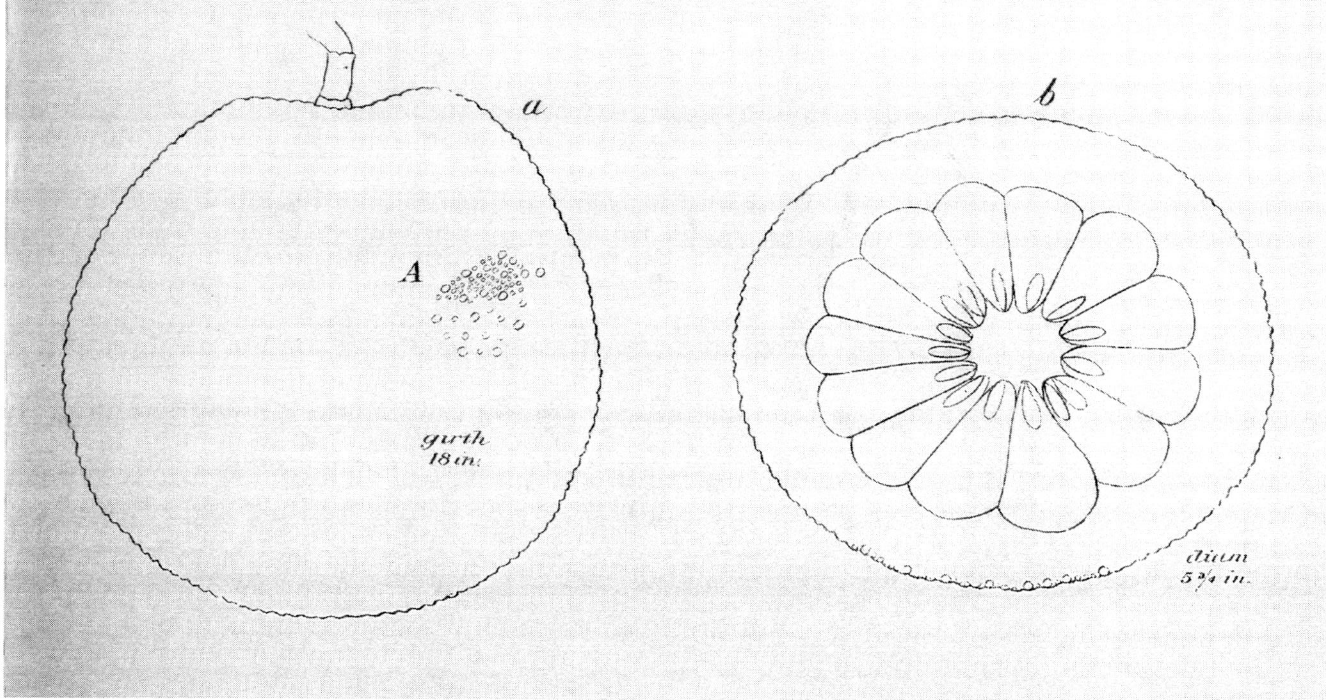

PLATE LXXVI.

c and *d* show the leaves of the *Jambòle* pummelo of Ceylon, shown on the foregoing Plate LXXV.

c is the largest pummelo leaf I have seen, excepting that of Plate LXXXV. ; its size being probably due to the abundant moisture and warmth of Ceylon ; *d* is a spring leaf; both crenate, and not so leathery as the leaves of the Indian pummelos. These leaves were of a light green, mottled faintly with yellow. The stem and mid-ribs were slightly pubescent. The oil-cells were distinct, and both the large and small ones distantly situated. In some parts none but the smallest oil-cells could be seen. Those of the edges, as usual, were quite distinct and large.

e is a longitudinal section of one of the pulp carpels. The juice-cells of the three different sizes are sufficiently clear, and shown in cross section. They are roughly of three sizes.

PLATE LXXVI.

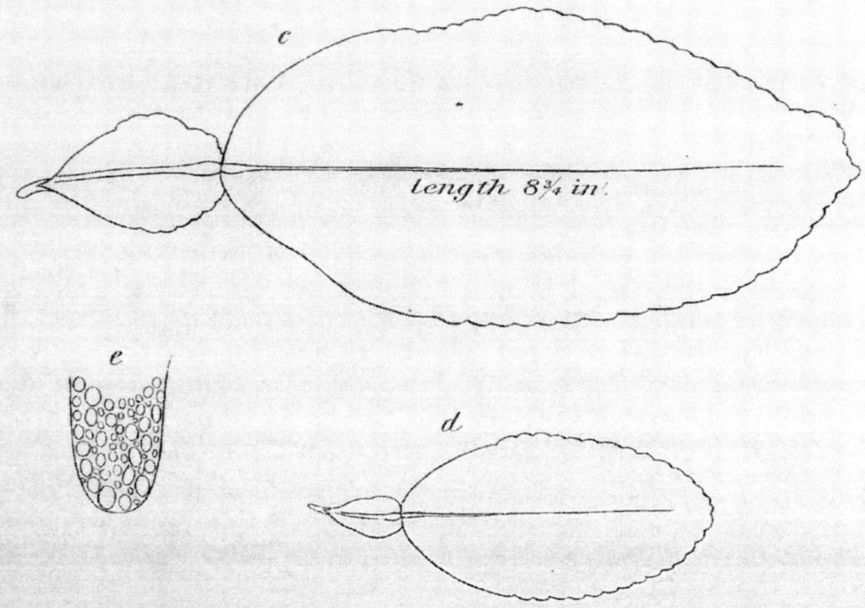

PLATE LXXVII.

Chakôtra Kalàn from Gundaroop Sing's Garden, Ajitmal, Etawah district.

a is the pyriform outline of this large pummelo. It is lemon-yellow, with a reddish tinge on one side. There are two sets of oil-cells, one concave like pinholes, shown by the dark dots at A, the others are miliary convexities, or little eminences between the former, as shown by the *light* dots at A. These miliary *convexities* near the peduncle are *also concavities*. In Rampur Rohilcund this sort of pummelo, I was told, is called *Át Anni Kalàn*. B B shows the zigzag minings of some insect, probably the larva of a minute moth. This is the only instance in which I noticed these minings under the epidermis of the fruit. Between the laminæ of the citrus leaves, in the rains, these minings are common, and give a glistening appearance to the leaves attacked; they injure the leaf. Probably the larvæ have a partiality to the essential oil of the leaves.

PLATE LXXVII

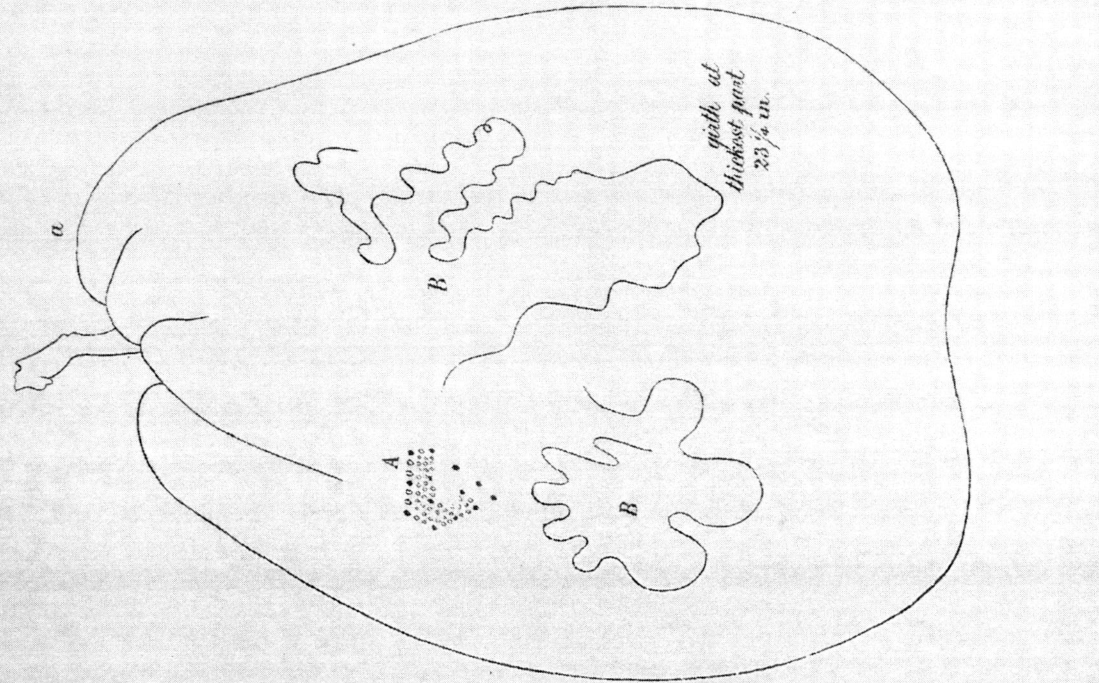

PLATE LXXVIII.

b is a section of the *Chakôtra Kalàn*, of the foregoing Plate LXXVII. It has a very thick skin and emarginate pulp carpels. The oil-cells of the rind are distinct. The pulp is red towards the circumference, and of a dirty yellowish colour elsewhere. The juice-vesicles of this specimen were dry, concrete, and tasteless. It had no seeds.

c and *d* are its leaves. The wings of the petioles in this variety, even in the young seedlings, are often continuous with the blade of the leaf, as shown in C C, the joint being in its normal position at C. Four leaves were sent, all with this character; *c* was only half so. All the leaves were tough and leathery.

PLATE LXXVIII.

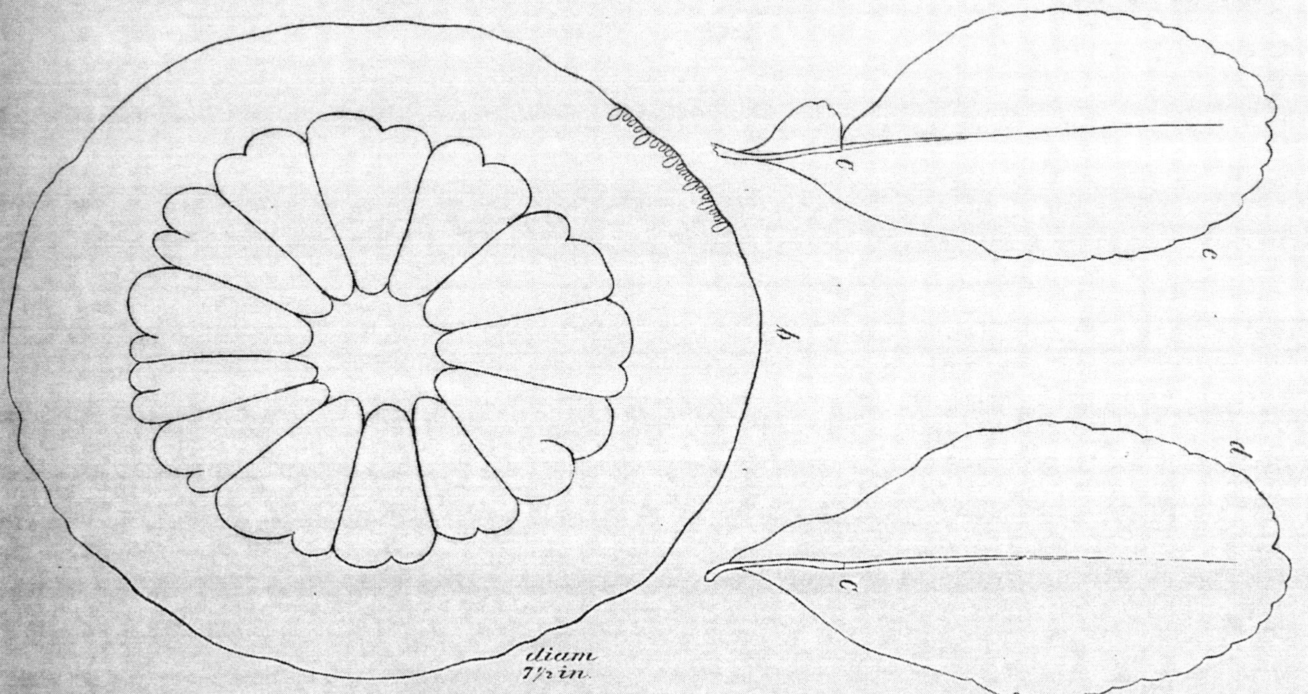

PLATE LXXIX.

Át Anni Kalàn of Rohilcuṇd.

This pummelo was pyriform and similar to the foregoing on Plate LXXVII., but larger. It had a girth of $25\frac{1}{2}$ inches at its thickest part; its section was rather oval, with a long diam. of $8\frac{1}{3}$ inches and a short diam. of $7\frac{1}{2}$ inches in the thickest part. The exterior was greenish lemon-yellow (perhaps not *quite* ripe), with very distinct foveoli depressions at certain distances, and everywhere between the former slight miliary convexities of the smaller oil-glands. The depressions gave it a uniform and faintly sub-warty surface. The apex had an outline of a *very* flattened mammilla.

a shows its section. The wavy outline indicates the depressions and elevations of the oil-glands, as shown at C. D D is the central column burst asunder.

b and *c* are the leaves of this pummelo. As before, *c* shows the union of the petiole wings with the leaf blade, and the joint at A.

The pulp was pale pink; juice abundant, sweetish sub-acid, with a pleasant aroma. The dissepiments or division walls of the pulp were of a dark rose colour. At B is shown the disposition of the juice-vesicles, which are mostly long and slender.

NOTE.—The ovality in section may possibly mean that it descends from a fruit made up of the *fusion of two ovaries*. (*Vide* Chapter on "Morphology," and Plates CCXXIII. and CCXXIV.)

PLATE LXXIX.

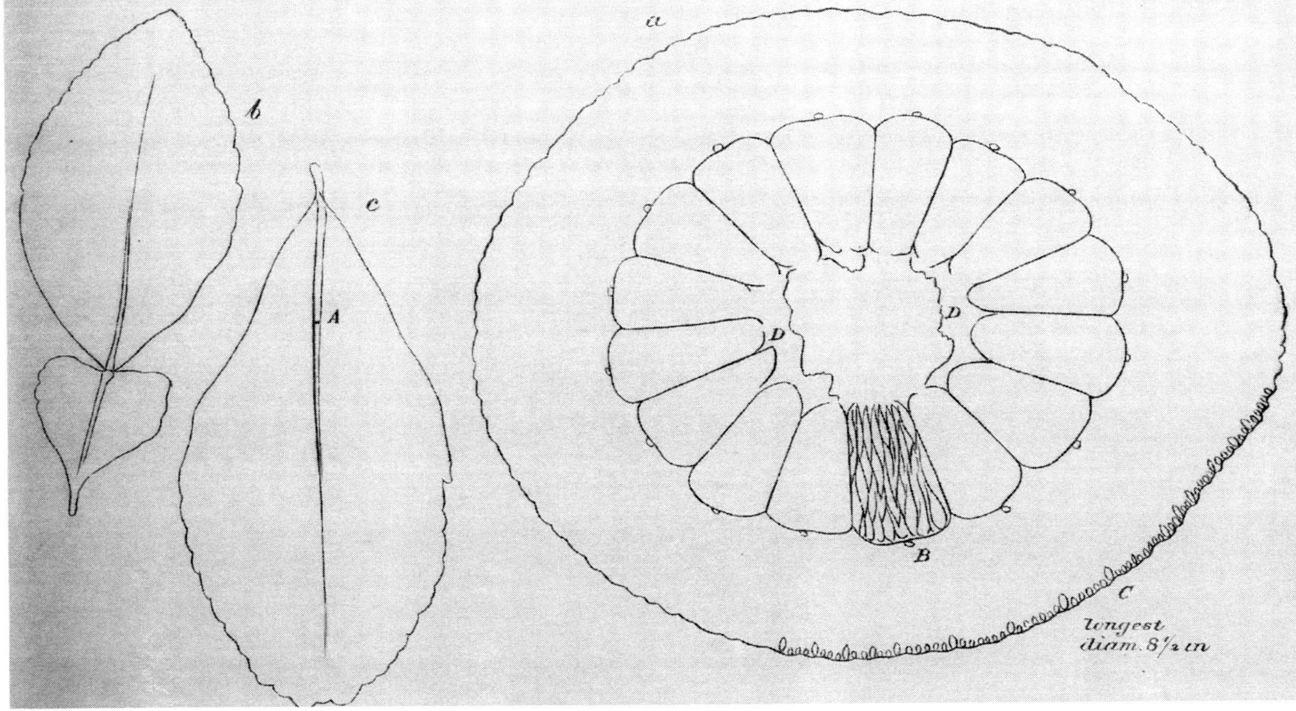

PLATE LXXX.

Large oblate pummelo, called "Chakôtra," from the Public Garden of Etawah.

a shows its outline, not unlike that of a gourd. When unripe, it is of a pale green, and when ripe, of a dull lemon-yellow. Its surface does not shine. It has large oil-glands at regular distances as shown at A, interspersed with innumerable small ones. This is the largest pummelo I have seen.

N.B.—The Bombay thin-skinned red pummelo is smaller than the above and more globose, with convex oil-cells of various sizes. The specimen I examined had a girth cf 22 inches. The thickness of its skin varied from $\frac{1}{4}$ *to* $\frac{1}{2}$ *inch*. Its pulp was of the colour of *raw beef*, and very juicy, and of a pleasant sub-acid, *sui generis* flavour, mixed with sweetness, and the merest *soupçon* of bitterness. The seeds when cut were white. It was by far the finest variety of pummelo I have yet seen, with an aromatic rind.

PLATE LXXX.

PLATE LXXXI.

Section of the foregoing huge pummelo given on Plate LXXX.

The pithy part of the thick skin is of the consistence of sponge cake, and has a pink blush.

The pulp is of a crimson pink, and hollow in the centre. The parts A A are the central column split up by the expansion of the fruit, and left adherent to the carpels. They are joined together by threads as shown in the centre.

The seeds are very numerous, and the carpels contorted in various ways, each having a very distinct emargination on its circumference side C C. In all other kinds these indentations were not so marked. The juice-vesicles are coarse, and their disposition shown at B. Taken singly, they are of a pale rose colour. The juice is an agreeable mixture of sweet, sub-acid, and just enough bitter to give it piquancy.

PLATE LXXXI.

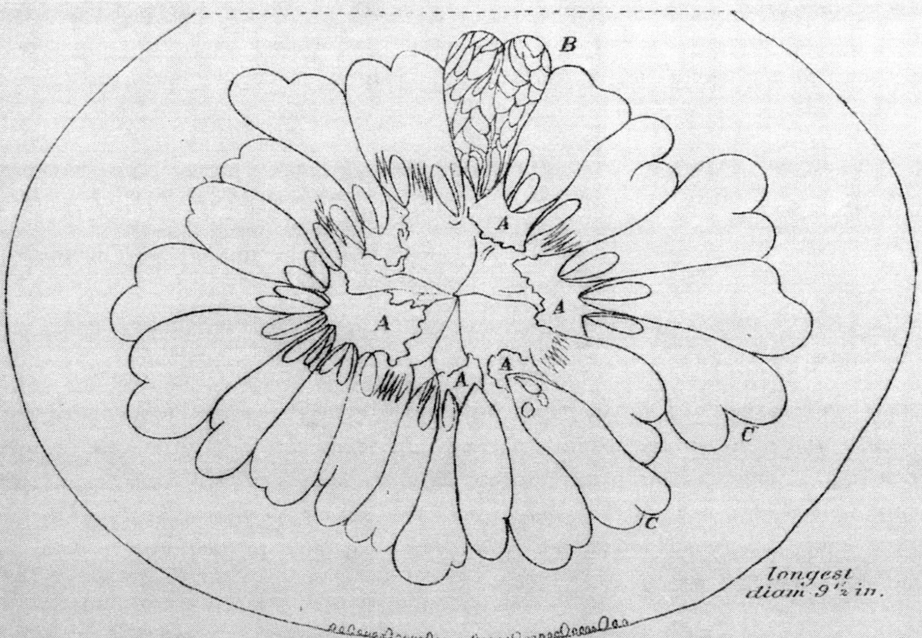

PLATE LXXXII.

Leaves of pummelos, in the Etawah Public Garden.

a is a well-developed rain leaf of the foregoing large pummelo given on Plate LXXX. The shoots of this tree and leaves are *quite glabrous*, so are the shoots and leaves of six other trees, which bear similar oblate fruit, but smaller. Their leaves are entire, with only an occasional indentation; nevertheless, on their edges, at stated distances, there are the remains of oil-glands, as if the leaves had been crenated. (*Vide* Chapter on "Morphology.")

These leaves are leathery, tough, and shiny; their scent is *nil*. The oil-cells of this blade appear to be all small, distantly situated, and almost indistinct, on account of the thickness of the leaf.

c is the leaf of a *fully pubescent* variety, with somewhat pyriform fruit, called *Mahtàbi* by the gardener. Its leaves are crenate, ovo-lanceolate, and of a duller and less shiny green than *a*. The petiole wings are smaller, and the oil-cells distinct.

b is an intermediate form, has a good deal of pubescence on young leaves and very young stem; less on older leaves and older stems, and none on the oldest leaves. The fully-developed but *young* leaves have a few scattered hairs here and there.

PLATE LXXXII.

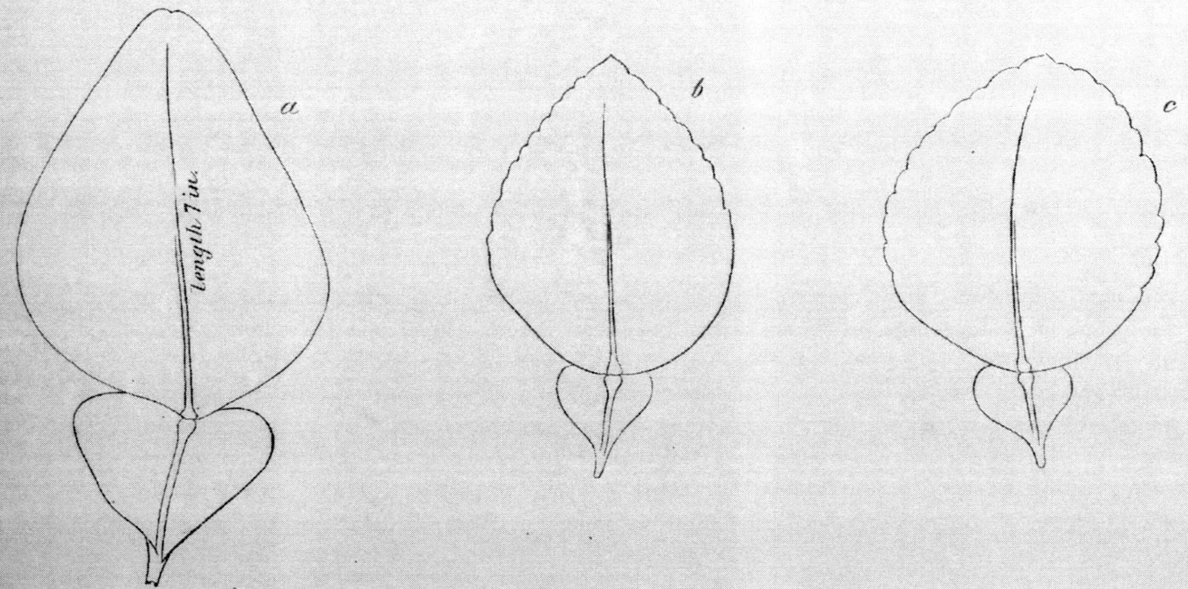

PLATE LXXXIII.

Chakótra, sent by Messrs. Carew & Co.

a and b show its outline and section. I here reproduce it because on its B side it was undeveloped. This produced a curious alteration in the oil-cells of the rind. Those shown on the developed, or A side, were simple depressions or *concavities*, not like pinholes, as in *Át Anni Kalàn* of Plate LXXVII. Between them were the small oil-cells, shown by the dots. On the contrary, on the undeveloped, or B side, the large oil-cells were closely set and *elevated*, that is *convexities*, while the small oil-cells were either not developed, or only here and there found, as shown by the few dots. Midway between the two sides the small cells became more apparent, and the convex larger cells became concave.

b shows the fully-developed oil-cells at A, and only the closely set large cells at B. This fruit had a rosy red pulp, sweet and sub-acid, imperfect and rather dry. The pulp carpels on B side also show a want of development. I think this specimen alone sufficiently proves that the coucave or convex oil-cells of the rind do not depend, as Risso said, on the acid or sweet nature of the pulp, but on a quite different set of conditions.

NOTE.—In this specimen also the elongated centre C probably comes from the fruit having originated in the fusion of *two ovaries*. (*Vide* Chapter on "Morphology.")

PLATE LXXXIII.

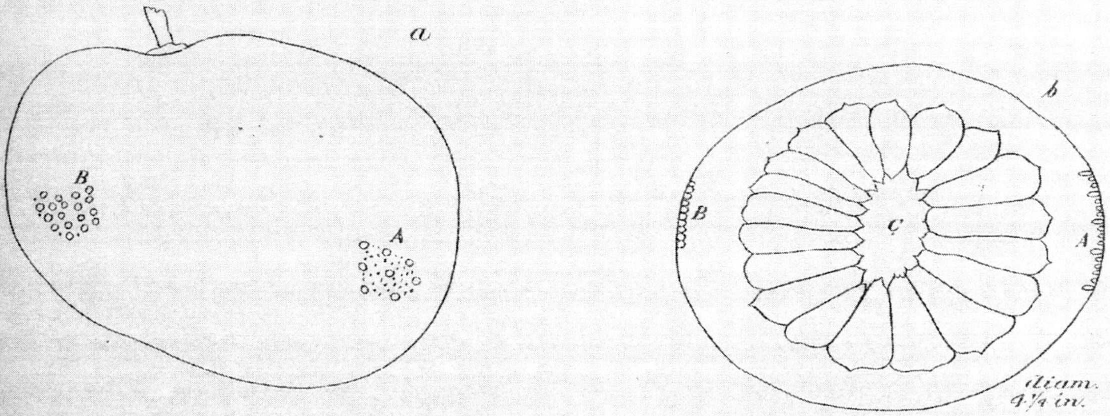

PLATE LXXXIV.

Leaves of the undeveloped pummelo given on the foregoing Plate LXXXIII.

c is a fully-developed rain leaf.

d is a spring leaf.

e, *f*, and *g* are also spring leaves, with margined petioles, *f* and *g* showing a deep emargination or division at the tip. The typical leaves of all the true pummelos I have seen always have a *large winged* petiole; but by search many types of leaves would be found on the same tree simulating the leaves of other varieties.

PLATE LXXXIV.

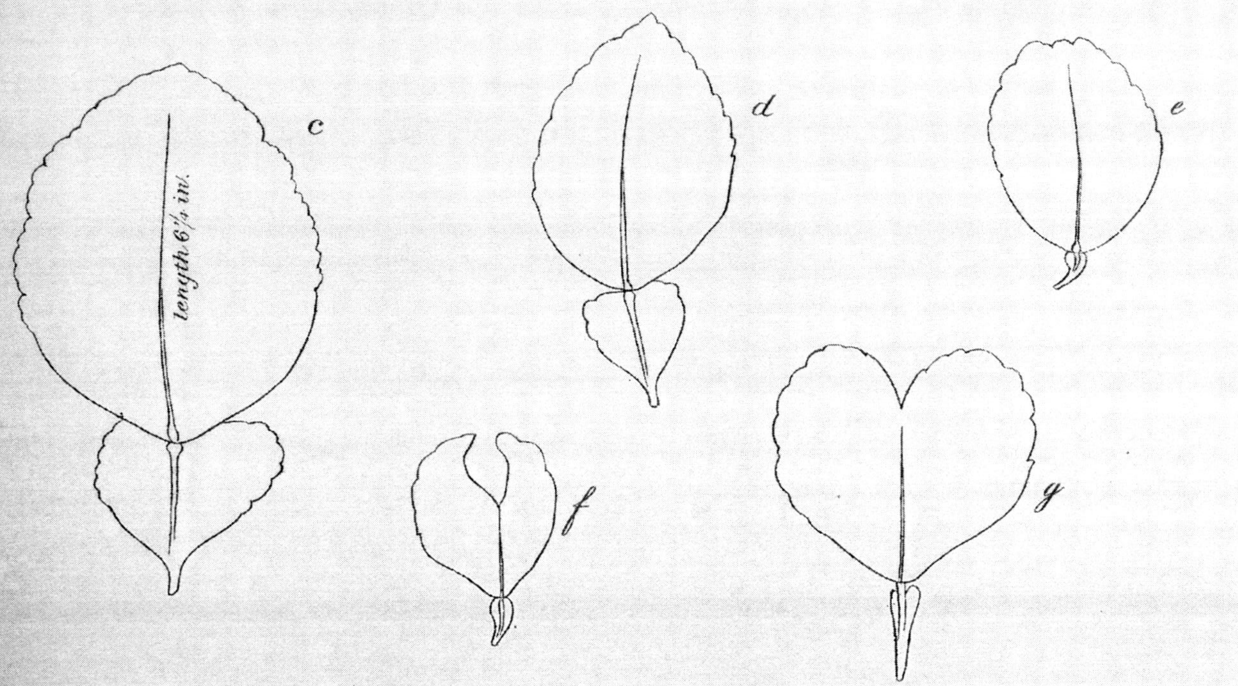

PLATE LXXXV.

Leaves of a citrus I obtained at Kandy, Ceylon.

These leaves were taken from a young tree which had no fruit. They had all the characters of pummelo leaves.

a resembled the fully-developed leaves of the Kandy *Jambòle.* The stems and leaves were quite glabrous, excepting the *minute unexpanded* leaf buds, which were decidedly tomentose. The large young leaves had only a few hairs on their edges, while in the tomentose forms the hairs were persistent on the edges even on the *old* leaves.

c is one of the spines I found on this tree. From its appearance the tree, I should say, was a seedling about three years old. If so, that would account for such a large spine. I have always found that *seedlings* of most citrus have more formidable spines than *budded* plants. These leaves had a faint lemon scent. Not having seen their fruit, I cannot say whether they were really pummelo trees.

PLATE LXXXV.

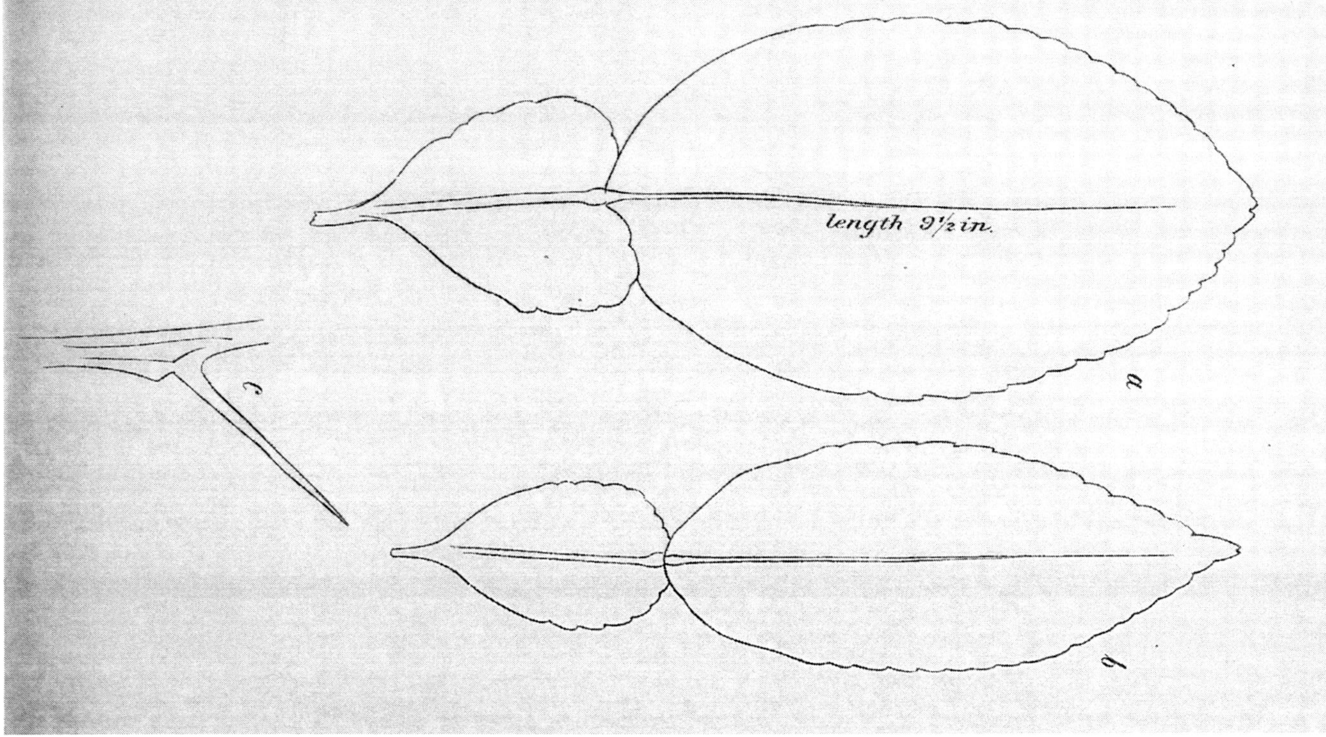

PLATE LXXXVI.

a, *b*, and *c*. All these three leaves are from *one* pummelo tree in Etawah; they are all glabrous, and apparently entire, but have oil-cells at their edges, with very minute, almost imperceptible indentations, showing that although entire they retain the remains of crenations. The scent of these leaves is almost *nil*. The oil-cells along the mid-rib and venations are very sparse.

PLATE LXXXVI.

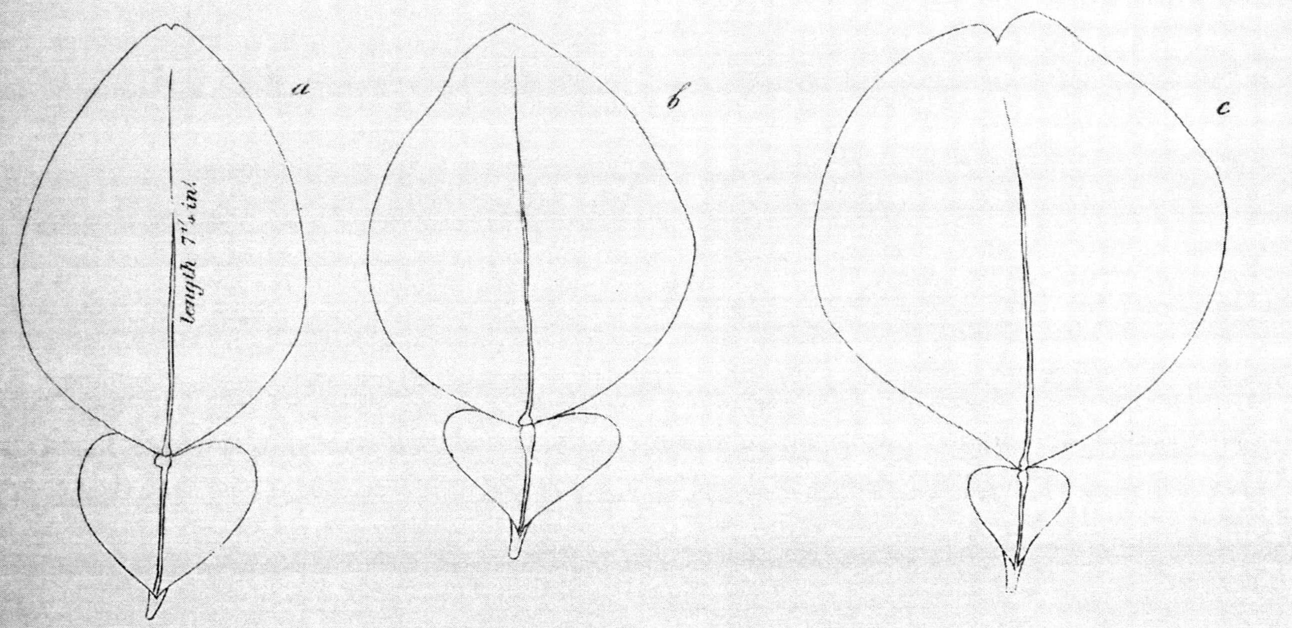

PLATE LXXXVII.

These are leaves of two pummelo trees I found in the "Taj" Garden. Their fruits were slightly different in size, but similar in shape. Their leaves were indistinguishable, except that those of *a* were tomentose, and those of *b* quite glabrous. The latter were slightly thinner, less crenate, and a little more shiny than those of the former. They had no scent.

The unexpanded buds of *b* had some hairs, as in other citrus, and the petiole wings of the young leaves a few scattered hairs on their edges. The young stems and mid-ribs were quite glabrous.

The oil-cells of *a* were minute and sparsely situated; crenations slight; mid-ribs and edges of petiole wings, and upper side of petiole base, and green stem were tomentose.

The oil-cells of *b* were also minute, very few and sparse, and scarcely visible; crenations obscure; all parts quite glabrous. (*See* Chapter on the "Pummelo and Amilbêd Group.")

PLATE LXXXVII.

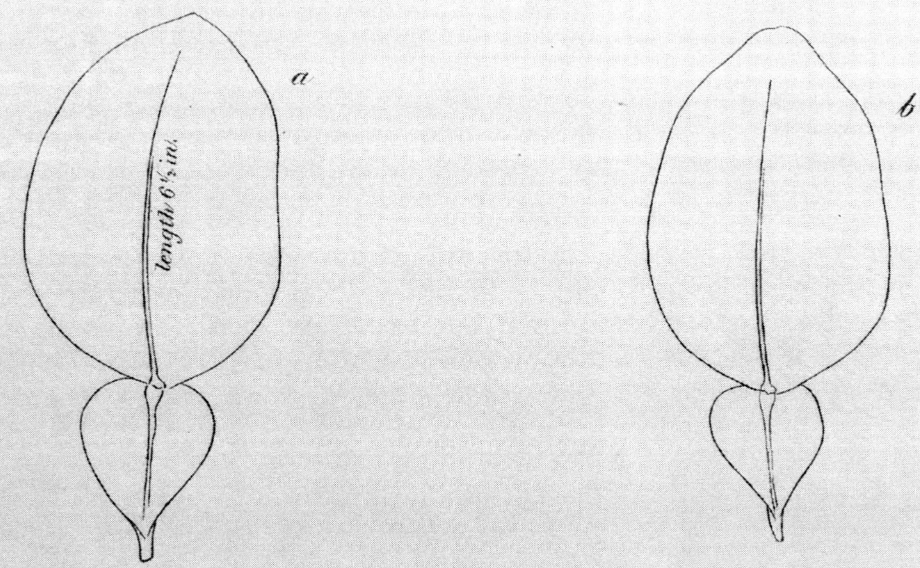

PLATE LXXXVIII.

This specimen was sent by the Secretary A. H. S. of India under the name of *sour pummelo.*

a and *b* are the same fruit. Externally pale yellow, and exactly like a pummelo of the *Mahtàbi* variety, only a little more shiny; generally smooth, with foveoli at stated distances, as shown at *c*, and smaller, and still smaller ones between them. The rind rather lemon-flavoured; pithy part very slightly sweetish, and not so spongy as is usual in pummelos; pulp pale transparent, like that of a lemon, acid, and quite seedless.

The letter which accompanied it stated, "I send you three fruits of a pummelo. We know it as 'No. 15.' It is said to be extremely acid. You will notice that the fruit contains no seed. Our garden people declare that anyone eating the fruit is certain to get fever! You must not suppose that our ordinary table-pummelo is anything like it."

I have tried the decoction of a number of sour kinds of citrus as an *antidote* for fever, including some *Amilbêds*. I found them all more or less useful for this purpose!

NOTE.—This and the following were received after the others were arranged, and therefore placed at the end of the group.

PLATE LXXXVIII.

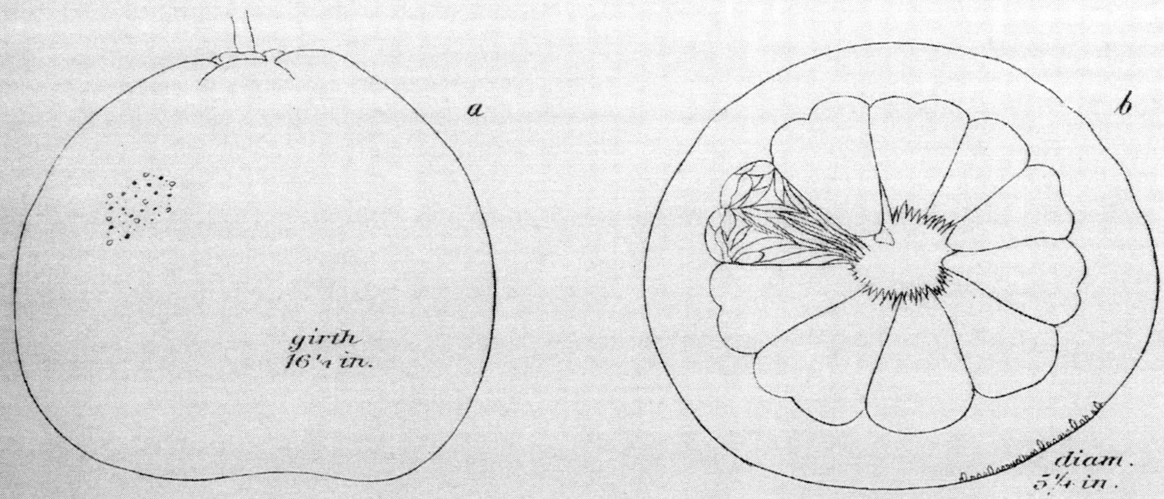

PLATE LXXXIX.

These are leaves of the sour pummelo, shown on the foregoing Plate LXXXVIII.

a, *b*, and *c* are fully-developed rain leaves, and *d*, *e*, and *f* are small spring leaves. They have some tomentum on the under side of the mid-rib, and round the edges of the petiole wings. The petiole wings of *b* are the largest; most of the other leaves have them much smaller, the petioles of the small leaves being only ridged. The petiole in all is short, and different from the long one of the pummelo. proper. The leaves are serrated rather than crenated, and the serrations commence from the base of the leaf as in lemons. The oil-cells are as usual, and the scent citrine, but feeble. If not an *Amilbêd*, this large pummelo-like citrus may be a lemon of the "Gulgul" variety; and, having been grown in Calcutta, may have got a thicker skin than usual. The spines *g* and *h* are not unlike those of the lemon tribe; but the winged petiole inclines me to think it an *Amilbêd*.

PLATE LXXXIX.

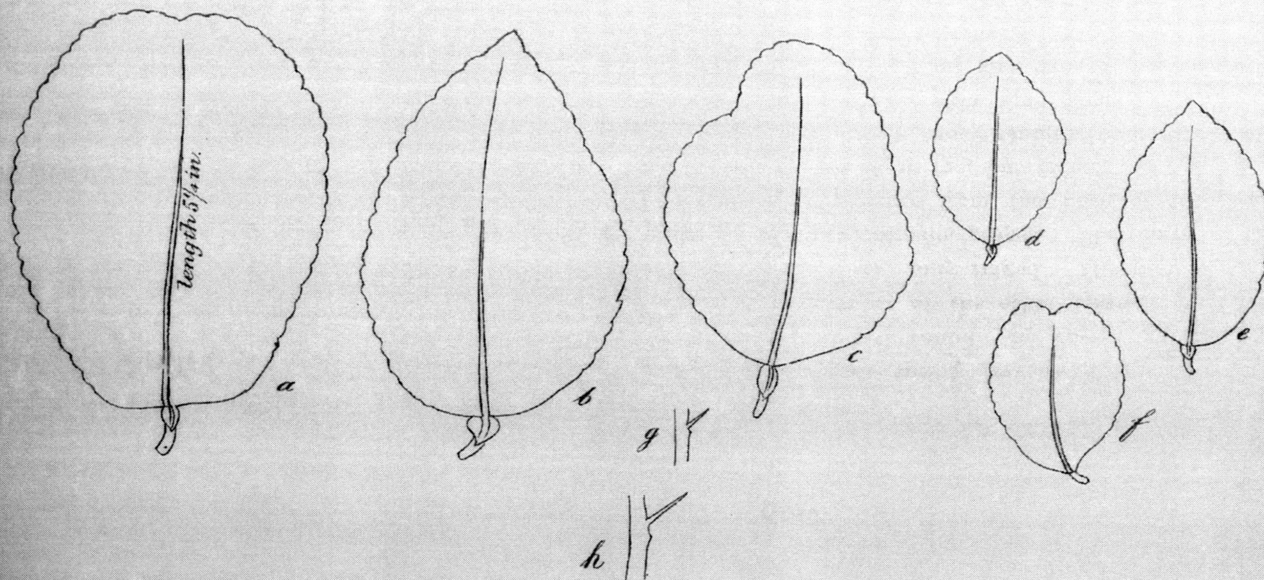

PLATE XC.

This specimen was taken from the Garden of the Maharaja of Ulwar. There it was called *Amilbêd*.

a and *b*. Externally lemon-yellow, like an *Amilbêd*, but with a tendency to sub-wartiness; the skin thickish, and of a lemon scent; pulp pale orange and sharply acid.

c is its well-developed leaf; thin, and its petiole only slightly margined.

If this is not an *Amilbêd*, it may not be impossible that it is a yellow-skinned variety of the *Khattà* orange.

PLATE XC.

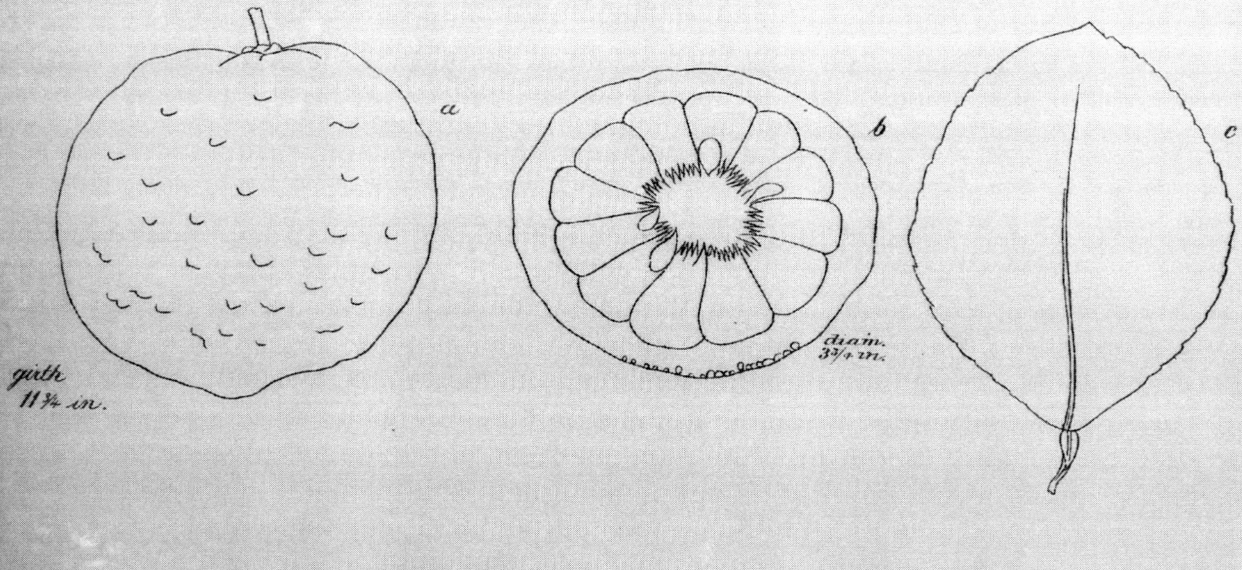

PLATE XCI.

a, *b*, and *c* are leaves from a tree called *Amilbêd*, from the Garden of the Maharaja of Ulwar.

Their serrations are indistinct; the oil-cells minute and distant, as in pummelo-leaves. The upper side of petiole base is distinctly tomentose; all had slight serrations at tips, and they are thinner than is usual in pummelos proper. The green stem is as tomentose as that of a tomentose pummelo.

The fruits are indistinguishable from small pummelos. The skin is $\frac{3}{4}$ inch thick and spongy; rind bitter; pulp pale, transparent and *sour*; it leaves a slight bitterness in the mouth. Seeds large, and rather like those of a pummelo, and white, when cut.

Taking into consideration the indistinctness of the leaf serrations and oil-cells, these leaves would appear to be of a *sour* pummelo. Its large petiole wings point also in that direction.

PLATE XCI.

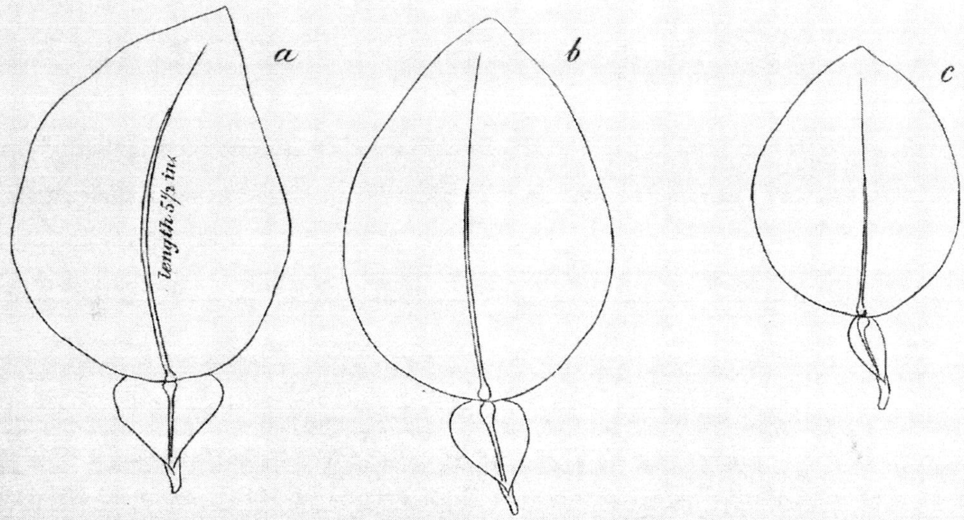

PLATE XCII.

These specimens were purchased from a shop in England. This kind is the shaddock, pummelo, or forbidden fruit of the English markets. The fruiterer said they came from Palestine. They are given for the purpose of comparison.

a. Skin quite smooth, with transparent oil-cells of different sizes; of a pale citrine colour, and from $\frac{1}{4}$ to $\frac{1}{2}$ an inch thick; centre solid; pulp pale, like that of a lemon, sub-acid and sweet, and slightly bitter; seeds many.

b is a smaller specimen of the same kind, and of a pyriform shape.

N.B.—The fine large red pummelos of India appear to be unknown in the English markets. They can be carried long distances without spoiling. The thin-skinned, dark red, and juicy pummelo of the Bombay market is the best I have seen.

It is doubtful whether this shaddock of the English markets is a pummelo proper. Gallesio says the Crusaders found the *Pomo d'Adamo* in Palestine, and that it is not the Pompelmoess, the latter being a new citrus introduced from the East Indies.

PLATE XCII.

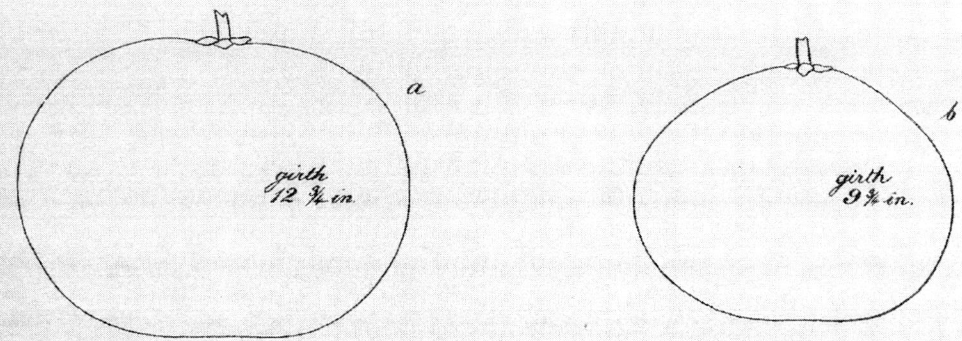

PLATE XCIII.

a is taken from the *Herb. Amboyn.* of Rumphius, vol. ii., Table xxxi. It is his *Limonellus Madurensis* (from *Madura*, in Java). (*Vide* Appendix, 41, *j*.) It is also called "Kimquit." Its tree is usually about 2 feet high. The fruit is not eaten raw, but preserved whole in sugar.

d is the smaller "Kumquat," or China orange grown in Lucknow. This branch had margined petioles; but *e* show leaves without the margins; *f* is a section of its fruit with five carpels, the smallest number I have ever met with in this genus. The skin is *very* thin; the pulp pale orange, and sour; seeds greenish-white.

g is a specimen of the "Kumquat" from Calcutta, used mainly as a decorative plant; both *d* and *g* were unripe specimens obtained in September. When ripe, the fruit is slightly larger, more oblate, and of an orange-yellow; *h* is a section with seven carpels. The leaves of the Calcutta specimen had linear petioles.

b is taken from Table xxxiv., vol. ii., of Rumphius (same as Plate CXVI. A of this group); *c* shows a margined petiole on the same branch. He calls it *Aurantium Sinense*. His description of it coincides with that of the "Suntara" orange of India. (*Vide* Appendix, 41, *l*.)

PLATE XCIII.

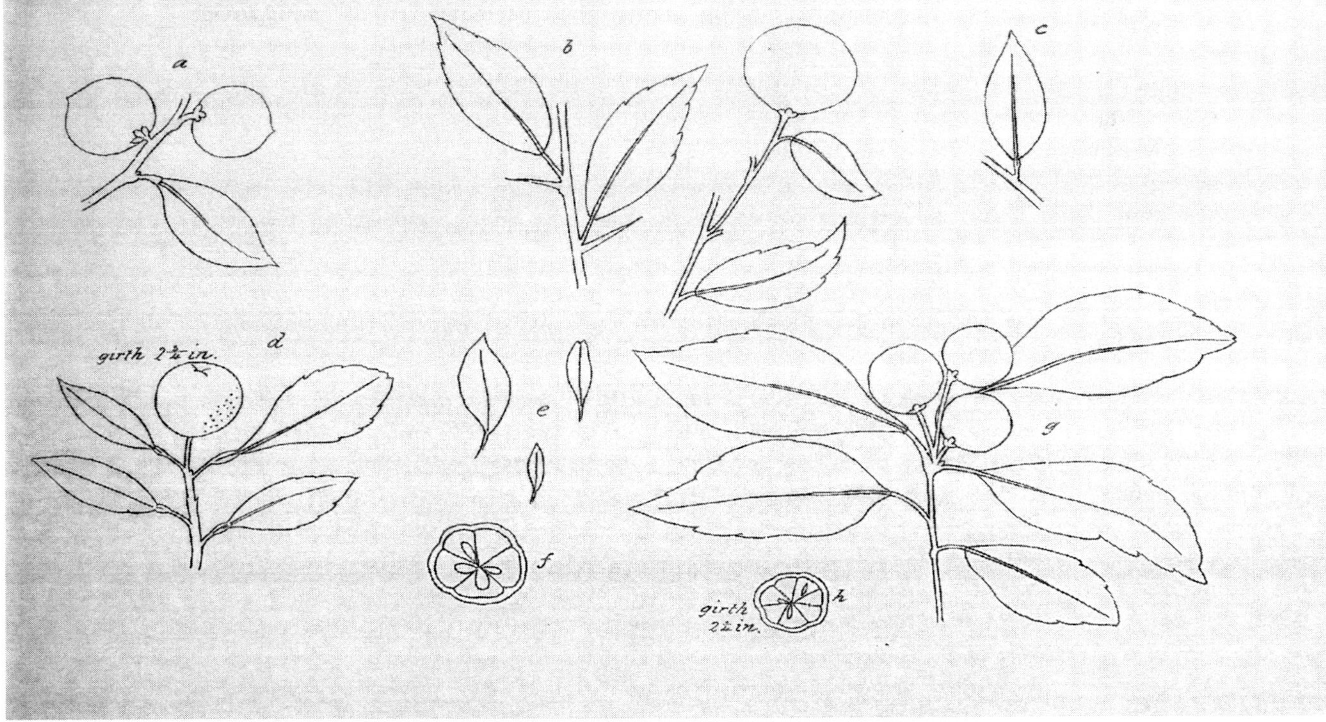

PLATE XCIV.

a, *b*, *c*, and *d* I obtained from a tree in Benares, called "Hazàra." It had innumerable oranges, both smaller and larger than the ordinary *Kumquat*. The name *Hazàra* comes probably from the thousands of oranges it produces. The tree in question was over six feet high, and was covered with oranges The colour is bright yellow-orange, like that of the "Suntara"; oblate, smooth, or chagrined, and foveolate. Pulp, orange, sour; juice abundant; seeds green, when cut; rind loosely attached; aromatic, but not agreeably so; flowers small, white, five-petalled, scented.

e, *f*, and *g* are its leaves; some having a linear, others a margined petiole; scent feeble.

h and *i* came from Rohilcund, under the name of *Hazàra naringhi*. Its leaves had linear petioles. The fruit was orange-red, very finely chagrined, with minute foveoli and intermediate miliary elevations. Pulp orange, juice plentiful and very sour; never sweetens; seeds greenish, and rind very thin. There were no spines on this branch. These *Hazàras* appear to be no other than overgrown *Kumquats*.

j is taken from Risso's work. He calls it "Bigaradier Chinois"; acid, and slightly bitter. Probably it is the same as the *Hazàra* and *Kumquat*, enlarged from the effects of climate and cultivation.

PLATE XCIV.

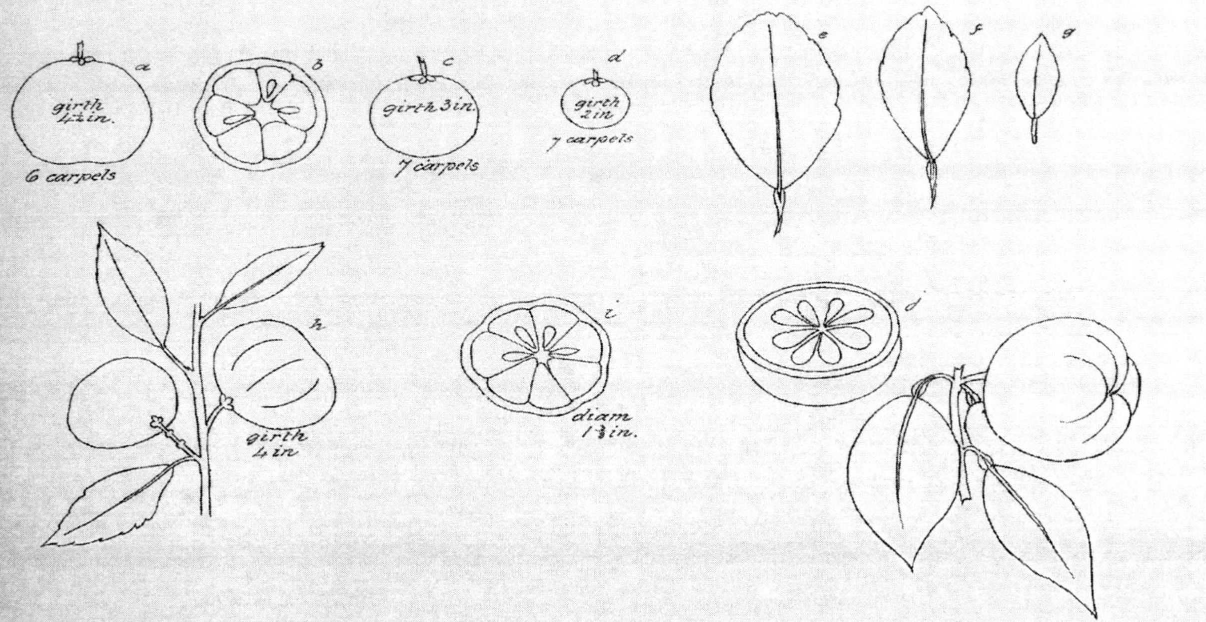

a
girth
$4\frac{1}{2}$ in.
6 carpels
b
c
girth 3 in.
7 carpels
d
girth
2 in
7 carpels
e
f
g
h
girth
4 in
i
diam
$1\frac{3}{8}$ in.
j

PLATE XCV.

a came from Messrs. Carew & Co., Shahjahaupur, under the name of *Reshmi naranghi.* Thin skin, yellow-orange; pulp pale orange, sub-acid, with greenish seeds; *b* and *c* are its rain leaves; *d*, *e*, and *f* its spring leaves.

g and *h* came from Benares, under the name of *Reshmi narangi.* The exterior of the fruit is sometimes chagrined, like a mandarin; at other times much smoother; skin loosely attached; pulp pale orange and sour; seeds green.

i are the leaves that came with it. They are small spring leaves. The fruit shown had fourteen carpels.

These two specimens appear to be no other than "Hazàras," or overgrown *Kumquats.* As the *Kumquat* is grown from seed, it probably may vary a good deal. Then cultivation, and difference of soil and climate are almost sure to induce other changes.

PLATE XCV.

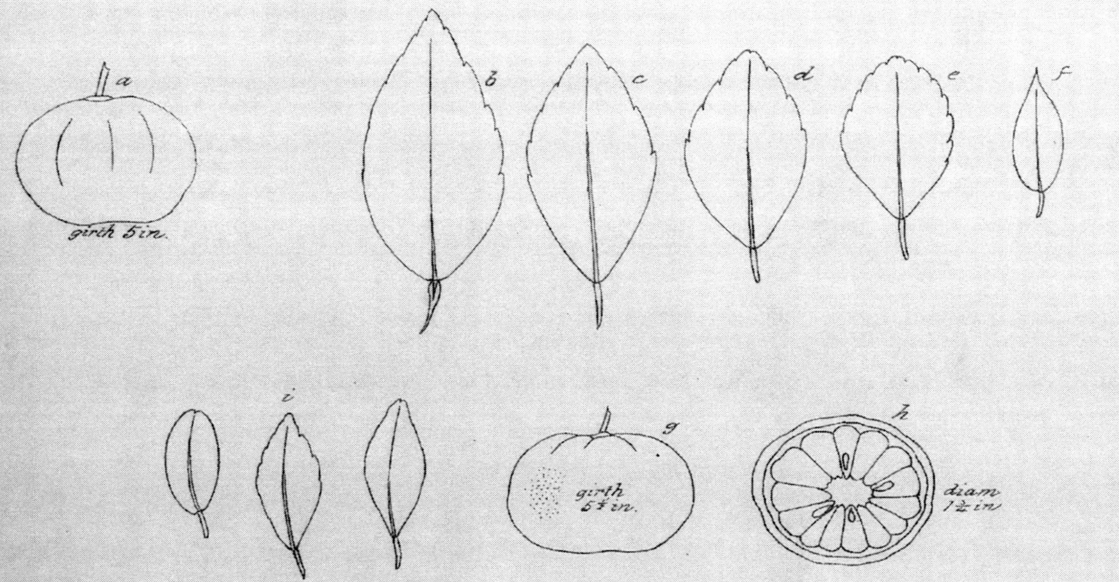

PLATE XCVI.

a and *b* I obtained at Kandy, Ceylon, under the name of *Nas-nàrun*. It was reddish yellow and foveolate, otherwise smooth. Pulp pale and greenish, and very acid; skin very thin, and seeds numerous; *c* are its leaves. At the Colombo Market I obtained a much smaller specimen than this, but with similar characters. It was there called *Oodoo-Dèhi*. (*Vide* Plate CCXXIII., Fig. *e*.)

d, *e*, and *f* are the *Surkh-nimboo* (red lime) of Lucknow; very smooth and polished; pulp orange-yellow and sour. The fruit, when ripe, is of a reddish orange.

g is a rain leaf, and *h* a spring leaf.

Whether this *Surkh-nimboo* is a distinct variety from the *Hazàra*, or an overgrown *Hazàra*, I cannot say. Although the fruit is larger, it has similar characters; and so have the leaves. Any differences there might be would be quite compatible with differences producible from seed.

PLATE XCVI.

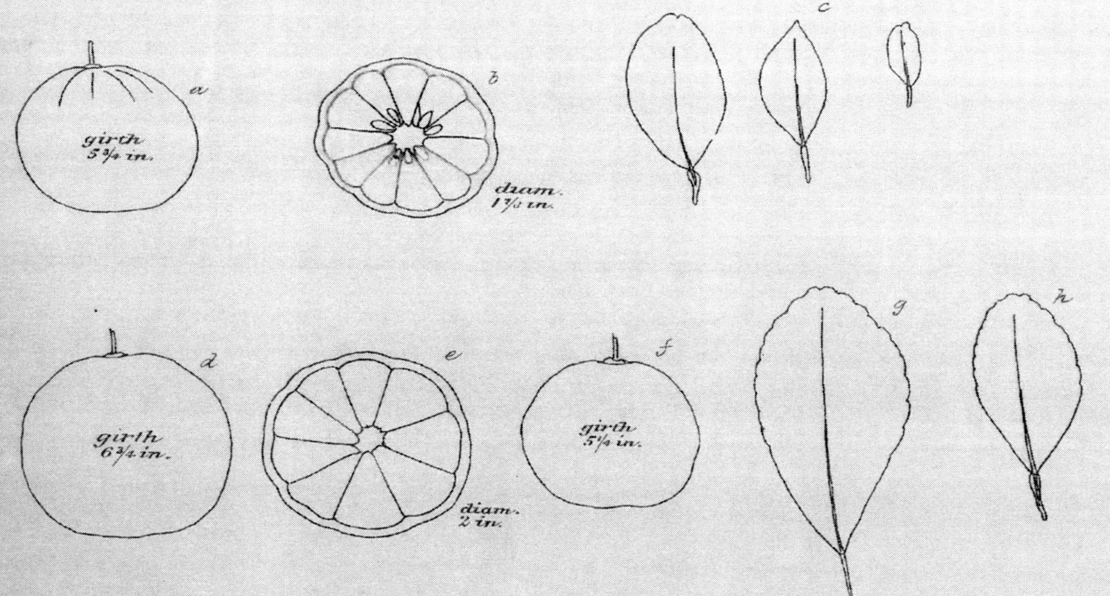

a
girth
5¾ in.
b
diam.
1⅓ in.
c
d
girth
6¾ in.
e
diam.
2 in.
f
girth
5¼ in.
g
h

PLATE XCVII.

a and *b* came under the name of *Bannàti-Benarsi-nimboo.* This name, I was told, was derived from its red-cloth colour, which natives call *Bannát.*

The surface was very finely chagrined, of an orange red colour. Pulp, orange; juice abundant and very sour; it never sweetens; skin very thin.

c, its rain leaf; *d*, its spring leaves. They resemble the leaves of the *Suntara* orange; *d* is the spine of the branch which came with it.

e and *f* is another specimen of *Bannàti-Benarsi-nimboo;* red-orange externally, foveolate and slightly chagrined. Pulp, orange; juice abundant, and very sour. It never sweetens; seeds green, when cut. The rind has a resinous aroma.

g and *h* are its leaves, like those of the *Suntara* orange, and with feeble aroma.

These two specimens do not appear to be different from the *Surkh-nimboo.*

PLATE XCVII.

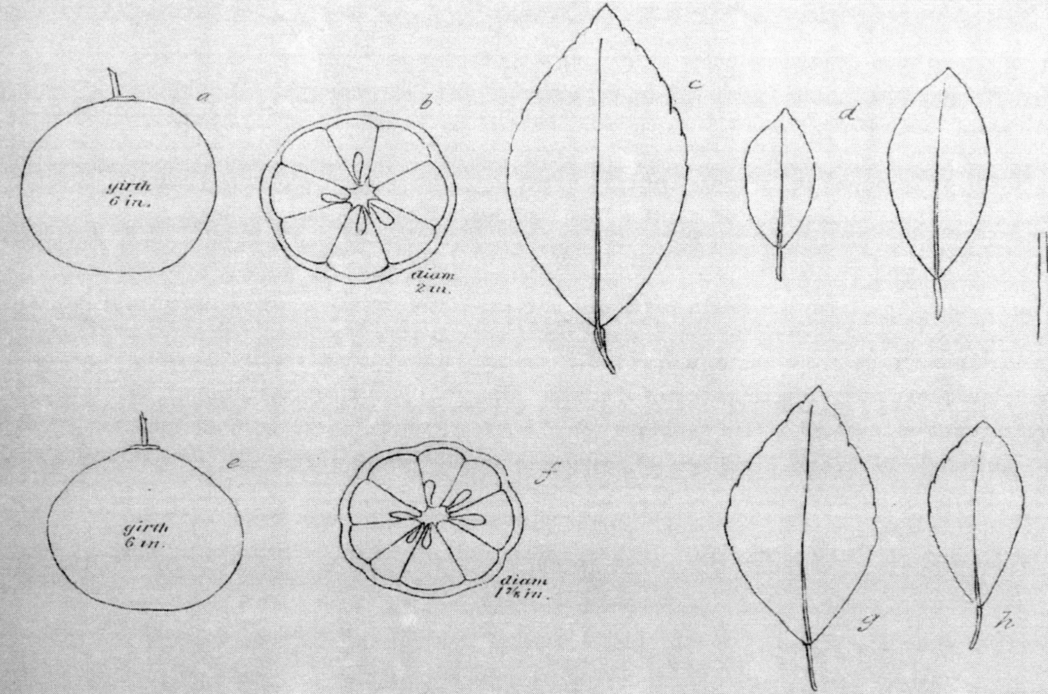

PLATE XCVIII.

a and *b* is a sour orange, which came from Gonda, under the name of *Khattà naringi.* It is said to have come there from Lucknow.

It is scarlet-orange and foveolate; rind not bitter or pungent, but with a slightly unpleasant resinous taste, and without any depressed mammilla at the apex, as in the sweet *naringhi.* Pulp, orange; juice abundant, and very acid, and with a slightly unpleasant flavour. Seeds green when cut; skin thin, and loosely attached.

c is its rain leaf, with marked nerve-furrows on the upper surface; *d*, spring leaves. They have a feeble scent.

The smallest of four oranges had a girth of $5\frac{1}{2}$ inches. This appears to differ from the *Surkh-nimboo* only in being slightly redder in colour.

e and *f* is a *Butwal* orange, received from Raja Siva Prasad, C.S.I. It was sent to him from Nepal. Colour of the Suntara; pulp, orange; juice very abundant and *sweet*; skin aromatic, thin, and loosely attached. I found twenty-one seeds in one orange. They were green when cut.

PLATE XCVIII.

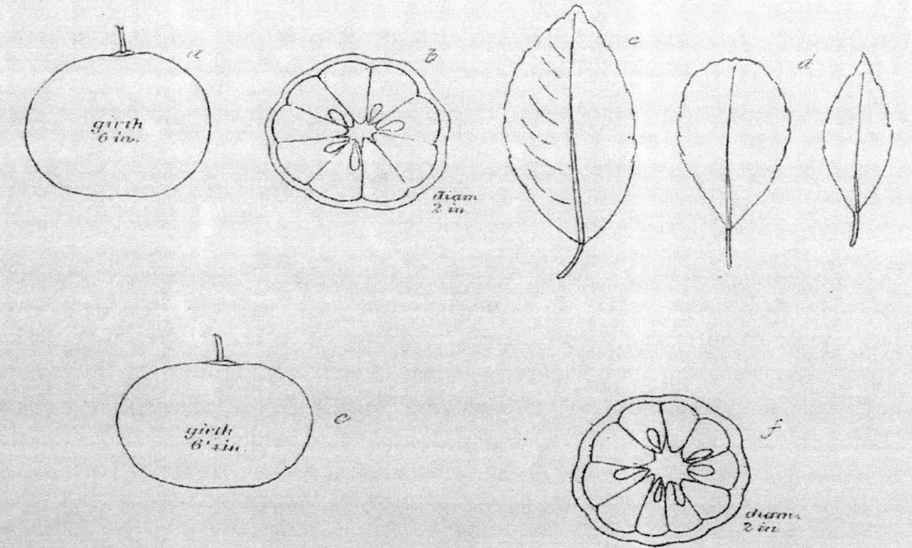

PLATE XCIX.

This is the interesting *Butwal* orange of Nepal sent by Major Buller from Gonda. It is the sweetest orange I have seen in India. Butwal is a Nepalese place near the borders of British India, and north of Goruckpore. Its proper name is *Sūntolah* or *Suntòwrea* orange. It is the colour of the *Suntara* orange, smooth and slightly foveolate; many seeded; but in some the seeds are empty. Skin, thin and closely fitting, but easily peeled off; pulp, deep orange, sweeter than any other kinds of *Suntara* when fully ripe, only very slightly mixed with sub-acid. Seeds green, when cut; centre hollow. *l* is the section of *k*.

i and *j* is a flat specimen, which came with the others; *d* is a rain leaf of the Butwal orange; *e*, *f*, and *g* are spring leaves.

h are the spines which came with them.

This is evidently a variety of the *Suntara* orange. It grows in a semi-wild state in Butwal, and appears to get no cultivation whatever. Externally some are more or less rough, and more or less foveolate, especially round the base and apex.

PLATE XCIX.

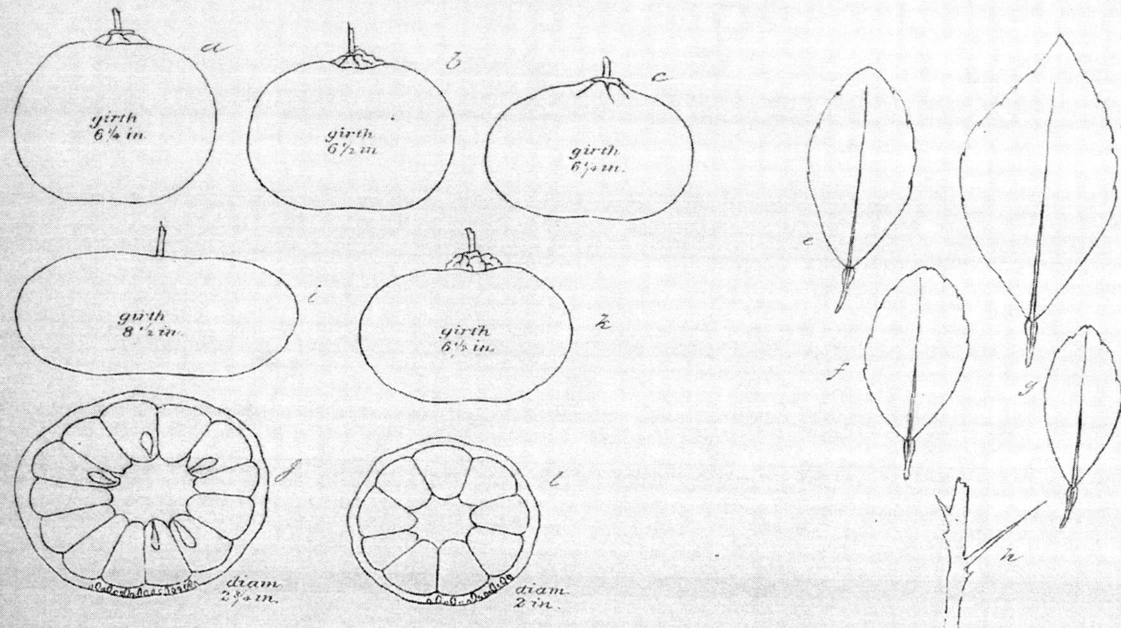

a
girth 6¼ in.
b
girth 6½ in.
c
girth 6¼ in.
i
girth 8½ in.
k
girth 6⅓ in.
j
diam. 2¾ in.
l
diam. 2 in.
d
e
f
g
h

PLATE C.

a and *b* is the *Sùngtara* orange of Mooltan, kindly sent by the Deputy Commissioner of that district. It was smooth and very slightly chagrined, with large and small foveoli closely set. Pulp, orange and sub-acid and sweet; juice abundant; thin skin. Like the *Keonla* orange, the juice-vesicles are mostly sessile. At the angles between the dissepiments, and the back of the carpel, there are some pedicelled vesicles.

c and *d* are rain leaves, the former with a broadly-margined petiole, and *e* and *f* spring leaves. On the branch sent there were no spines.

g and *h* is a specimen I purchased at the Colombo market, and called there *Heen-nàrun.* It was orange-yellow, smooth, except round the apex, and with shallow foveoli. Pulp, deep orange; juice abundant, and of a pleasant flavour, with large vesicles; seeds green, when cut. The oil-cells were of various sizes, the largest occupying the whole thickness of the skin.

This appears to be like the *Konda-nàrun* of Kandy, and the Nagpore orange of India. *i* was a smaller specimen, at the apex it had an obliterated mammilla.

PLATE C.

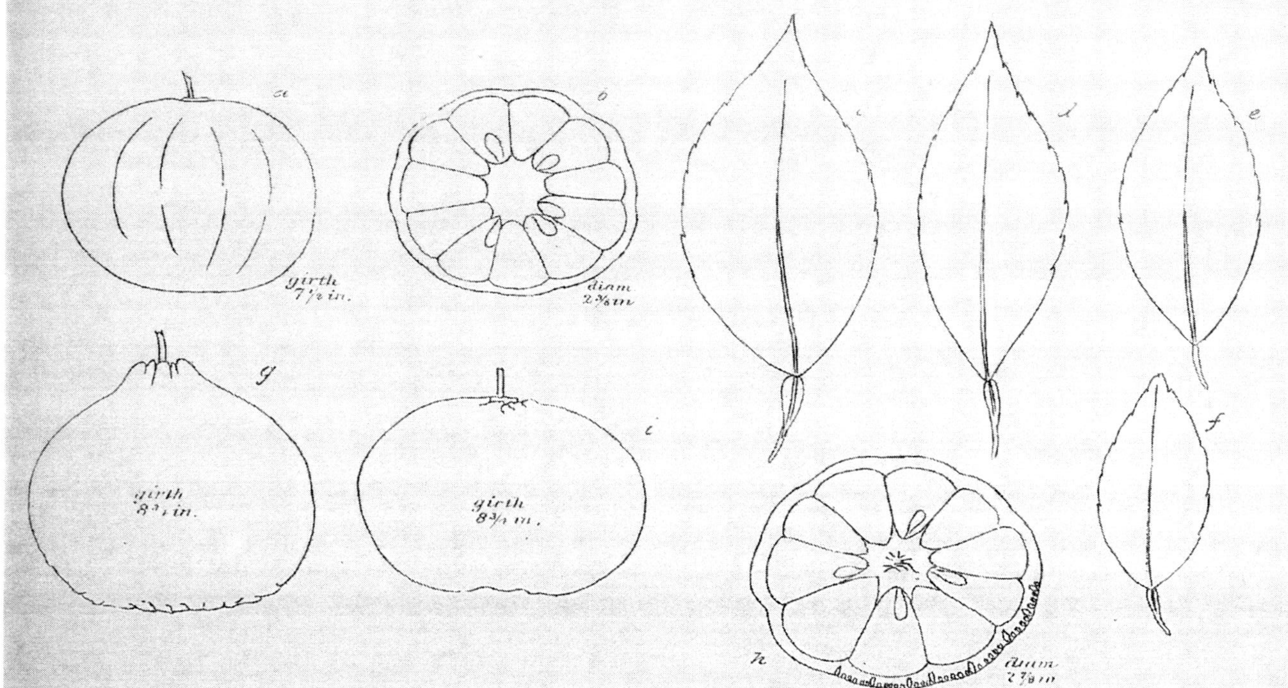

a
girth 7½ in.
b
diam 2⅜ in
c
d
e
f
g
girth 8¾ in.
i
girth 8¾ in.
h
diam 2⅞ in

PLATE CI.

a and *b* is the *Konda-ndrun* of Kandy, Ceylon; mostly pyriform, chagrined, and foveolate, more so round both base and apex; oil-cells of rind distinct; pulp, deep orange, and well flavoured; seeds green, when cut. This was an unripe specimen. Its centre was filled with a cottony fibre, which probably disappears when the fruit ripens; although the exterior was green the larger oil-cells of the rind were already turning orange.

c is its rain leaf; *d* and *e* its spring leaves.

f, *g*, *h*, and *i* are other specimens of the same *Konda-nárun*.

j is the section of *i*. This *Konda-nárun* of Ceylon appears to me to be identical with the Nagpore orange, or merely a variety of it.

There is a notion in Ceylon that this orange never gets coloured, and they consequently look upon it as a *green* orange. Indeed, it is not possible to obtain an *orange* one at the market. It is sufficiently well flavoured in its green state in December. However, I purchased some on the 11th December, and took them with me to Etawah, which I reached on the 1st January. Most of them, by that time, had turned of a *yellow-orange*. Probably this is a variety which, even in Ceylon, colours late. It is well flavoured when fully ripe, and travels well.

NOTE.—Rumphius, in his chapter on "Aur. Sinence," mentions a *green* orange, which, if left on the tree till it becomes *orange*, is worthless.

PLATE CI.

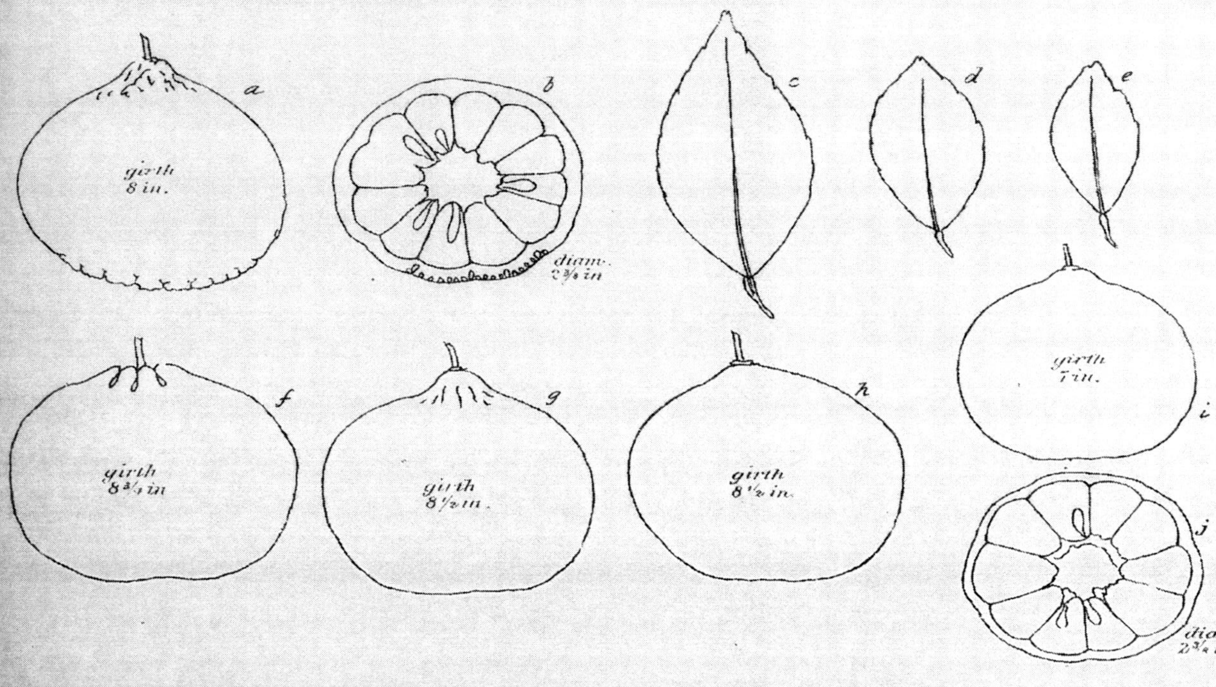

a
girth
8 in.
b
diam.
2 3/8 in
c
d
e
f
girth
8 3/4 in
g
girth
8 1/2 in.
h
girth
8 1/2 in.
i
girth
7 in.
j
diam.
2 3/4 in.

PLATE CII.

a and *b* is the Nagpore orange, grown in Nagpore, and which I purchased at one of the railway stations in the Central Provinces. The skin is thin; pulp, deep orange, deeper coloured than the rind; juice very abundant, and of a pleasant flavour; rind loosely adhering, the white tissue of the skin being very scanty. Surface smooth, only foveolate round the base and apex. All Nagpore oranges are neither so smooth nor so regular in form as this. The mammilla at the base is rather typical of one of the Nagpore varieties. I saw some with the mammilla so flattened that it was practically obliterated; others were oblate at both base and apex. One had an areola, or remains of a mammilla on the apex. The Nagpore orange is one of the best *Suntaras* of India.

c and *d* is the Nagpore orange, grown in Etawah. It has the *Suntara* colour, with abundant juice, a very pleasant mixture of sub-acid and sweet. When ripe the rind is aromatic, not bitter, loosely attached to the pulp; centre hollow; seeds greenish, when cut; *e* and *f* are its rain leaves; *g* and *h* its spring leaves. Usually the Nagpore orange tree has no spines, but *i* shows what it can sometimes produce.

PLATE CII.

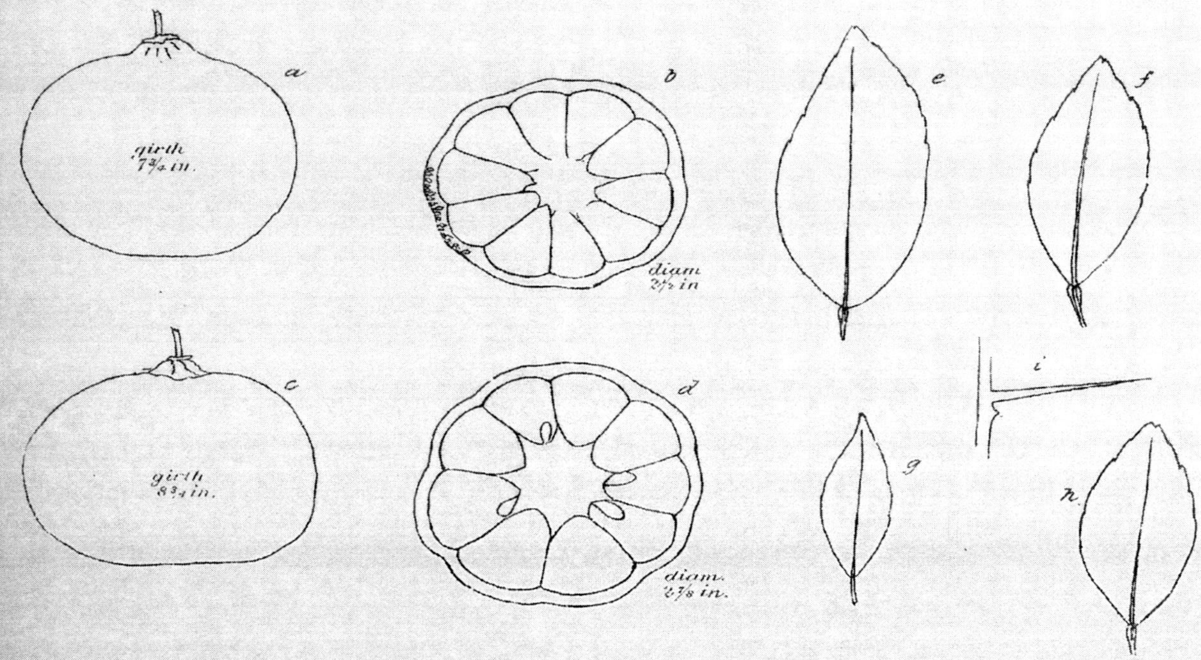

PLATE CIII.

a and *b* is the Nagpore orange, grown in Lucknow. It has the same surface and colour of the *Suntara*. It is baggy, with the apex much depressed; most specimens have a prominent base, but not all. Pulp, a shade deeper than the ordinary *Suntara* ; carpels loosely adherent, with a space between them and the skin; centre hollow; seeds green, when cut.

c and *e* are rain leaves; *d* and *f* are spring leaves; their scent is like that of the *Suntara* leaves.

g and *h* is the Sylhet orange, as grown in Lucknow from seed. Exterior exactly like a baggy *Suntara*; pulp also similar; carpels loosely held together, with a space between them and the pulp-ball; centre hollow; seeds green, when cut.

The original Sylhet oranges of Lucknow were seedlings raised from seeds of the Calcutta Sylhet oranges, or *Kamlà lemboo*. The tree does not spread horizontally as much as the Nagpore or *Suntara* proper, but straight upwards. It is the most productive of the *Suntara* group, and appears to suit the climate and soil of Lucknow better than either the Nagpore or *Suntara* proper varieties. It has larger leaves than the latter.

j is a rain leaf, and *i* is a spring leaf.

PLATE CIII.

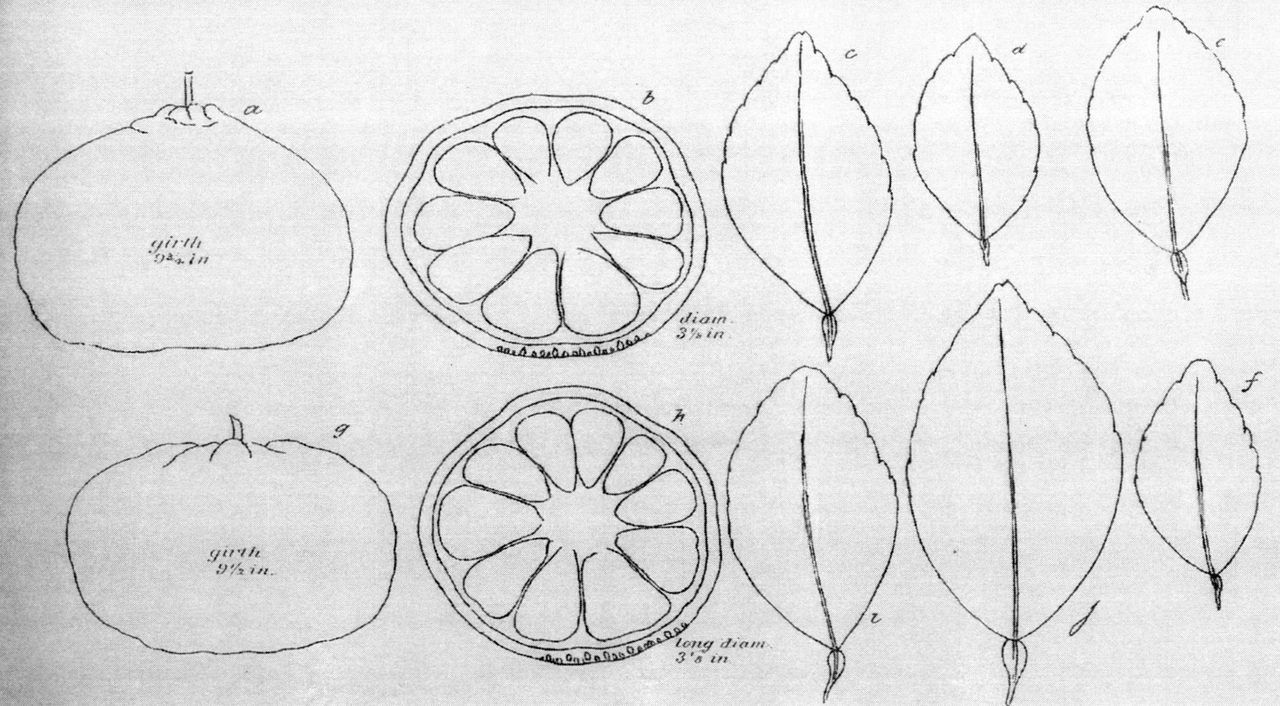

PLATE CIV.

a and *b* is the *Suntara* orange proper, as grown in Lucknow. Of a smooth yellow-orange colour, with scarcely any foveoli, and with minute miliary projections. Apex much depressed; most of these oranges have also a depressed base. Pulp, orange, of about the same shade as the rind; very juicy, and, when ripe, of a pleasant sub-acid and sweet flavour; centre large and hollow, with a space between skin and pulp-ball; seeds green, when cut. The hollow space beneath the skin makes it feel baggy. All these *Suntara* oranges are very good floaters.

c is a rain leaf, and *d* a spring leaf.

e and *f* is the *Suntara* proper of Delhi. It is also called *Rungtra*, *Sungtra*, and *Suntra*. It is of a bright orange-yellow, with a smooth surface as before. The base has often a flattened mammilla. The oil-cells of the skin are distinct, and their rotundity quite visible on the inside of the skins, as it has little pith; *g* is the section of *f*, with a thin skin, and very small space between it and the pulp-ball; pulp, transparent orange, of a pleasant mixture of sweet and sub-acid; centre hollow; seeds green, when cut.

h and *i* are spring leaves, with the usual scent of all leaves of this *Suntara* group.

PLATE CIV.

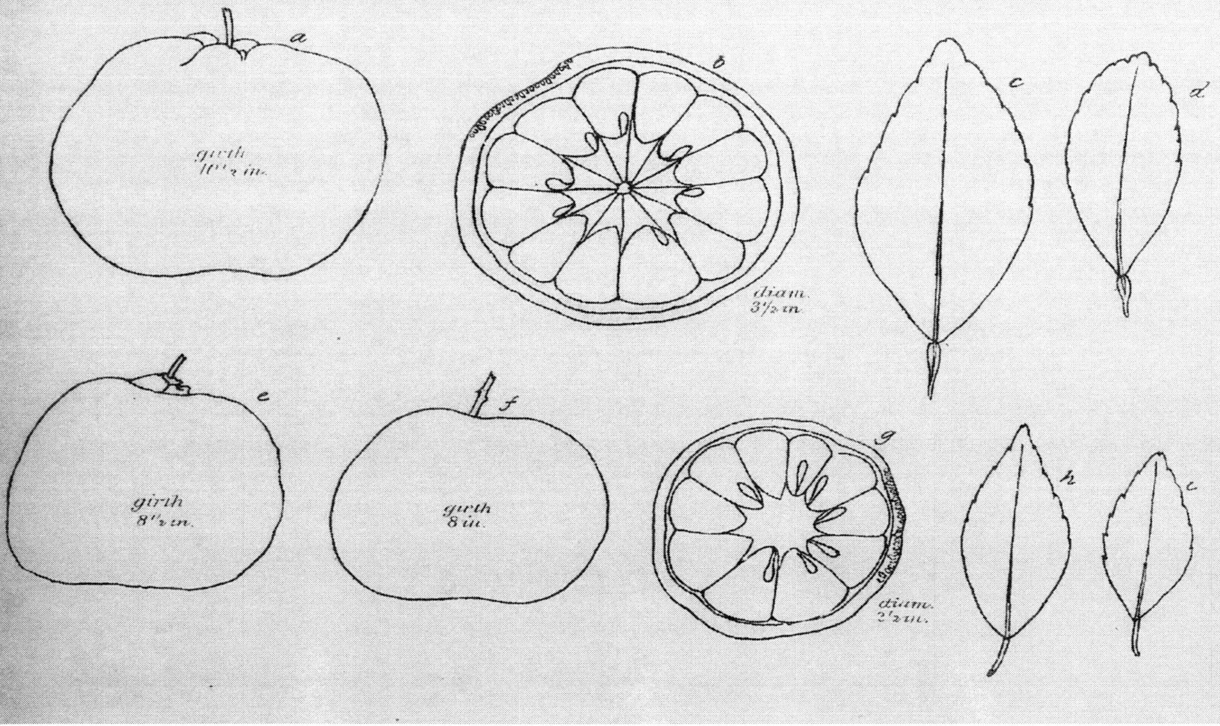
a
girth
10½ in.
b
diam.
3½ in.
c
d
e
girth
8½ in.
f
girth
8 in.
g
diam.
2½ in.
h
i

PLATE CV.

a and *b* is a *Suntara* orange from Rohilcund, with all the characters of the *Suntara* orange. This was an unripe specimen, obtained in October, of a bright green, turning yellowish in parts. It floated well. (*Vide* Chapter on "Derivations of Vernacular Names.")

c are small spring leaves of the same. The specimen sent had no spines.

d and *e* is the *Narànghi*, from Rohilcund. It was unripe, and of a bright green, turning reddish in parts. It had all the characters of a *Suntara* orange, perhaps with a more chagrined exterior. It floated very well.

f are its spring leaves. The specimen sent had no spines.

I could see no decided difference between these two oranges, although they came with distinct names. The colour of the "Naranghi," when ripe, may be redder, and the surface rougher; but such variations are frequently found on the same tree.

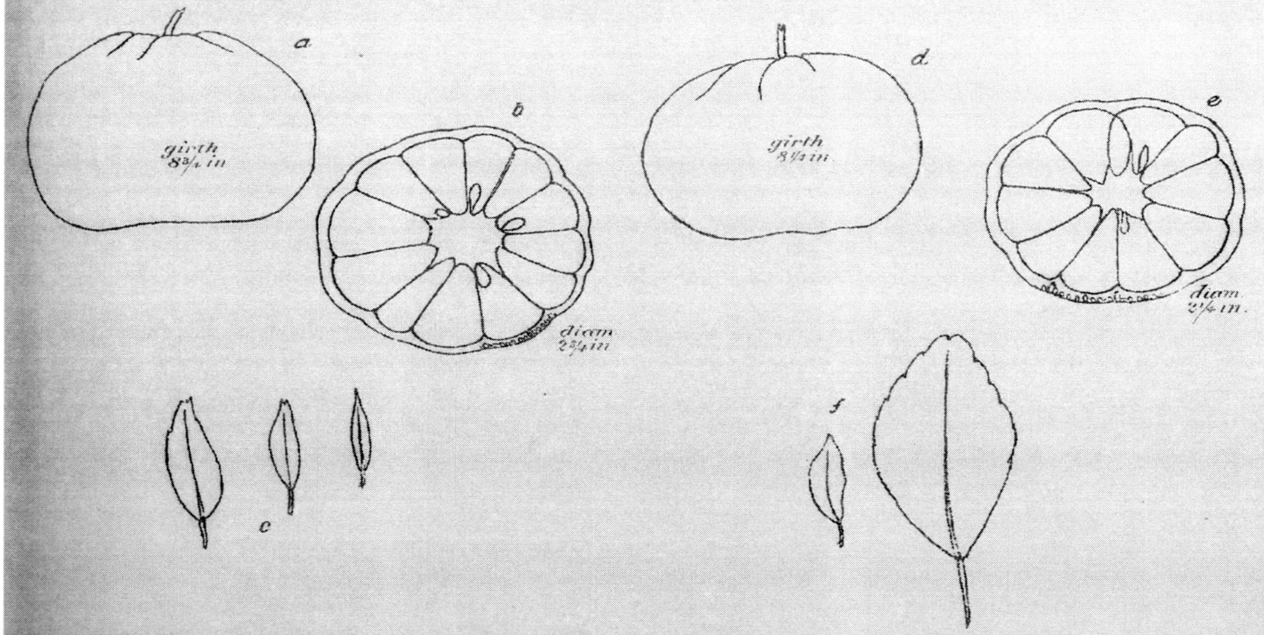
a
girth
8¾ in
b
diam
2¾ in
c
d
girth
8½ in.
e
diam.
2¼ in.
f

PLATE CVI.

a and *b* was kindly sent to me by Dr. J. Shortt, from Yercaud, in the Shevaray Hills, S. India. He stated it is there called the *country* orange. Natives call it *Kolinje*, and about Madras it is called *Kitchlee*.

Externally deep orange, smooth; slightly foveolate. The rind had a peculiar scent, with the aroma of the "Lantana." It was faintly five-sided, and had fourteen carpels. The pulp was rather pale orange; the juice thick with mucilage, and did not taste like that of ordinary oranges; with a *sui generis* flavour. The skin was loosely attached, and the flavour was not what I should call pleasant, with a *soupçon* of bitter.

c shows its juice-vesicles, with pedicelled ones only at the circumference angles of the carpels.

d and *e* are oranges I purchased at Mangalore. I was told they came from Coorg. They appeared to be *Suntara* oranges of the Nagpore variety. The pulp was deep orange; juice abundant and sweet, and the seeds were few. The exterior was of a pale orange and fovelate; the centre was hollow; *f* is the section of *d*, which had a flattened mammilla at the base.

At Calicut and Cochin I found small oranges of the same stamp as those of Mangalore. Probably they came also from Coorg, although at Cochin they said they came from Madras. I was informed that in Canarese the orange is called *Kitle-hannoo* (*hannoo*=fruit).

PLATE CVI.

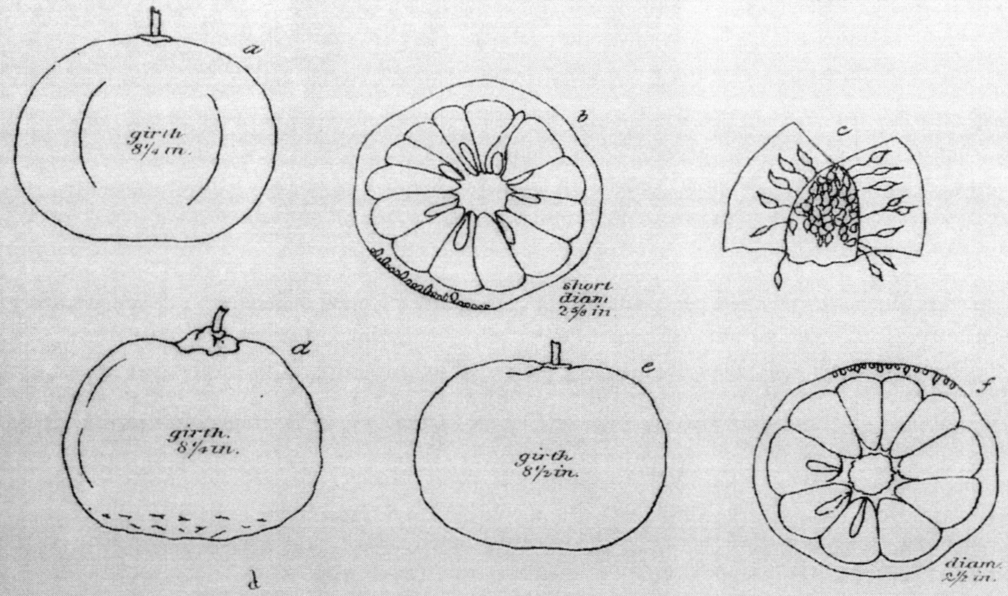

a
girth 8¼ in.
b
short diam 2⅝ in.
c
d
girth 8¼ in.
d
e
girth 8½ in.
f
diam 2½ in.

PLATE CVII.

a and *b* is the Buxa orange (Bhootan), kindly sent at the request of Colonel Rutherford, 33rd Regiment, N.I. It is of the Suntara type, with yellow-orange exterior, and with large distant foveoli, more pronounced in the south half; skin loose, and in every way as good, but not better, than the Slyhet orange.

c was smaller and smoother, and externally much like the Butwal orange.

Probably this Buxa orange may be the "sweet orange" alluded to in De Candolle's *Origin of Cultivated Plants*, p. 185, where he says, "Turner's expedition gathered 'delicious' wild oranges at Buxadooar, a locality to the N.E. of Rungpur, in the province of Bengal."

d and *e* is the Bhootan orange from Gonda, Oudh. It has all the characters of a *Suntara*, though not baggy; sub-warty round the apex; pulp, deep orange, with a good sub-acid and sweet flavour; juice abundant; centre hollow; seeds green, when cut. The skin was closely adherent, but *easily* separated; *f* are its spring leaves, with the *Suntara* scent.

This orange came on the 24th January, and was still green, only *tinged* with orange. If not a *dumrez*, it is a good *late* orange; or perhaps of a variety similar to the *green* orange of Kandy.

PLATE CVII.

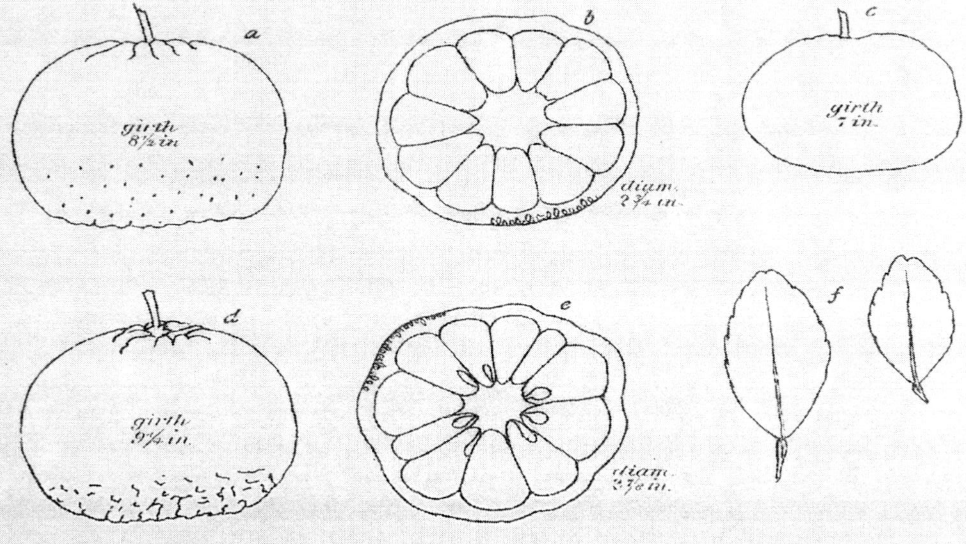

PLATE CVIII.

a, *b*, and *c* is the *Suntara* orange of Poona, light orange colour, and puffy to the feel. Apex greatly depressed, and rather warty all round it. It had an irregular mammilla at the base, depressed, and with furrows all round it as seen in longitudinal section *c*. Foveoli not very distinct, except among the warts. The small oil-cells are represented by minute miliary convexities. It floats very well. Pulp, deep orange, deeper than the rind. The white tissue of the skin is almost absent, except at the angles between the pulp carpels; centre hollow; juice abundant, and of a pleasant sweet and sub-acid flavour. Juice-vesicles large, and attached also to the sides of the carpel, a little way up.

d and *e* is the *Jáwa-ndrun* of Kandy, Ceylon. This is also of the *Suntara* type, orange-yellow when ripe. The oil-cells of the skin distinct; pulp, orange and juicy; seeds green, when cut; agreeable flavour, and in every way like a *Suntara*.

f is its rain leaf, and *g* its smaller spring leaves, with the *Suntara* scent.

PLATE CVIII.

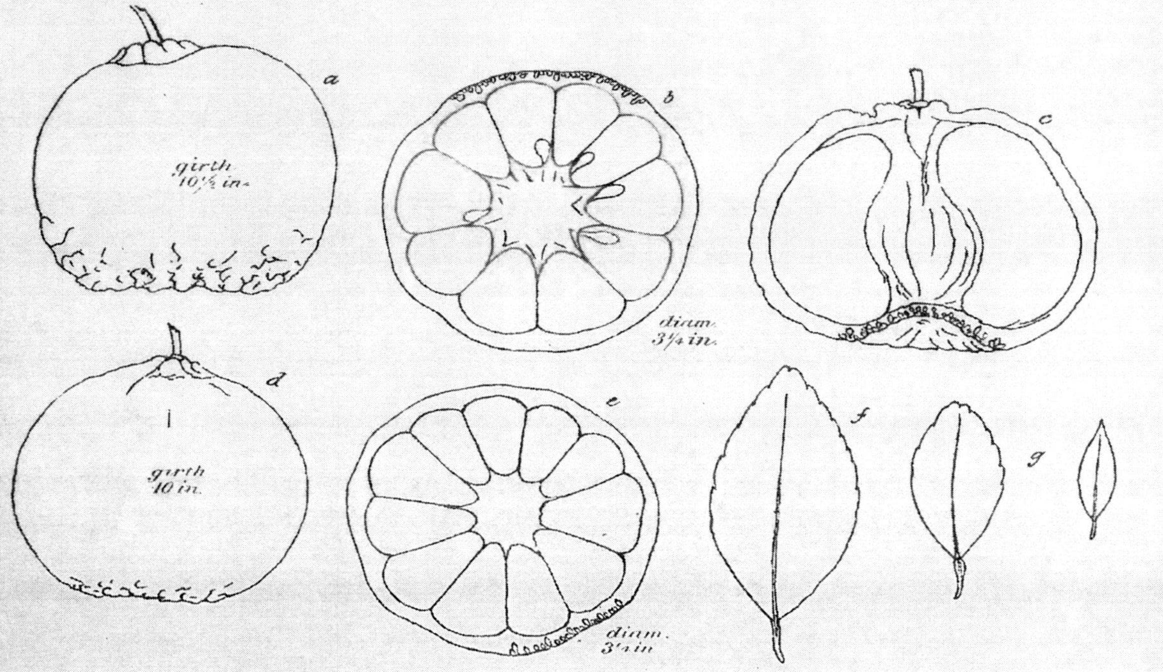

PLATE CIX.

a and b is the *Jàwa-nàrun* of Colombo, called also by some *Jamboo-nàrun*. It has an orange-yellow exterior, all up and down, uneven and baggy, gathered up into folds, and with a pronounced mammilla at the base; much chagrined, with miliary convexities, but hardly foveolate at all. It floats well. The oil-glands of the skin are very pronounced, of various sizes, the largest touching the pulp-ball. Even when the exterior is still green, the oil-cells are of an orange colour, and resemble juice-vesicles. Pulp, deep orange, with large vesicles; juice abundant, and very pleasant; hollow centre; seeds slightly greenish, when cut; apex depressed. *b* shows the size of skin oil-cells, and also that of juice-vesicles. *c* is a smaller and less uneven specimen.

d and *e* is the *Sungtara* of Lahore, wrongly named also *Karna*. This is the most pyriform of all specimens I have seen, and a distinct variety; bright yellow-orange, finely and closely chagrined, with miliary convexities; round and shallow oil-cell depressions. When shaken the pulp-globe wabbles inside. The section *d* shows how loosely the pulp carpels are attached to one another and to the skin. Pulp, pale orange, and, from being kept too long on the tree, rather dry, with the juice-vesicles somewhat concrete; seeds green, when cut; centre hollow. Two specimens were sent, both very pyriform. *f* is a fully-developed rain leaf with large crenations. *g* are spring leaves, all with the *Suntara* scent.

NOTE.—In No. 266 of Miss North's gallery of oil-paintings, Royal Gardens, Kew, are given pictures both of this *Jàwa-nàrun* and of the *green orange* of Ceylon.

PLATE CIX.

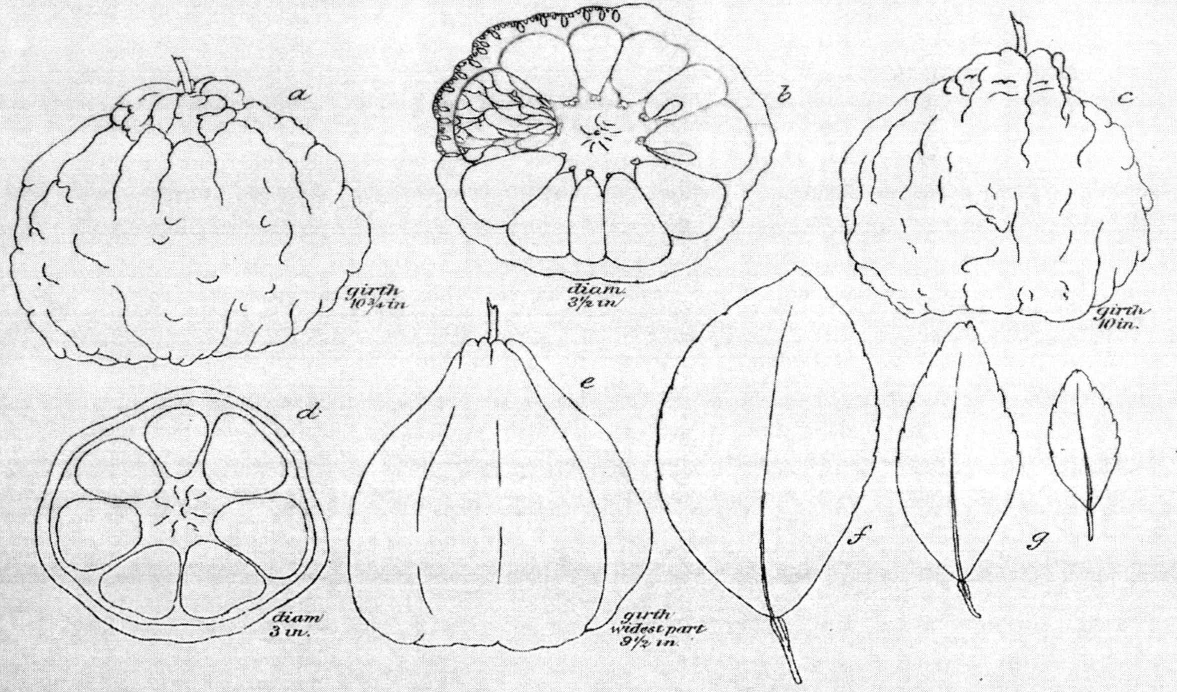
a
girth
10¾ in
b
diam.
3½ in
c
girth
10 in.
d
diam
3 in.
e
girth
widest part
9½ in.
f
g

PLATE CX.

a and *b* is the *Át Anni* of Rampur, Rohilcund. Its name, I am told, comes from its being about half the size of a pummelo—from *Át Anna* (eight annas = half a rupee). This specimen was unripe, and quite green. It had a very curious exterior. The large and almost equi-distant foveoli A A are connected one with the other by means of slight and sinuous furrows, as shown at A A, mapping the whole surface into irregular squares or triangles. The intermediate spaces are filled with miliary convexities, representing the smaller oil-cells, while the depressions represent the larger oil-cells, as shown in section *b*. The pulp is pale pinkish-orange; the juice is plentiful, and of a rather pleasant sweet and sub-acid flavour. The juice-vesicles are rather large. The oil-cells of the skin appear distinctly of three sizes. Those most deeply placed are the largest, and correspond to the large foveoli or depressions above mentioned. The pulp carpels are all emarginate in section.

c and *d* are spring leaves; they were thin, and resembled those of the *Suntara*. Some were slightly margined at the petiole. I found no spines on the branch sent.

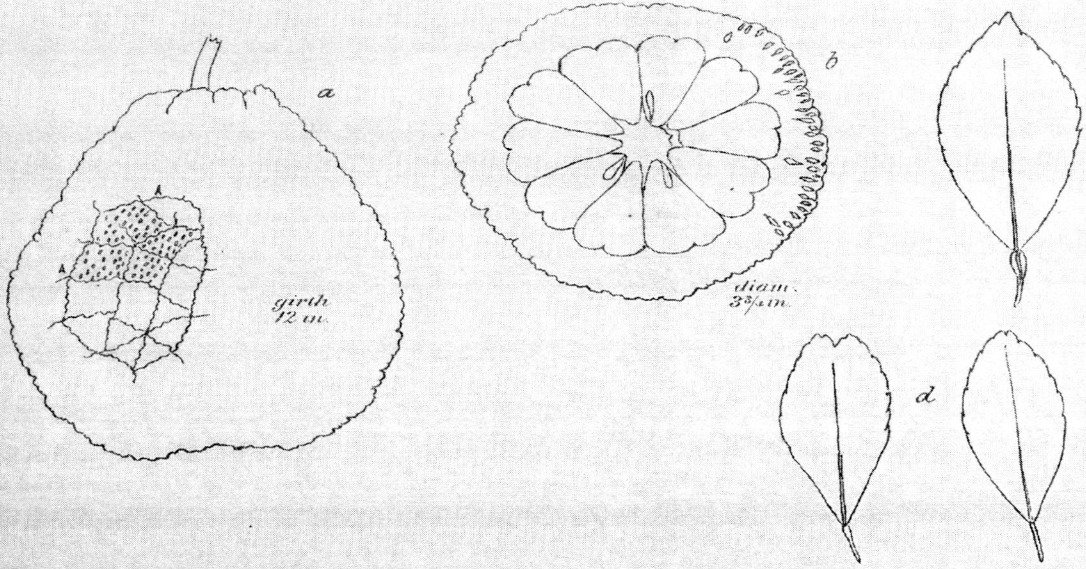
a
girth
12 in.
A
A
b
diam.
3¾ in.
c
d

PLATE CXI.

a and *b* is a ripe *Át Anni* from Mr. Kinloch's garden, at Etawah.

It is of a yellow-orange colour externally, much chagrined, with large foveoli at certain distances, with sinuous broken furrows radiating from them. Between the large foveoli are smaller ones, as shown at A. Some specimens were smoother than the one given. The rind is aromatic and pungent, but scarcely bitter. The pulp is a pale orange, streaked with lighter shades, of a pleasant rather sweetish acid; centre solid and filled up; seeds greenish white, when cut.

c is a rain leaf; *d*, *e*, and *f* spring leaves. The young leaves have a scent of the *Keonla* orange leaf. The old leaves are leathery. Flowers are rather large, four or five petalled. Those I saw on the tree were single and axillary. The young shoots are of a yellowish-green.

N.B.—The young stems and leaves are *pubescent*. The white tissue of the skin is thick and spongy.

PLATE CXI.

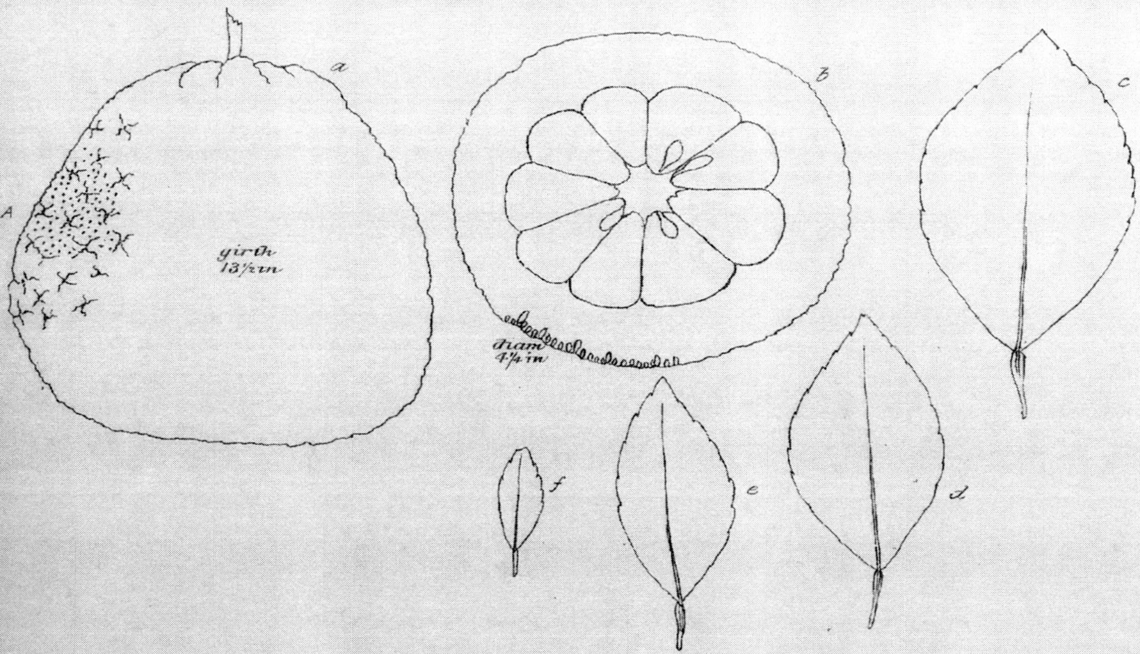

PLATE CXII.

Shows a large *Át Anni* from Gonda, Oudh, which came under the name of *Naringi*. Externally it was of a maize-orange colour, very rough and sub-warty. At certain distances there were depressions, and sinuous furrows radiating from them; then intermediate foveoli, with smaller sinuosities converging towards them, and finally between these again there were miliary oil-cells, as shown at A. All over the surface there was, in addition, what appear to have been minute cracks, which had healed up.

The character and scent of this *Át Anni* leaves, and the looseness of its skin indicate, I think, relationship with the *Suntara* orange. Not improbably it may be a *Decumana* variety of the *Suntara* group.

It is very suggestive that on this "Decumana" variety the young shoots and leaves should be also found *pubescent*, as in some varieties of the pummelo.

PLATE CXII.

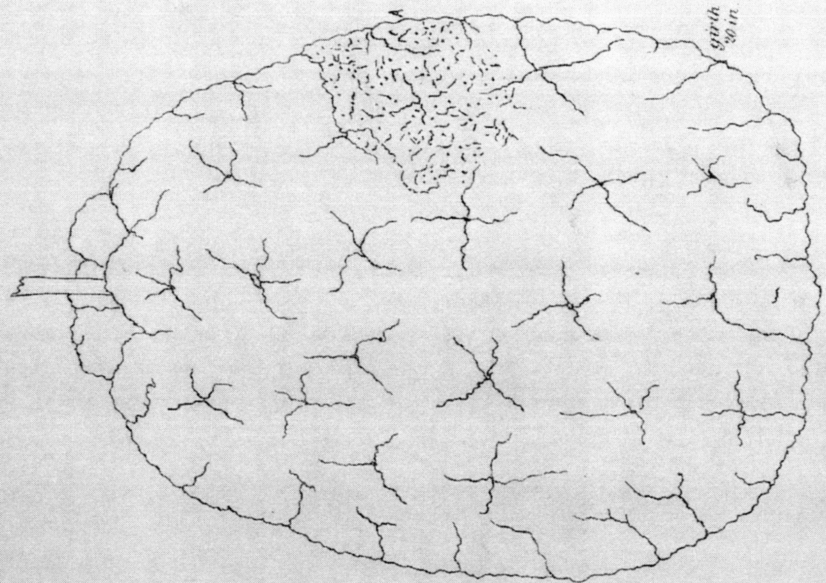

PLATE CXIII.

a is a section of the preceding large *Át Anni* from Gonda (Plate CXII). The oil-cells of the skin are large; the white portion of the skin is very thick and spongy. The skin is easily separated from the pulp-ball. The pulp is pale orange, of a pleasant sub-acid. Eaten with sugar it is very nice. The juice-vesicles are large and like those of a pummelo. The juice is abundant; the seeds are large and of a cream, or greenish-cream, colour, when cut. They are more like those of an orange than of a pummelo.

Under the name of *Nimboo Shirnee,* two small specimens were sent from the Maharaja's garden, at Mathora, Gonda. They had the same characters and the same flavour as this *Át Anni.* Some of the carpels were burst open towards the centre, as shown in section *a*, and the juice-vesicles projected into the hollow centre, as shown at A A. The central pith column, by expansion, was separated into four pieces, as shown at B B.

b and *c* are rain leaves; *d* and *e* spring leaves. All leathery, and with a *Suntara* scent. *f* is the spine which came on the branch.

PLATE CXIII.

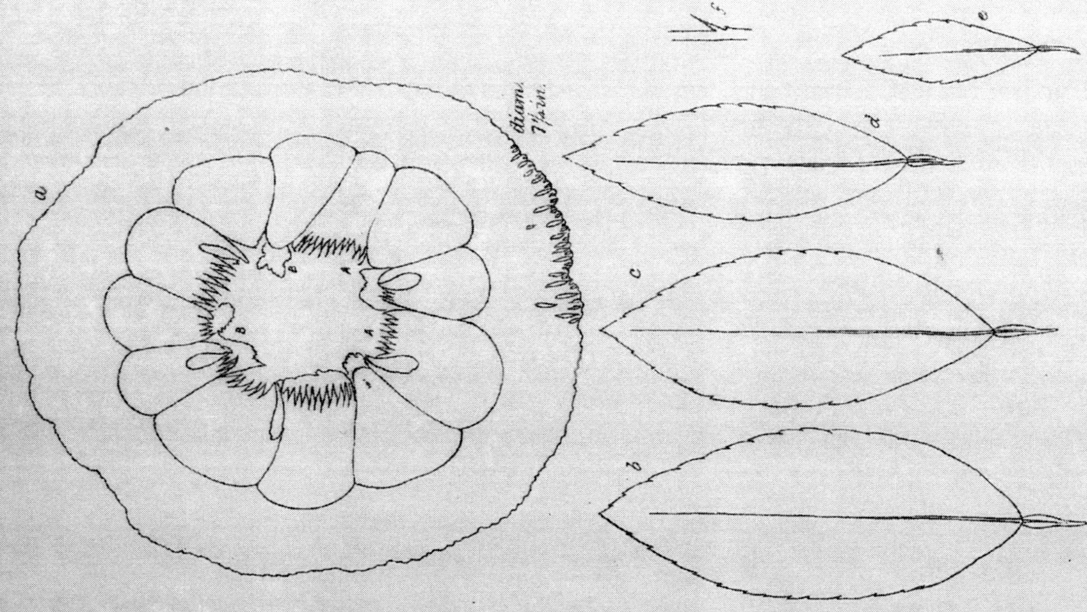

PLATE CXIV.

Is the Rungpur lime from Saharunpore Botanic Garden, called by the native gardener *Rungpolang*; which is nothing but a transformation of "Rungpur lime."

a and *b* are the same fruit, of a lobster-red round the apex, and of a yellow-orange round the base; smooth and very slightly foveolate all over; has an elastic feel, and no sign of mammilla at the apex. Skin, although closely-fitting, is easily removed. The section *b* is exactly like that of a Nagpore *Suntara* orange; juice abundant, and very sour; centre hollow; seeds of a greenish-cream colour, when cut. *d* and *e* are the spring leaves of *a*, with a very faint scent.

c was smooth like a *surkh-nimboo*, very thin-skinned; pulp, pale orange, and very sour; of a rather orangy flavour. When unripe the skin adheres to the pulp, like that of a sweet lemon.

f, *g*, *h* are the leaves of *c*. Both these specimens came from the same garden. The former was sent to me; the latter was unripe in October, and which I plucked myself.

NOTE.—This and the following specimens I obtained late, and are, therefore, placed at the end of the group.

PLATE CXIV.

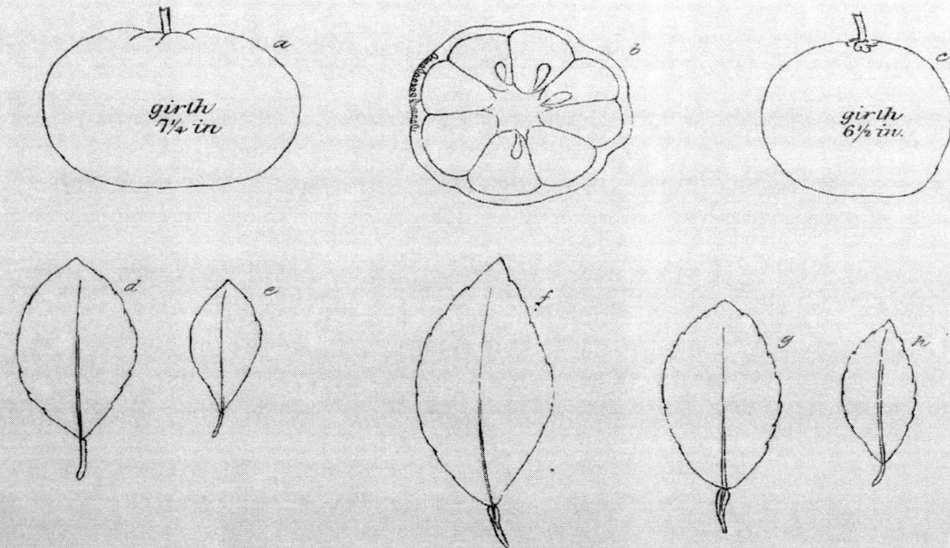

PLATE CXV.

This is the *Shôr* orange of Almora, Kumaon. Plucked in October, and therefore rather unripe. It is the *Suntara* orange of Kumaon, sent by Mr. A. Harris.

a and *b* are one fruit, much chagrined, green, turning yellowish; skin with flavour of *Suntara*; pulp deep orange, sour-sweet; centre solid, probably because *unripe*; seeds green, when cut. Skin rather thick and solid; always so in the unripe *Suntara*. By further ripeness and expansion the centre would become hollow, and the skin thinner and looser. The seeds have a rather long beak.

c is a slightly smoother specimen. This orange of Kumaon is called indifferently *Shôr*, *Sitòwli*, or *Gàngoli* orange of Almora. There appears to be no difference between *a* and *c*. The names are taken from the *places* where they are grown.

d is the leaf of *a*.

e and *f* came with *c*. They were pale green, with deeper green veins.

PLATE CXV.

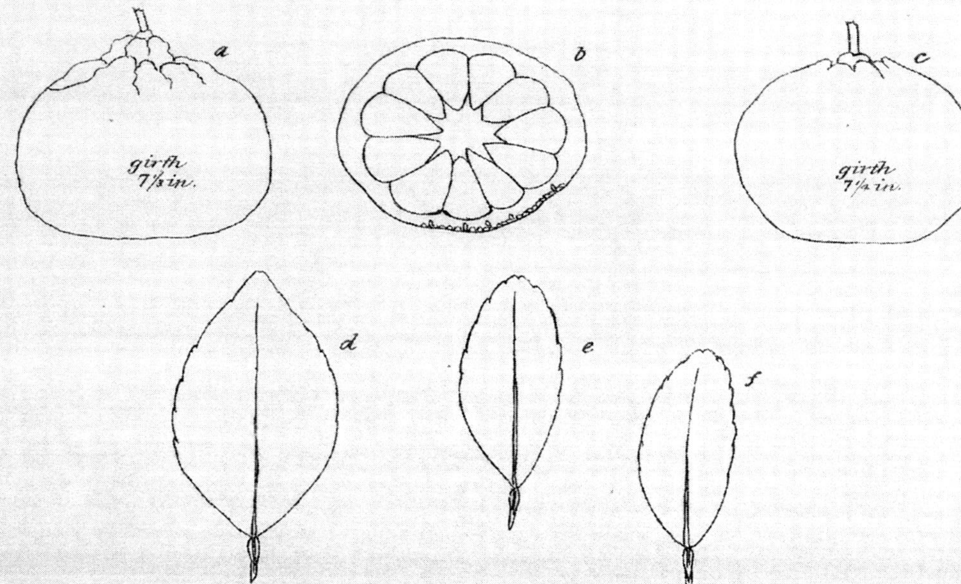

PLATE CXVI.

This is an *Át Anni*, which I plucked from the *Roshnàra bagh*, Delhi. I got it in October, and unripe.

a. The exterior is not clearly marked out by furrows, as in the other specimens of Plates CX. and CXI.; but the prominence of the small oil-cells in the would-be intermediate spaces is very distinct. The surface is deeply chagrined.

b is from the same tree, but not so pyriform; the large oil-cells are depressed, and the intermediate smaller ones very prominent, giving the surface a chagrined appearance.

c is the leaf of this *Át Anni*. It has a feeble scent; petioles distinctly pubescent on upper side of their base; young stems also distinctly pubescent, under the magnifying glass.

The pulp of this citrus has a pale orange tinge; juice of a pleasant acid flavour. (The pulp of a ripe *Át Anni*, eaten with sugar, is nice.) Its centre was solid, probably because unripe, and it was full of seeds.

PLATE CXVI.

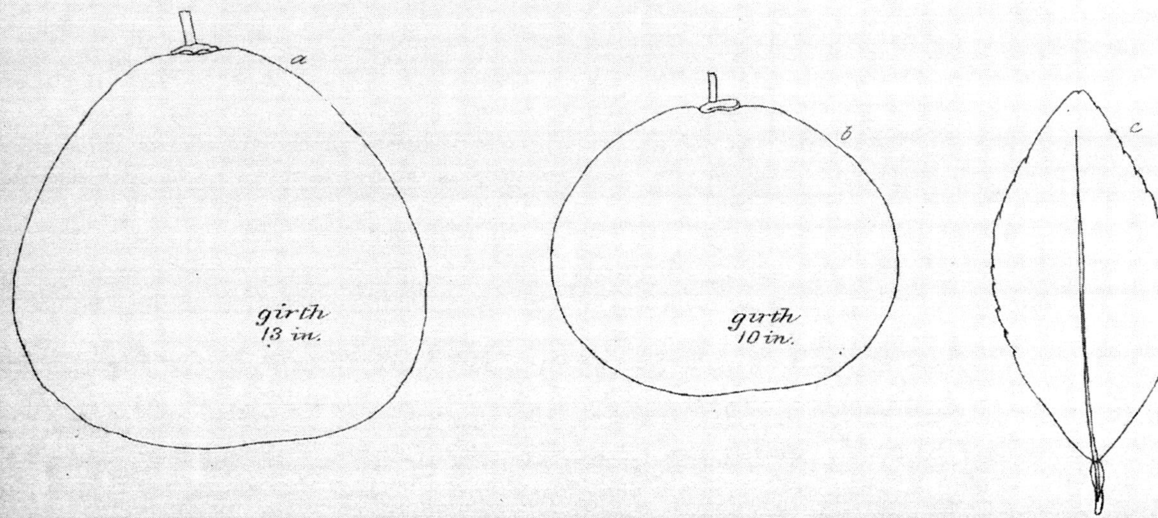

PLATE CXVI A.

This Plate shows the Aurantium Sinense of Rumphius more fully than Plate XCIII., Figs. *b* and *c*.

a and *b* show the leaves of adult trees; *b* shows them with margined petioles; *c* shows the leaves and spines of a young branch.

d is a separate and enlarged fruit, to show its proper form.

From this description of Rumphius, I have no doubt whatever that this is identical with the "green" *Suntara* orange of Kandy—the *Kònda-nàrun*.

Rumphius describes two varieties of this *Suntara*, a larger and a smaller. In the copy of the Royal Botanic Garden of Seebpore there are notes on the back of this plate, written by Buchanan Hamilton. He writes: "The *large* kind is the *Sylhet* orange; and the small kind is the *Midnapore* orange." In India there are now many varieties of the *Suntara* type.

PLATE CXVI[A].

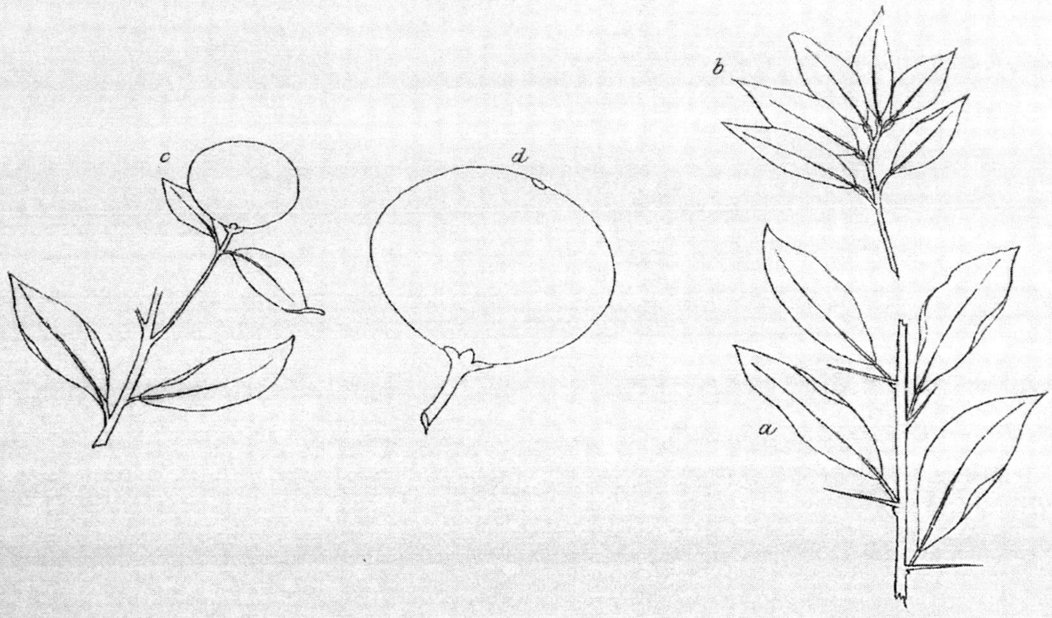

PLATE CXVII.

a and *b* is a true Mandarin orange, plucked at Etawah, in the unripe state in September. The exterior is deep green, coarsely chagrined, and *shiny*, as if varnished. Pulp, when unripe, is pale orange-yellow ; juice abundant, of a pleasant sweetish sub-acid.

c is a typical rain leaf, decidedly and distantly serrated in its tip-half with spine ; *d*, *e*, and *f* are spring leaves, apparently entire. A whole branch had leaves averaging from *g* to *h*.

On the same branch I found spines from ½ an inch long to less than ¼ inch.

i is a *myrtle* leaf of the rainy season. A leaf of myrtle and one of Mandarin could scarcely be distinguished by the eye.

j is taken from Risso's monograph. He called it "Bigaradier à feuilles de myrte." "It has a shiny chagrined skin, sometimes larger than that pictured ; pulp orange-yellow, sweet and sub-acid."

It appears to me not improbable that this Bigaradier of Risso and the Mandarin orange are identical.

NOTE.—In Andrew's Repository there is a picture of a Mandarin orange called C. nobilis. It has immense leaves and very large flat fruit. *If this be a true Mandarin*, climate and culture have made a great change, both in its leaf and fruit.

PLATE CXVII.

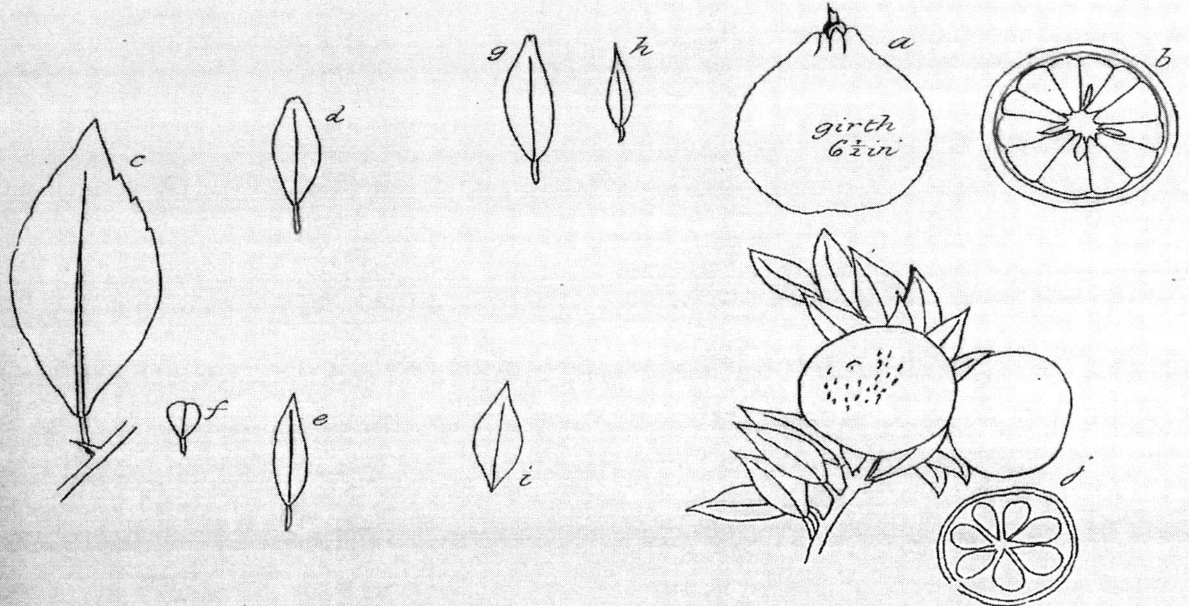

PLATE CXVIII.

a and *b* is a ripe true Mandarin, plucked from a tree in the Peradeniya Botanic Garden, Ceylon. Dr. Trimen told me that in 1847 H.H. Ibrahim Pashà, of Egypt, sent a collection of orange plants to Peradeniya, and that probably these Mandarins were descendants of some of them. The rind and leaves of the true Mandarin have an aroma distinct from all other orange trees that I have seen, although it is allied to that of the *Keonla* of India. The exterior of this orange was smooth and *shiny*; oil-cells distinct, as shown at A. It was not *perfectly* ripe, and the colour was orange-yellow (December); skin thin, and loosely adherent to the pulp; the latter being orange-yellow, with large cells, as shown in one of the carpels; seeds green, when cut. The rind had an aroma distinctly that of a true Mandarin; juice abundant, and of a very pleasant flavour. The oil-cells of the rind project like little balloons into the scanty, and white loose areolar tissue.

c is a rain leaf, and *d* and *e* spring leaves, both with a *sui generis* aroma.

f and *g* is a ripe Mandarin orange from the Etawah Jail Garden, introduced from Lucknow. Exterior bright orange, foveolate and chagrined, especially round the apex. The typical shape is slightly pyriform; some are more globose. Pulp orange; seeds green, when cut; centre hollow. In this and the Lucknow climate and soil the pulp is dryish. *h* is a rain leaf; *i*, *j*, and *k* are spring leaves; *l* its spines. Often it is spineless.

PLATE CXVIII.

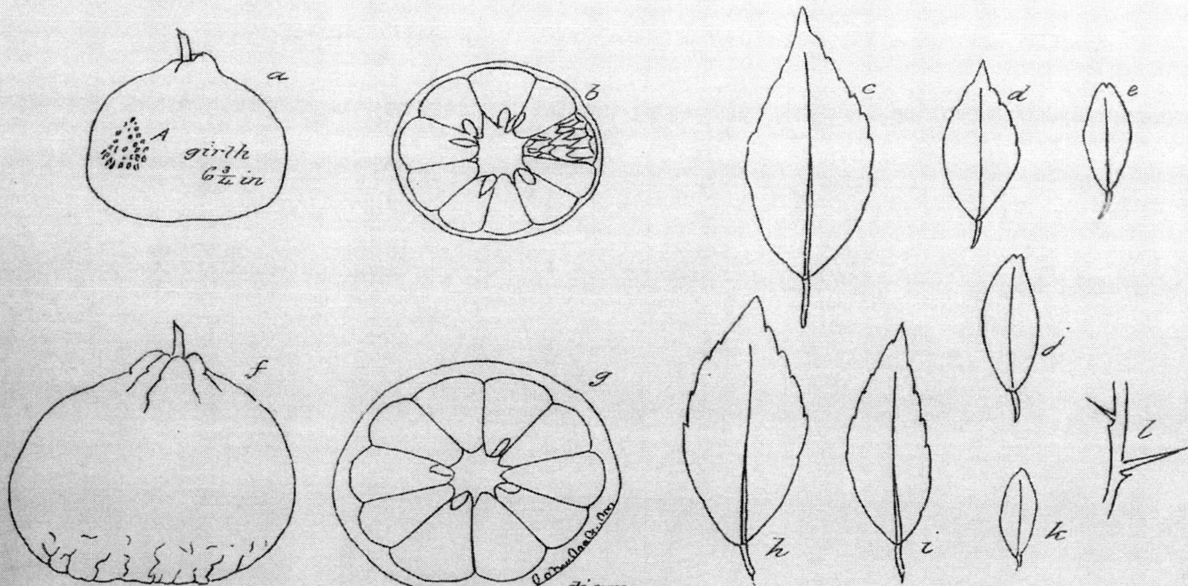

PLATE CXIX.

a and *b* is a globose Mandarin orange from Lucknow, with a close but loose skin; bright orange, smooth, and simply foveolate; pulp orange, paler than the rind, with a special aroma. The pulp is dry; the centre hollow and small.

c is a rain leaf; *d* and *e* spring leaves. The petioles are linear and without wings. The scent of the leaves reflects somewhat that of the rind, but it is a *sui generis* scent, and allied to that of *Keonla* leaves.

In a suitable climate and soil the flavour of the Mandarin orange pulp is exquisite, and the juice abundant.

f and *g* was obtained from Auraya, unripe in September. It is what natives call *Naràngi*; loose-skinned and about the size of a *Keonla* orange, but said to be sweeter. The glandular portion of the rind is thick, and the white portion thin; pulp, in its unripe state, is pale orange-yellow and sour; seeds numerous, and conspicuously green, when cut.

PLATE CXIX.

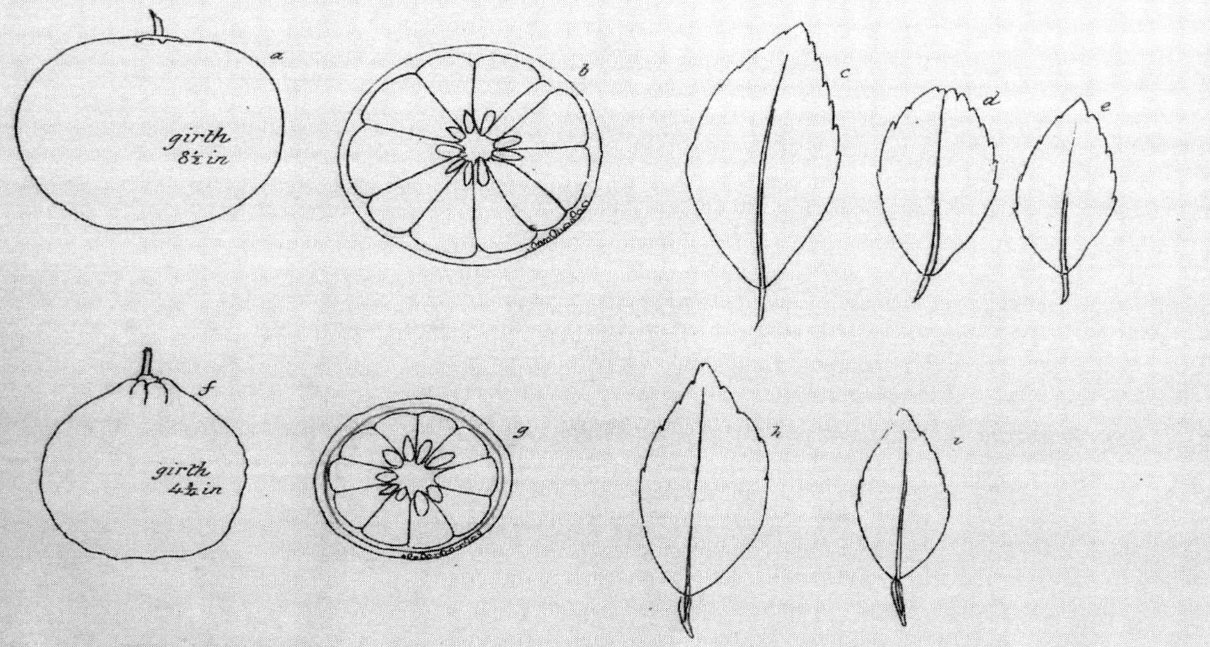

PLATE CXX.

a and *b* is a *Naràngi* orange, sent by Messrs. Carew & Co., of Shahjahanpur; chagrined and covered with foveoli. The intermediate spaces have small cells, decidedly convex. The rind of the unripe fruit is deep green; pulp pale orange, sub-acid, and sweet. *c* is a rain leaf, and *d* and *e* spring leaves.

f is a *Naràngi* orange from Gonda. Exterior scarlet, and foveolate, with a depressed mammilla; oil-cells of rind large and distinct; pulp orange; juice abundant, and more like a *Keonla* orange; centre hollow; seeds green, when cut.

h and *i* are spring leaves, with the scent of *Keonla* leaves. This appears a small form of *Keonla*, All these *Naràngi* oranges are more chagrined than those of the *Suntara* type, and frequently they have a depressed mammilla. They appear a sweeter variety than the common *Keonla*.

PLATE CXX.

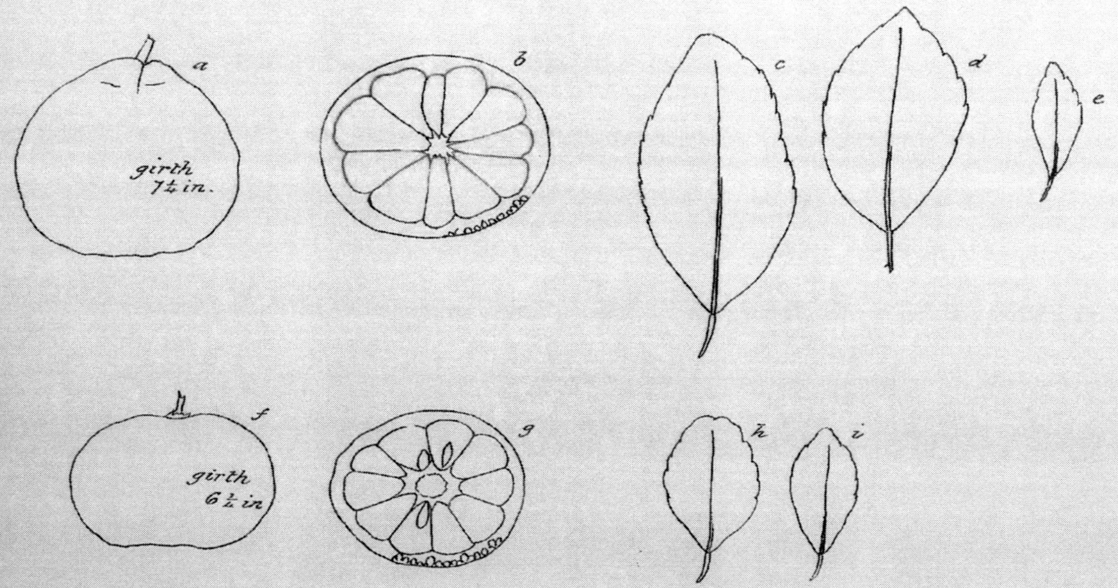

PLATE CXXI.

a and *b* is the *Nas-nârun* of Colombo, called there Mandarin. Externally it is deep orange, smooth and pitted all over with minute foveoli. The intermediate cells are not distinct. Skin loosely attached to pulp. The pulp is orange, and large celled. The juice has a pleasant flavour, and the seeds are green, when cut. This orange appeared to me to have the character of the *Reshmi* orange of Upper India. It is not a true Mandarin. I was told that its juice is used medicinally, mixed with other things, and poured into the nose, for headaches, &c. It is also eaten.

c and *d* is the *Heen-nârun* of Kandy. Shaped like a tomato, with surface distinctly foveolate. It is depressed at both base and apex, and the colour, when ripe, is that of a boiled lobster. The oil-cells of the rind are large and distinct; pulp deep orange; juice-cells large; flavour not unpleasant—sub-acid and aromatic; seeds green, when cut.

e is a smaller one of the same variety; *g* and *h* are its leaves; *f* is another form, and *i* and *j* are its leaves. The leaves of these two had the scent of the *Keonla* orange; *c*, *e*, and *f* were distinctly like the *Reshmi* orange of India.

PLATE CXXI.

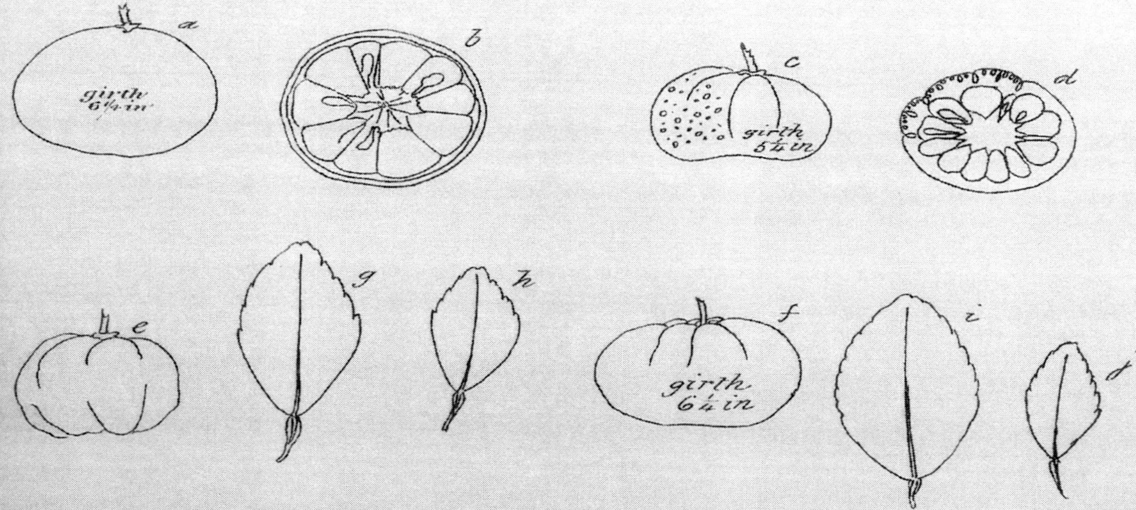

PLATE CXXII.

a and *b* is a *Reshmi Narángi,* taken from Raja Siva Prasad's Garden, at Benares, flat and tomato-like; depressed at both base and apex; colour, when quite ripe, of a lobster-red. On the apex especially it is often as red as a tomato. Pulp orange, and juice abundant; it does not sweeten completely, but remains sub-acid; juice-cells stout and short; seeds green, when cut. The rind is loosely attached, and has the scent of Lantana; aromatic, but not agreeably so.

c and *d* are the leaves of this orange, rounded and crenated, like those of a *Keonla.* The scent of the leaves is also similar, but not so pronounced.

e and *f* is the same *Reshmi* orange from Lucknow; does not sweeten till late. *g* is a smaller and smoother form.

h and *i* are its rain and spring leaves.

k is the section of a *Keonla* orange from Gonda; externally sub-warty, with a thickish, loose skin, containing the largest oil-cells I have seen. The juice-cells were of an orange-colour; juice sweetish acid; seedless. Leaves had the scent of the *Keonla.*

PLATE CXXII.

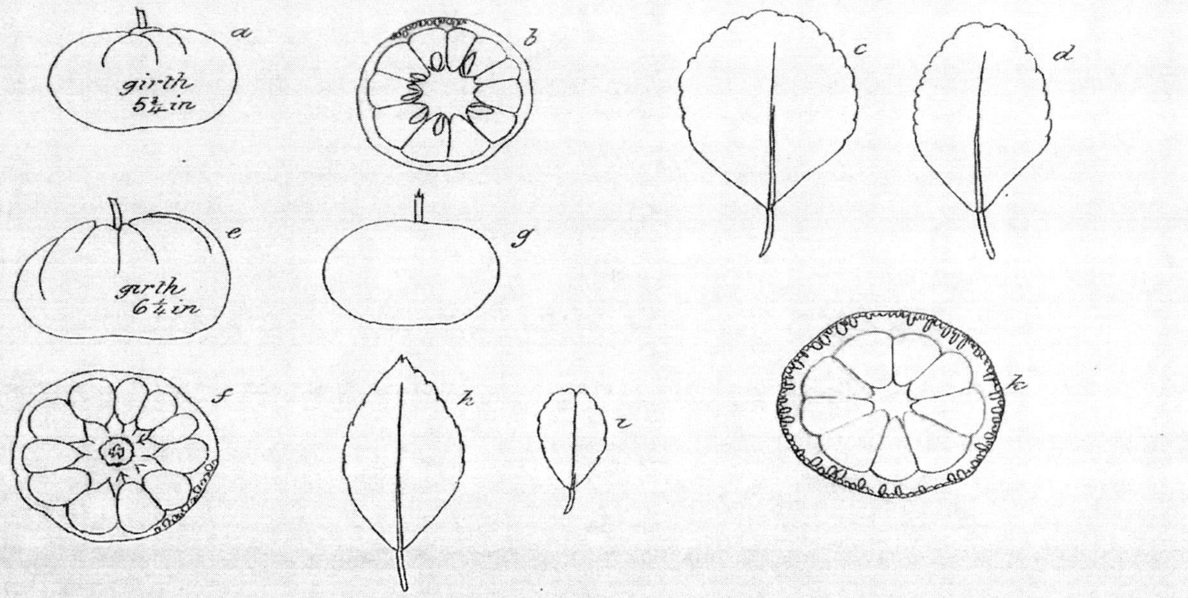

PLATE CXXIII.

a and *b* is a *Keonla* from Bulrampur, Gonda; of a lobster-red colour on its apex half; chagrined and foveolate; with a flattened mammilla on the apex. It felt baggy, from the skin being very loose.

c was a smaller one from the same place.

d and *e* are their leaves. The oil-cells, as shown in *b*, are very large and distinct, and the pith around them easily removed so as to expose the globular orange-coloured oil-cells, the largest of which had a diameter of $\frac{1}{8}$ inch. The rind was sweet and pungent; pulp orange and sub-acid; juice-vesicles coarse; seeds very few, and green, when cut.

f and *g* is a *Keonla* from Lucknow; deep orange and chagrined, more like a Mandarin than a *Suntara*, but of a deeper red, rather a lobster-red. On the apex there is often a flattened mammilla. Pulp is of the same colour as the *Suntara*, but not so juicy, and more sour. Seeds green, when cut.

PLATE CXXIII.

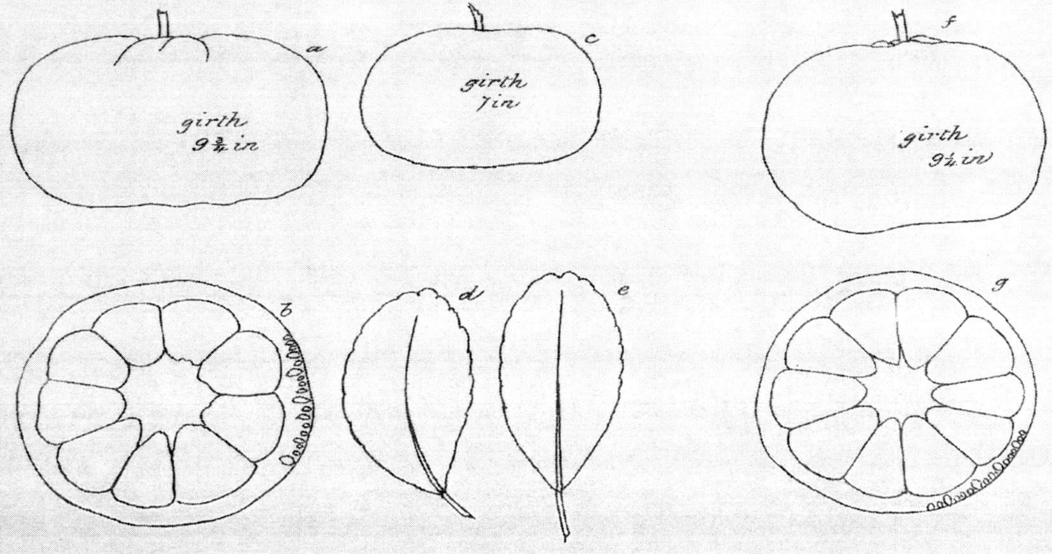

PLATE CXXIV.

a and *b* is a *Keonla* orange from Benares. This is a good average-sized *Keonla*; others are smaller, $7\frac{1}{4}$ inches in girth, and a few still larger. When quite ripe, of a red orange, inclining to lobster-red. This specimen was sub-verrucose; rind strongly aromatic, rather resinous, and loosely attached. The pulp was distinctly sour, otherwise it did not differ from others of the same type. *c* and *d* are its leaves; rounded and often emarginate, crenate, and with a distinct aroma.

e and *f* is an unripe *Keonla* from Etawah. The apex is rough, sinuous, and sub-warty, with a pushed-in mammilla. Oil-cells large, and easily dissected from the white pithy tissue; pulp bright orange; juice-cells coarse, and, when fully ripe, sweetish.

g are some of the juice-cells; very few were pedicelled, they were mostly sessile, and some not larger than the oil-cells of the rind.

h and *i* are well-developed rain leaves; and *j* and *k* well-developed spring leaves. The young canes from the bottom of the trunk have spines like the Sylhet and *Suntara* varieties.

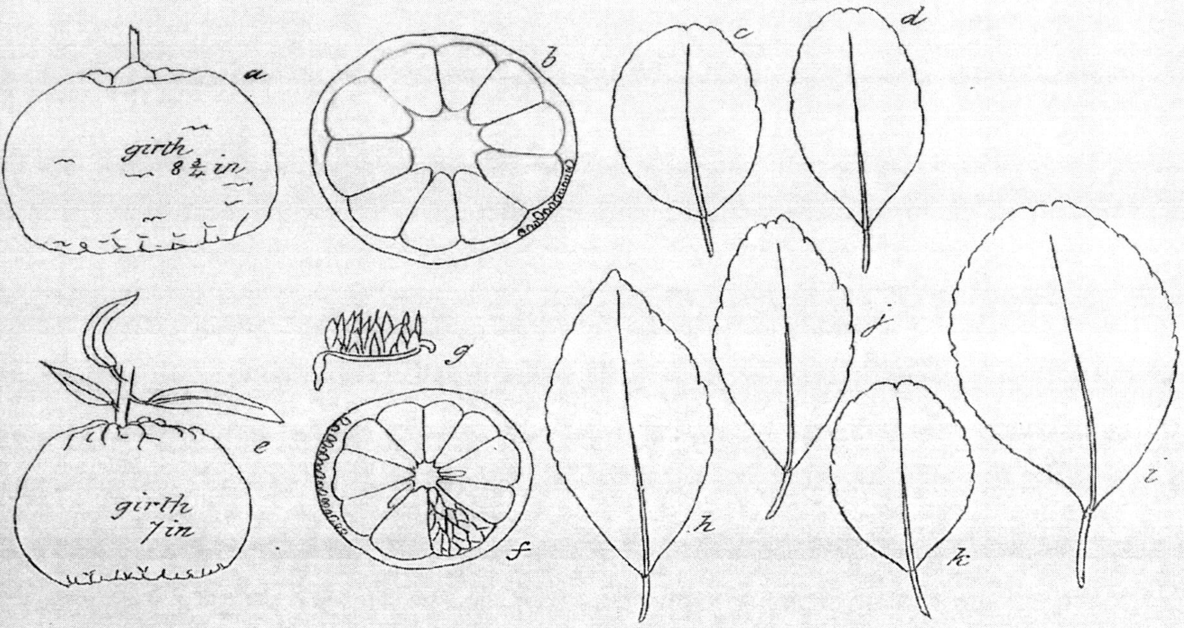
a
girth
8 3/4 in
b
c
d
e
girth
7 in
f
g
h
j
k
l

PLATE CXXV.

a and *b* I purchased at the Bombay market. I was told it came from Aurungabàd, Deccan. It is the most warty orange of the *Keonla* type I have seen. Externally deep orange, with its apex half very warty. The apex has a distinct mammilla, also warty, pushed in, and depressed in its centre. Each wart of this orange has usually one or more distinct foveoli. The base half is slightly rugose and foveolate. Pulp deep orange; juice fine-flavoured, and abundant; juice-vesicles large, and attached also to the *sides* of the carpels. This appears a desirable variety of the *Keonla* type. It has few seeds, and a *fine flavour*.

c shows the interior surface of the rind, with the pithy white tissue dissected off. There was a space between the skin and pulp-ball.

d and *e* is a *Keonla* from one of the Poona orchards. On the apex it had only a warty and depressed *aureola*, not a distinct mammilla; it had a large space between the skin and pulp-ball, with connecting pith-fibres, as shown in section; pulp deep orange, distinctly sub-acid; seeds green, when cut; centre hollow.

f and *g* are its leaves, distinctly crenate, with all the characters of *Keonla* leaves.

PLATE CXXV.

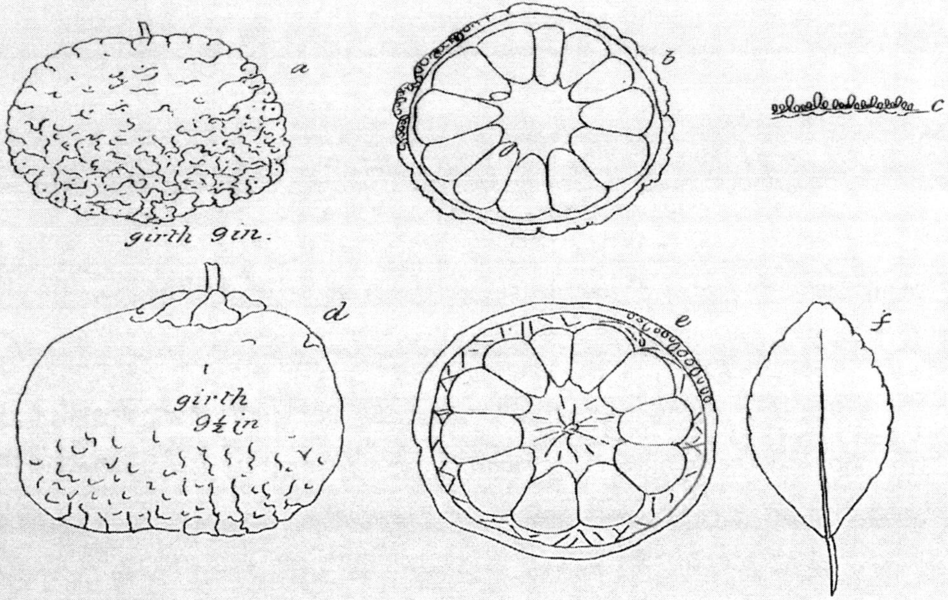

PLATE CXXVI.

a and *b* is a variety I obtained also in one of the Poona orchards. It is there called "Laroo." It is quite flat, with a prominent mammilla at the base. The apex is much depressed. It is of a lobster-red, bladdery, and loose-skinned; foveolate all over very markedly and deeply; between the skin and pulp-ball there is a large space, as shown in section, with connecting fibres. The pulp is orange, large-vesicled, sub-acid, and not very sweet; seeds green, when cut; centre hollow; seeds few.*

c, *d*, and *e* are its leaves; rounded and distinctly crenate, with a distinct *Keonla* scent. On the petioles of the young leaves I found scattered hairs.

f and *g* I purchased in the Bombay market. I was told it was a *Keonla* from Delhi. Its colour was lobster-red, much chagrined and sub-warty, and foveolate. It had a depressed mammilla on the apex; skin loosely attached, and the quarters, or carpels, loosely adhering; pulp orange; vesicles coarse; juice not very abundant, and distinctly sub-acid; centre hollow; seeds greenish, when cut.

* Can this be the same as the large flat Mandarin pictured in the Botanical Repository?

PLATE CXXVI.

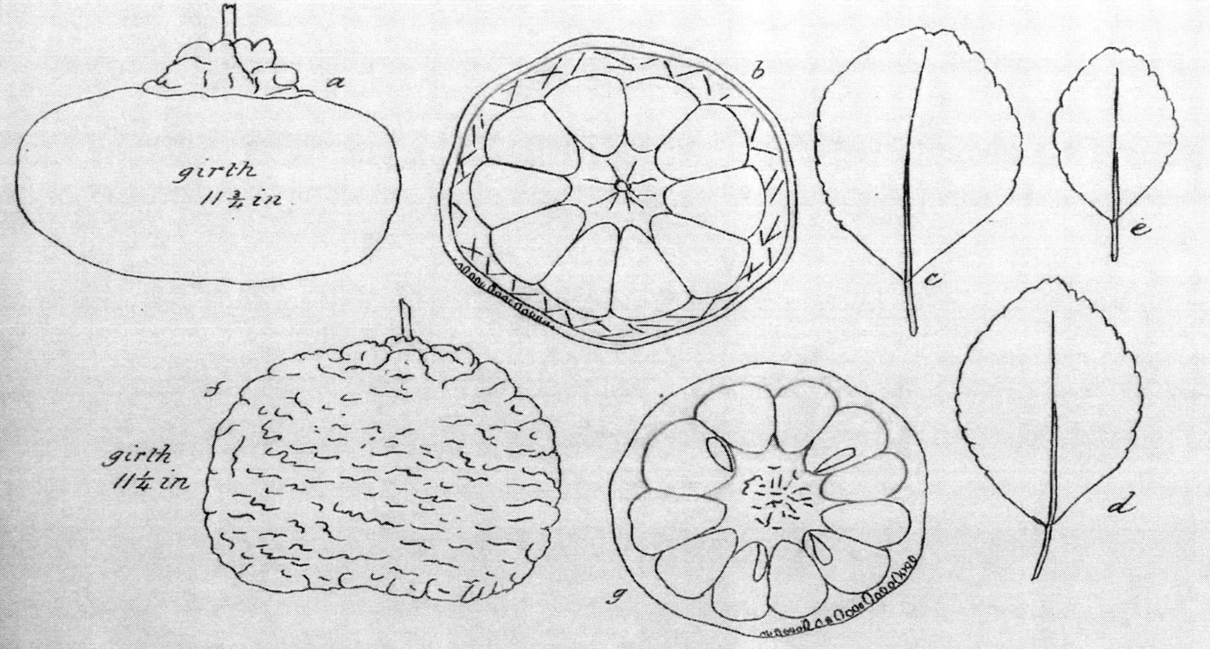

PLATE CXXVII.

This shows the *Kôkni* orange of Saharunpore and Delhi.

a and *b* are one fruit; chagrined, especially round the apex. I only saw it when unripe, in October. The skin is loosely adherent, and strongly aromatic; pulp orange, juicy, and sub-acid, when unripe. It is said to sweeten, when ripe; centre solid in October; seeds green, when cut,

c is a smaller specimen, with some of the smallest leaves on.

d and *e* are well-developed leaves; and *f* and *g* are small spring leaves. The scent of its leaves corresponds more to those of the *Keonla* than any other. It is redder than the *Kumquat* when ripe.

I believe in Saharmpore its English name is "China orange." Rumphius mentions a small orange of China. It may be this.

PLATE CXXVII.

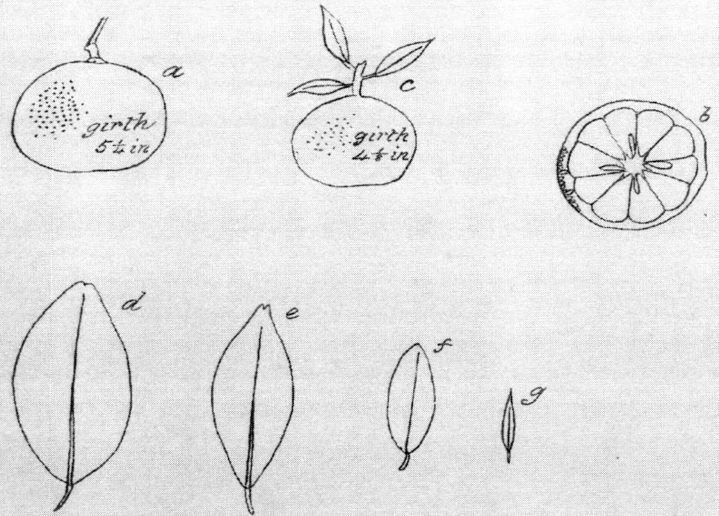

PLATE CXXVIII.

These four oranges are all true Mandarins, purchased at an English shop, given here for purposes of comparison. Each is from a different firm, and probably all come from Spain.

They all have the same character; pitted all over with foveoli, and *shiny*.

a had the brand of "Vives navarrete; Oliva." Firm, A. Barraca.

b was "Mandarina Catarroja; Valencia." Firm, Pedrer.

c "Mandarine Extra; Espagne; Abaran." Firm, D'Ginestar et fils.

d "Sinibaldo Gutierez; Gandia; 50 milms."

a, *b*, and *c* were simply enveloped in thin tissue paper, and each orange wrapper had the brand of the firm.

d, besides a wrapper of tissue paper, had a second one of *fine tin foil* to each orange. This flat tomato shape is typical of the true Mandarin, when grown in a suitable soil and climate.

PLATE CXXVIII.

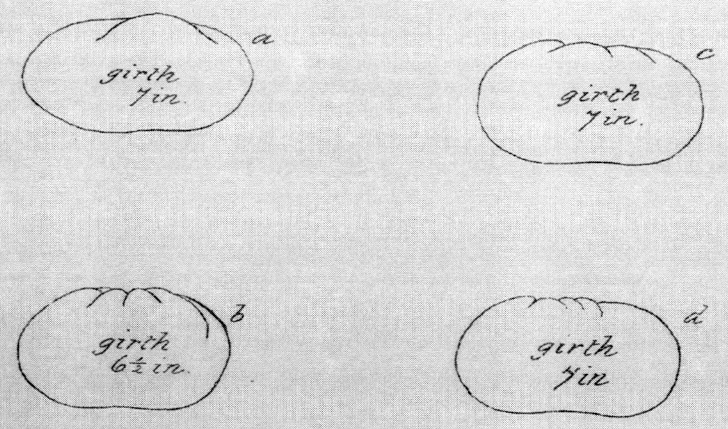

PLATE CXXIX.

b and *c* is the "Jamir" of Almora, sent by Mr. H. Harris. It had a somewhat ventricose appearance, but the general outline was that of a typical Malta lemon; not improbably it may be a link between the two types. Exterior lemon-yellow, studded closely with minute foveoli; inclined to be sub-warty, or verrucose; slightly aromatic. Skin thick, pulp pale, with a tinge of orange-yellow; juice abundant, and very acid; seeds many, but all shrivelled and without a kernel.

d is a typical rain leaf; *e* and *f* typical spring leaves; and *g* its spines.

c is taken from the Flor. Amboin. of Rumphius, vol. ii., Table xxvi., Fig. 2. He calls it *Limo tuberosus*, or Lemon Martin. He says it is allied to Limo ventricosus (Plate XXVI., Fig. 1), but that the former has very different leaves from the latter. It is impossible, from Rumphius's plates, to judge of the size of the fruit. Probably this Limo tuberosus is of the lemon group, but *may* have some connection with the *Jambiri*.

PLATE CXXIX.

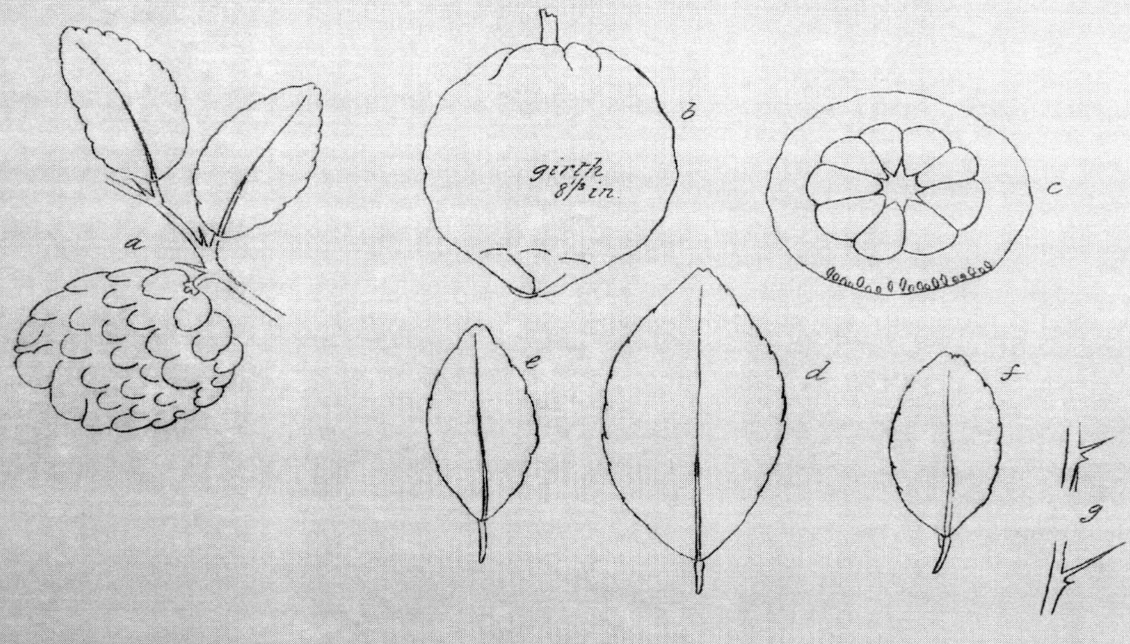

PLATE CXXX.

Two forms of *Jhambiri*.

a and *b* is the *Jhambiri* from Dhama Chowree, Gonda, one of the late Maharaja's gardens. The exterior is lemon-yellow, inclining in parts to orange-yellow; rind verrucose and aromatic; pulp lemon-yellow, and very sour, with the structure of a *Keonla* orange; seeds green, when cut; rind lemon-flavoured, but unpleasant. It had no prominent mammilla.

c and *d* are the leaves of the same.

e and *f* is the *Jhambiri* lime of the Saharunpore Botanic Garden. It is lemon-yellow, with an elastic feel; foveolate all over, and with here and there a slight eminence, as if it tried to be verrucose. It has a flattened mammilla. The skin is loose like that of a *Keonla* orange. The appearance of the pulp is also that of the *Keonla*, excepting that it is very pale yellow; juice abundant and pure acid; centre hollow; seeds greenish white, when cut.

g, *h*, and *i* are its spring leaves; flowers small, half inch diameter, faintly tinged purple; young shoots green; spines mere feeble points. In all respects this *Jhambiri* is like a *Keonla* orange, excepting colour of rind and pulp. The scent and shape of the leaves, and the colour of the seeds, are more like those of a lemon.

PLATE CXXX.

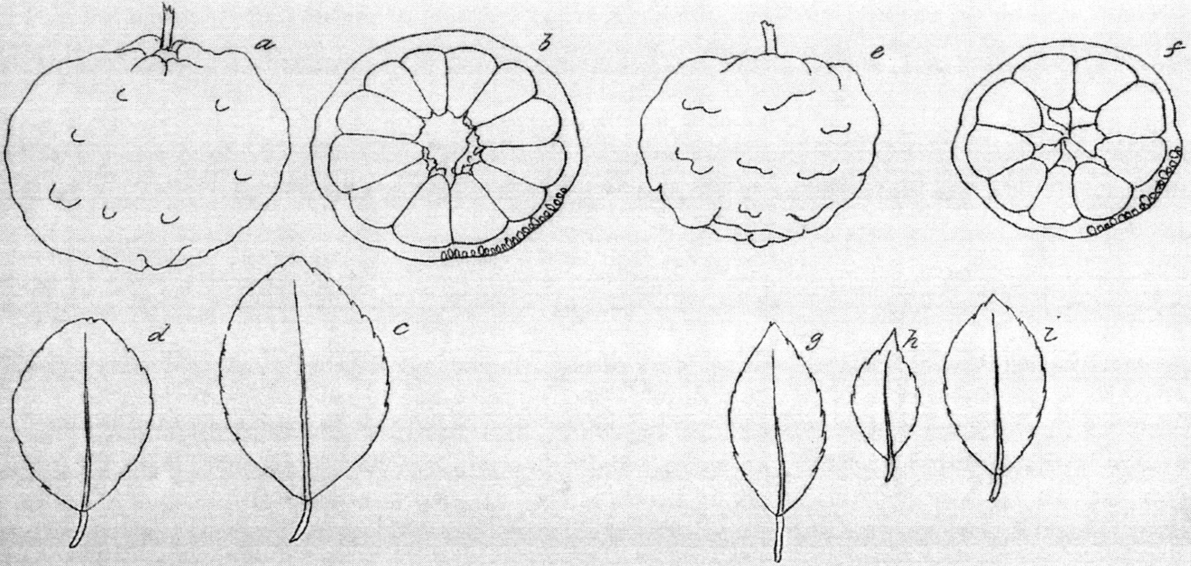

PLATE CXXXI.

Other forms of *Jhambìri.*

a and *b* I obtained at one of the G.I.P. Ry. stations in the Central Provinces. I was told it is called *Jhambìri.* It is shaped like a *Keonla* orange; surface rough, gathered into folds round the base, with a pronounced and flattened mammilla on the apex, and a deep furrow all round it, as shown in section *b*. Externally of a clear lemon-yellow, deeply pitted all over with foveoli and intermediate indistinct oil-cells. *b* is a longitudinal section, showing its hollow centre and the small and large juice-vesicles very distinctly. Cells of rind very distinct; pulp with a pale orange tint; juice-cells rather large, like those of the *Keonla*; juice abundant and sour. It reminded me, both in flavour and sourness, of an unripe *Keonla* orange.

c and *d* rain leaves; *e* and *f* spring leaves. All leaves were emarginate on the branch I took. They were rather lemon scented. In shape they were similar to those of the *Keonla*; *g* is its spine.

h, *i*, and *j* is the *Jamìri* of Rohilcund; pale lemon-yellow; chagrined. The mammilla is flattened and pushed in, as shown in *j*; pulp pale and very sour, never sweetens; centre hollow.

k, *l*, and *m* are the leaves that came with it. *n* is its spine.

PLATE CXXXI.

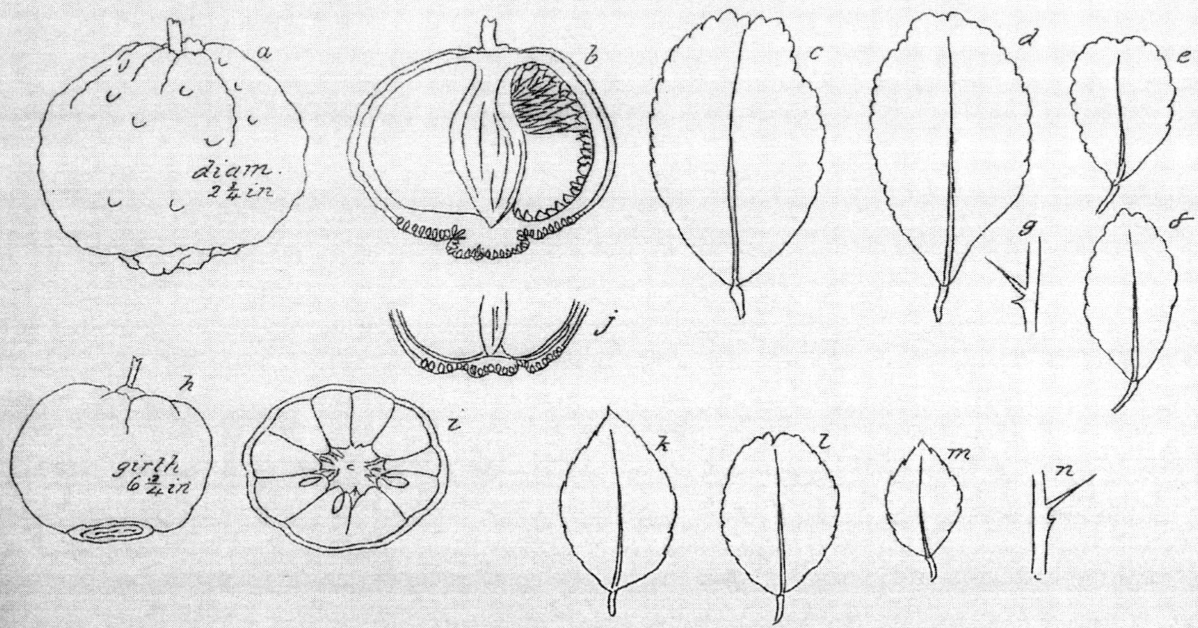

PLATE CXXXII.

Other forms of Jhambìri.

a and *b* is a Jhambìri from Lucknow, which came marked No. 1. Its exterior is lemon-yellow, much chagrined; with folds round the base, and a depressed mammilla on the apex. It has the shape of an orange of the loose-skinned type. Pulp pale, like that of a lemon, and very sour. It never sweetens; centre hollow; flowers very faintly tinged purple.

c is a smoother specimen.

d is a spring leaf, with distant and scarcely perceptible serrations.

e is a rain leaf, with distinct crenations.

There is a yellow and a red variety of Jhambìri in Lucknow, and the flowers of both are faintly tinged purple, and the young shoots are green.

f and *g* is a citrus, which came from Benares under the name of "Another Nepâlee." I believe it is nothing but a Jhambìri, much chagrined round the base and apex, otherwise smooth, with a flattened mammilla; pulp pale and very sour. It was sent without leaves. Its section is more like a "Keonla" orange than a Nepâlee lemon.

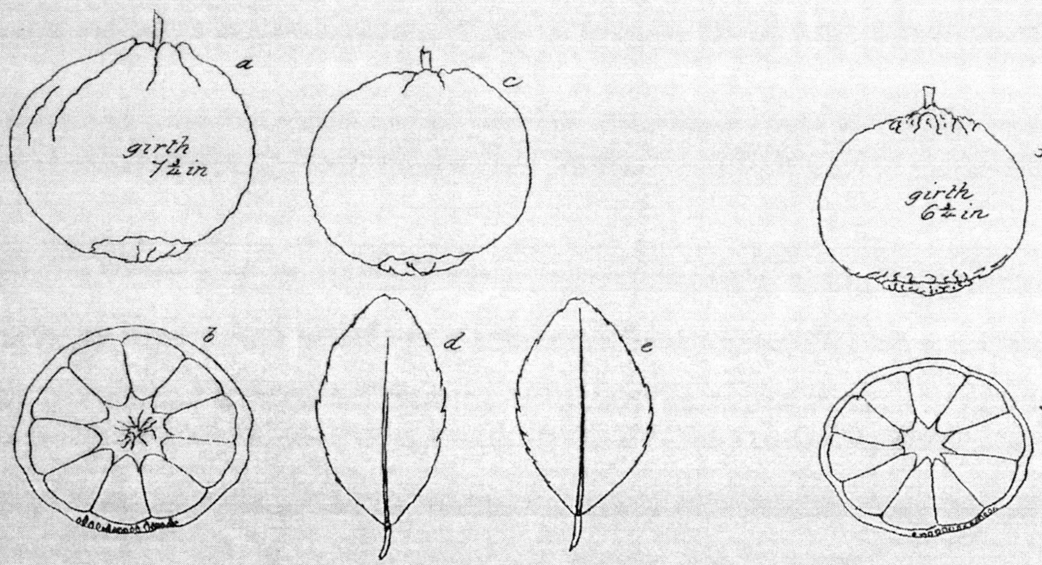
a
girth
7¼ in
c
f
girth
6¼ in
b
d
e
g

PLATE CXXXIII.

Other forms of *Jhambiri*.

a and *b* came from Calcutta, under the name of *Gorá* lemon (Vide Appendix, No. 55) (2nd kind). Its exterior is slightly chagrined, with a depressed mammilla, like that of other *Jhambiri*. It has large and small foveoli, with intermediate oil-cells. This specimen was turning pale yellow. Pulp pale, with an orange tinge; juice abundant, sub-acid, with an orange flavour.

c and *d* are the leaves which came with it.

e and *f* came from Allahabad, under the name of *Kunra*. Its exterior is pale yellow, and chagrined, with foveoli closely set; the intermediate spaces are filled with miliary convexities, representing the smaller oil-cells. The pulp is pale, with a very slight tinge of orange, and sour. The rind has more the taste of orange rind than lemon rind. The mammilla is flattened and pushed in, with a sulcus all round, as shown in section.

N.B.—*Kunra* may possibly be a corruption of the Bengali name *Gorá*. The small juice-vesicles of *f* are vere distinct.

PLATE CXXXIII.

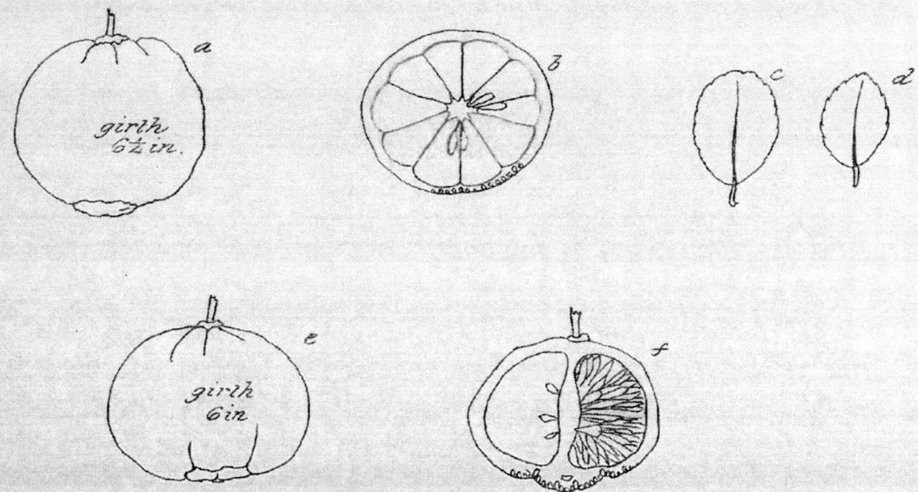

PLATE CXXXIV.

a and *b* came from Benares, under the name of *Shunkhàdràv*. Exterior smooth, but not so smooth as the *Kalan Kaghzi nimboo*. The oil-cells are close to each other. Pulp pale orange, very sour, and with a lemon orange taste.

c and *d* are the leaves that came with it, and *e* the spine.

f came from Dhama Chowree, Gonda, one of the Maharaja's gardens. Exterior of a fawn-coloured orange, quite chagrined, and with a curious epidermis, which may give it this fawn colour. It has a flattened mammilla; skin thin and puffy; pulp very pale orange, very sour, and juice abundant, with a slightly orange flavour; skin has an orange taste; centre hollow; seeds green, when cut.

h and *i* are the leaves which came with it, they had no scent; and *g*, its spine.

Another came from Toolshipur, Gonda. It was yellow, with an orange-skin flavour; pulp very pale, with only a *soupçon* of orange tinge; very sour; others were like a *Keonla*; seeds greenish cream.

j and *k* is a *Jambìri* from Lucknow, which came ticketed No. 2, smoother than No 1, and more globose; mammilla scarcely visible; its skin is thin and closely fitting; when ripe, lemon-yellow. It is full of sour juice, and has a *sui generis* aroma.

PLATE CXXXIV.

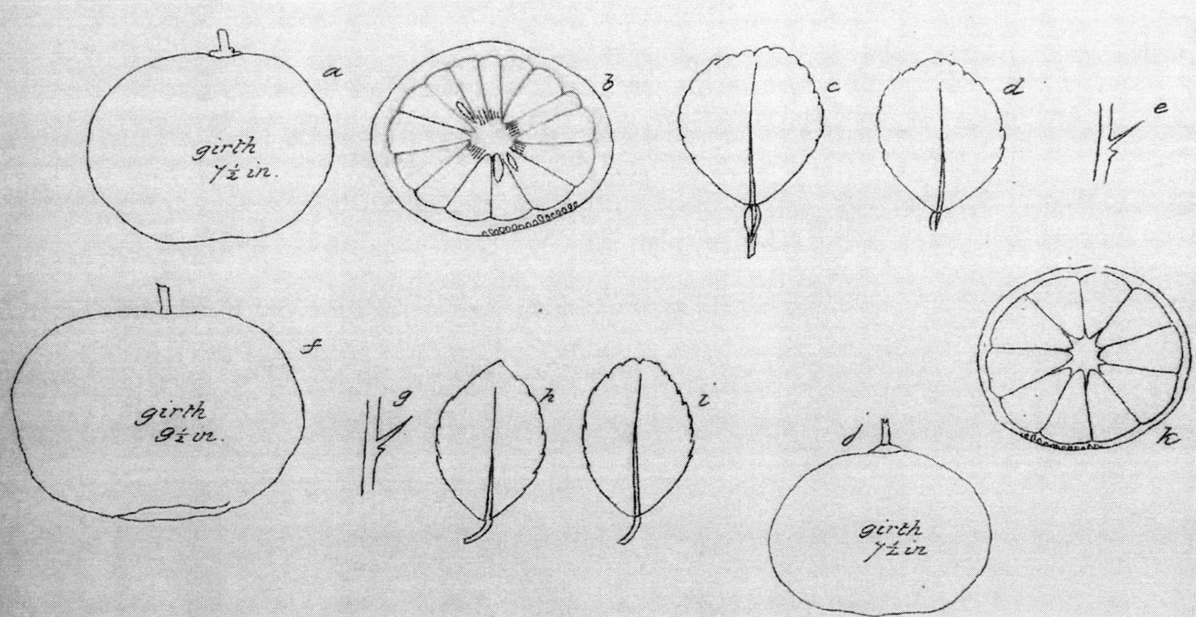

PLATE CXXXV.

a and *b* is a *Jambiri* from Rosa, Shahjahanpur; externally pale yellow, and closely studded with foveoli.

c is an ovoid form, with the mammilla represented by a point. The pulp is pale and very sour, with a faint bitter taste.

d and *e* are rain leaves.

f and *g* spring leaves.

It is doubtful whether this is a *Jambiri* proper or a citrus like the ones from Mooltan, Khoorja and Calcutta (*Vide* Plates CCVII. and CCVIII.), which are also with a slightly bitter taste in their juice.

h and *i* came from Baghelkund, Toolshipur, Gonda. It came ticketed *Mitha nimboo*. The colour is deep yellow on apex half, and yellow orange round base, and foveolate all over; pulp pale yellow, with a tinge of orange; perfectly sour; centre hollow; seeds greenish cream, when cut. It is certainly not a *Mitha nimboo*, or sweet lemon. The skin fits closely, but is easily detached. It has all the characters of a *Jambiri*. *j* is a rain leaf, and *k* a spring leaf. The spines were mere points.

PLATE CXXXV.

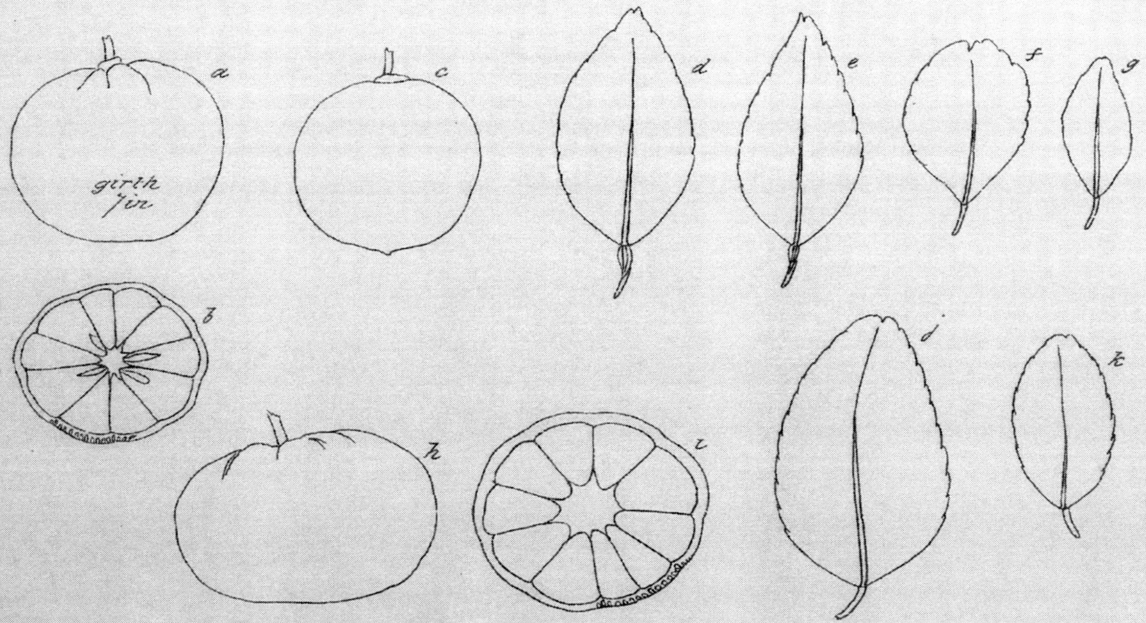

PLATE CXXXVI.

a and *b* is a citrus I found on a tree in Hagkala, Ceylon; colour lemon-yellow, and foveolate all over, and with a flattened mammilla. The rind had not a very pleasant scent. The pulp was pale orange, juice abundant, and sour; centre solid; seeds white, when cut.

c is a fully-developed rain leaf, with only ridges on upper side of petiole, like those of the Malta lemon leaf.

d is an old spring leaf, and *e* a young leaf (December). Both were slightly margined.

The flowers were tinged purple, and the youngest leaves also tinged purple. Not improbably this is of the *Jambiri* type. The large size of leaf *c* is accounted for by climate, and by its having been taken from a young cane.

f I purchased at the Bombay market, and said to be grown in Bombay. It is pyriform, chagrined, and foveolate. It is said to be yellow when ripe.

g is one of the leaves which were attached to it. This was distinctly crenate and lemon scented, others were distinctly emarginate. Not impossibly it belongs to the *Jambiri* type.

PLATE CXXXVI.

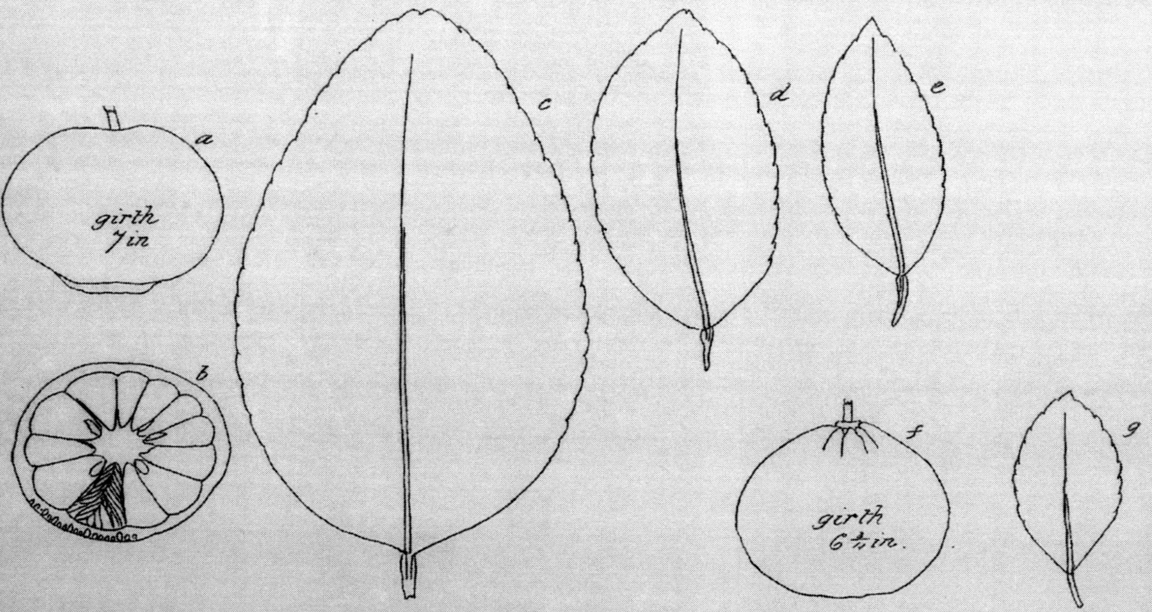

PLATE CXXXVII.

a and *b* is a *Jambiri*, from the Botanic Garden, Saharunpore. It was unripe when I plucked it in October. Probably this is the reason why it is so chagrined. The pulp was white and sour, with abundant juice. The seeds were greenish, when cut, and with a brown pellicle beneath the outer shell; rind aromatic, but not pleasant; oil-cells closely packed, possibly from being unripe and insufficiently expanded.

c and *d* are rain leaves; *e* and *f* spring leaves; and *g* the spine.

PLATE CXXXVII.

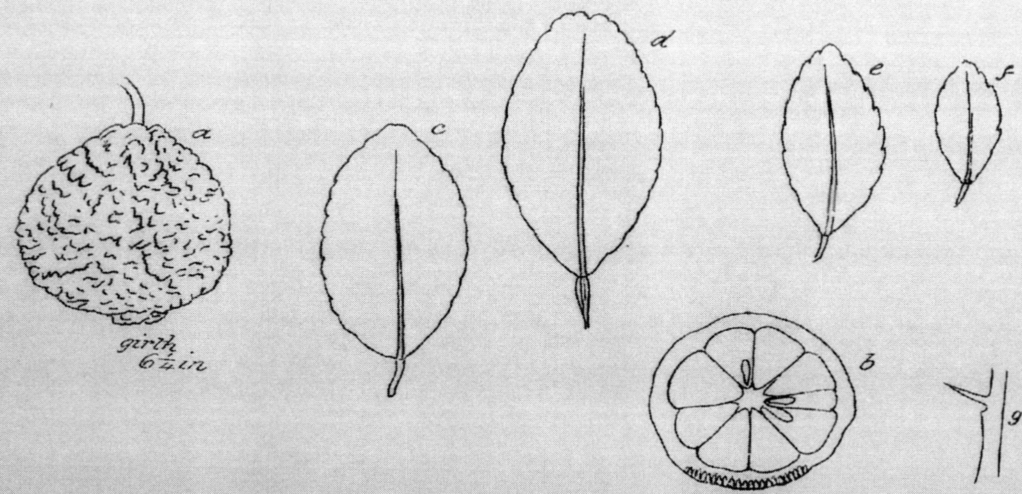

PLATE CXXXVIII.

a and *b* is the *Jamir* of Almora, grown at Sitowli, by Mr. H. Harris. When I got it, it was green turning pale citron colour; chagrined like an unripe *Keonla* orange; the aroma of the rind, neither citrine nor pleasant; pulp pale transparent, with a slight orange flavour. It was full of seeds, which were longer than usual.

c and *d* are its rain leaves, thin and rather like those of the *Suntara* orange.

PLATE CXXXVIII.

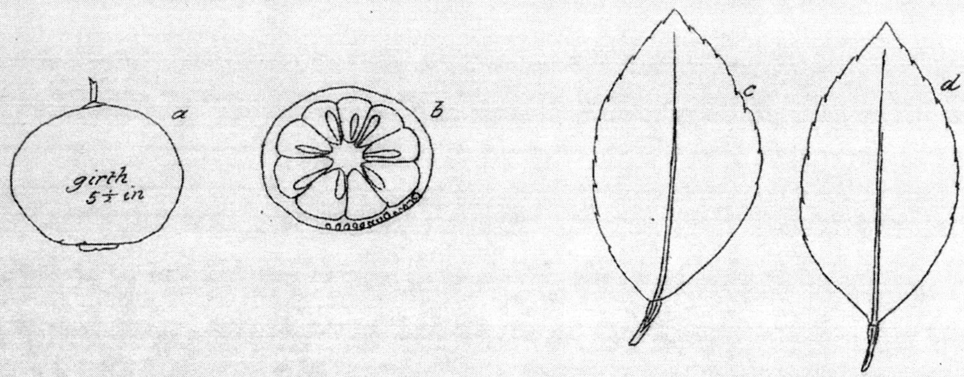

PLATE CXXXIX.

The *Chhàngurà* (literally, six fingers) or primitive (?) pulpless citron.

a gives an idea, as I think, of this most interesting and primitive attempt of nature at evolving a citrus fruit. The carpels, although distinct, are united at their base, and *free* at their extremities. This digitate citron consisted of *two whorls*, an outer one of 13 carpels, and an inner one of 7 or more carpels. In section, more than ten are visible.

b is a section across the solid part, and *c* across the part which is just above the union of the carpels. It should be observed that the inner whorl of rind carpels at A is that which at a later period, according to my view, developed into the citrus *pulp*; the oil-cells of the rind of the inner whorl becoming the *juice-vesicles* of the pulp. (*Vide* Chapter on "Morphology.") The hollow space at A was filled up with some withered carpels.

d, *e*, and *f* are the leaves of this citrus, and *g* its spine. The leaves have a lemon scent.

PLATE CXXXIX.

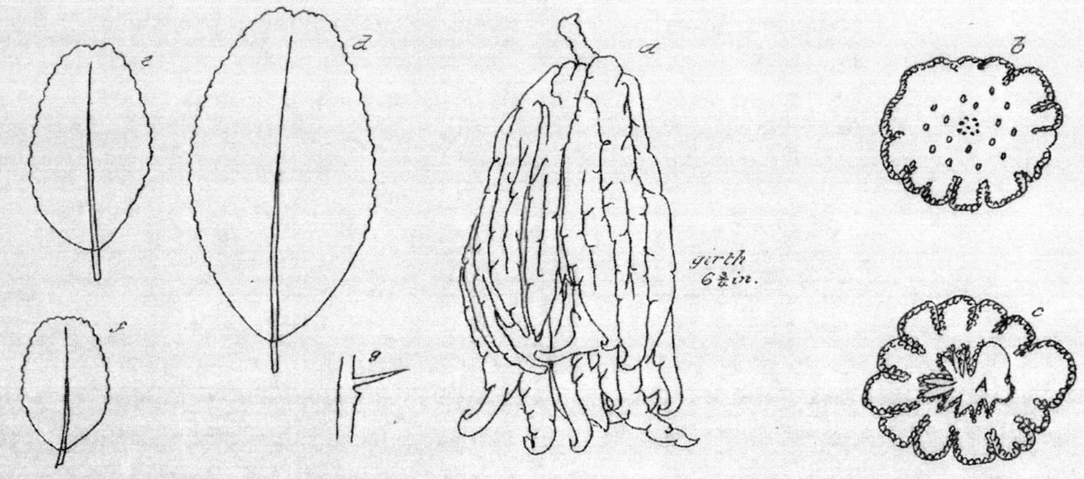

PLATE CXL.

Represents another *Chhdngurd*.

a had also two whorls; the inner consisted of 9 carpels, and the outer of 11 carpels. In the same way that a flower can become *double*, by an additional whorl of *petals*, so I think a fruit can double itself, by an additional whorl of *carpels*.

b is a section across the base. At A there appear to be oil-cells or rudimentary carpels.

c is a section close to the base of the fingers. At B there appears to be a ring of oil-cells, or a rudimentary inner rind.

d was an unripe, but still more interesting specimen of a *Chhàngurd*. It appears to indicate a later period than *a* in the morphological history of the citrus. Its digits are still *ununited*, but closed upon themselves, like the fingers of a closed fist, preparatory to complete union and formation of the modern closed rind of the fruit.

e is a longitudinal section of *d*, showing no indication of an inner whorl. This specimen appeared to be a *single* fruit.

PLATE CXL.

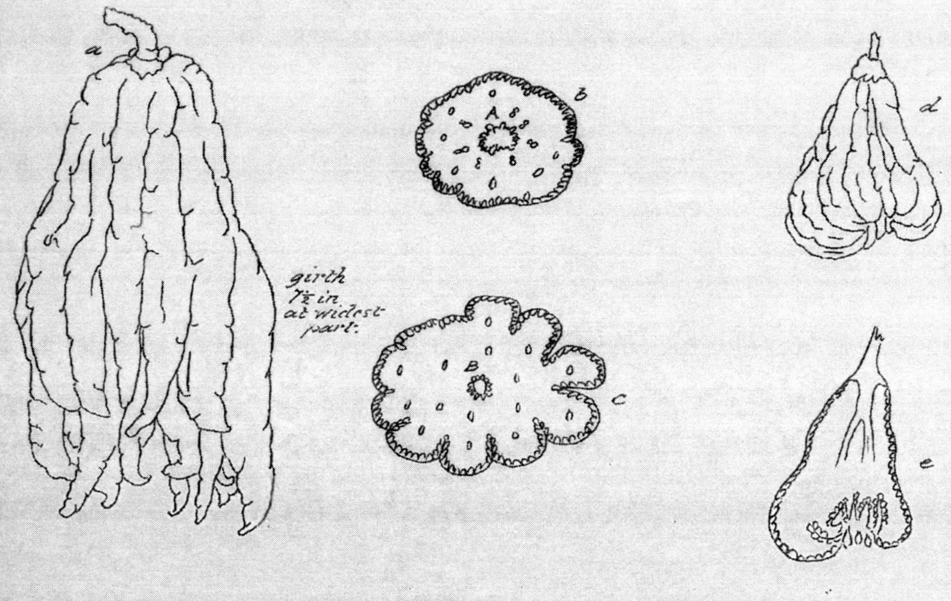

PLATE CXLI.

a and *b* are taken from the Flor. Amboyn. of Rumphius, vol. ii., tab. 25. *a* is the warty form, and *b* the smooth form and called by him Malum Citrium.

J. de Loureiro, in his Flor. Cochin Chin., p. 465, refers to this plate, under the head of Citrus Medica, and says that the petioles are linear, flowers *white* (no purple or pink colour mentioned), pulp white, often acid; skin thick, externally yellow, hard, and unequal. Eaten raw, and preserved; *cultivated* in Cochin China.

c is taken from Risso's monograph. It is a section of the fruit of his "Cedratier à gros fruit." It is only given to show the enormous thickness of its skin. The dots round the carpels are probably their feeding vessels.

PLATE CXLI.

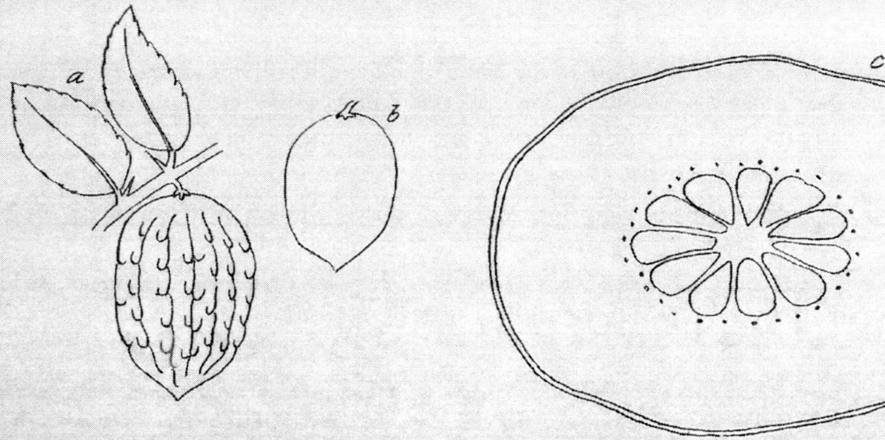

PLATE CXLII.

Is a *Turunj* from Mangalore. I was told that in Concani it is called *Mauling*, and in Tulu it is called *Ma'palá*.

a shows the very warty exterior of this citron proper. I was told that this was a small specimen, and that the first fruits are larger than those of the subsequent crop. Externally it was lemon yellow, with deep transverse furrows in the middle, and deep longitudinal furrows in the lower half; the warts prominent, especially in the middle part. The surface was dotted all over with oil-cells of various sizes; in some parts *concave*, in others *convex*.

b is a longitudinal section. The oil-cells were large and distinct; the pulp pale yellowish; juice not abundant, and pure acid. At A is shown a pretty example of the large, medium, and small juice-vesicles, corresponding, as I think, to similar sizes of the oil-cells of the rind and leaves of the citrus. (*Vide* Chap. on "Morphology.")

PLATE CXLII.

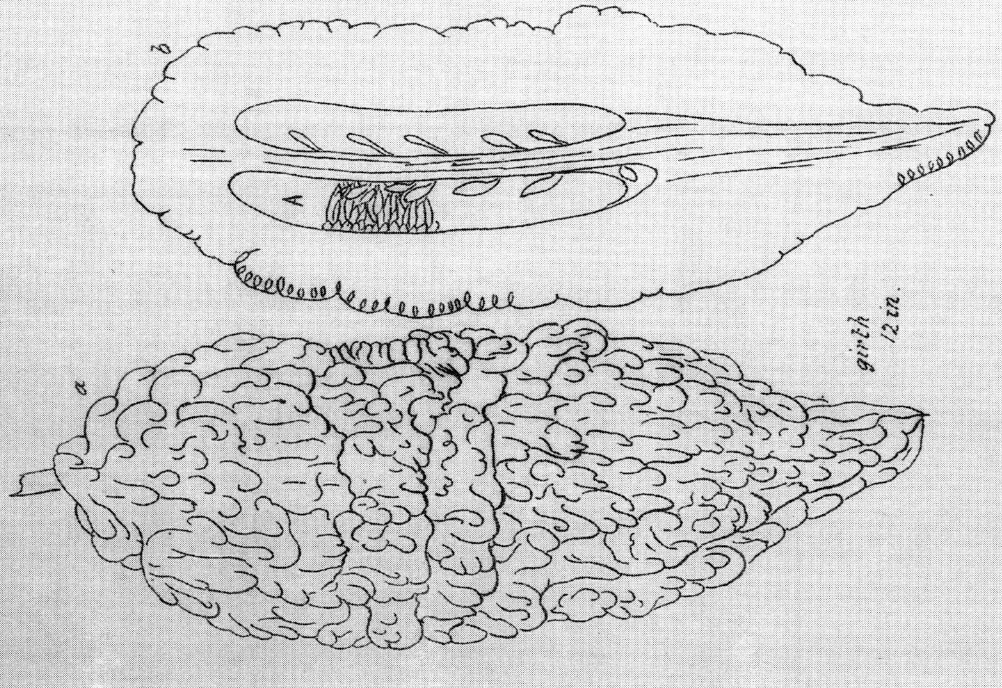

PLATE CXLIII.

A *Turunj* from Bassein, near Bombay, purchased at the Bombay market.

a gives an idea of this curious citron. Externally it was almost of a sulphur-yellow, dotted all over with oil-cells, as shown at A. This citron had a constriction all round its middle, as shown at B, with transverse lines and small warts; round the base the warts were comparatively smooth, but round the apex they were prominent and large. The rind was very aromatic.

b is a section across the most warty part, close to A, cutting across the ends of the pulp carpels.

c is a section across the constriction. The skin is solid white, and sweetish; pulp pale yellowish white, dry and sour, and many-seeded.

PLATE CXLIII.

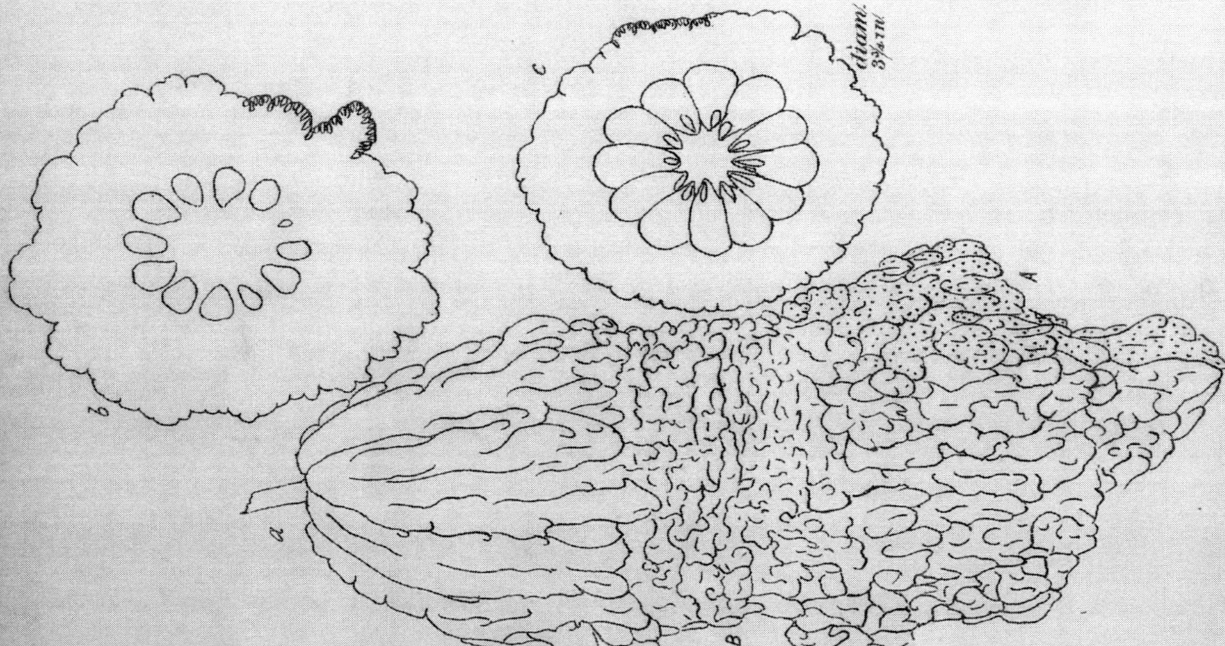

PLATE CXLIV.

A *Turunj* from Alibagh, near Bombay, purchased at the Bombay market.

a represents its external appearance. It was rather flattened as shown in section. Externally it is lemon-yellow, striated transversely, and studded with *concave* oil-cells, which in certain parts became *convex*. The oil-cells were not distinct to the unaided eye. The lower portion was rather warty, and the mammilla inverted.

b is the same in section. The oil-cells of the rind were distantly located; the rind aromatic; skin white and sweet; pulp pale yellowish; juice rather abundant, and pure acid.

PLATE CXLIV.

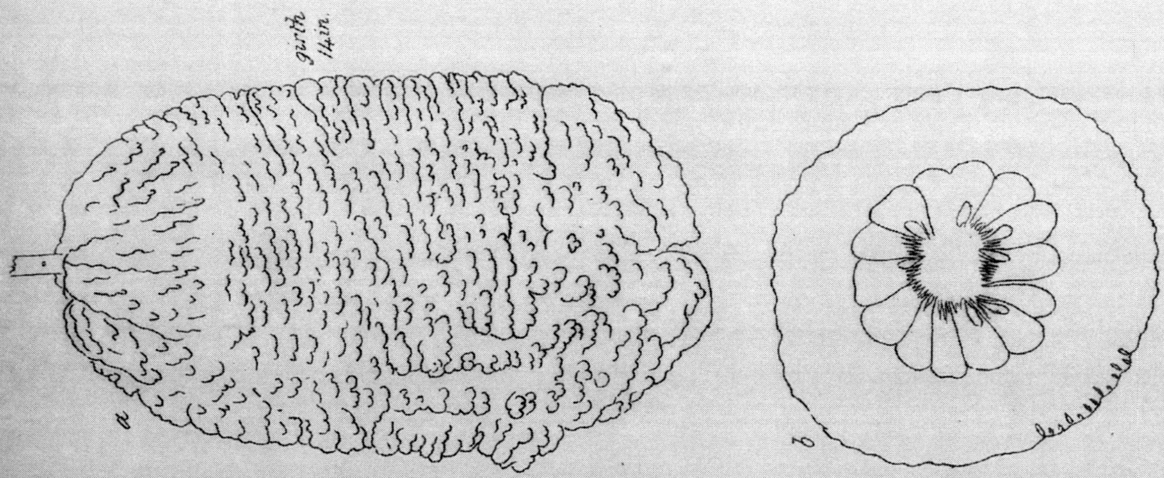

PLATE CXLV.

Shows another *Turunj* from Bassein, near Bombay.

a shows its form, with the repetition of the constriction and transverse striæ in its middle. The exterior was pale yellow, rough and sinuous, but not decidedly warty. The constriction was more pronounced on one side than on the other. It was deeply pitted all over with oil-cells.

b is its section across the constriction. Skin very thick and white; pulp white, dry, sour, and many-seeded. Rind aromatic.

I have not been able to account for the constriction, which occurs so often in these Bombay specimens, and which is connected with transverse striæ, nor is the cause of it in any way apparent in the sections.

PLATE CXLV

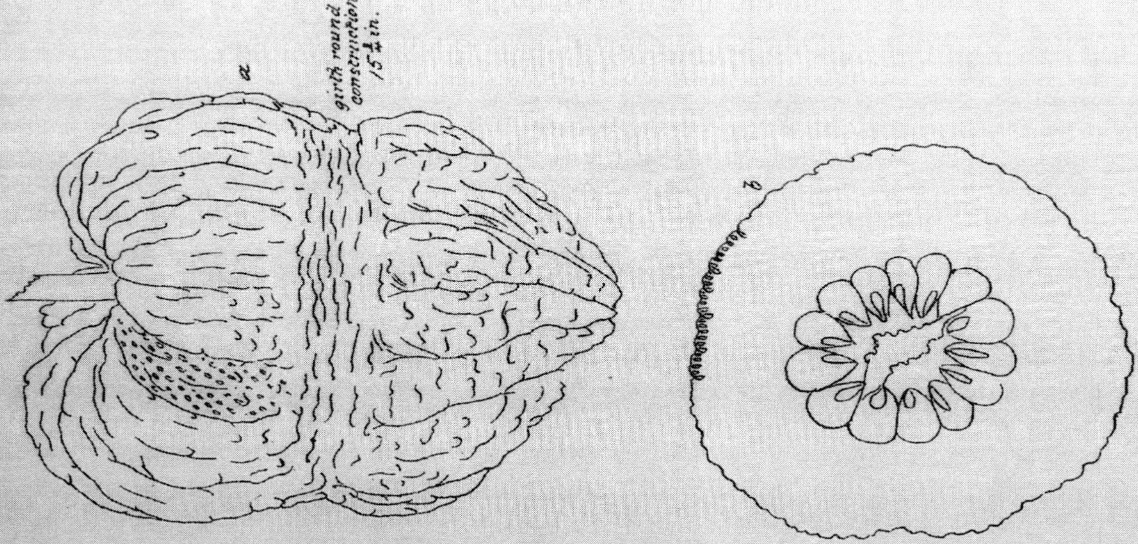

PLATE CXLVI.

A *Turunj* from the Saharunpore Botanic Garden.

a represents its form. On the bulged-out side B, the warts are larger, while on the rather contracted side A, the warts are small and placed among the transverse striæ, apparently the same striæ, for which I could not account, in the Bombay citrons, shown on the foregoing plates. In the section *b*, there does not appear much difference in the two sides. The oil-cells of the rind, on the contracted side, may be perhaps more closely packed than on the opposite side. The rind is aromatic, the skin white and *sweet*; pulp pale yellow, sour, and juice scanty; seeds white, when cut, edged with white and brown lines, from the brown pellicle under the outer shell.

c and *d* are spring leaves—not typical—that came with it, and *e* its spine. The leaves are serrated from the base, and the petiole is barely ridged. They have a faint lemon scent.

PLATE CXLVI.

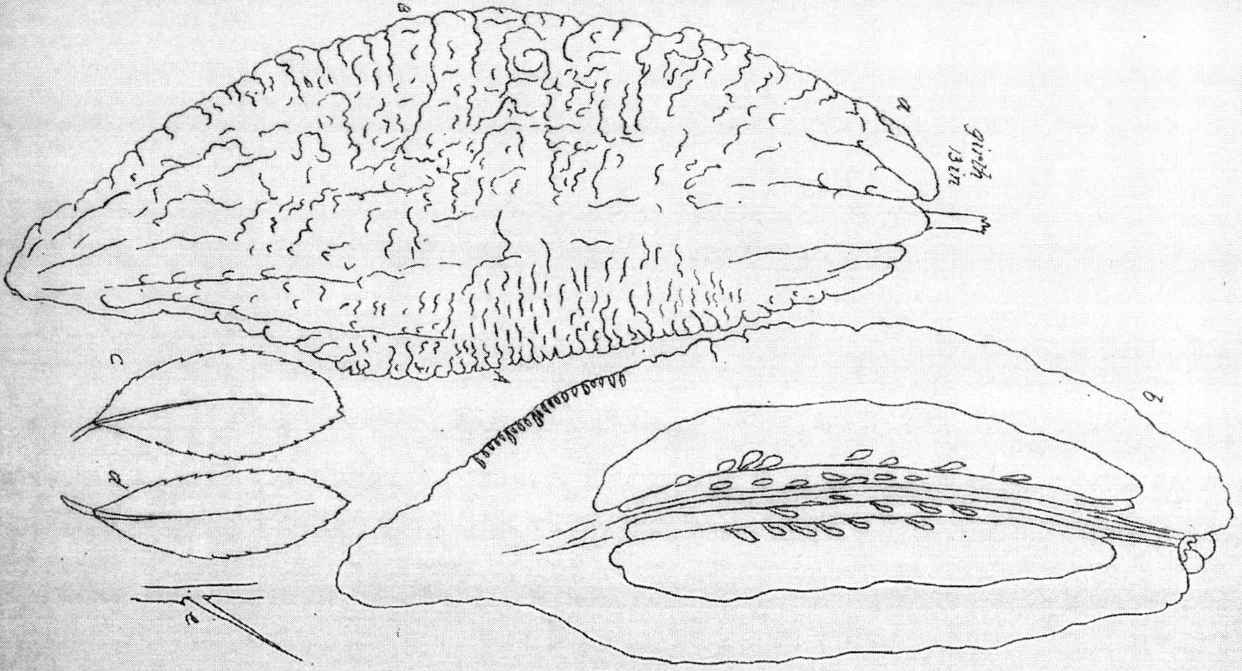

PLATE CXLVII.

Shows another *Turunj* from Alibagh, near Bombay, purchased at Bombay.

a shows its long and slender form. Its exterior was almost of a canary yellow, with shallow longitudinal furrows. The warts were small projections, mostly towards the apex. In this case also we find a belt of transverse striæ, as if there were a tendency to a constriction. This appears to be inherited, otherwise the same feature would hardly appear in so many. The surface is dotted with oil-cells, which, if anything, are slightly *convex*. This is against Risso's theory, as the pulp is *very sour*.

b is the section of the same. Skin white and sweetish; pulp yellowish white; juice not abundant, and very sour.

PLATE CXLVII.

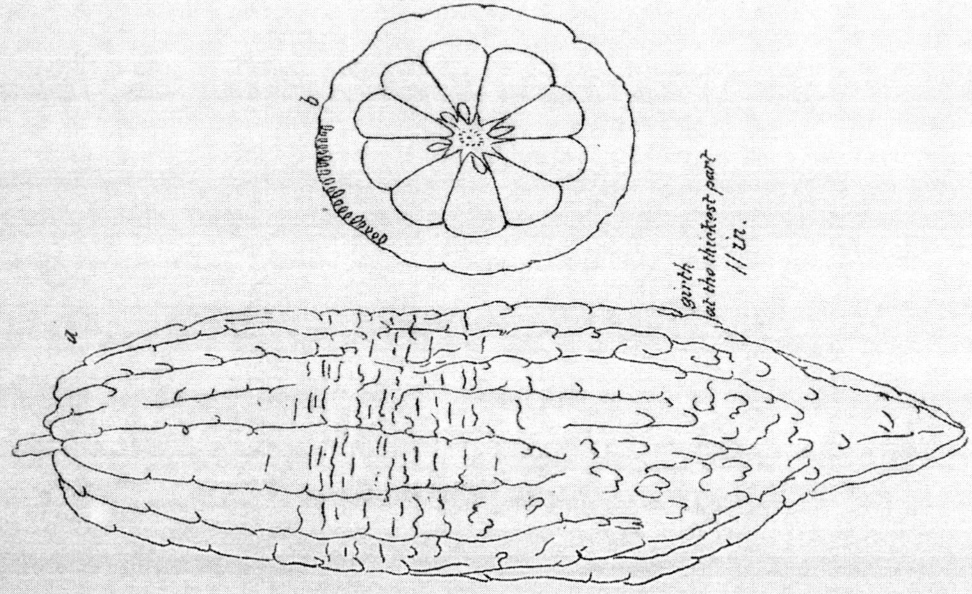

PLATE CXLVIII.

Turunj from Goa, said to grow also in Mysore, called there (at Goa) *Mauling*; purchased at Bombay.

a shows its smooth, melon-like form, with a lemon-yellow exterior, only slightly furrowed. The warts are hardly traceable. Mammilla not pronounced. It was dotted with large oil-cells, generally *plane* with the surface.

b is its section, with scattered oil-cells. The outer rind *was not at all bitter*; skin very thick and *sweet*; pulp white, dry, and sour. Natives eat its thick sweet skin, after removing its outer rind. This is probably a variety that has been selected for its thick sweet skin. In section, the oil-cells of the rind are not distinctly made out.

PLATE CXLVIII.

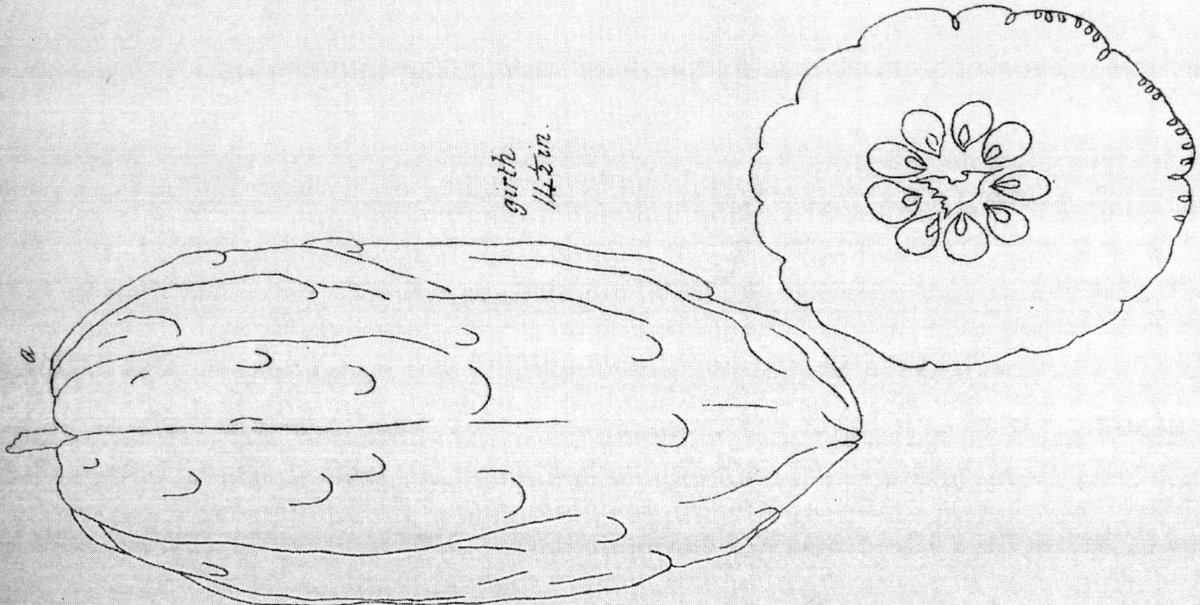

PLATE CXLIX.

A *Turunj* from Lucknow (ticketed sweet lime).

a shows its exterior conformation, scored with longitudinal furrows, the warts being represented only by undulations, of a deep yellow colour, and pitted all over with oil-glands.

b is its section. The oil-rind was aromatic, with large oil-cells; the skin sweetish, and the pulp dry, with an insipid *sweetish* taste. The pulp carpels were open towards the centre, which was hollow.

is a rain leaf, and *d* a spring leaf, both serrated.

Note.—On account of the sweetness of the pulp, this should, by rights, be called *Mudhkünkur*.

PLATE CXLIX.

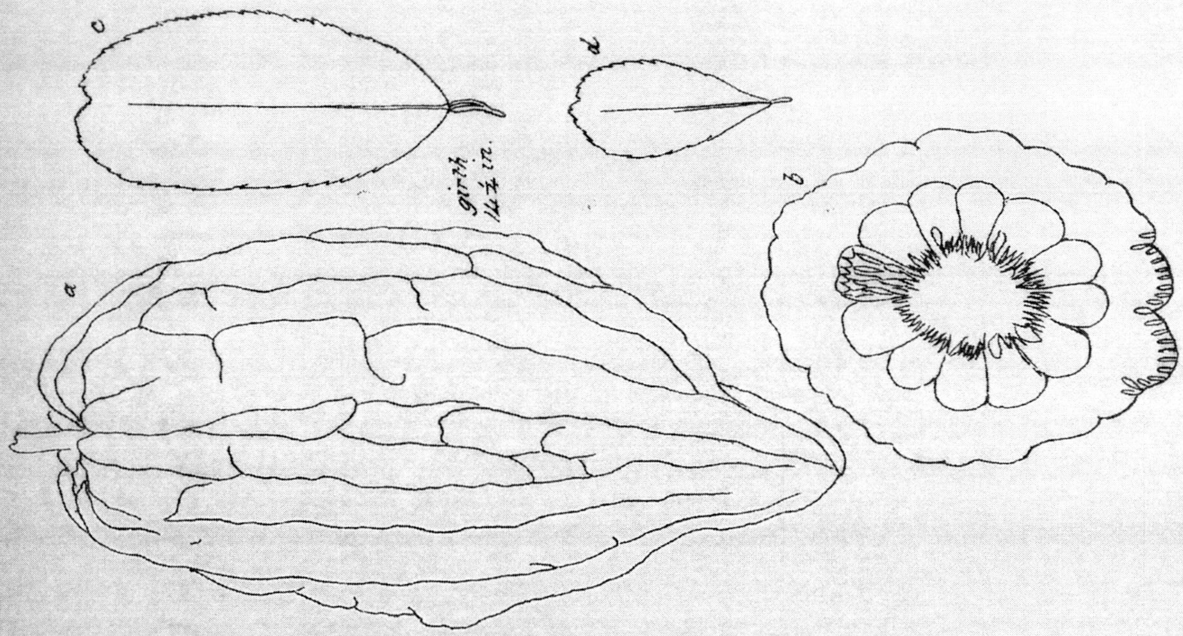

PLATE CL.

A *Turunj* from Khoorja, in the Bolundshuhr District.

a shows its size and appearance, with the curious transverse striæ in the middle. The warts were not prominent, and were covered with the little depressions of the oil-cells. I tried this citron in water, and it floated, in spite of its solid centre. The tranverse striæ are quite plain.

b is the section, with sour pulp, of the colour of a lemon; juice not abundant. The feeding vessels of the carpels were distinct. The skin was not very thick; and on the side A the oil-cells were of one size and closely packed, as if not sufficiently developed.

c and *d* are the only leaf and spine which came with it. They are not typical.

PLATE CL.

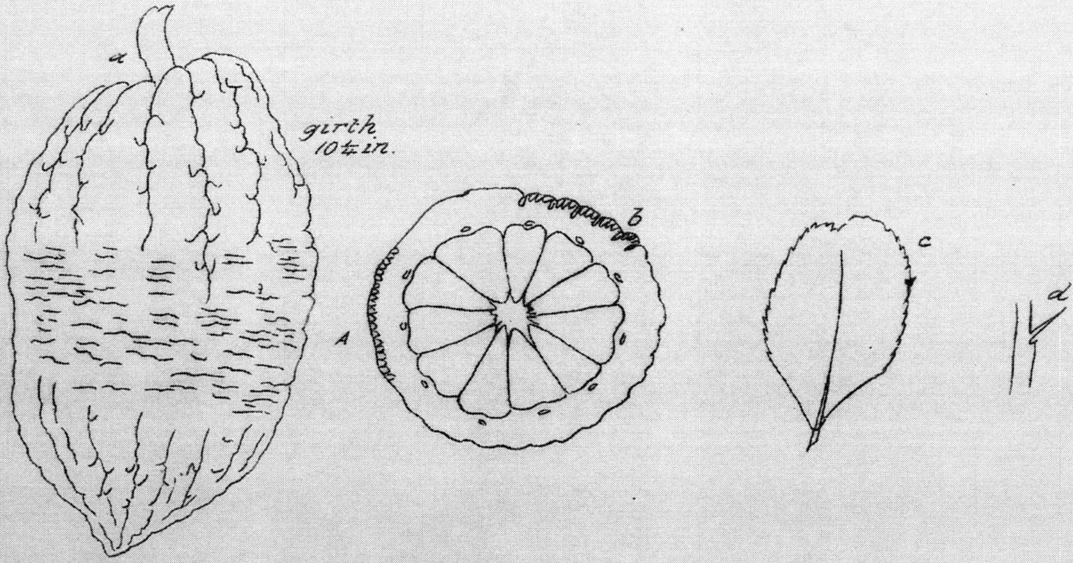

PLATE CLI.

Represents the citron of Kandy, Ceylon. Some call it *Siderun*, others *Nàtterun*.

a and *b* give an idea of its exterior. The small-sized one is not unlike the *Cedrato* of Italy. The exterior was lemon-yellow, slightly furrowed, and warty and pitted all over with shallow cavities.

c is a section of *b*, with sour and scanty juice; skin solid, and rind aromatic.

d was a leaf, without a jointed petiole, of which there were several, with the serrations commencing near the petiole.

e had a jointed petiole of the usual type. The young unexpanded leaf-buds of this citrus were decidedly *tomentose*, and the upper side of the petioles of the large leaves had also a few scattered hairs.

f represents its spine.

PLATE CLI.

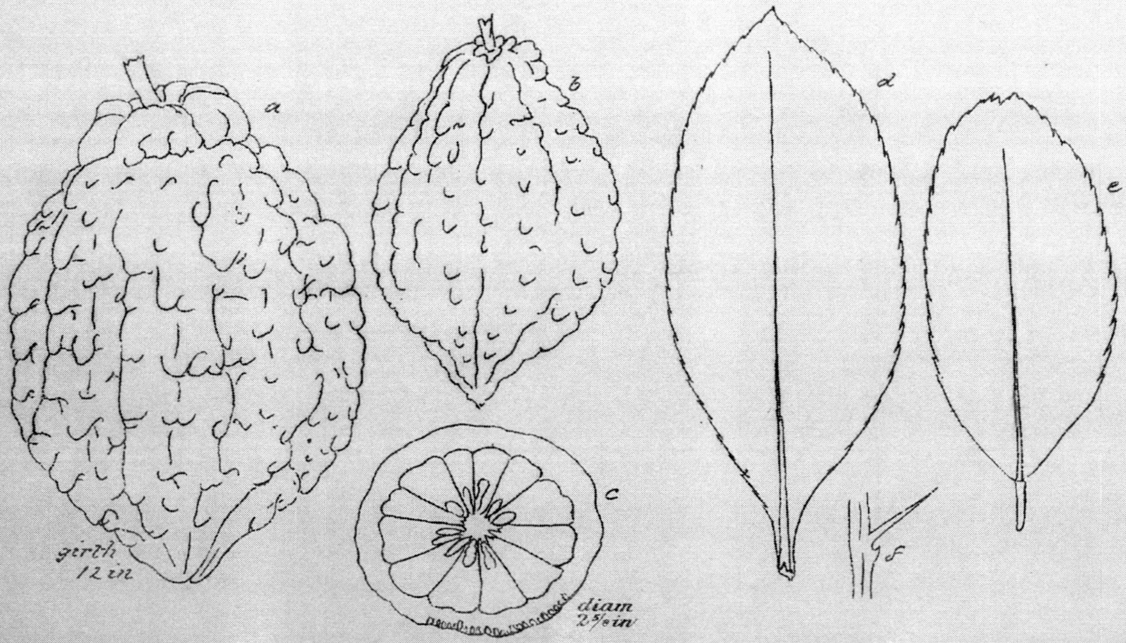

PLATE CLII.

Another *Turunj* from Lucknow.

a shows its exterior, with an undulating surface, and shallow furrows pitted with oil-glands.

b is its section, with a sweet skin, dry and sweetish pulp. The juice-vesicles were coarse, like those of the pummelo, and the pulp carpels were open towards the centre. The seeds were smooth like the *Amiltas* seeds (Cassia fistula); the centre hollow.

c represents the seed.

PLATE CLII.

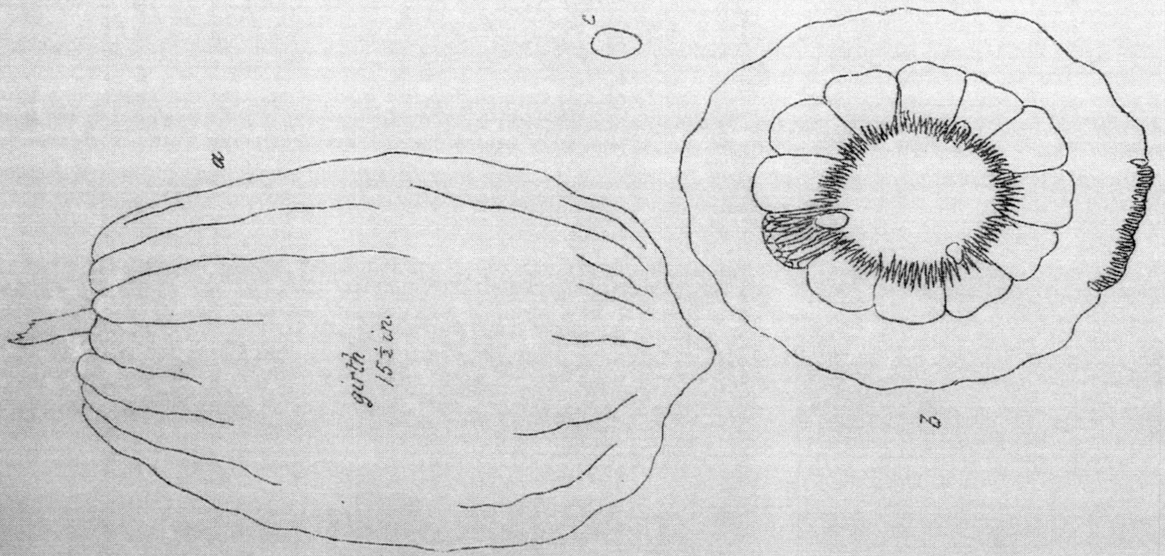

PLATE CLIII.

A *Turunj* from Rampur, Rohilcund.

a shows its exterior, with an occasional wart.

b is its section, with insipid pale pulp, inclining to sweetish.

c, *d*, and *e* are spring leaves, and the only ones which came with it.

I think all the citrons proper, with a sweet or acidless pulp, should be called *Mudhkùnkur*. (*See* Chap. on "Derivations of Vernacular Names.")

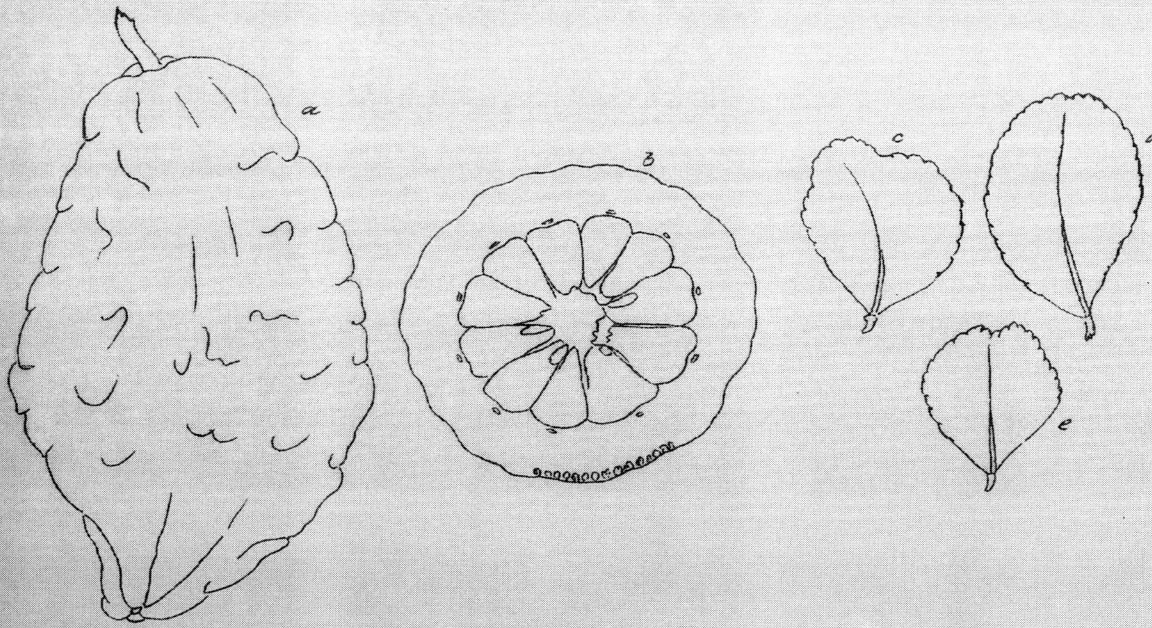
a
b
c
d
e

PLATE CLIV.

A smooth *Turunj* from Agassi, near Bassein, purchased at Bombay.

a shows its curious shape, like an inverted pear. The surface was uneven, as shown in section, gathered in folds at the base.

b is its section, through the thick part. The interior was perfectly white everywhere; skin solid; rind very aromatic; juice not abundant and very sour. The juice-vesicles were very slender, numerous, and closely packed. The majority were long and spindle-shaped; others were small, contorted, and compressed, as if there were too many for the space.

c shows the different forms of juice-vesicles I found in this citrus.

PLATE CLIV.

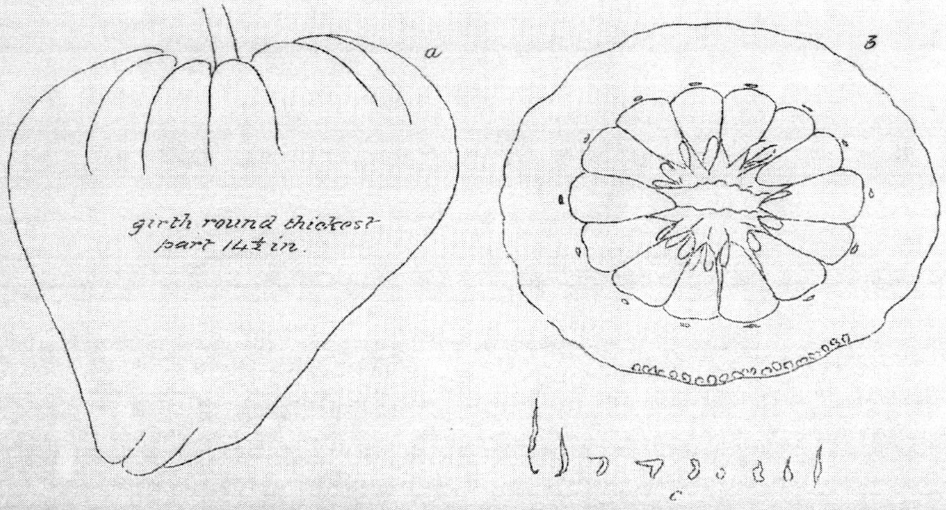

PLATE CLV.

Turunj from Rosa, Shahjahanpur.

a shows its shape and size. The exterior was slightly rough and sub-warty, especially towards the apex. This specimen was unripe, but turning pale-yellow in places.

b shows it in section. Pulp very pale, dry, and sweetish.

c, *d*, and *e* are the leaves that came with it, and *f* its spine. Many leaves of the citron proper are found, like *e* and *d*, without margins or wings to their petioles.

PLATE CLV.

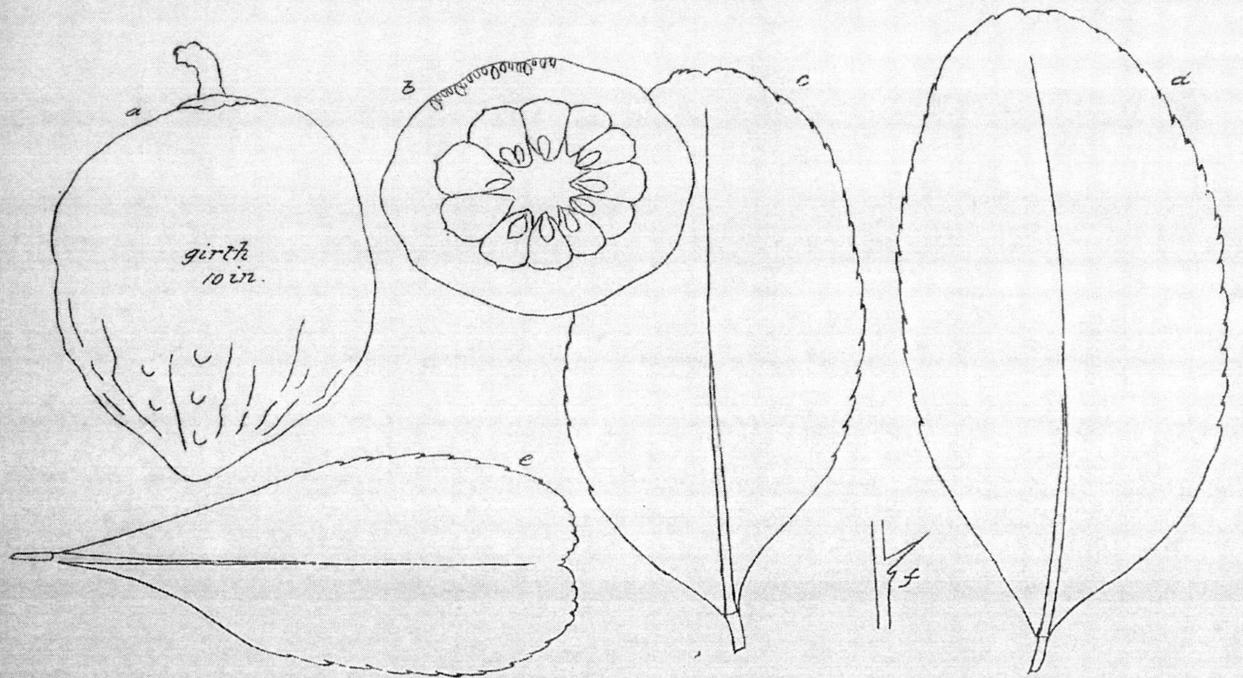

PLATE CLVI.

Mudhkùnkur from the garden of the Maharaja of Bulrampur, Muthoora, Gonda.

a and *b* had ridges converging to the apex. *a* was more warty than *b*, which was almost smooth and shiny. The rind was citron-scented, pale-lemon colour, with shallow foveoli all over.

c is the section of *a*. Pulp pale and sour, and therefore the name *Mudhkùnkur* is *inappropriate.*

d and *e* are spring leaves which came with it. They were slightly lemon-scented, and the joint of the petiole not distinguishable in most leaves.

Why this was called a *Mudhkùnkur*, and not a *Turunj*, or a *Bajoura*, I do not know.

PLATE CLVI.

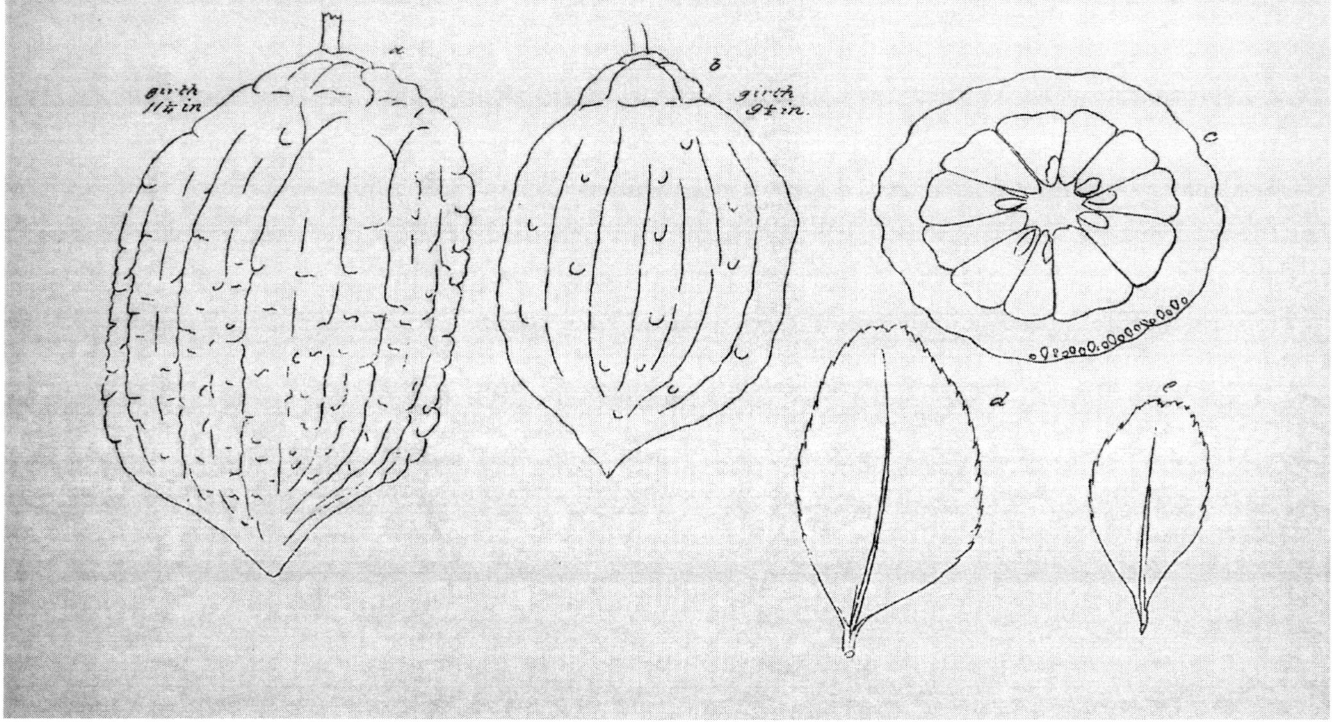

PLATE CLVII.

Mudhkùnkur from Lucknow. (In Almora this name is changed into *Mudkakrée.*)

a shows its form; exterior light yellow; surface deeply pitted with oil-glands; rough but not warty. Surface *dull*, not shiny.

b is its section. Pulp rather dry; juice scanty and sweet, more so than that of the sweet lemon; pulp-vesicles coarse. Skin white and sweet; oil-rind very aromatic, but oil-cells not very distinct.

c and *d* are rain and spring leaves. The junction of petiole and leaflet is not distinguishable.

PLATE CLVII.

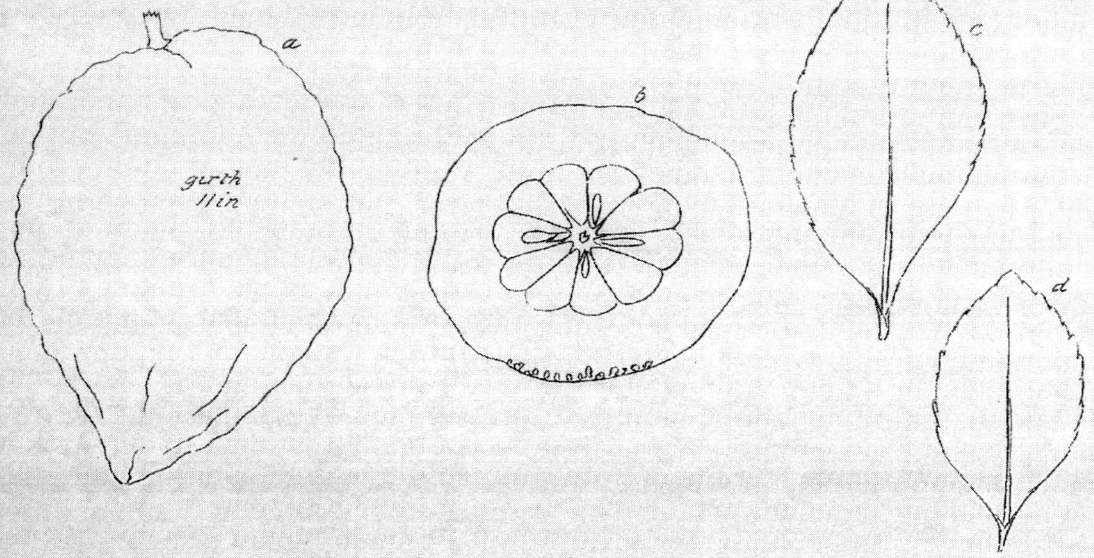

PLATE CLVIII.

The *Bhimra* of Nepal.

a is its shape, much like the *Cedrato* of Italy.

b is its section, with the pulp white, dry, and acid.

c and *d* are rain leaves, of a pale green, with lemon scent.

e and *f* spring leaves.

g its spines.

The flower-bud and calyx which came with it had a purplish tinge. The petioles of the leaves had also a purplish tinge, so probably the young shoots had also the same tinge. The fruit is said to grow to 7 inches long. A small specimen was probably sent from Katmandoo for convenience of carriage. For all the Nepal specimens I am indebted to the kindness of the resident at *Katmandoo*.

PLATE CLVIII.

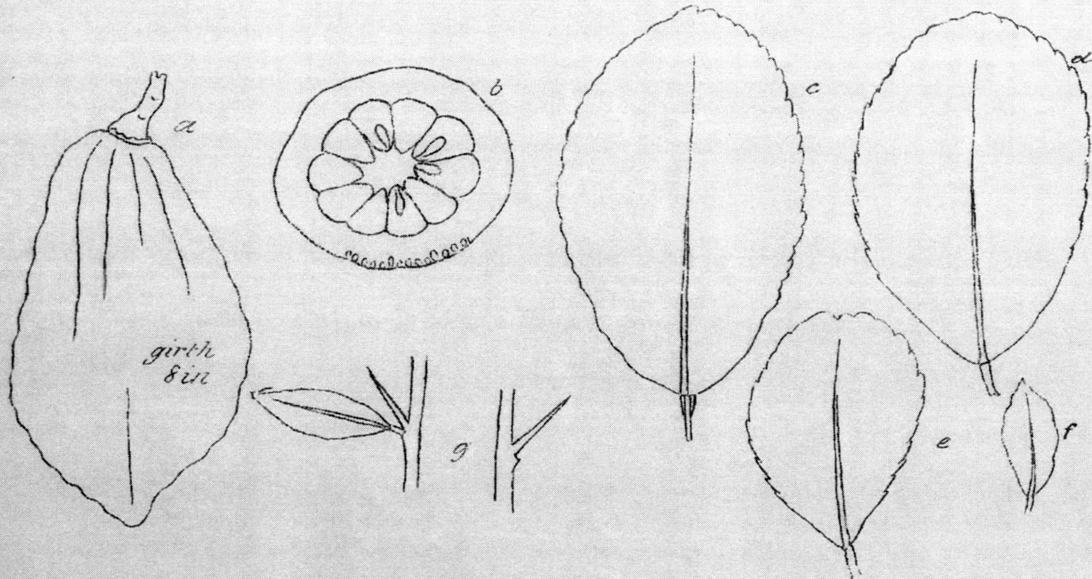

PLATE CLIX.

Bajoura from Mr. Kinloch's garden, Bholi, Etawah District.

a and *c* were of a pale lemon-yellow, rough and furrowed towards the mammilla.

b is a section of *a*. Pulp pale; juice rather abundant, and very sour.

The larger foveoli depressions are not distinct in these *Bajouras*. The oil-cells resemble those of the Malta lemon, and there are uniform slight depressions studded all over the surface.

d and *e* are rain leaves.

f, *g*, and *h* spring leaves.

PLATE CLIX.

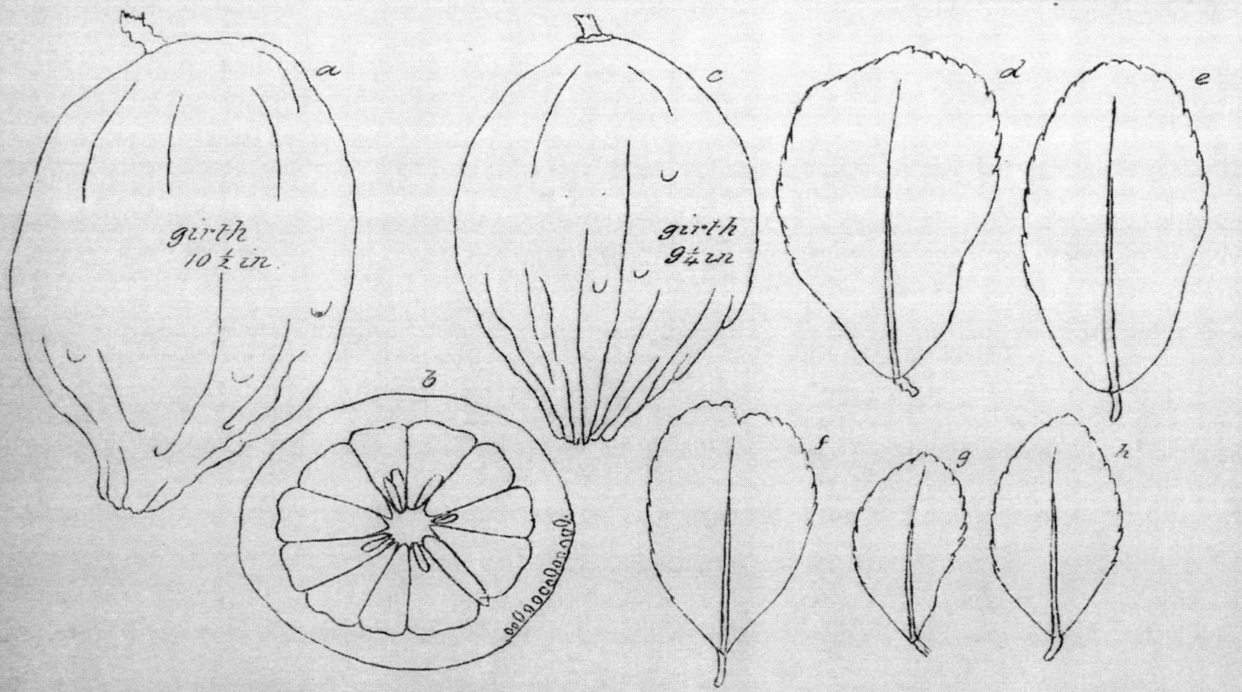

PLATE CLX.

Bajoura from the garden of Gundaroop Sing, Auraya, Etawah District.

a shows its form, with small isolated warts in its upper half. Exterior lemon-yellow, studded with closely-set oil-cells, as shown at A.

b is its section, with pulp like that of a lemon; juice abundant, and very sour.

This *Bajoura* comes near the *Limonier à grappe*, *L. Amalfi*, and *L. à deux mammelons* of Risso. At one time there were citrus collectors in Europe, as now there are orchid collectors in England, and it is not impossible that either Portuguese, Dutch, or other traders with the East introduced some of the Indian *Bajouras* and other citrons to Europe, if those in Risso were not all raised in Europe. The fruit of these citrons will keep a long time.

c is a rain leaf; *d* and *e* spring leaves. Some have the petiole slightly winged; others only margined.

is its spine.

PLATE CLX.

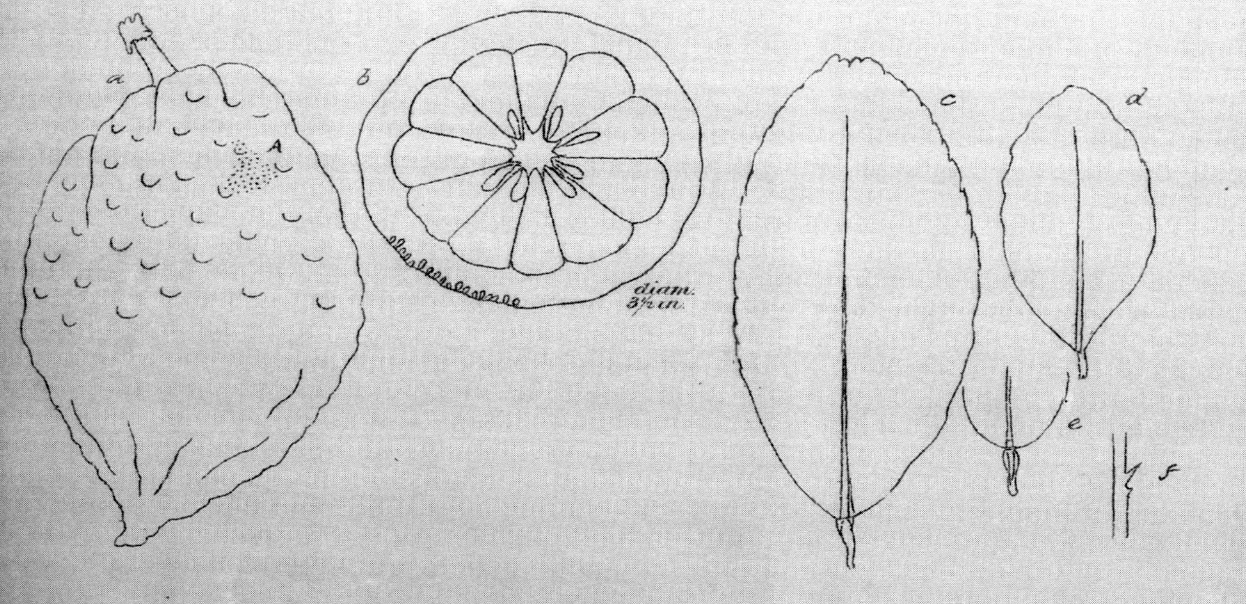

PLATE CLXI.

Bajoura from Mr. Kinloch's garden, Etawah.

a shows its furrowed character. Colour pale lemon-yellow; foveolate and polished. When unripe, it is of a pale green. It was not warty.

b is the section. The rind has a pungent lemon aroma. Skin white and solid, like that of a carrot, and sweetish; pulp pale, like a lemon; juice pure acid, not abundant; seeds white, when cut, edged brown.

c is a rain leaf; *d* and *e* spring leaves. They have more the character of lemon than citron leaves; large ones serrated, small ones crenated. Petioles short and yellow, rarely margined. Young unexpanded leaves have only scattered hairs on them. Young shoots and flower-buds purple.

PLATE CLXI.

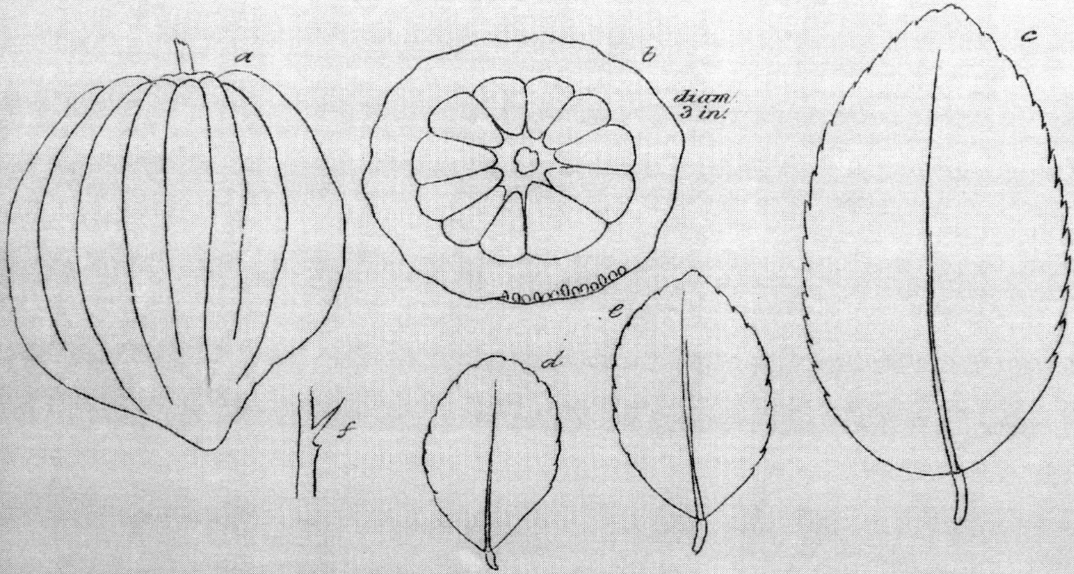

PLATE CLXII.

Bijòra from one of the gardens of the Maharajah of Bulrampur, Gonda.

a and *b* are their form, slightly furrowed longitudinally with shallow foveoli; colour lemon-yellow. They had no warts.

c is the section of *b*. Pulp pale, juice scanty and sour; skin solid; seeds white, brown edged.

d and *e* are the leaves that came with it; lemon-scented, with naked yellow petioles; flowers purple.

f is its spine.

PLATE CLXII.

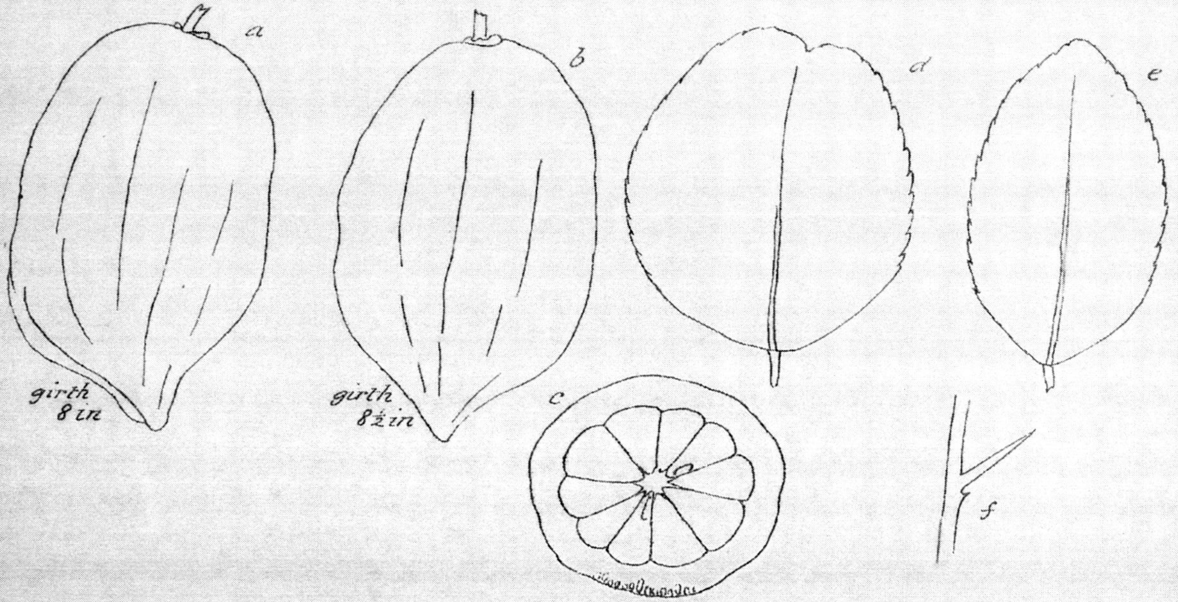

PLATE CLXIII.

Bajoura from Public Garden, Etawah.

a and *b* are one form. } Exterior slightly rough and pale yellow; pulp pale, like that of a
d and *c* are another. } lemon, and as sour; juice-vesicles coarse; white part of skin sweetish.

e and *f* are the leaves. The former shows also the spine.

PLATE CLXIII.

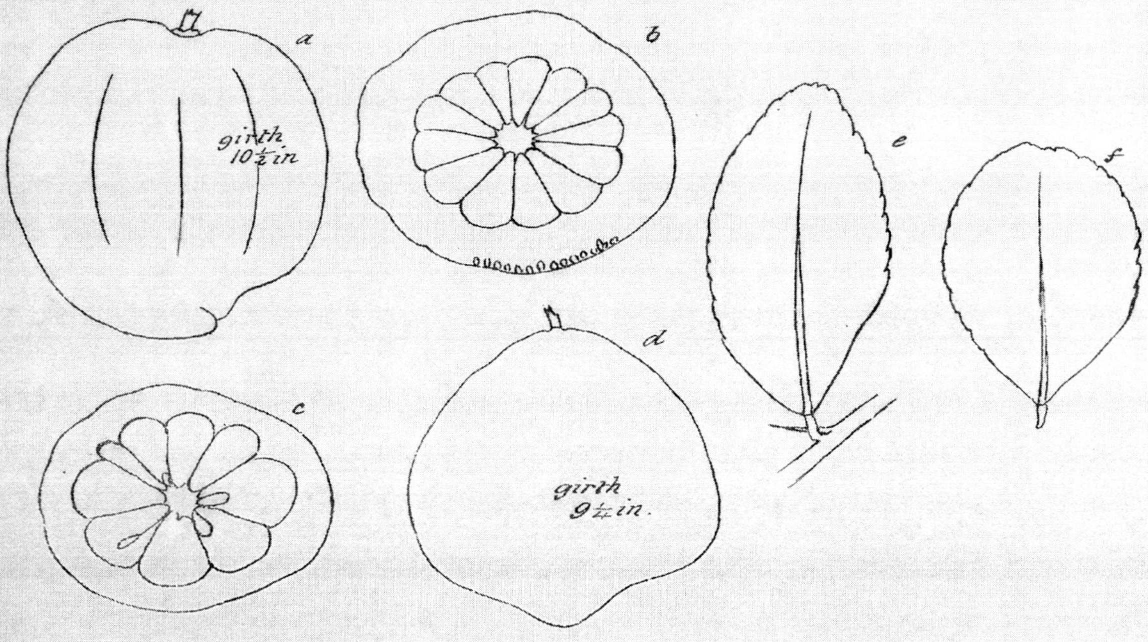

PLATE CLXIV.

This is the *Sunkhdaràz* of Nepal. Probably this word is a modification of the Sanscrit (?) *Shunkhdaràv*, or "shell splitter," owing to its extreme acidity.

a and *b* show its form and section. The pulp is very acid and many-seeded. The exterior is smooth.

c is a rain leaf, and *d* and *e* spring leaves.

f its spine.

Shunkhdaràv is the name of one of the Indian sour citrus. Its juice is said to melt shells, in the same way that the *Sui-gul* is said to melt needles.

PLATE CLXIV.

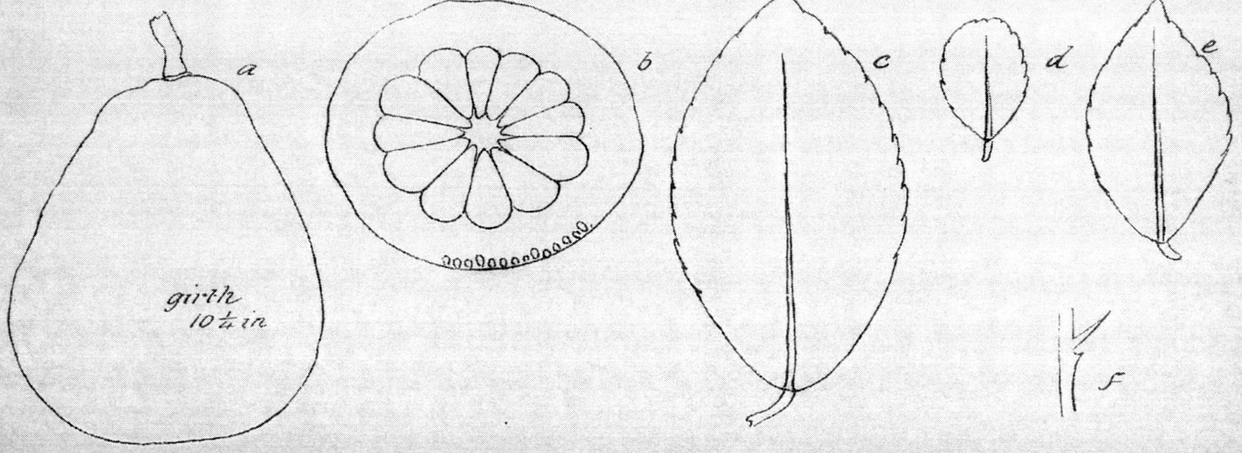

PLATE CLXV.

This is the *Nibooa* of Nepal. (This name is evidently a modification of *Nimboo.*)

a and *b* show its shape and section. I have little doubt that other forms might be found on the same tree. This often happens. The pulp is pale and acid. It was smooth.

c and *d* are rain and spring leaves, both slightly winged.

e its spine.

PLATE CLXV.

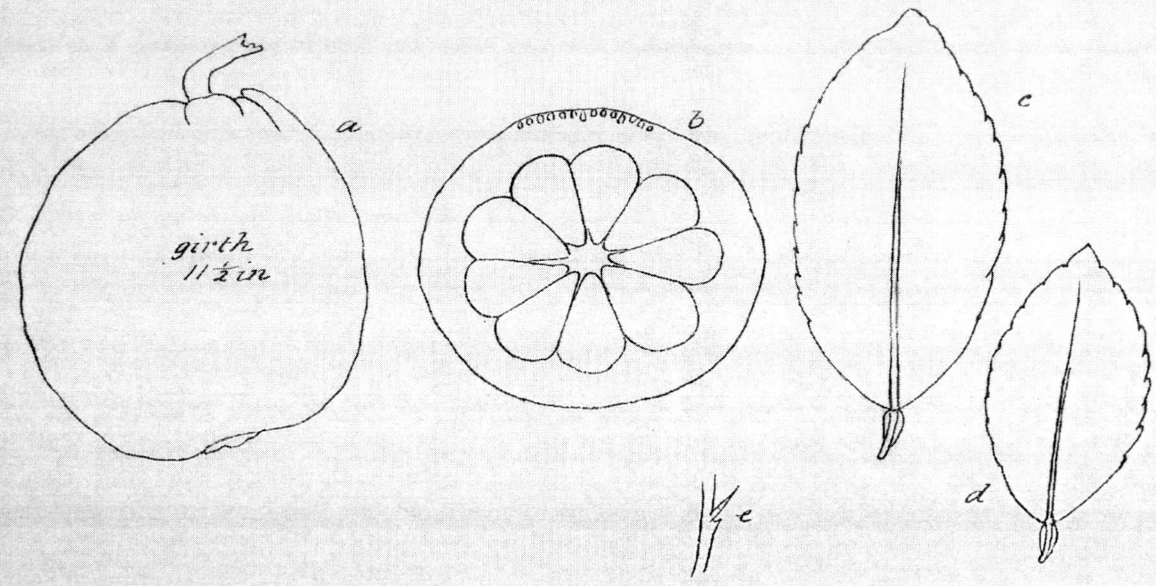

PLATE CLXVI.

The *Kalámba* of Calcutta.

a shows its curious peg-top shape. The extérior is of a shiny pale yellow, with distant foveoli and smooth interspaces, filled with smooth oil-cells.

b is its section. Pulp pale, and pure acid; white part of the skin solid and sweetish; many-seeded.

c and *d* are the serrated leaves that came with it, and *e* its spines.

I am informed that in Sanscrit they have the word *Kalamba*, which means the pumpkin used as a float for swimming purposes, and not improbably this *Kalamba*, which may be of a much larger size than that shown, is derived from that, being not unlike a pumpkin.

PLATE CLXVI.

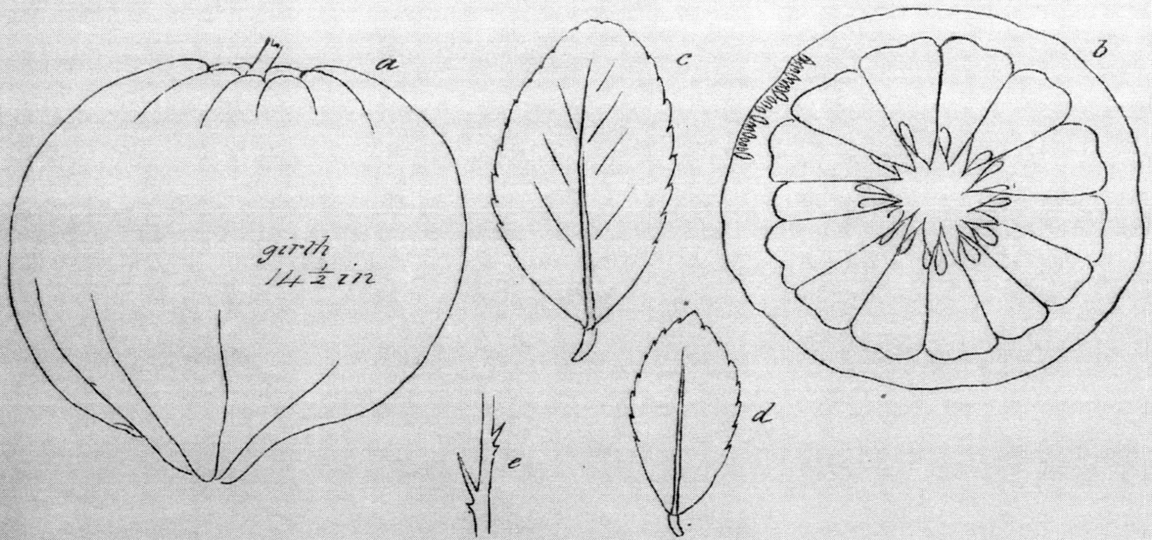

PLATE CLXVII.

Other forms of *Bajoura*.

a and *b* are a *Bajoura* which came from Benares. It looks like a large elongated lemon. The upper $\frac{3}{4}$ were smooth, and only warty round its mammilla. It was of a deep lemon-yellow, with pulp like a lemon, and sour (but not very much so). It had a rather thin skin, but considering the amount of pulp, the juice was rather scanty.

c and *d* are a *Bajoura* received from Allahabad. Externally pale yellow. The large and small oil-cells not distinct. It was studded all over with minute depressions. The pulp was pale; juice rather abundant and sour; many seeded.

PLATE CLXVII.

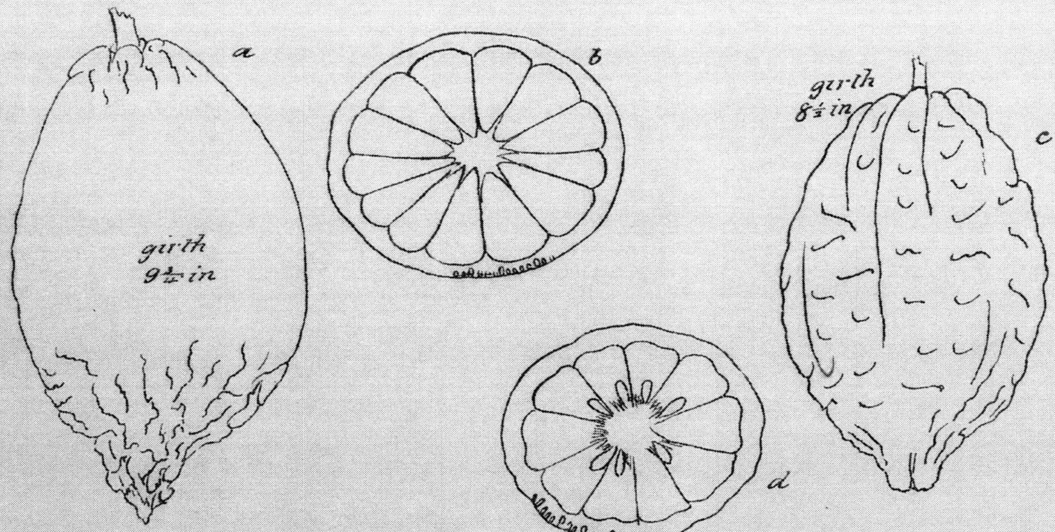

PLATE CLXVIII.

a and *b* are the *Kaldma* of Calcutta. This was an unripe fruit, sub-warty, with both deep and shallow foveoli, and undulations of the surface. The pulp was pale and pure acid.

c and *d* are the leaves that came with it.

The name *Kaláma* bears a family resemblance to *Kalâmba*, which see. (Pl. CLXVI.)

a´ and *b´* are an oblong lemon, which I found in the Benares Public Garden, said to have come from Calcutta. Colour lemon-yellow, pitted with large and small oil-cells, as shown at A ; pulp pale, juice abundant, and pure acid.

c´ is a rain leaf and *d´* a small spring leaf; the former quite lemon-like, only serrated like that of a citron, while that of a lemon is often crenated ; *e´* is its spine. The young leaves and flower-buds are of an *intense maroon purple*, deeper than any I have seen. The young leaves are amply covered with hairs, and the young calices have hairs also. Traces of ridges (abortive wings) on the petiole, only visible by a magnifying glass. The leaves had a faint lemon-scent.

PLATE CLXVIII.

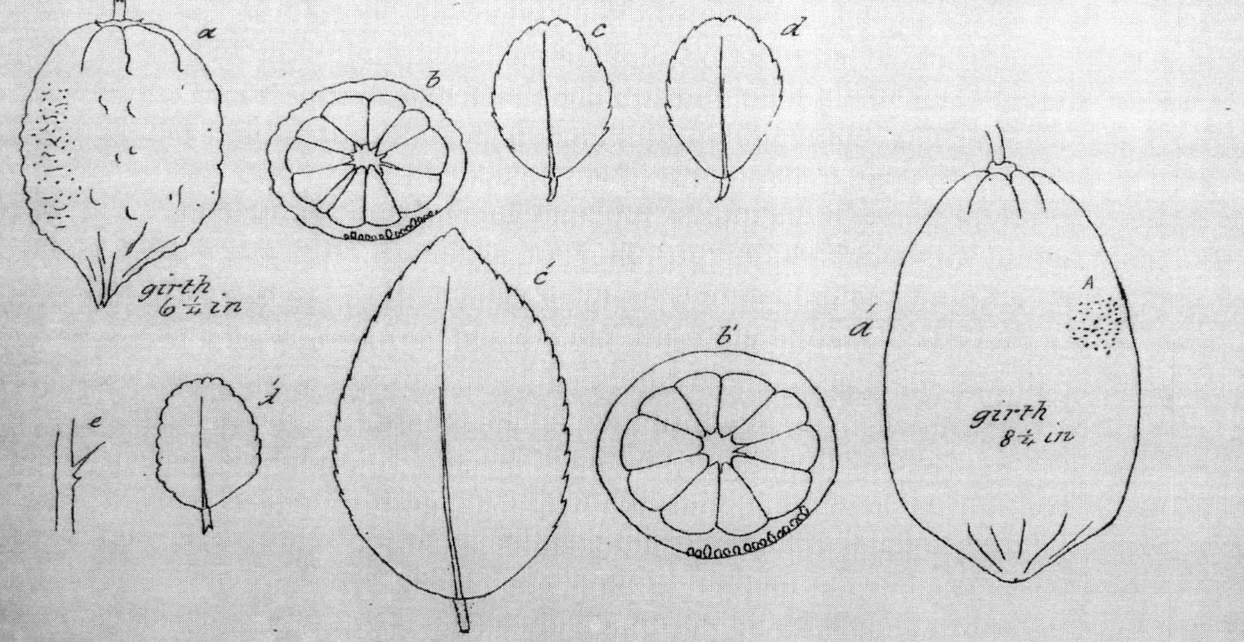

PLATE CLXIX.

Saròtee Nimboo from Gonda, Oudh (said to have come from the East).

a and *b* are the forms of this citrus. Exterior sub-warty, of a beautiful *pale* lemon colour; surface polished; foveoli not distinct; rugæ round the apex.

c is the section of *a*; pulp very pale and *Bajoura*-like; juice not very abundant, and pure acid; many-seeded; seeds white when cut.

d, *e*, and *f* are its leaves, of a pale green, like those of *Nepalee Nimboo*; petioles generally margined and lemon-yellow; scent faint and hardly that of lemon leaves.

g are its spines.

(*Vide* Chap. on Derivations of Vernacular Names.)

PLATE CLXIX.

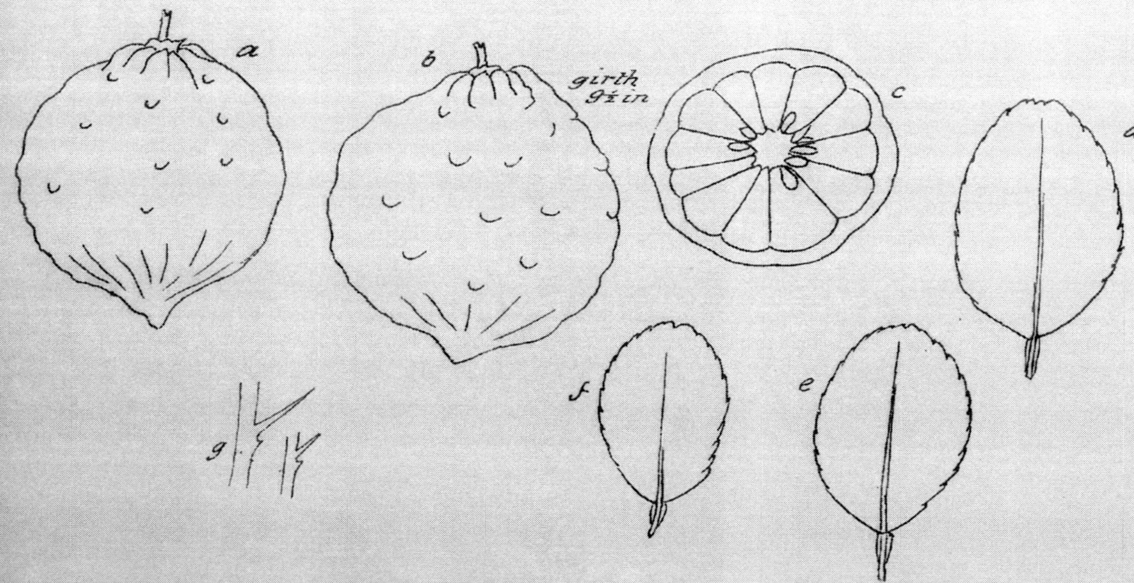

PLATE CLXX.

This is the *Bijouri*, received from the Saharumpur Botanic Garden.

a and *b* show its form. Colour lemon-yellow, foveolate all over, and rather rough round the apex, with a pronounced greenish-yellow mammilla. The scent and taste of the rind are different from those of the Malta lemon.

b is its section, with a rather thin skin; pulp pale greenish, unlike that of the Malta lemon. In this specimen I found no seed. Juice abundant and acid; it differs in taste from that of a Malta lemon.

c and *d* are spring leaves, serrated and rather curly; petiole just margined, and they have only a faint lemon scent.

Note.—This citrus and the foregoing one are so near to the lemons that they might have been as well placed in the lemon group. I have placed them at the end of the citron proper group, to show the gradations by which the citron may have passed into the modern lemon.

PLATE CLXX.

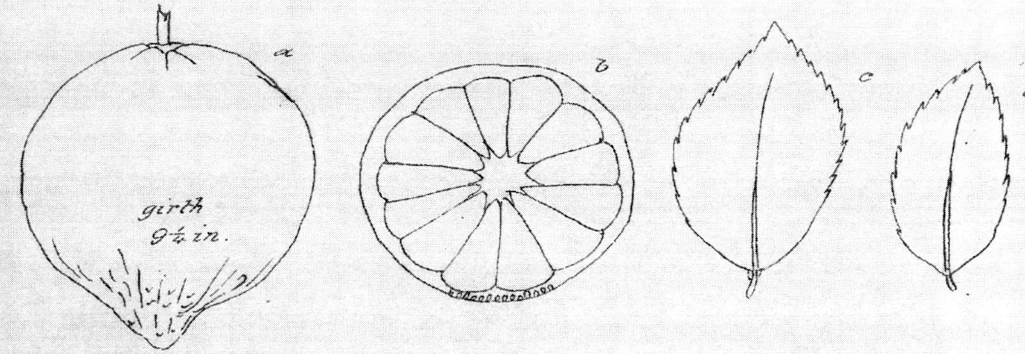

PLATE CLXXI.

This is the *Madhkakree* of Almora, sent by Mr. H. Harris.

It was almost smooth, the surface being *slightly* undulating, with slight eminences, as at A, and covered with oil-cells of various sizes, as at B. The rind was pale green, turning citrine, and very aromatic. It was like a melon, and having a sweet pulp; the name *Madhkakree* is not inappropriate.

NOTE.—Some of the skin of this made the best candied citron-peel I ever tried.

This and the following specimens were received after the citron-plates were arranged, so I placed these fine citrus at the end of their group.

PLATE CLXXI.

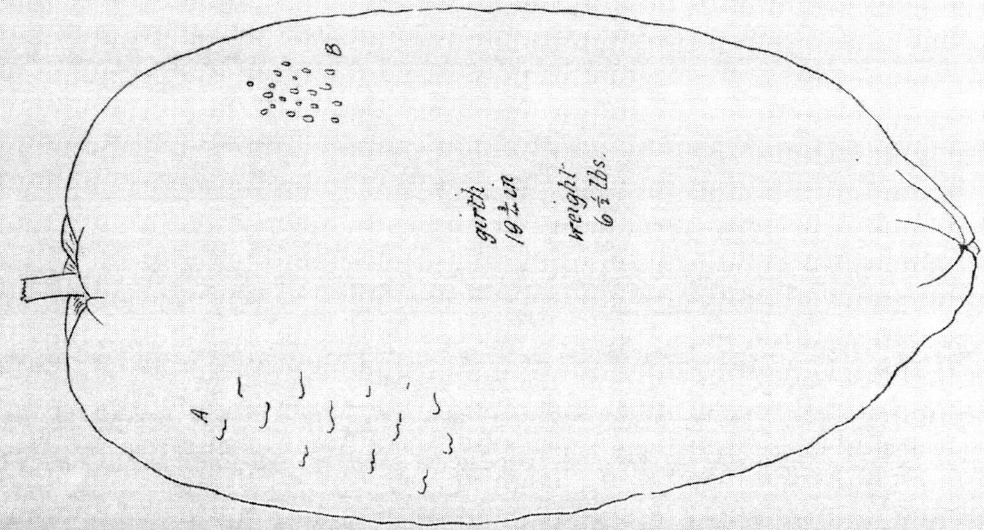

PLATE CLXXII.

a is a section of the *Madhkakree* shown on Plate CLXXI. The oil-cells of the rind are very indistinct in section, although quite otherwise on its exterior surface. The rind is aromatic, but not bitter. The white part of the thick skin is sweet, and resembles the flesh of the *Pètha* (Benincasa cerifera). The juice-vesicles are perfectly white, dry, and sweetish. They are attached only to the circumference part of the carpel. Some are pedicelled, others sessile; some short and stumpy, others long; but the majority are of a uniform length, as shown in *b*. They do not, however, fill the carpel to its central edge.

c shows a cross view of a carpel with the juice-vesicles seen in section, and a seed at the apex.

d is the natural size of the seed. This citrus is full of seeds; in *half* a carpel there were *nine*, arranged on each side alternately like peas in a pod, along the line of union, which is a furrow. The seeds are flat and white, when cut.

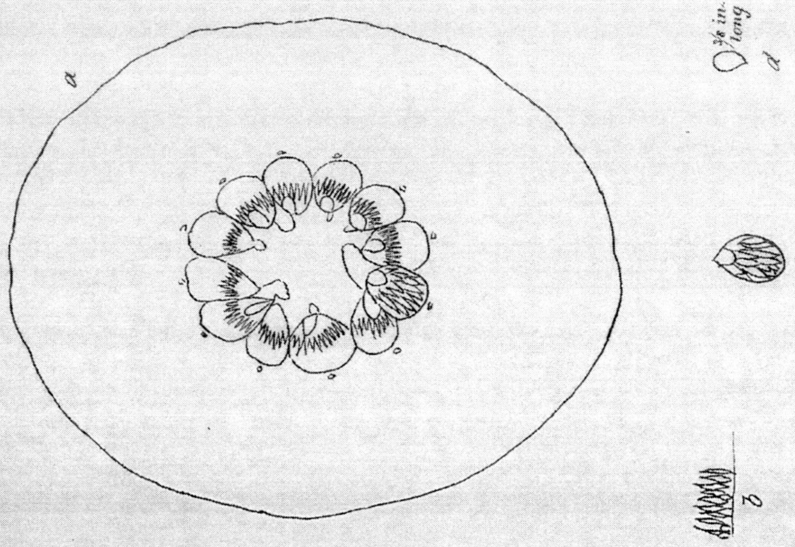
a
b
c
3/8 in. long
d

PLATE CLXXIII.

This is another specimen of the *Madhkakree* of Almora, also sent by Mr. H. Harris. Whether it grew on the same tree as the smooth one, shown on Plate CLXXI., or not, I do not know; but, judging from the oil-cells, it is probably another variety.

Externally it was pale citron-yellow, very fragrant, and covered *all over* with *convex* oil-cells, like miliary projections, as at *b*. They were more closely packed round the apex. They appeared of uniform size. This specimen alone would suffice to disprove Risso's theory that a sweetish or "fâde" pulp carries with it plane oil-cells. Under a magnifying-glass these cells resolved themselves into large, smaller, and smallest, the latter not being numerous.

A, A are deep furrows, the rest are shallow and broad. The rind appeared made up of eight carpels, the space between the deep furrows A, A consisting probably of three distinct carpels.

girth 17 inches
in thickest part
weight 4 lbs.
A
A
A
A
b

PLATE CLXXIV.

a is the section of the *Madhkakree* shown on the foregoing Plate CLXXIII. The rind is aromatic and not bitter; the pulp is white, dry, and sweetish; the seeds are white, when cut. The thick skin is also sweetish. In section the larger oil-cells are distinct, but not the small ones. The arrows indicate deep furrows, of which the three A, A, A are deeper than the others. They appear to be the joinings of the carpels, while the indentations shown by the crosses appear to correspond to the *midribs* of the carpels. In that case the rind whorl would consist of about nine carpels; while the pulp consists of eleven, or probably twelve, as *a′* appears to be a fusion of *two* carpels, as it has two nourishing vessels or midribs. It is evident that twelve pulp carpels and nine rind carpels can neither be *opposite* nor *alternate*, but sometimes the one and sometimes the other.

b is the base or peduncle end, showing more distinctly the joinings of the carpels. Probably *b′ b′* is the fusion of two carpels. In that case the rind would consist of about nine carpels. *c* shows the division of the apex in eight or nine distinct carpels. In the *body* of the citron the carpels are more or less fused, and their number is counted with less certainty. These points are noted in connection with Phyllotaxis, mentioned in the Chapter on "Morphology."

PLATE CLXXIV

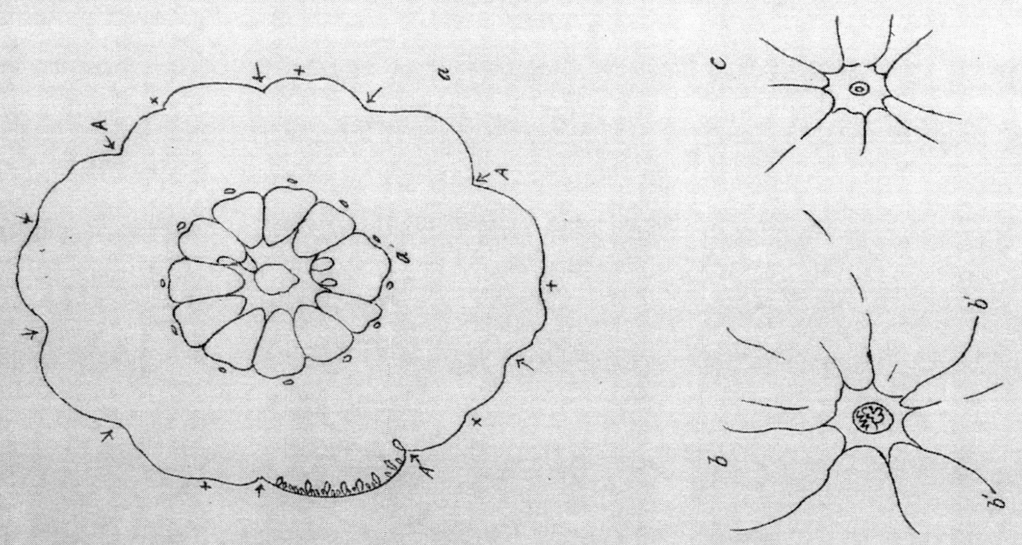

PLATE CLXXV.

a and *b* are the rain leaves of the *Madhkakree* of Almora.

c is a spring leaf.

d is the spine that came with its branch.

PLATE CLXXV

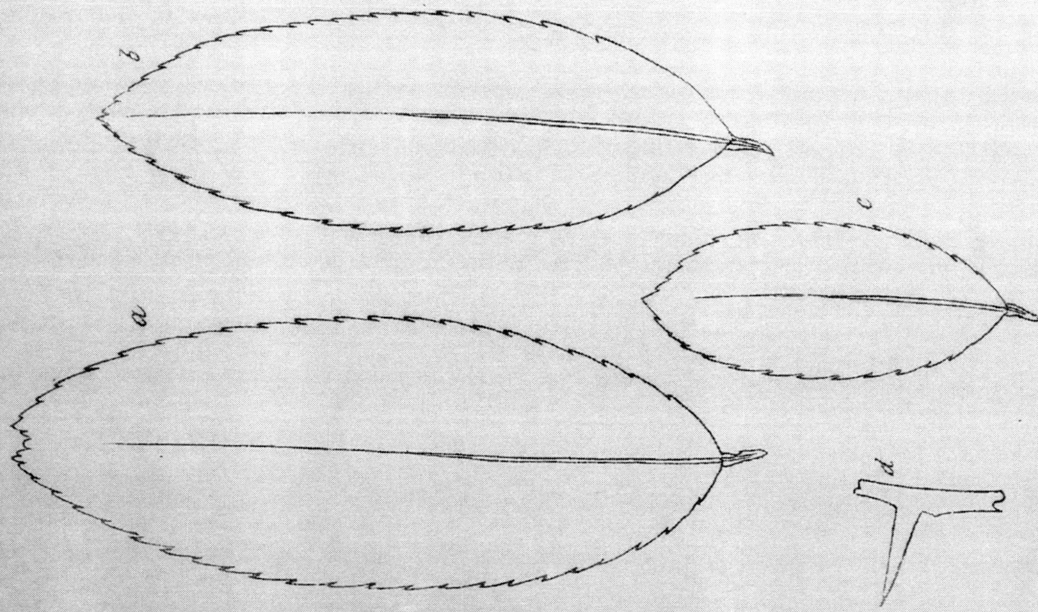

PLATE CLXXVI.

This is a *Bajoura* from the garden of the Maharaja of Ulwar. It is warty on the side *a*, and smoother on the opposite side. It is more like a "Turunj" than a "Bajoura."

b is one of its leaves. The upper surface of all the leaves is channelled, in correspondence with the nerves, but the general outline differs as in the following plate.

PLATE CLXXVI.

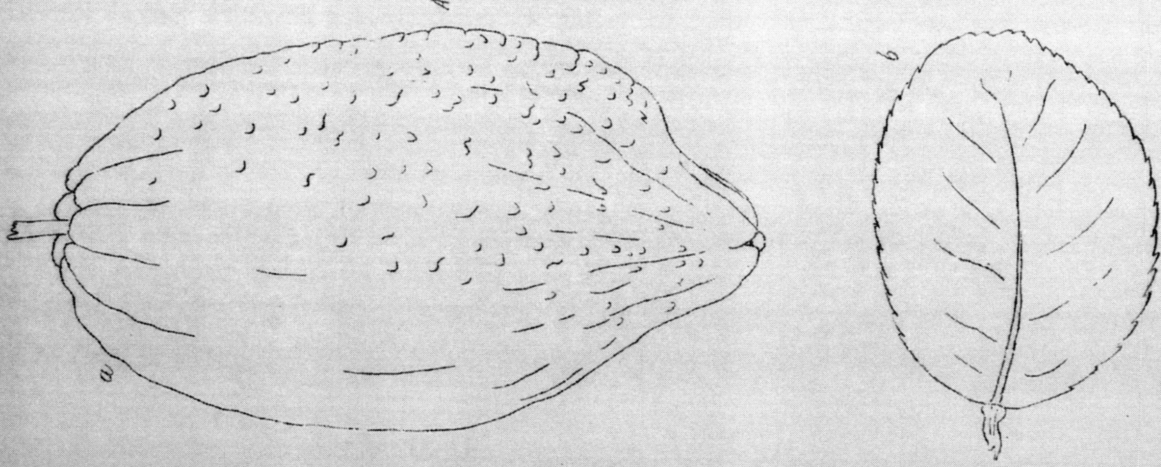

PLATE CLXXVII.

a is the section of the foregoing citrus, Plate CLXXVI. The joinings of the carpels of the rind are obliterated, excepting at the base and apex, and therefore it is impossible to make out whether they are opposite to or alternate with those of the pulp. (*Vide* reference to Phyllotaxis in Chapter on "Morphology.") In some leaves of this citron, such as *b*, there is no sign of division between the petiole margin and the edges of the blade, and no sign of a joint, while in others, as in *c*, the separation between the two is imperfect.

d is its spine.

PLATE CLXXVII.

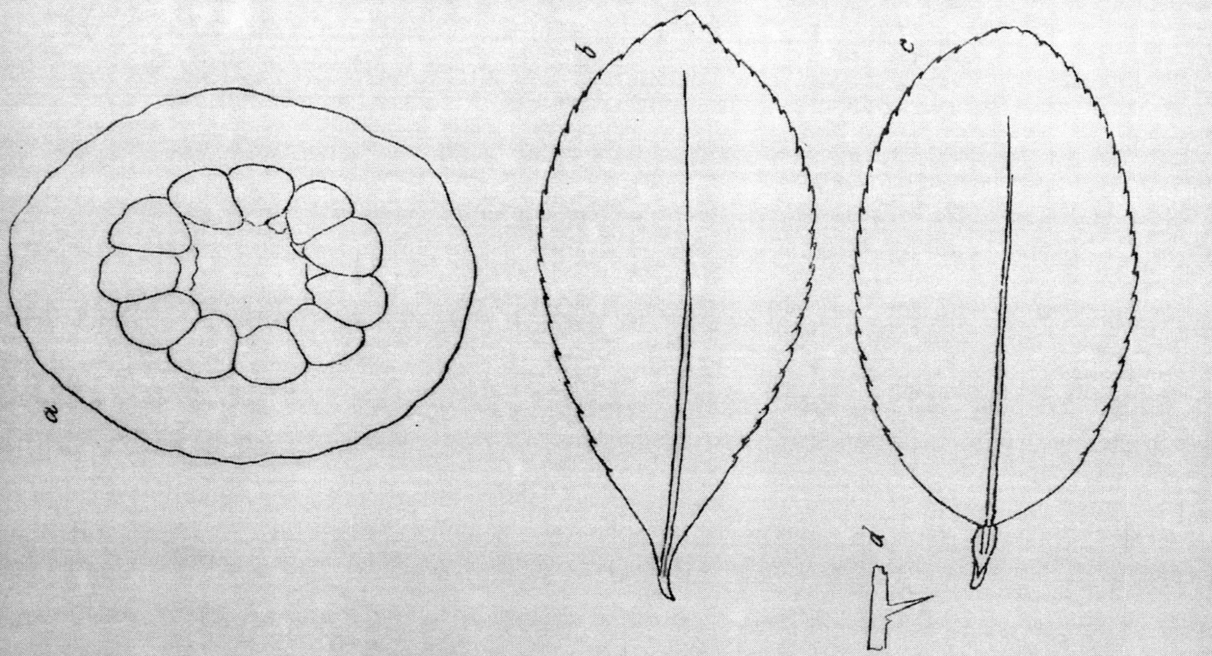

PLATE CLXXVIII.

a is the "Limonier à fruit digité" of Risso. Many years ago I remember seeing one like it in India. It has no pulp, and is composed of a single or outer whorl of carpels, with their ends free at the apex.

b is the "Limo tuberosus Martinicus" of Rumphius, taken from his Flor. Amboyn, vol. ii., tab. 26, fig. 2. He says it is allied to Limo ventricosus, *but has very different leaves* from the latter. Its leaves are distinctly those of the lemon; I consider it a warty lemon, or citron, of a globose form. I have given the same figure in Plate CXXIX., so that it may also be readily compared with the *Jambiri* forms.

c and *d* are the fruit of the "Limonier ordinaire" of Risso—the Citrus limonum vulgaris of the same author. It is the same as the Malta lemon. It has a very slightly rough surface.

e is its leaf, taken from Risso.

f and *g* are also taken from Risso's monograph. It is the "Limonier à fruit rond." It is not unlike some specimens of the Indian *Kaghzi Kalàn*.

PLATE CLXXVIII.

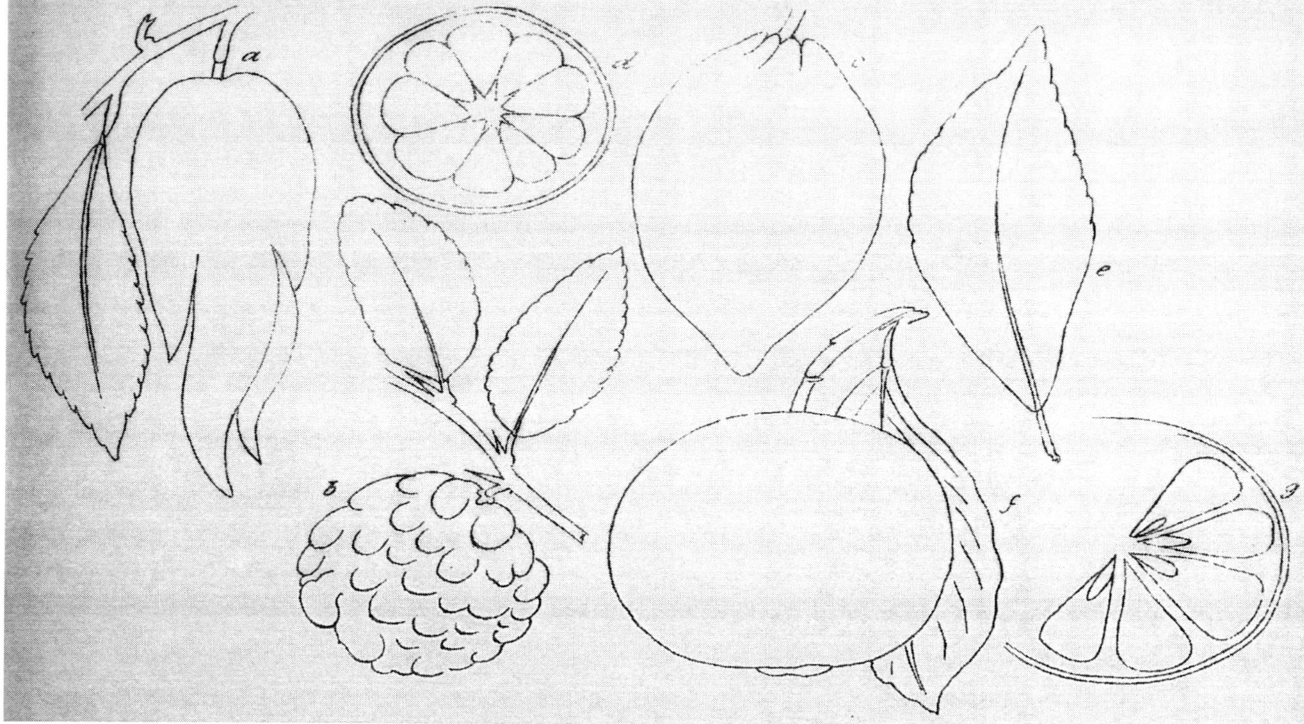

PLATE CLXXIX.

Various specimens of the Malta lemon from the Jail Garden, Etawah.

a is typical of the spring crop, which ripens in November and December. Skin slightly rough, with depressions of oil-glands.

b is an exceptional form; so is *c*. They are *Dumrèz*, or rain-crop fruit, which ripen in the ensuing hot weather. *d* is the section of *c*. These two were plucked in the rains. They were smooth and very juicy.

e, *f*, and *g*, *h* were plucked from the same tree. They had few seeds. Risso mentions that the C. limonum vulgaris varies in form, especially in its after crop. With management and proper cultivation ripe fruit may be taken from this lemon tree all the year round. It fruits abundantly, and grows luxuriantly everywhere, provided the climate is not too cold for it.

PLATE CLXXIX.

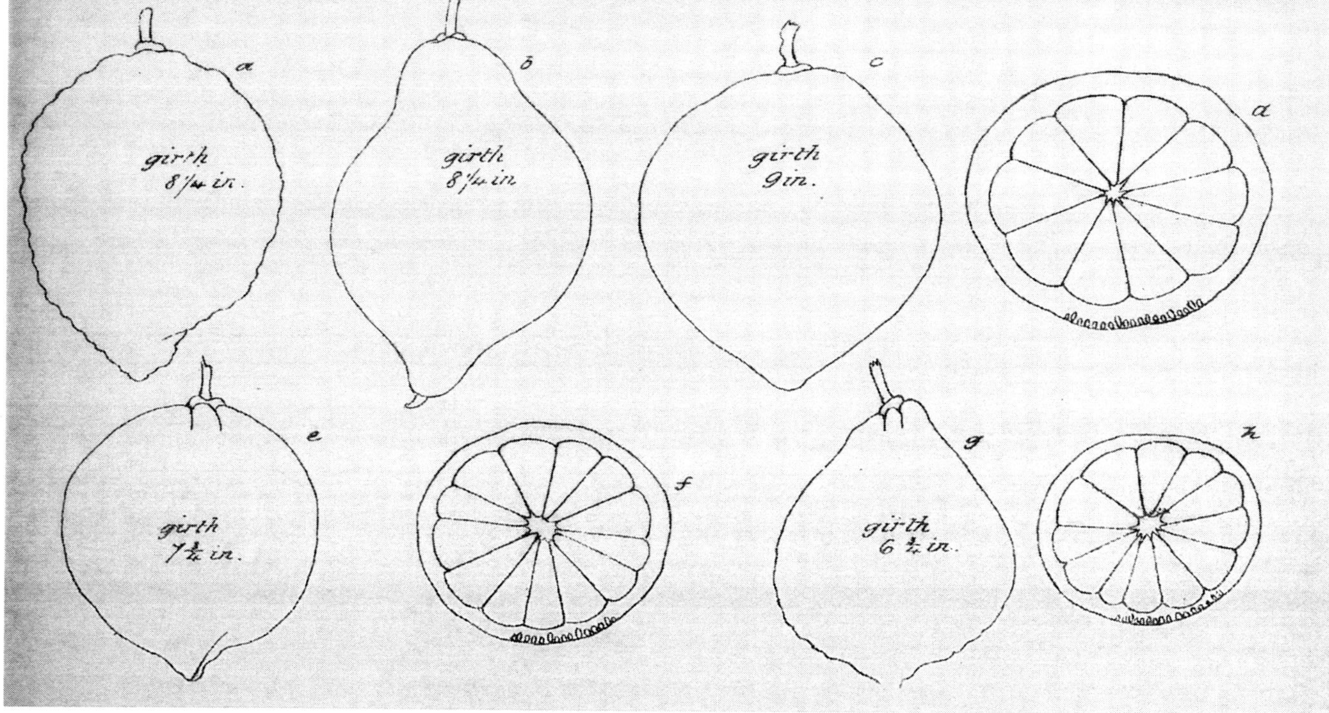

PLATE CLXXX.

Other forms of Malta lemon from Jail Garden, Etawah.

a was plucked in September. It was almost ripe. It resembles in shape the *Kaghzi Kalan* and *Sherbetee Nimboo.*

b is a *Dumrèz*; smooth, and pitted with oil-glands.

c and *d* are a globose specimen. This had a *faint* tinge of pale orange in its pulp. The exterior was smooth. Besides the deep foveoli and lesser ones, it had numerous dots, which looked like undeveloped oil-cells, for want of space.

All the Malta lemons are pale yellow at first. The colour becomes deeper by ripening.

PLATE CLXXX.

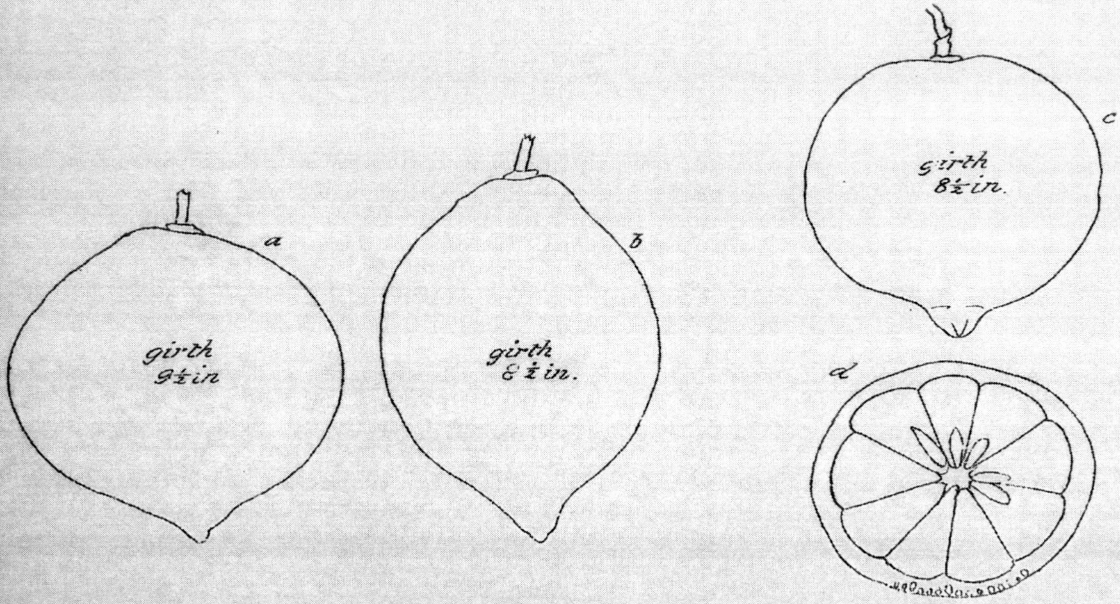

PLATE CLXXXI.

Leaves of the Malta lemon, from the Etawah Jail Garden.

a is a new fully-developed rain leaf, thin and transparent. Its petiole has no sign of wings or margins. Two minute ridges on the upper part, indicated by two lines at A, are the remnants of ancestral petiole margins. On this sketch are shown the three sizes of oil-cells, which are repeated on the crenations. The crenations, large and small, are exact copies of the original. The Malta lemon leaf and rind have very fine and distinct aromas. The main nerves branch towards the edge, and their branches anastomose. This is the character of all the citrus leaves I have examined. On the upper surface the larger oil-cells can be seen as low miliary projections. On the under side the two larger sizes can be seen as dark green dots on a light green surface. The third and *smallest* size can be only seen by transparency.

b and *c* are rain leaves, and *d* a typical spring leaf.

e is the spine.

In fig. *a* the open rings represent the largest oil-cells; the large black dots, the medium-sized oil-cells; and the mere points represent the oil-cells of the smallest size.

PLATE CLXXXI.

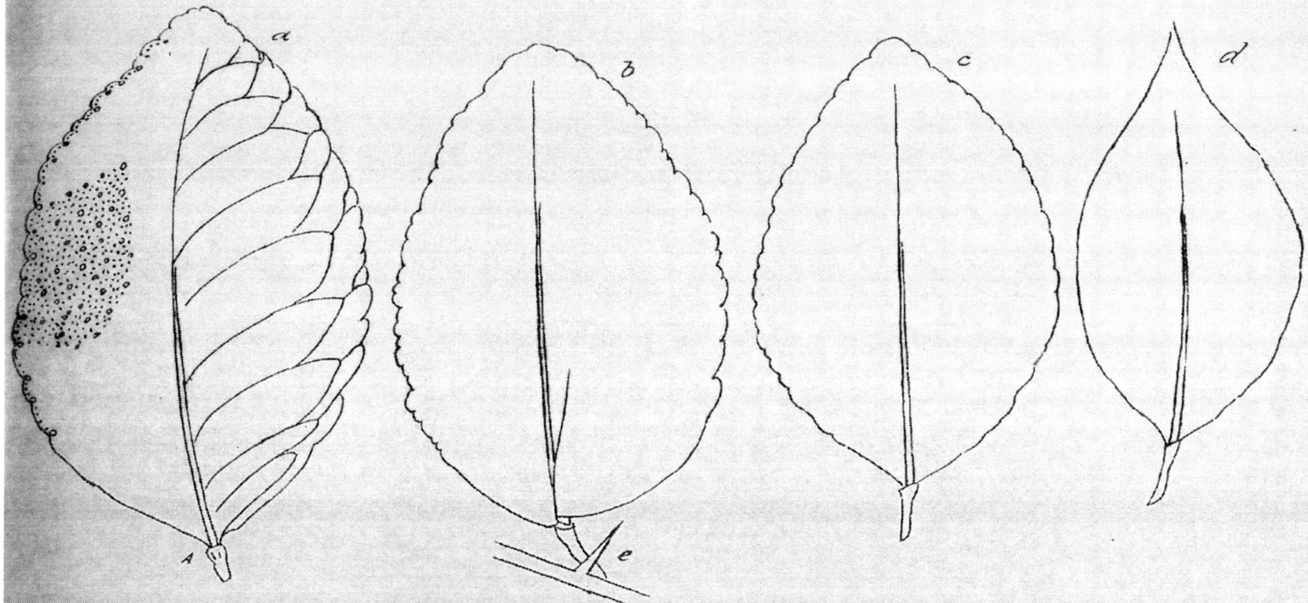

PLATE CLXXXII.

Malta lemons sent by Messrs. Carew & Co., of Rosa, under the name of *Amalbêd*, or *Amilbêd*.

a and *b* show their shape. They were chagrined with large and small foveoli. The skin of both was $\frac{1}{8}$ of an inch thick.

c is a rain leaf.

d, *e*, and *f*, spring leaves. The "petit grains" or essential oil-cells were very distinct.

g is the spine.

There was no doubt in my mind that these were of the Malta lemon type. They had its aroma and its pure acid juice. Probably they had been obtained from Lucknow.

NOTE.—The Malta lemon is the same as the Palermo and Messina lemons that come to the English markets. I have observed many specimens in the shops that bear traces of their *citron* origin, in having a rough, channelled, and thick skin.

PLATE CLXXXII.

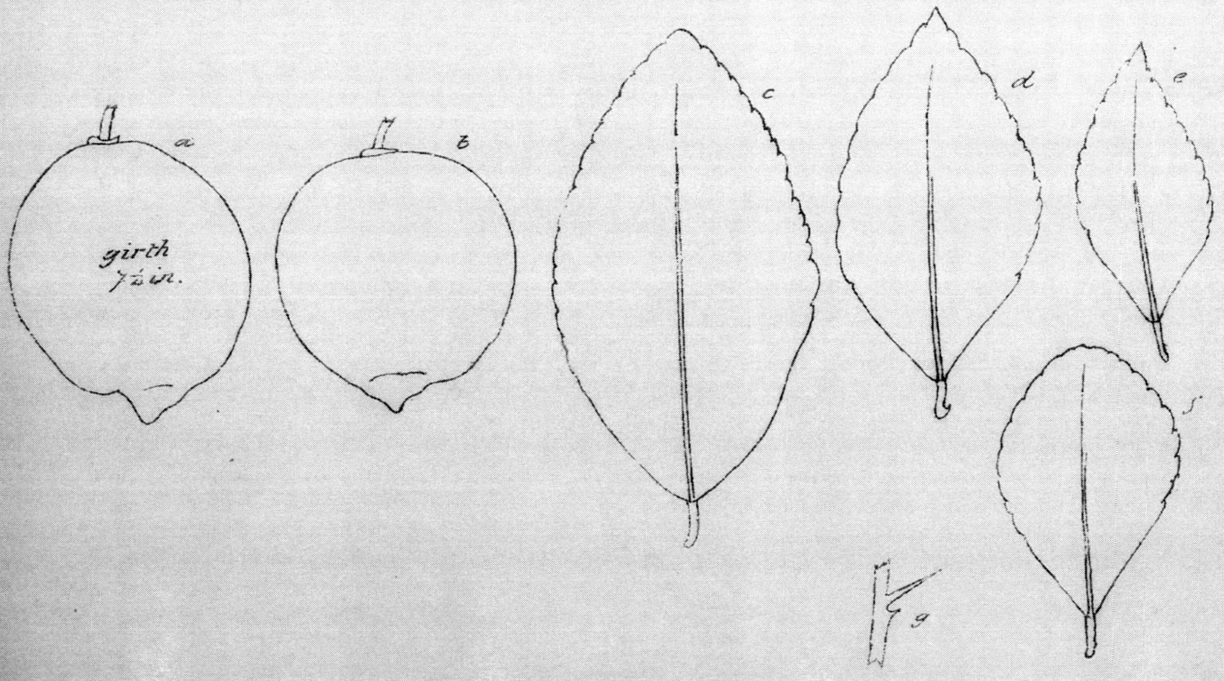

PLATE CLXXXIII.

Specimens of the Malta lemon type, received through Mr. R. Blechynden, Sec. A.H.S. of India, and grown in Mr. Stalkartt's garden at Goosery.

a, *c*, *d* are forms usual in the Malta lemon. They came in July, and were ripe. Therefore, they are probably of the *Dumrez* crop. Mr. Stalkartt states those of the spring crop are rougher.

b is the section of *a*; *e* is a typical spring leaf; *f* and *g*, other spring leaves; *h* is the spine of the branch that came with them.

I at first thought this stock may have been obtained from Lucknow; but it is not so. Mr. Stalkartt vouches for the trees having been in his garden since he came to India, in 1833. Mr. Blechynden thinks it probable that the old plants in the Society's garden may have been obtained from him. He adds that Firminger alludes to this lemon, and thinks it the "common Spanish," and gives *Korna neeboo* as the native name. And that, in the *Hortus Bengalensis* of Roxburgh, published in 1814, the *Korna neeboo* is given as the Citrus medica, "common lemon," and the date of its introduction into the Botanic Garden is given as 1796. The Goosery lemon trees are not improbably some of its descendants. All the characters of the Goosery lemon are those of the Malta or Spanish lemon. Nevertheless, it may be also an improved form of the Assam lemon, *Jóràtenga* (?). (*Vide* Plate CCXXXIX., fig. *a*.) The Goosery lemon just floats in water.

PLATE CLXXXIII

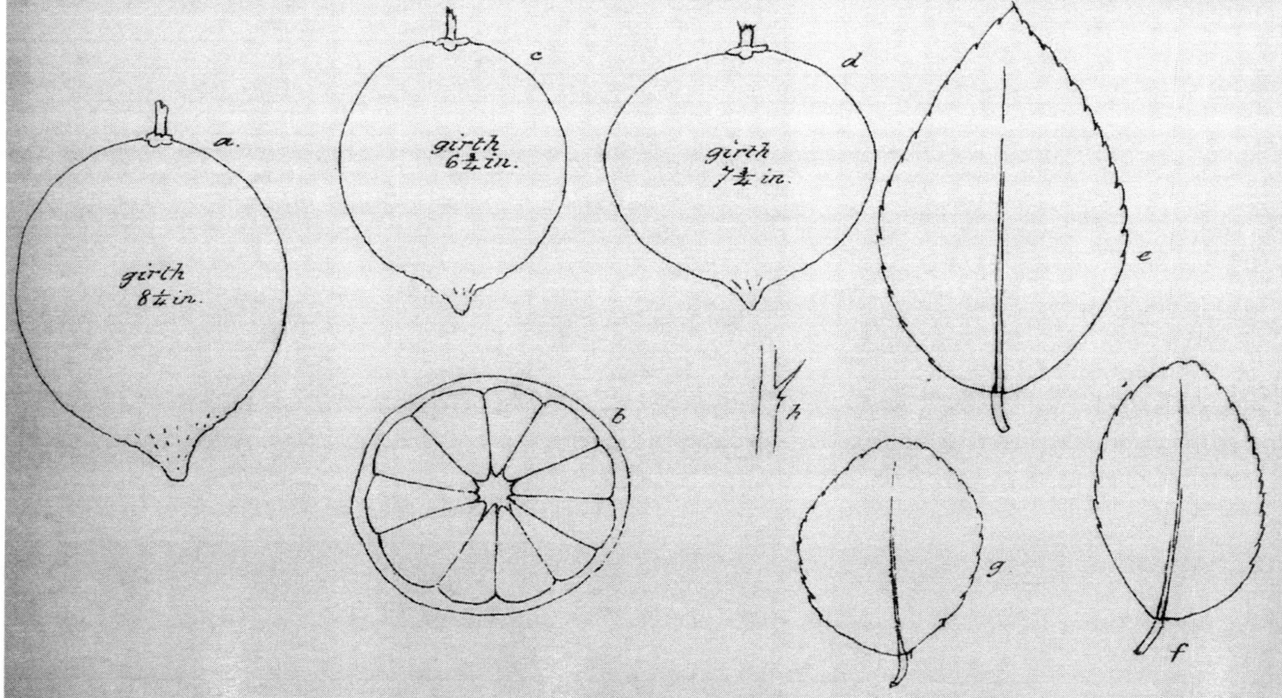

PLATE CLXXXIV.

a and *b* are Pondicherry lemons. *a* had concave oil-cells, and *b* convex cells. They are called "citrons" by the French there. Both had thin skins, and very pale and sour pulp. Their flavour had something of the *Kaghzi Nimboo* taste in it. The seeds were greenish, when cut. I obtained both in the market. In the Horticultural Garden of Pondicherry I was shown a plant, said to be that of the "citron." Its leaf is shown at *c*. It struck me as being more like that of the *Turunj*. The Eurasian superintendent, however, who had been to Italy, told me that the Pondicherry lemon was exactly like the Italian lemon. The Italian and Malta lemons are one thing. It is not improbable that the French introduced this lemon from Europe. I saw it nowhere else in S. India.

d and *e* are the Malta lemon, from the Saharunpur Botanic Garden.

f is an unripe one; *g* and *h* are its typical leaves; *i* an abnormal spring leaf; and *j* the spines. The history of the Saharunpur lemon trees is not known. Mr. Gollam states they are between sixteen and eighteen years old. Probably they were obtained from Lucknow.

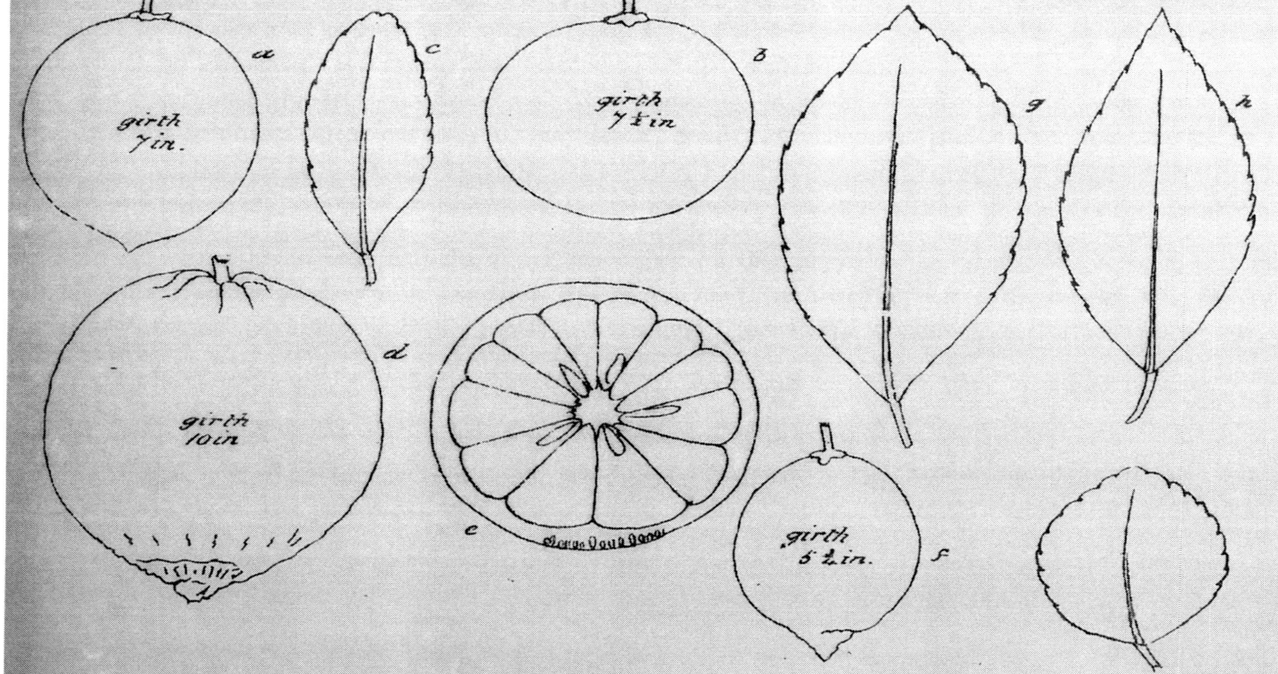
a
girth
7in.
c
b
girth
7¼ in
g
h
d
girth
10in
e
girth
5¼ in.
f

PLATE CLXXXV.

Variety of the Malta lemon, received from Mr. C. Nickels, Passèwa Factory, Jaunpore.

a and *b* show the shape of this lemon, with a pale yellow exterior, pitted with deep and shallow foveoli, with whitish dots between them. The aroma of the rind did not appear to me so fine as that of the Lucknow lemon.

b is the section of *a*. The pulp is pale, and pure acid, with abundant juice of a fine flavour.

d is a rain leaf; *e* and *f* spring leaves; *g* a spine. The only difference I could see in this lemon from that of Lucknow was that it had its mammilla a little to the one side, and its leaves perhaps more mucronate or pointed.

Mr. Nickels says that in 1872 he brought out from England some blood orange trees. The stock on which one was budded gave out a shoot. Thinking that in England they budded on the lemon stock, he removed the shoot, and struck it under glass. It gave the fruit shown. It may, perhaps, be of some use to distinguish this variety as the *English* or *Jaunpore* lemon.

PLATE CLXXXV

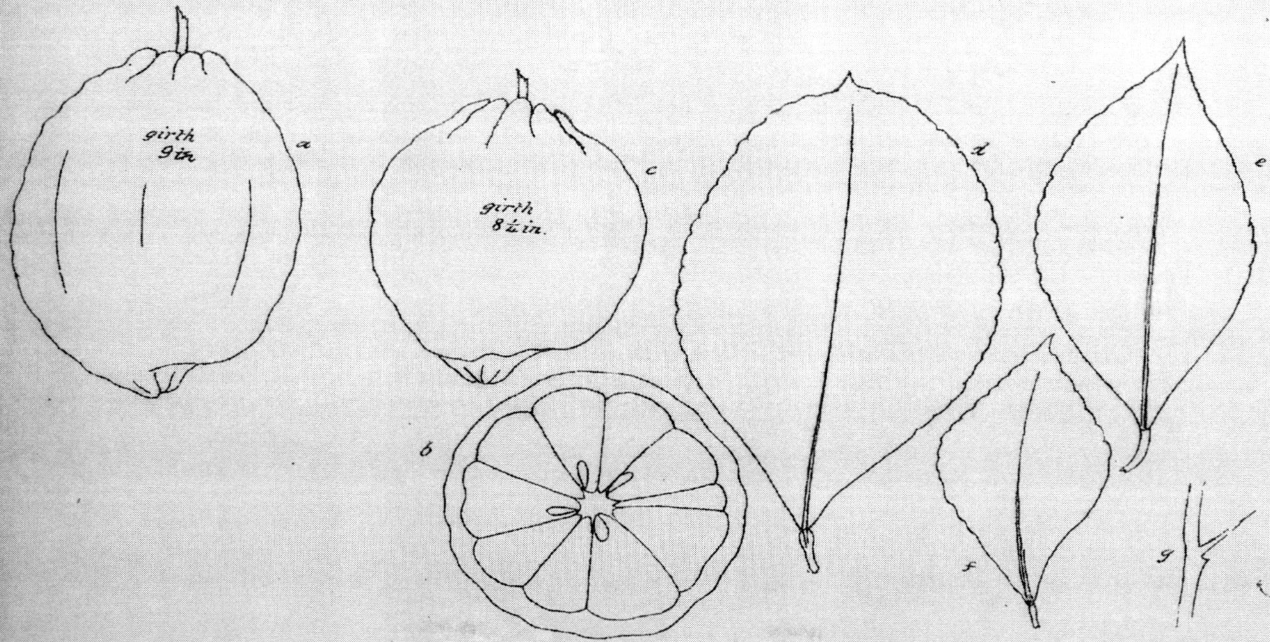

PLATE CLXXXVI.

Gulgul from Raja Shiva Parshad's garden at Benares. He says it abounds in Lahore.

a indicates its form. It is of a lemon yellow, closely foveolate all over; apex depressed.

b is its section. The pulp is pale, like a lemon; the juice abundant, and pure acid; centre hollow.

c is the *Gulgul* leaf, with a slightly margined petiole. The leaves are crenate, and thin; rather like those of a *Khatta* orange. The young leaf buds have hairs on them.

d is the *Gulgul* spine.

e and *f* are two *Gulguls* purchased at Jagàdri. They look much like the *Kilkil* or *Kulkul* of the Emperor Baber's memoirs. He says: "It is like a goose's egg, but does not, like that egg, taper away at the two extremities. Skin thin, like the *Sangtereh*. It has a remarkable quantity of juice." The skin is quite smooth, and of the texture and colour of *Kaghzi nimboo*, and marked longitudinally with shallow depressions opposite the divisions of the pulp. Juice very sour, very abundant, and slightly aromatic.

g is the section of *e*.

PLATE CLXXXVI.

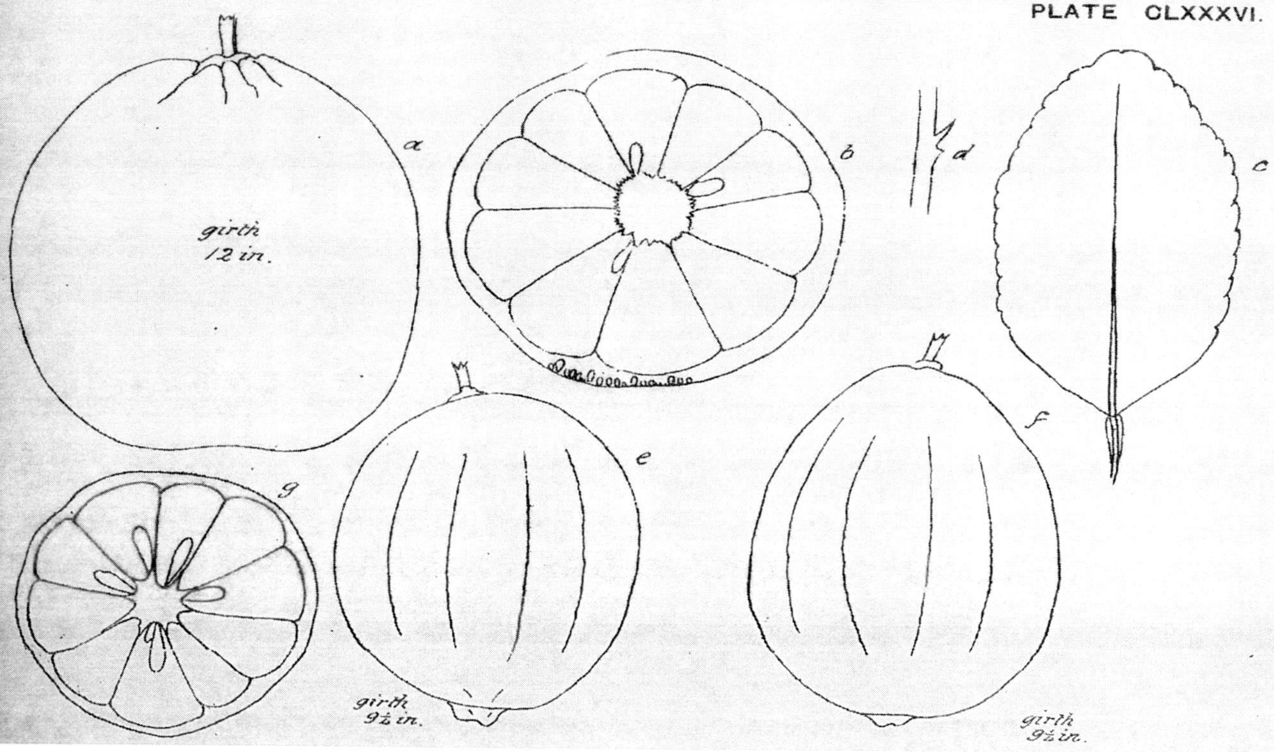

PLATE CLXXXVII.

Meetha Gulgul of Saharumpur, Botanic Gardens.

a is the shape of this lemon. Its colour is lemon yellow; foveolate all over; is rather smooth, and has an elastic feel. It looks like a large Malta lemon.

b is its section, with a thick skin. The oil-cells are large and distinct. The pulp is pale and lemon-like. Although it is called *Meetha* (sweet), this specimen is not so, but *sub*-acid. The juice is abundant, and the vesicles coarse. The centre is hollow.

c and *d* are spring leaves, with a *faint* lemon scent. The petioles are only slightly margined. The spines were mere points. Flowers large white, tinged purple.

PLATE CLXXXVII.

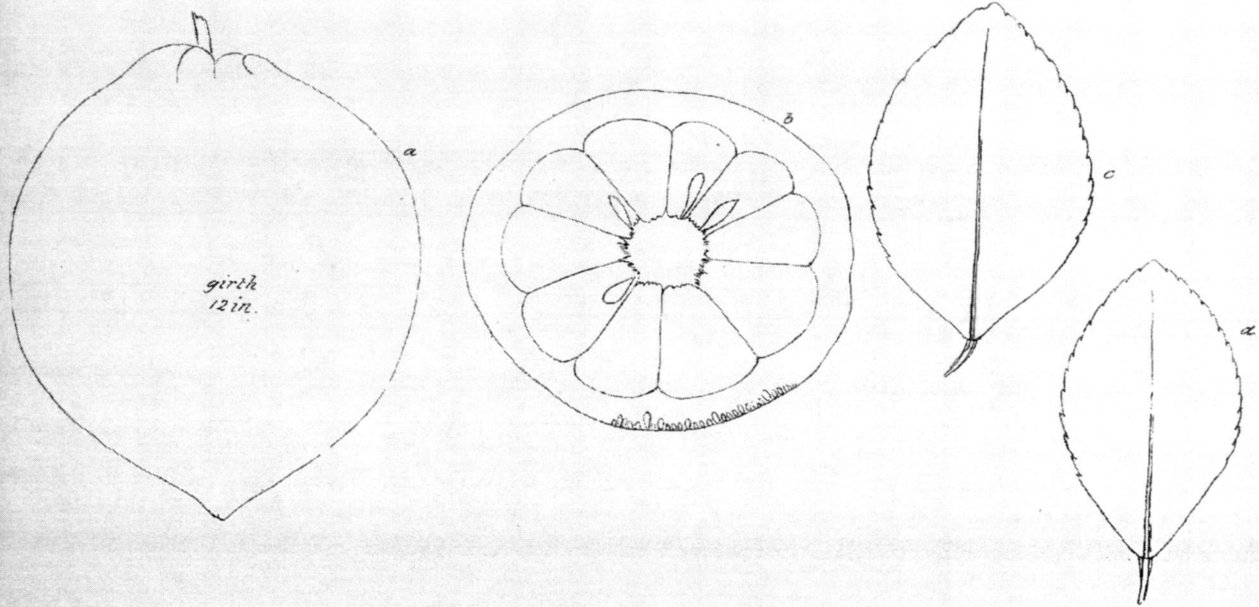

PLATE CLXXXVIII.

This is what is called the Kumaon lemon, or lime. It was sent by Mr. John Martin, proprietor of Douglas Dale, Nynee Tal.

a is its shape, like a very large Malta lemon, and not unlike the *Meetha nimboo* of the foregoing plate. The exterior is lemon-yellow, with a rough surface. The large oil-cells are depressed, and the intermediate small ones are like pinholes. It is slightly sub-warty round the apex.

b is its section, with thick skin; oil-cells distinct; pithy part white and sweetish; the rind has not the fine aroma of the Malta lemon. Pulp transparent, and of a *faint* orange-yellow; sour, but not the pure sourness of the Malta lemon; juice very abundant; centre hollow; seeds white, when cut. This appears to be a true lemon of the *Gulgul* type.

c is a rain leaf, and *d* a spine; *e* is a bit of the rind, with the pith shaved off, showing sections of the oil-cells of three sizes. The young leaves are bronze-coloured, and the blossoms bronze-reddish-brown.

PLATE CLXXXVIII.

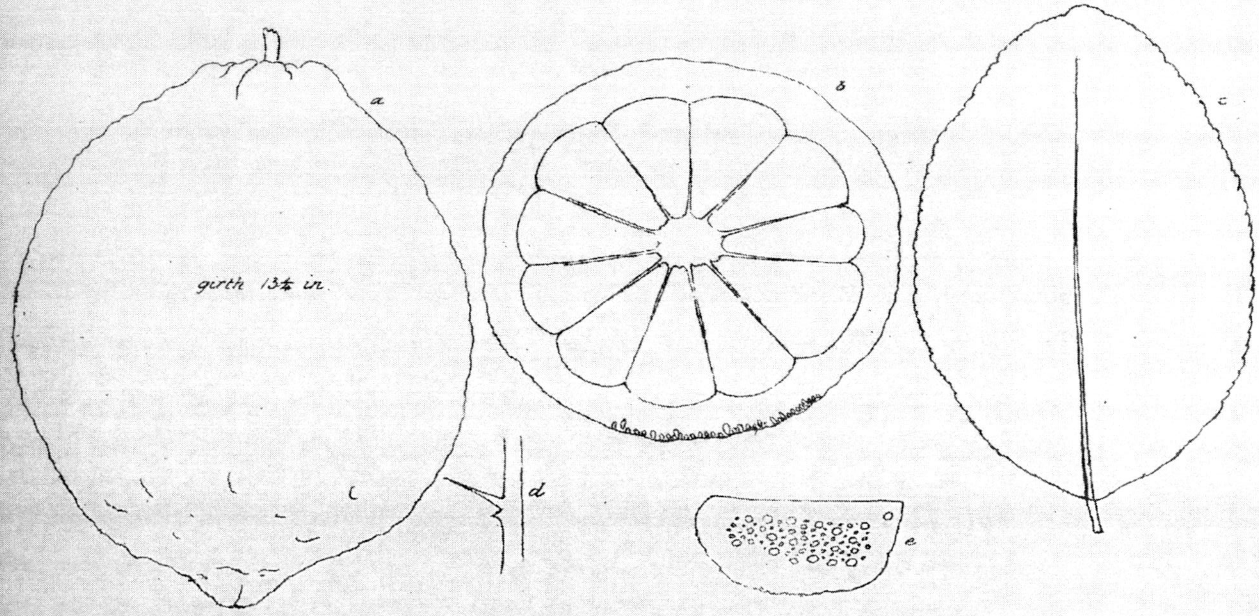

PLATE CLXXXIX.

Kaghzi Kalàn lemons, from Gundaroop Sing's garden, at Ajitmal, Etawah District.

a, *c*, and *e* differ only slightly in form and size. Their exterior is pale yellow, and quite smooth, only marked with faint foveoli at certain distances. The intermediate spaces being filled with smaller oil-cells, which are neither raised nor sunk.

b is the section of *a*, and *d* the section of *c*. The skin is very thin; pulp pale; juice abundant, and very sour.

g is a typical rain leaf, and *f* an abnormally shaped one.

h is a small spring leaf. I could see no difference between these leaves and those of the sweet lemon, or *Sherbetee nimboo*. The spines were mere points.

This lemon tree is said to have been obtained from Saharumpur. The name *Kaghzi* only means that it has a very thin skin, that is, *paper-like*.

PLATE CLXXXIX.

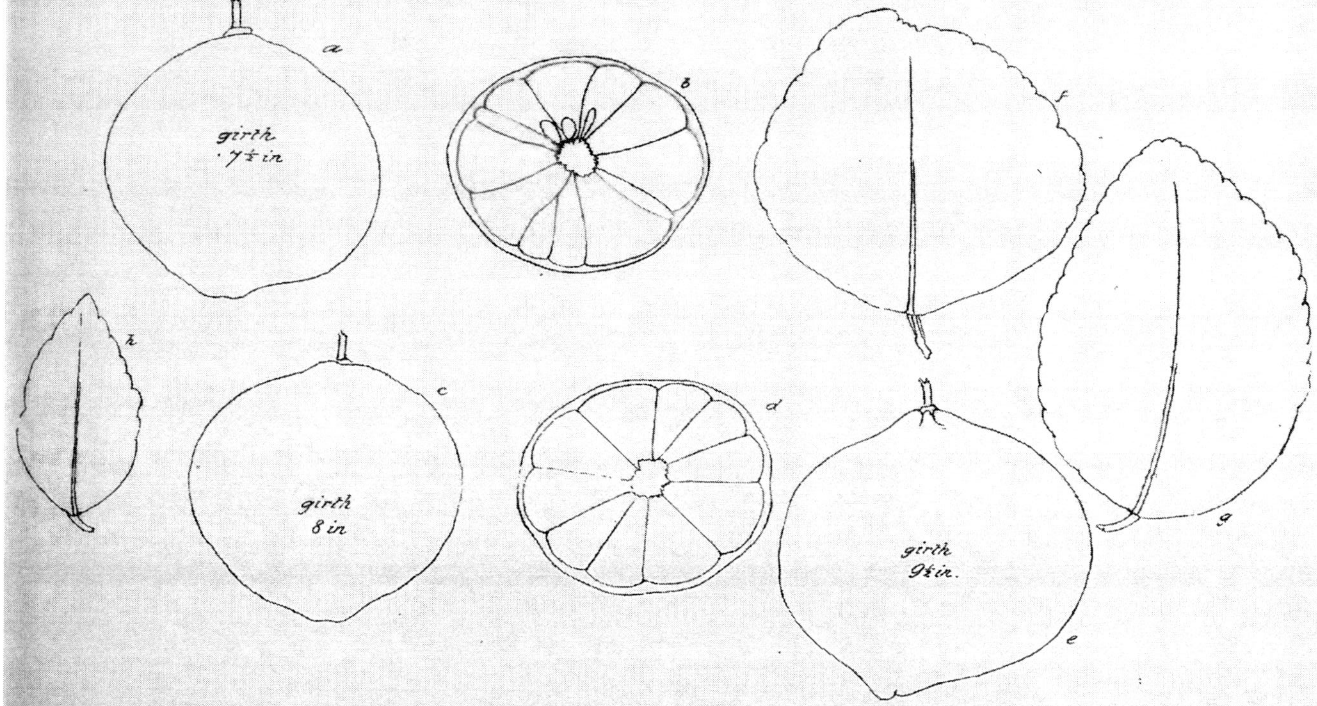

PLATE CXC.

Mitha nimboo, or sweet lemons; also called *Sherbetee nimboo* and *Amruphál*.

a is the sweet lemon of Mooltan; pale yellow and smooth, the furrows being tinged with red. The specimen was rather dry. The skin was very thin, as shown in section *b*. The juice was abundant, and of a nicer flavour than other sweet lemons I have tried. Probably the dryness of the Mooltan climate may have influenced its flavour.

c is an abnormal rain leaf; *f* an abnormal spring leaf; *d* and *e* typical spring leaves. The leaves have a slender petiole, without a trace of wings or margins, which are represented by two minute ridges on the upper part. The very youngest leaf-buds have a little down. There were no spines on the branch sent.

g and *h* is a sweet lemon from Khoorja. On the apex the oil-cells are concave, in other places quite plane. It floats in water, but not well; it first sinks and then rises slowly to the surface.

i are abnormal spring leaves, and the only ones that came with it. It is curious that from Khoorja I received both small *Sherbetee* and also small *Kalán Kaghzi* lemons. This, however, might be a small specimen of an ordinary tree.

PLATE CXC.

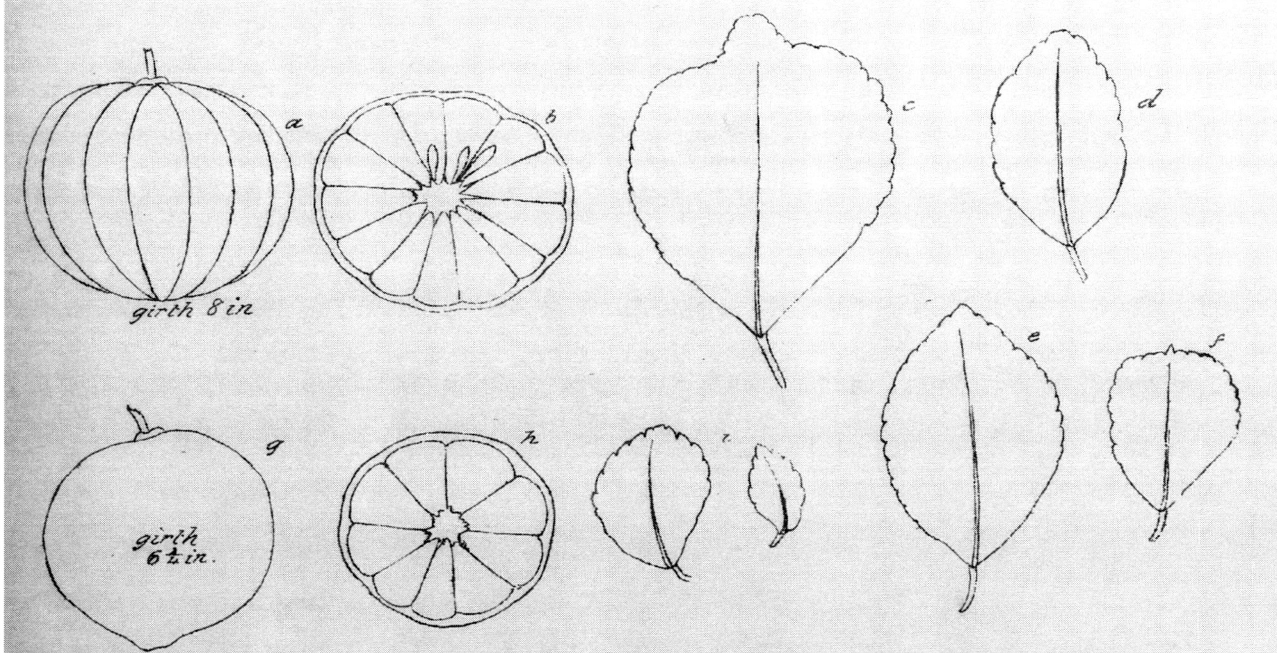

PLATE CXCI.

Other forms of lemons.

a is the usual form of sweet lemon.

b its typical rain leaf; and *c* its typical spring leaf, with their spines.

d and *e* are *Kalán Kaghzi*, or sour lemons, from Lucknow. The former was as round as a cricket-ball, and the latter had an oblate form.

f is a rain leaf of the same; and *g* a spring leaf. The wings of the petioles were mere margins.

The flower of the sweet lemon is *pure white*, and the young shoots green, with scattered hairs on the young leaf-buds.

The flower of the *Kalán Kaghzi* is *very slightly* tinted with red, and the young shoots green.

Judging from the fruit and leaves, one would say the *Sherbetee* is an acidless variety of the sour *Kalán Kaghzi*.

Judging from the flowers, one would say the *Sherbetee* is a lemon-coloured *orange*

PLATE CXCI.

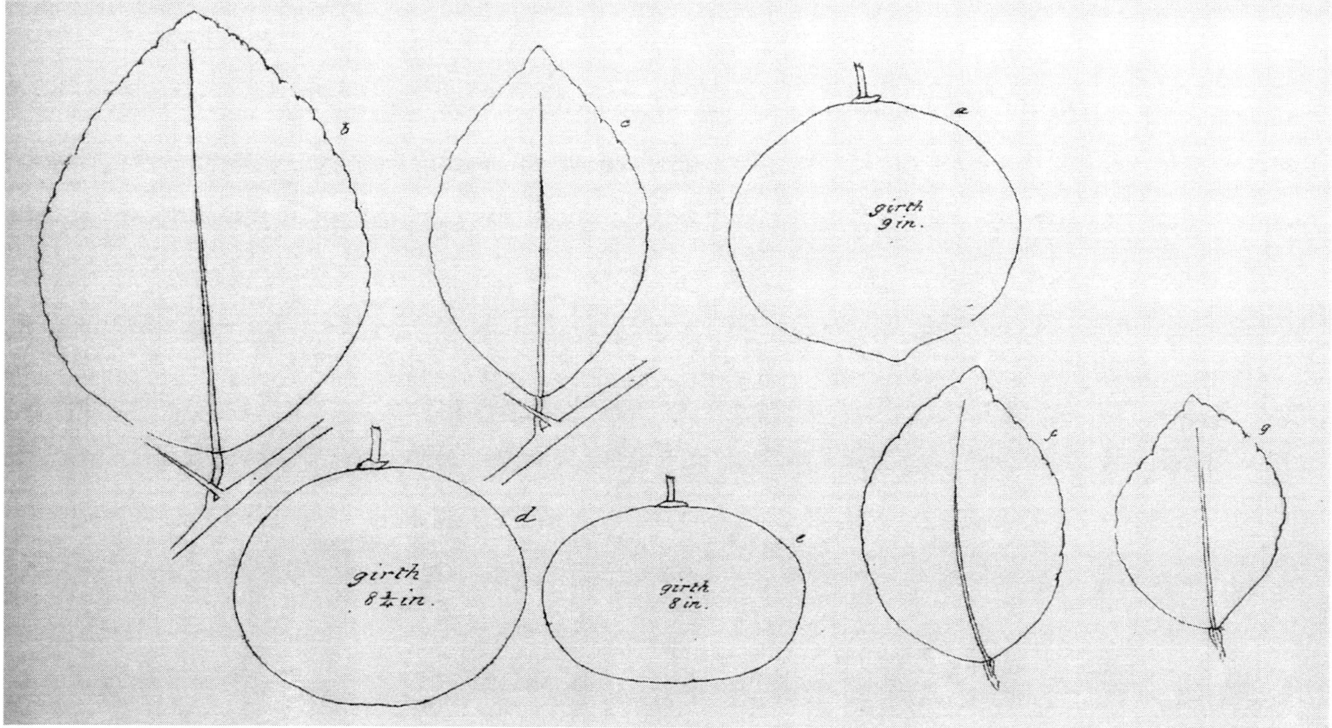

PLATE CXCII.

Other sweet lemons.

a and *b* came from Benares, under the name of *Nepâlee*. This was a *sweet* lemon, an ordinary *Sherbetee*. The *Nepâlee* proper is a *sour* lemon.

c is the *Mitha nimboo* I purchased at Bombay, and said to come from *Nagpore*; *d* is the leaf that was attached to it. It appeared quite a lemon leaf.

e, *f*, *g*, and *h* are leaves of a *Sherbetee* which came from Rosa, Shahjahanpur; *e* is a rain leaf, and the others small spring leaves.

The fruit of this Rosa *Sherbetee* was smaller than ordinary sweet lemons, with thin skin, pale pulp, and sweetish abundant juice; otherwise it did not differ from other sweet lemons.

PLATE CXCII

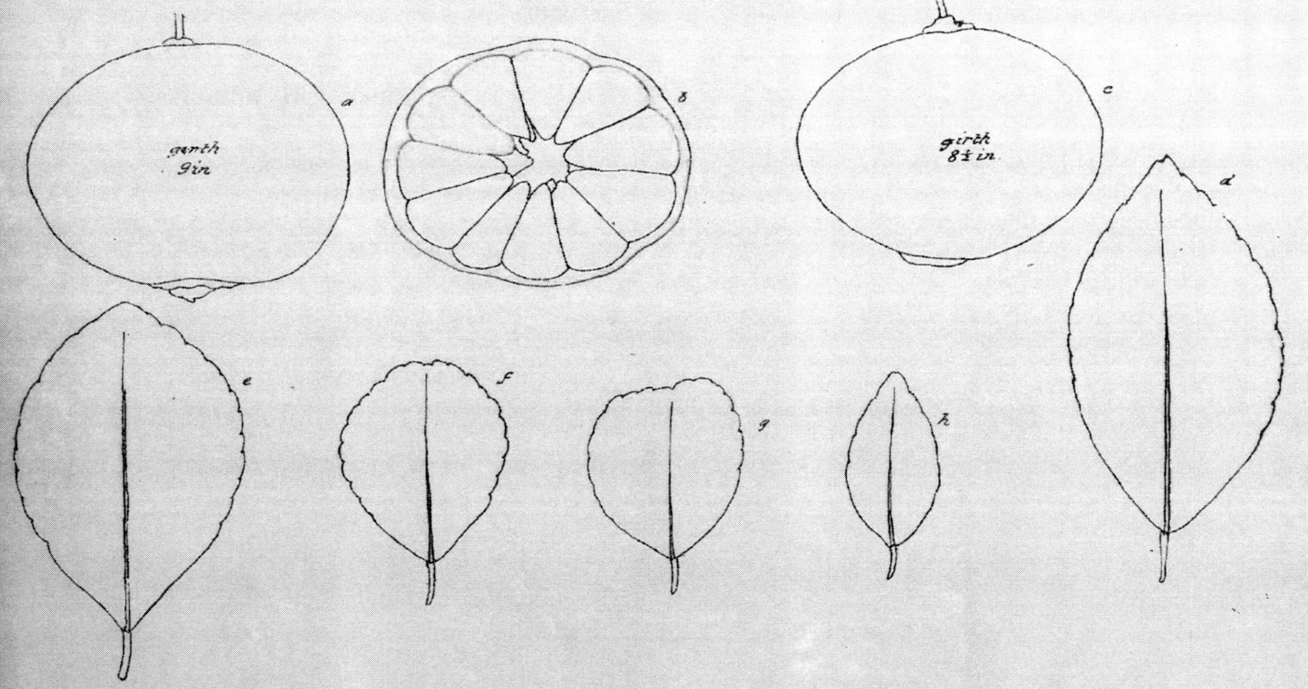

PLATE CXCIII.

Other sweet lemons.

a and *b* is a *Sherbetee nimboo* from Mr. Nicholson's garden, Gonda. It has a thicker skin than the usual, with a solid centre, oil-cells of rind very distinct. The seeds, when cut, were white, tinged green.

c and *d* are its leaves; their petioles had a slight pubescence, even in old leaves; the leaves had a faint lemon scent.

e is a *Sherbetee* from Bhilawa, Auraya. The oil-cells present neither concavities nor convexities. They are mere transparent dots; neither the tip of the finger nor that of the tongue can detect any unevenness.

All the sweet lemons are more or less smooth, globose, or oblate, and generally with a small indistinct mammilla, and usually marked with shallow longitudinal furrows, corresponding to the divisions of the pulp. This is probably owing to the tightly-fitting thin skin.

f, *g*, and *h* are the leaves which came with *e*.

PLATE CXCIII.

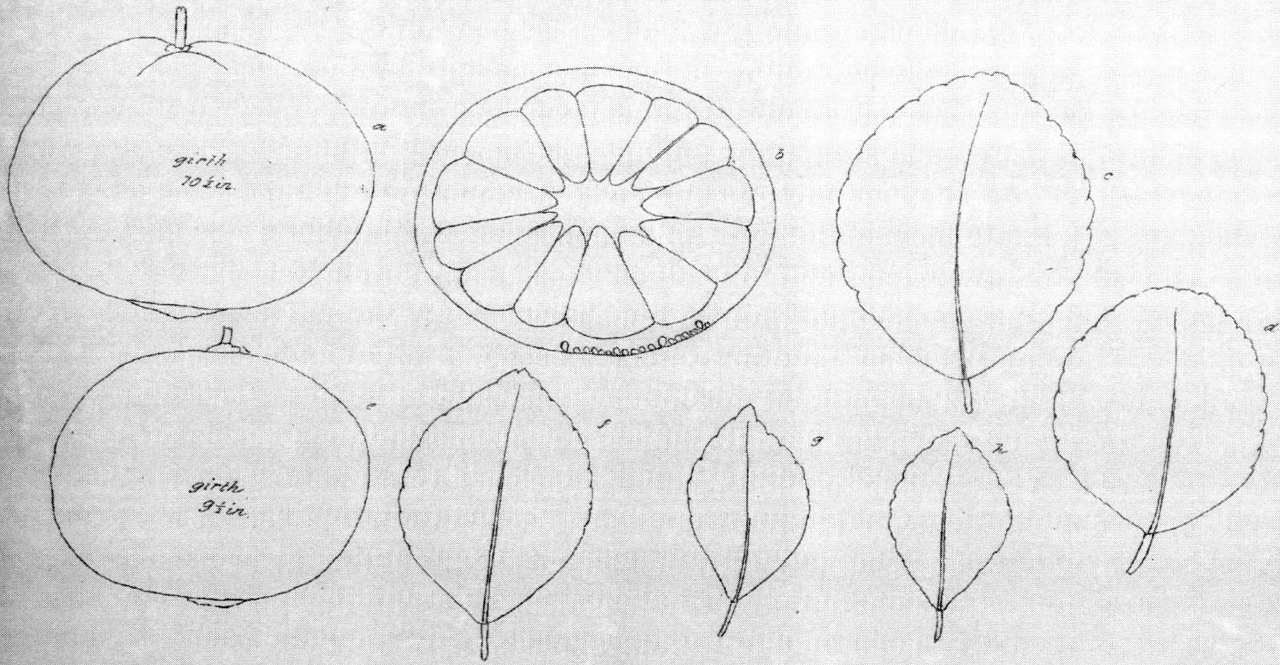

PLATE CXCIV.

Other sweet lemons.

a and *b* are the only ovoid sweet lemon I have met with in India. It came from a tree which bore *globose* fruit, in the Public Garden, Benares. It was lemon yellow, and closely foveolate with *concave* cells; rather thick-skinned. The *Dumrez Sherbetee* has a thicker skin than that of the spring crop. The rind of this was more aromatic than usual.

c is a globose *Sherbetee* from Raja Siva Parshad's Garden, Benares. Deep lemon yellow, and also rather thick-skinned.

d is its leaf, rather serrated than crenated. Petiole only margined; young leaf-buds much covered with hairs.

e is its spine.

PLATE CXCIV

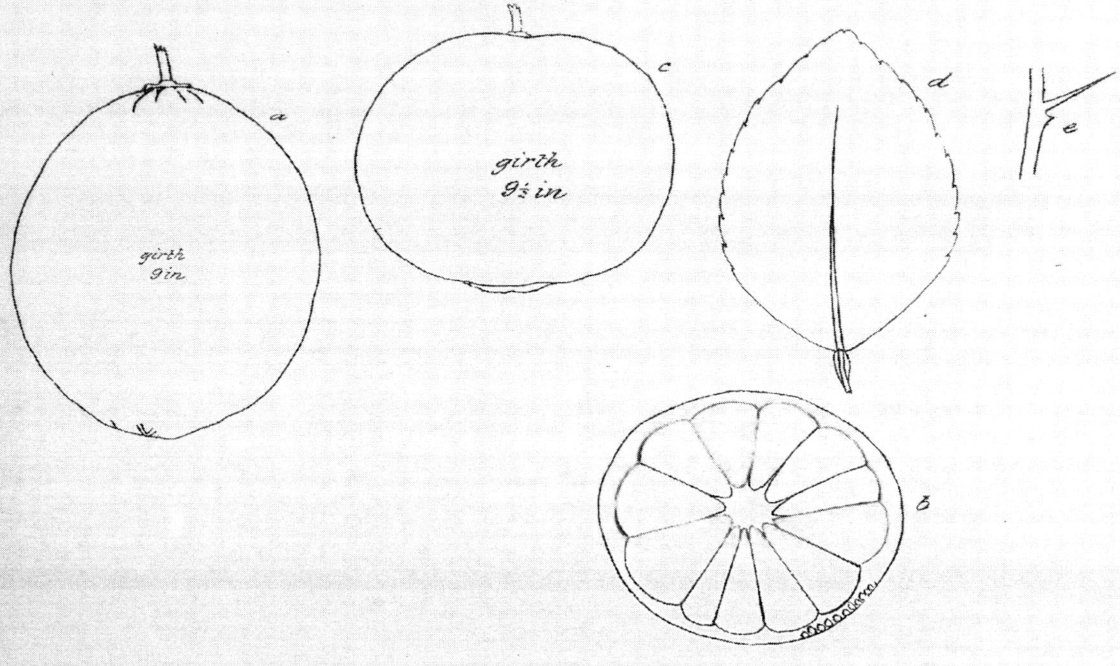

PLATE CXCV.

Other forms of sweet lemons.

a and *b* are a sweet lemon from Muscat, which I purchased at the Bombay market. Its flavour, unlike that of Mooltan, appeared to me of the ordinary *Sherbetee*. Why they import them from Muscat, when they are largely grown in India, is impossible to say. It had few seeds.

c is another Muscat sweet lemon. For a sight of this I am indebted to Mr. A. Y. Gubboy, of Ezra Street, Calcutta. He was travelling in the same carriage with me from Bombay. He showed me this enormous sweet lemon, which he purchased in Bombay, under the name of "Muscat sweet orange." I could not see its interior, as he was taking it to his friends in Calcutta. I, however, took an outline drawing of it, and measurements. It had a diameter of about 4 inches, and was of a canary yellow. Mr. Gubboy afterwards kindly sent me its seeds. They germinated, and I sent some of the plants to Lucknow and some to Saharunpur.

d and *e* are a pyriform *Sherbetee* from Auraya. It was unripe, and that may account for its smallness and thick skin. It had pure white flowers; *f* is its rain leaf; and *g* its spring leaf.

PLATE CXCV.

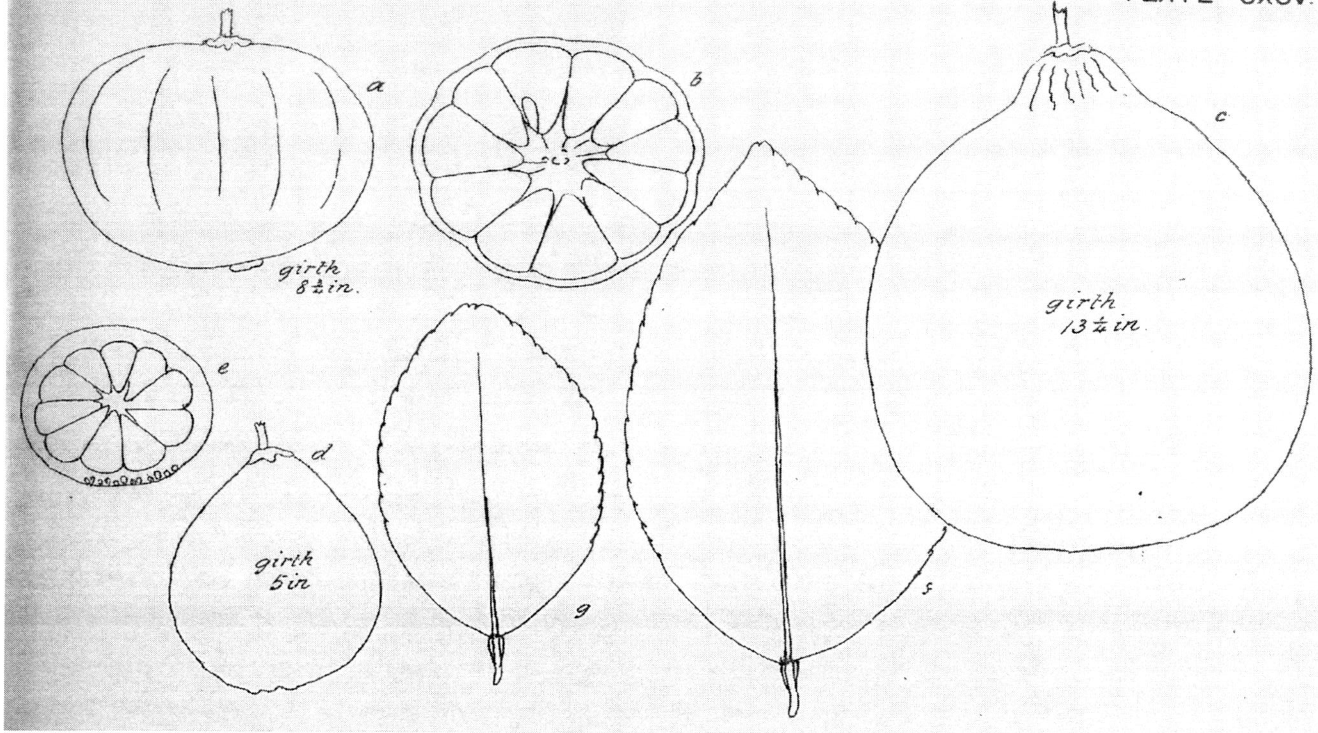

PLATE CXCVI.

a and *b* are a citrus sent by Major Buller from one of the gardens of the late Maharaja of Bulrampur, Gonda. It is a very distinct variety, and I regret that no leaves were sent with it. It was deep yellow, rough, elastic, and puffy; shaped like a large Malta lemon, but with the feel of a spongy-skinned pummelo. The oil-cells were very large; skin sweetish, and loosely attached. The angles A A were not filled up as in all other citrus, but *hollow*. The pulp was yellowish-white; the juice-vesicles loose and sour; the carpels were loose and open at the centre. The centre was hollow, and the seeds white, when cut. It may possibly be a yellow mamillate variety of *At Anni*. It came under the name of *Qism Bajoura Turshee*, but it is *not* a Bajoura.

c and *e* are the *Barā Nepālee nimboo*, or Nepal lemons. The exterior is of a beautiful *pale* lemon yellow, and regularly dotted with foveoli and intermediate oil-cells. *d* is the section of *c*. Pulp lemon-like; juice abundant and acid, and leaves a rather unpleasant aroma in the throat. These lemons had the shape and colour of *Guavas*.

f, *g*, and *h* are their leaves, rather serrated than crenated, with the scent of lemon leaves. Some had margined petioles, others not. Young shoots purple; flower-buds tinged purple. The Nepal lemon is often *seedless*.

PLATE CXCVI

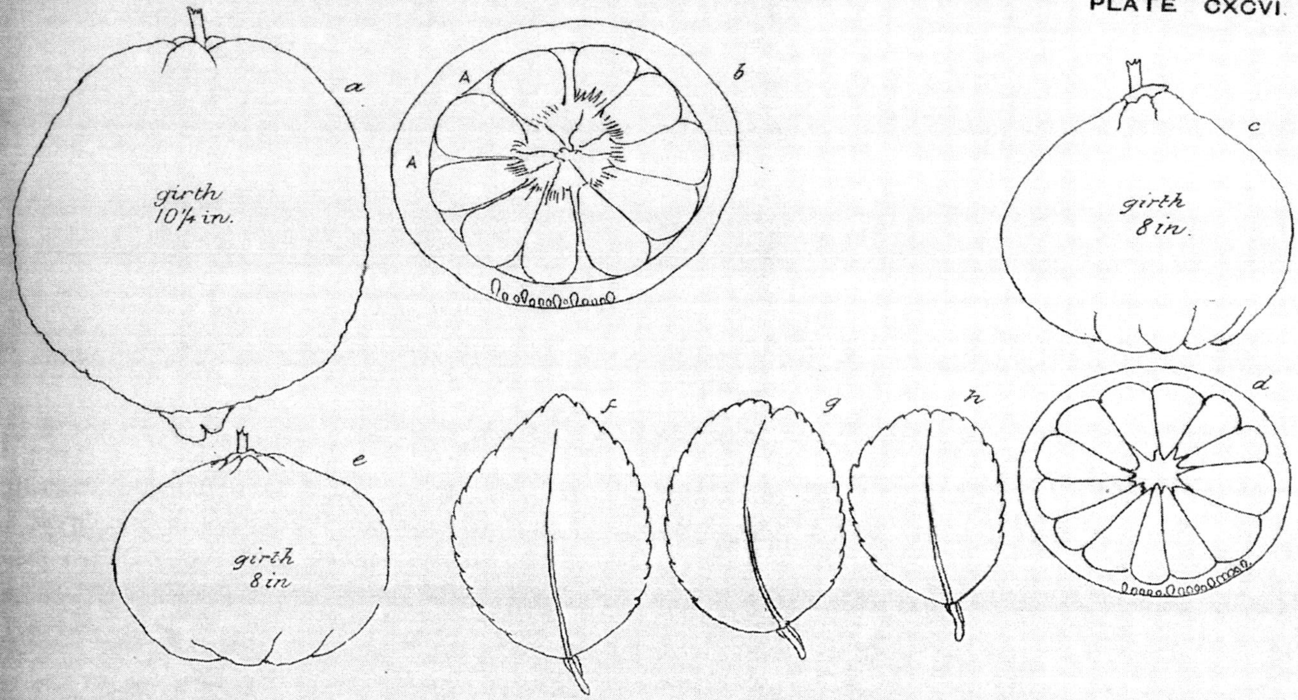

PLATE CXCVII.

Nepal lemons from Gonda.

a and *b* came under the name of *Nepàlee Kaghzi nimboo*—as round as a cricket-ball; pale lemon yellow, smooth with shallow foveoli. Rind aromatic, pulp pale, juice abundant and very sour, and slightly aromatic; almost seedless; centre hollow. It appears a globose form of Nepal lemon.

c is a small spring leaf, and the only one that came with it. It had a faint lemon scent, and with a naked petiole. The spines were mere points.

d and *e* came under the name of *Kaghzi nimboo* (*Nepàlee*); very pale lemon yellow, globose and minutely foveolate all over; deeper yellow round the apex. Rind lemon flavoured, pulp pale, inclined to greenish; thin skin, seedless; centre solid; juice abundant, with much the flavour of the *Barà Nepàlee nimboo*, and, like it, leaves an unpleasant taste in the throat.

f, *g*, and *h* are its spring leaves, and have the character of lemon leaves. They are *lemon* scented, not *lime* scented. It has all the characters of the larger Nepal lemon, and appears to be a small form of it.

PLATE CXCVII.

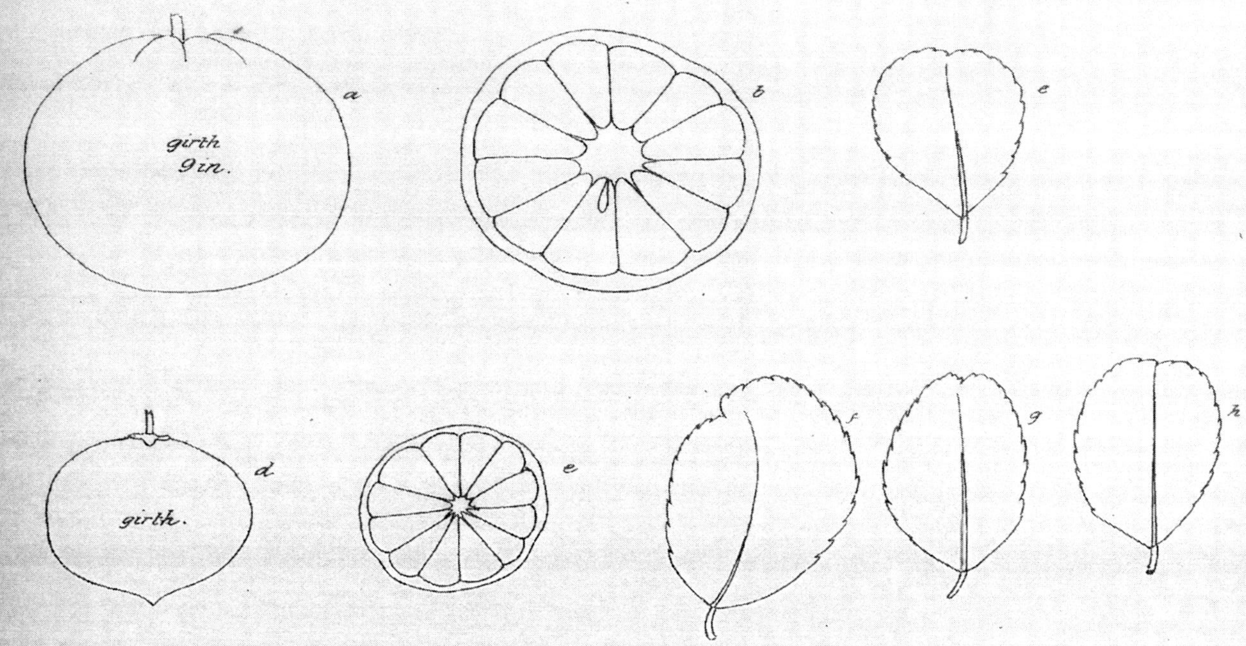

PLATE CXCVIII.

Pahdree nimboo sent by Major Buller from the late Maharaja's garden at Sheopura, Gonda.

a, *b*, and *c* are its form; *c* had a small flattened mammilla. Curiously enough, they both had those transverse striæ on one side that I found in various citrons (which see). They made no difference in the section. Exterior lemon yellow, smooth (excepting the striæ), with shallow foveoli. They looked like smooth and large Malta lemons. Thin skin, pulp pale, like a *Sherbetee*; juice abundant, not very sour, only sub-acid. When cut, they gave the scent rather of an orange than a lemon; rind with a faint lemon flavour; seeds white, when cut. It seems a desirable variety. It appears allied to the thin-skinned *Gulgul* of Jagàdri.

It is not quite clear whether by the term *Pahdree* is meant a *mountain* lemon, or a mistake for *Behàree*, from Behàr.

PLATE CXCVIII

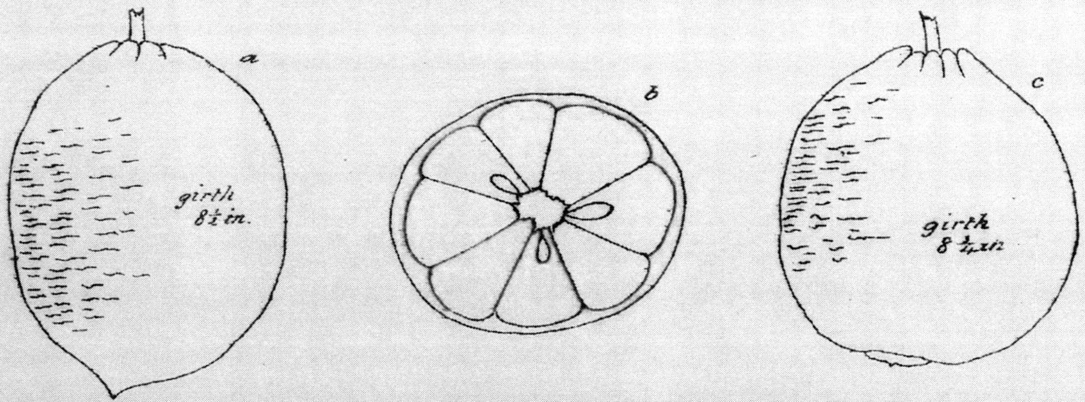

PLATE CXCIX.

Gungolee lemons, sent by Major Buller, Gonda.

a and *b* came from Sheopura. Another of the same shape had a girth of 8 inches. Externally it was of a dull clayey yellow, and in parts with an epidermis not unlike that of a potato. Whether this may have been the work of some insect I do not know. The oil-cells were *convex* and large, like those of the Ceylon pummelos. Rind lemon scented; skin hard and citron-like; pulp pale, like that of the *Bajouras*; seeds many, white, when cut; some were edged with brown, on account of the under pellicle of that colour; juice abundant, and very acid.

c and *d* are spring leaves, which came with it; serrated from the base, tough, and with scarcely any scent.

e is its spine. This lemon appears close to the *Bajouras*.

f and *g* are a *Gungolee nimboo* from Bulrampur. Exterior of a dull fawn yellow; oil-cells indistinct, and very small. In the hand it feels like a potato; slightly aromatic, when scratched; pulp pale, like that of a lemon; juice abundant, and very sour; seeds white, when cut; centre solid.

h and *i* are spring leaves that came with it.

NOTE.—I have met with a *Jhambiri* citrus also of this fawn colour; and I have been told that in Monte Video there is an *orange* which is *always* of this colour.

PLATE CXCIX.

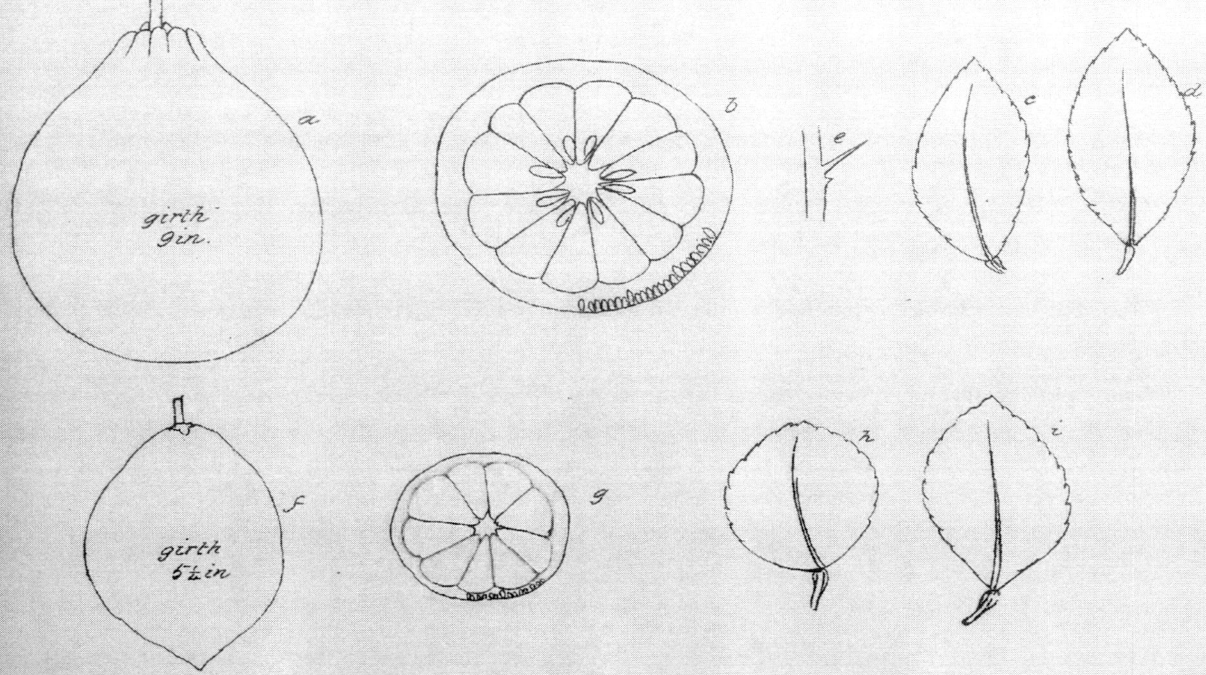

PLATE CC.

Citrus sent by Mr. H. B. Webster, B.C.S. He states he found a thicket of these lemon trees growing wild in a heavy tree jungle in the Taràì, near Barèni, N.W.P. He said the thicket was 10 or 12 feet high, and the trees had 2-inch spines, so that his elephant refused to face it. There were several ripe lemons, but, owing to the spines, only one could be reached. He had never met with wild lemons before. He said the leaves were large, broad, and glossy; he had collected some, but lost them.

a and *b* show the shape of this citrus. Externally deep lemon yellow, quite smooth, with transparent oil-cells of various sizes, neither concave nor convex. In section the oil-cells were indistinct; skin sweet, with lemon aroma; pithy part yellowish-white; pulp pale, transparent, yellowish; juice abundant and very sour, with a *sui generis* flavour. Afterwards, through the directions of Mr. Webster, Mr. MacDonald, C.S., of Moradabad, kindly obtained for me the leaves of this wild lemon. It is situated in the Bazpur tehsil. They are shown in *c*, *d*, and *e*. They appeared to be rain leaves, lemon scented, with a yellow naked petiole, having only two ridges on its upper side. They had a coarse surface, and were more like citron leaves. The flowers were large and tinged with red, and the young shoots were green. The young unexpanded leaves had scattered hairs on their midribs. *f* is the spine I found on the branches.

PLATE CC

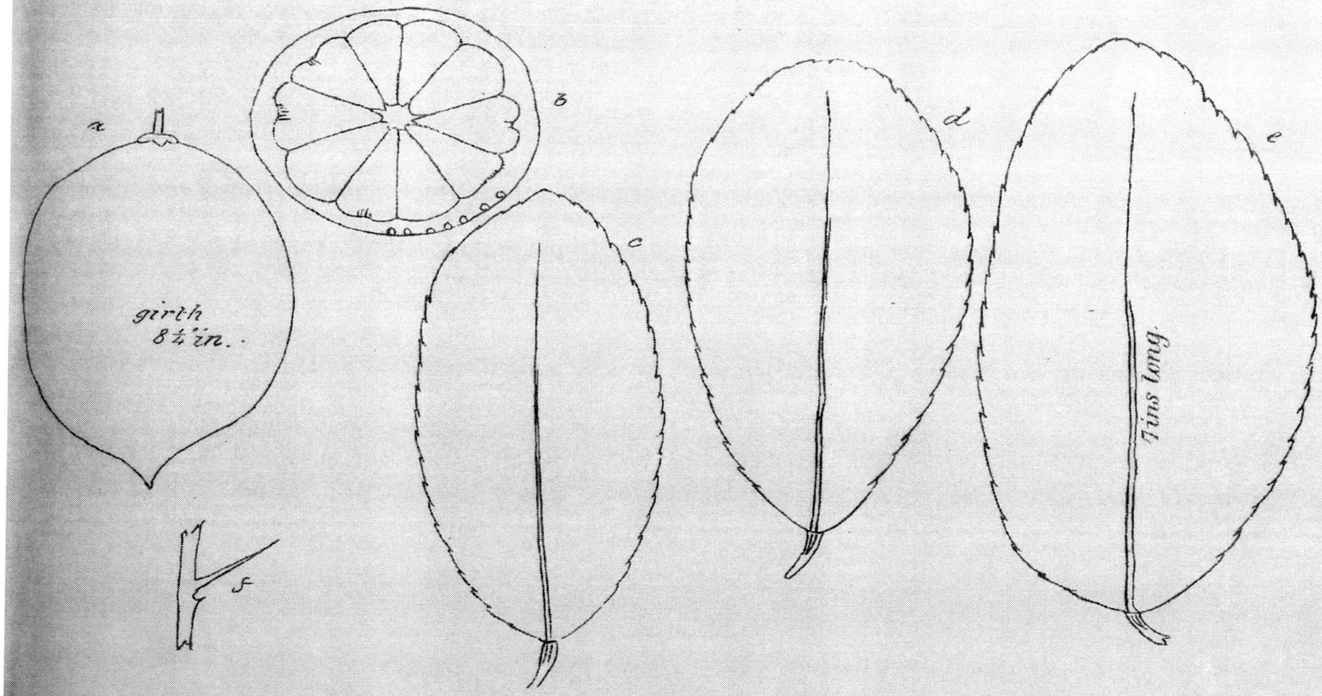

PLATE CCI.

Other forms of lemons.

a, *b*, and *c* came from Calcutta, under the name of *Kagchi lemboo* (long kind). Exterior, when unripe, has distinct foveoli and minute intermediate oil-cells; pulp pale; juice not abundant and sour, with an aroma something like the *Kaghzi nimboo*. Three sizes of oil-cells were visible in the section. *c* is the section of *b*.

d, *e*, and *f* are spring leaves that came with it, and *g* the spines. There was no sign of margins to the petioles.

h, *i*, and *j* came from Lucknow, under the name of *Gungolee nimboo*; surface very smooth and polished, exterior yellow, pulp pale and pure acid; flowers small, very faintly tinged red.

k is a spring leaf, and *l* a rain leaf. Both had a slightly margined petiole.

Note.—Not impossibly the long kind of *Kagchi lemboo* of Calcutta shown at *a*, is of the variety shown in Plates CCV. and CCVI.

PLATE CCI

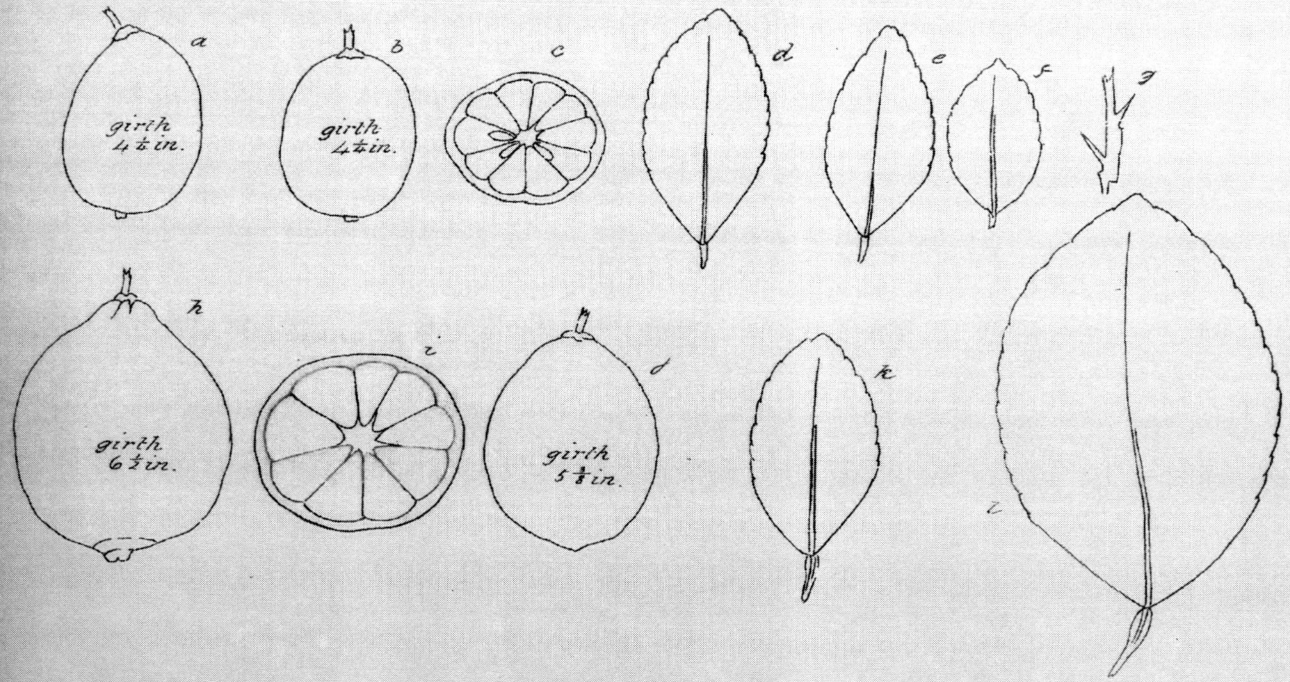
a
girth 4 1/2 in.
b
girth 4 1/4 in.
c
d
e
f
g
h
girth 6 1/2 in.
i
j
girth 5 3/8 in.
k
l

PLATE CCII.

Other forms of lemons.

a, *b*, and *c* are *Behàri nimboo* from Lucknow. Yellow and rather rough; pulp very pale and sour.

d and *e* are its leaves. They did not come with it, but afterwards, so I am not quite sure that they belong to this *Behari nimboo*. The flowers are said to be tinged red.

f and *g* came from Nepal, ticketed *Zamiri*. It was rather unripe, and, if I remember rightly, the pulp was pale and sour. I omitted to note this.

h and *i* are its rain and spring leaves, which were sent afterwards.

PLATE CCII.

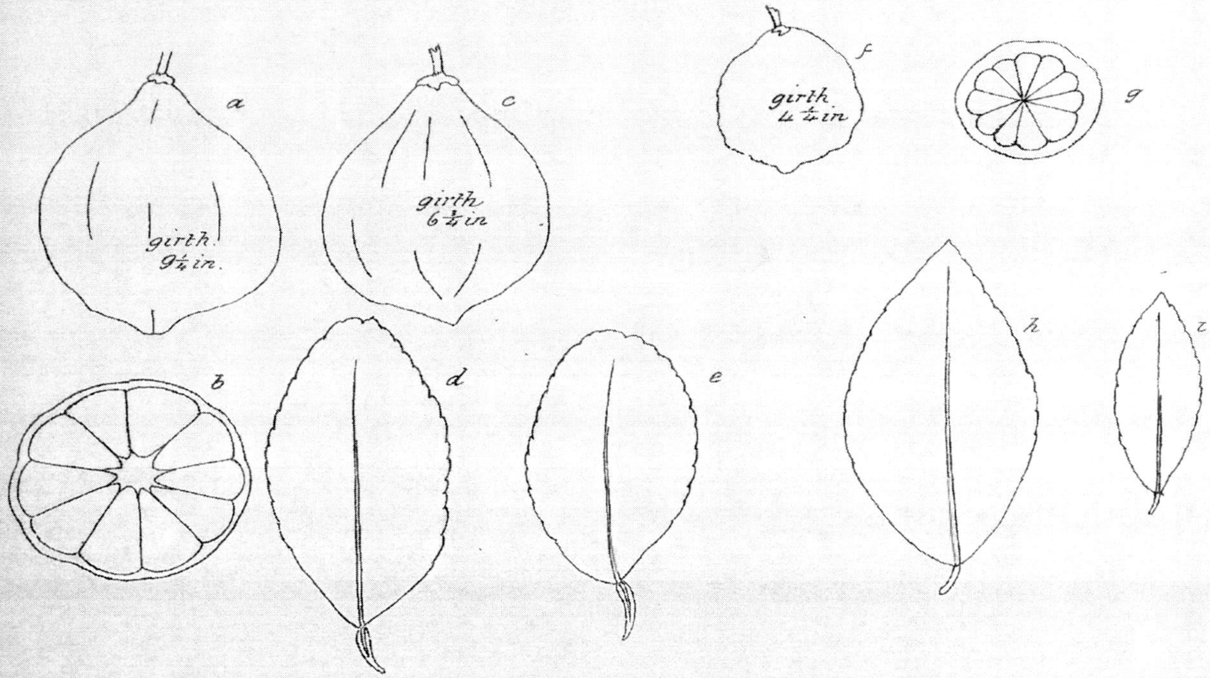

PLATE CCIII.

Behari nimboo, from Messrs. Carew & Co., Rosa, Shahjahanpur.

a and *b* are its shape. Exterior lemon yellow, neither rough, nor very smooth. Skin not thin; pulp pale; juice sour, with the aroma of a *Kaghzi nimboo.*

c is a rain leaf; *d*, *e*, and *f*, spring leaves.

g is its spine.

PLATE CCIII.

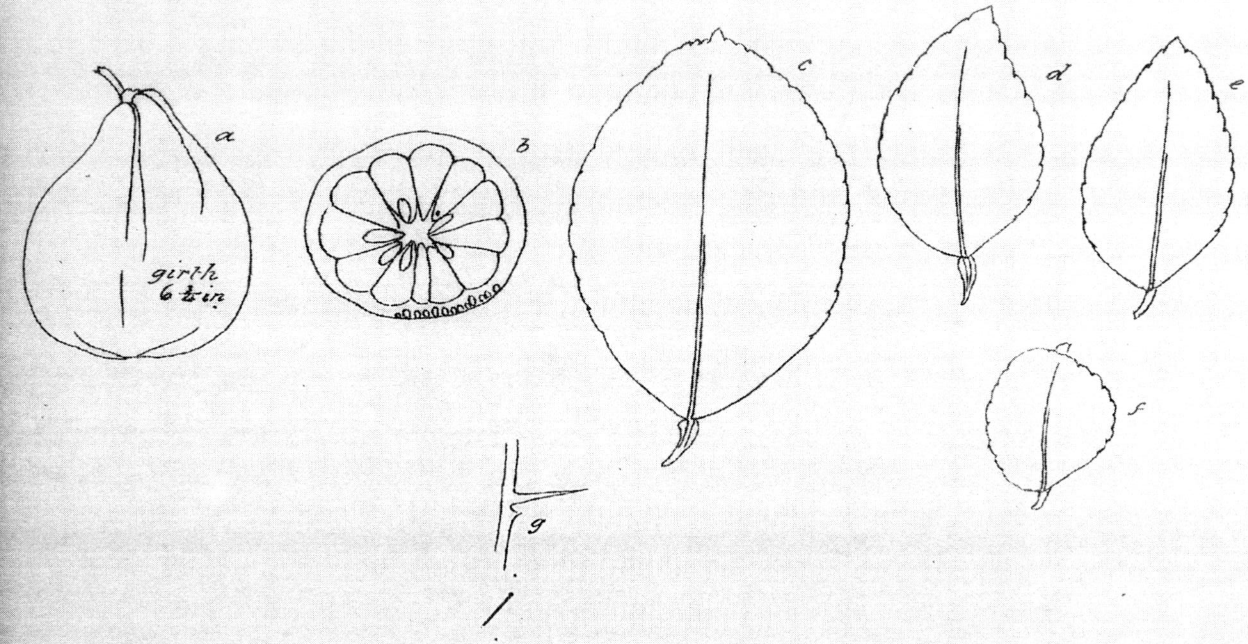

PLATE CCIV.

Behàri kalàn of Lucknow. This is the only place from which I got this variety. It was sent by Mr. Ridley.

a, *b*, and *c* are its forms, rather purse-shaped. The exterior was smooth, but not shiny, pale yellow or buff, studded with oil-glands. It looked like a large lemon; *c* was smoother and yellower than *a*.

b is the section of *a*; skin not thick; pulp pale and lemon like, and as sour, with an aroma *sui generis*; juice-vesicles rather coarse—a desirable variety; centre hollow.

d and *e* are its leaves. They were sent afterwards, and in such cases there is always some doubt as to their belonging actually to the specimen. In *e* there was no joint between the petiole and leaflet, and it is like that of a citron proper. The flowers are said to be large, and coloured red.

PLATE CCIV.

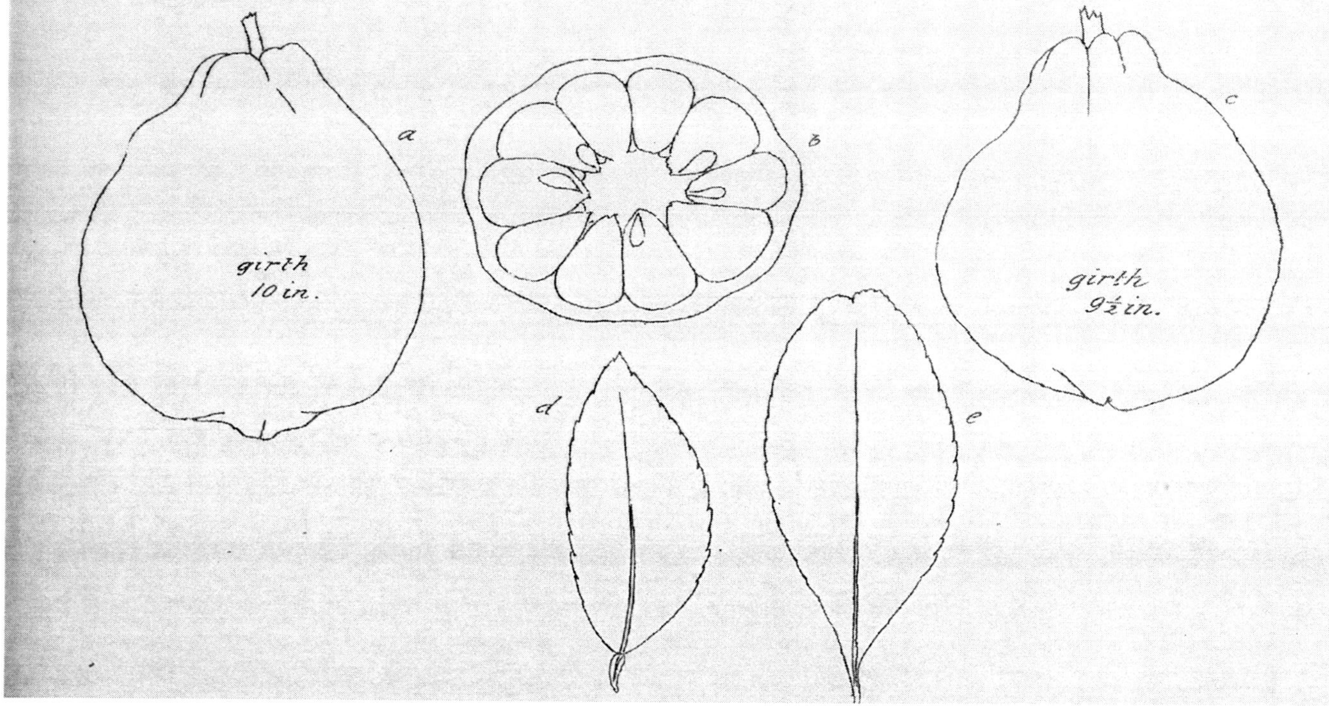

PLATE CCV.

Other forms of lemon.

a and *b* came from Benares, under the name of *Jamiri*. This name and *Zamiri* are evidently a modification of *Jambiri*. It has been given, like *Karna*, to many different varieties of citrus. It is, therefore, impossible to identify any variety from its *native* name. It resembles either the *Behāri* or *Gungolia nimboo*. It is lemon yellow; pulp pale and sour; a good variety.

c, *d*, and *e* came from Allahabad, also under the name of *Jamiri*. This is more like the *Gungolia* of Lucknow and *Gulgul* of Auraya. It is pale yellow. There is no apparent distinction between large and small oil-cells. The surface is closely studded with the minute depressions of the oil-cells; skin thin; pulp pale; juice abundant and very sour. No leaves were sent with either this or the so-called *Jamiri* of Benares. *e′* is a long form of the same. It seems a desirable variety.

f and *g* were sent in August by Dr. Duke, Civil Surgeon of Jhansi. They are of the same var. as *c* and *d*. *h* is a rain leaf, and *i* and *j* spring leaves. *k* is their spine. The branch sent had both the leaves and fruit attached. The branch was very spiny, and the leaves had *not* the *sui generis* aroma of *lime* leaves. The fruit had many seeds, and not the distinctive aroma of *Kaghzi nimboo*. It is known in Buldelcund as *Gangolee*, or *Gulgul*, and in Rohilcund as *Behāri nimboo*.

PLATE CCV.

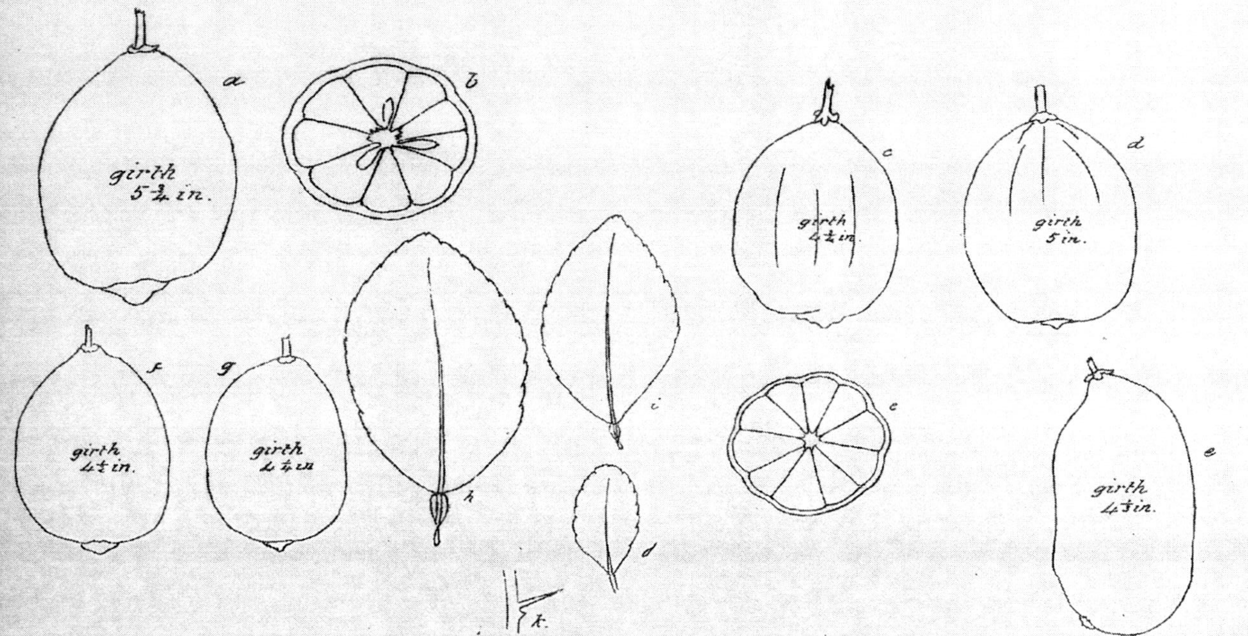
a
girth
5¾ in.
b
c
girth
4½ in.
d
girth
5 in.
f
girth
4½ in.
g
girth
4¼ in
h
i
d
c
e
girth
4⅓ in.
k.

PLATE CCVI.

a and *b* were brought by a friend from Jhansi, purchased in the bazaar there. He did not know the name given there. Inquiries made by letter in Jhansi elicited the reply that this elongated citrus was probably a *Kaghzi nimboo*. This word may mean a distinct variety, or that the variety has a very *thin* skin. *c* is the section of *b*; seeds white, when cut. Pulp pale, with abundant pure acid juice.

d, *e*, *f*, and *g* I purchased at Auraya, Etawah district, under the name of *Gulgul*. No one knew where they were grown. They were evidently brought there for sale. *g* is the section of *f*. In section, both this and the foregoing have the stamp of a *Kaghzi nimboo*. Almost all the specimens had the mammilla to the one side; *f* had it exactly in the middle; pulp greenish-yellow; juice abundant, very acid, with a *sui generis* aroma of a *Kaghzi*.

I tried to get specimens of these elongated limes, with their leaves, and *h*, *i*, *j*, *k*, and *l* were sent to me. It is probably a small specimen of the same. If so, the leaves (spring leaves) appear like those of true limes. Surface of *h* is pale yellow and quite smooth. It is very probable the *Jamiri* of Benares and Allahabad belong to *this* variety (*a* and *d*).

P.S.—On the 17th June, 1886, Mr. J. F. Holcomb sent me *c′* and other similar leaves, stating that he took them off a tree, with fruit like the oblong Jhansi lemon *a* and *b*, from the Government garden at *Bárwa*, twelve miles from Jhansi. This leaf is different from the true lime leaf, and is nearest that of a *lemon*.

PLATE CCVI.

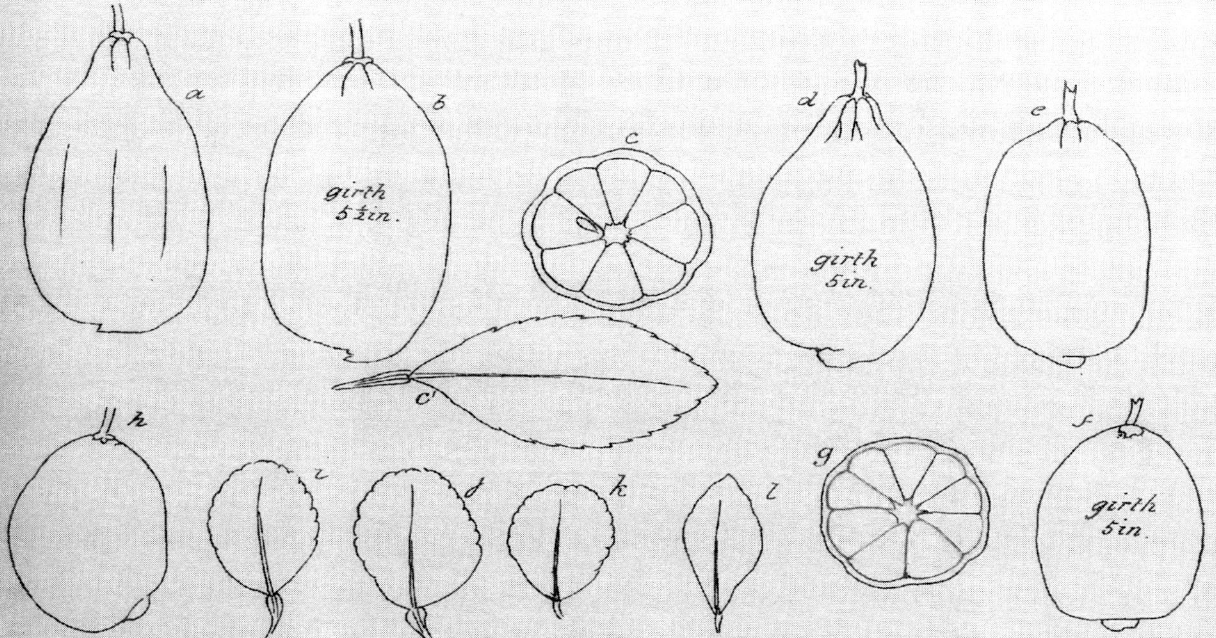

PLATE CCVII.

a and *b* is a globose citrus, which came from Mooltan, under the name of *Niboo*. Exterior pale yellow, studded with minute depressions, so closely set that some ran into others by twos and threes. The surface of this citrus was tinged red, as if inclined to take on the colour of an orange. In some places the colour was decidedly red, in others only suffused with red. This is the only red-cheeked lime or lemon I have seen.

c, *d*, *e*, *f*, and *g* are the leaves which came with it; they appear those of a true lime, and so do the spines *h*. The pulp was pale, juice abundant and acid, with a slightly bitter taste.

i and *j* is a citrus, which came from Calcutta under the name of *Shêrbetee pâti*. It was pale yellow, with a shiny surface; skin very thin, pulp pale, juice abundant, sour, and slightly bitter. The leaves *k*, *l*, and *m* are like those of the *Kaghzi*, and probably it is the same variety as that of Mooltan; *n* is its spine.

PLATE CCVII.

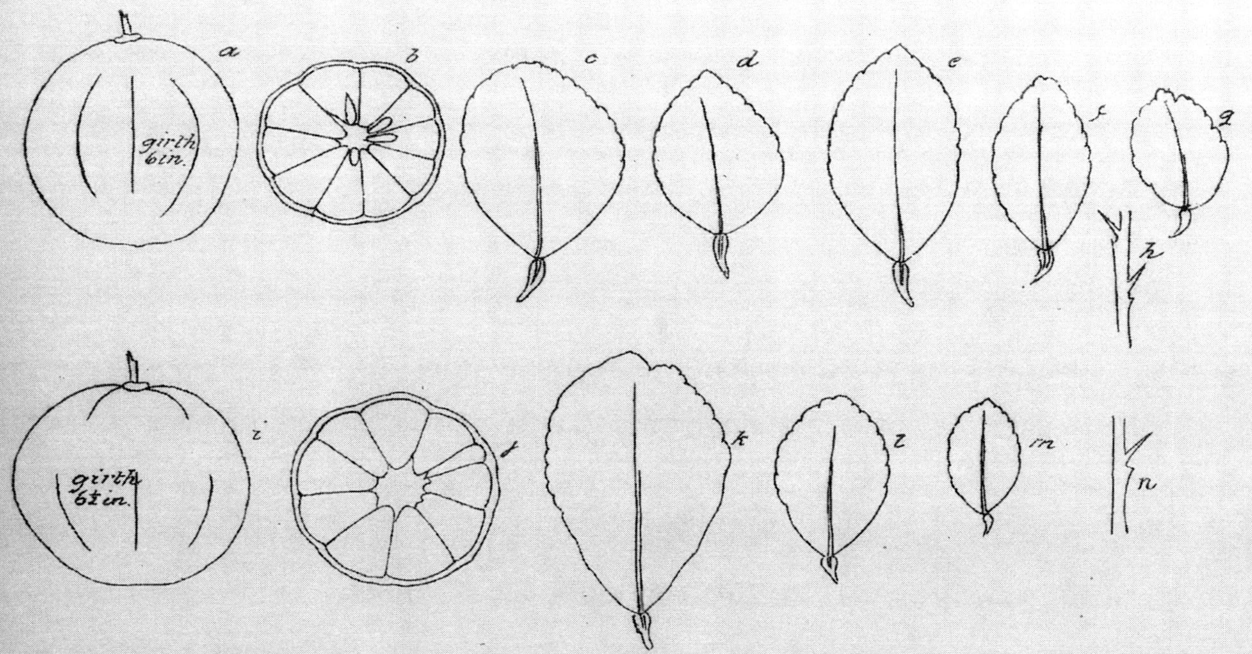

PLATE CCVIII.

A citrus from Khoorja, which came under the name of *Kaghzi nimboo*. (It should be remembered that "kaghzi" means with a skin of *paper*-thickness, and does not always mean any particular variety. It is used, also, for walnuts and *Bæl* fruit.)

a and *b* are its form; pale yellow, very smooth. It floats in water, but not well. It sinks and then rises slowly only to the surface. Pulp pale, juice sour, and slightly bitter, with an aroma *sui generis*.

c and *d* are probably large spring leaves, and *e*, *f*, and *g* small ones—all with a naked, lemon-like petiole.

This citrus, and the two previous ones from Mooltan and Calcutta, have many points in common, viz., the shape, thinness of skin, and a slightly *bitter*, sour juice, but the leaves of this one differ in their petiole from those of the other two. It is not impossible that all three belong to the variety called *Kaghzi kalàn*, which I think is a *lemon*. It is curious that from Khoorja I should receive both this (which may be a *small Khagzi kalàn*) and also a *small Shérbetee nimboo*. (Not improbably these two—the sour and the acidless, are variations of each other.)

PLATE CCVIII.

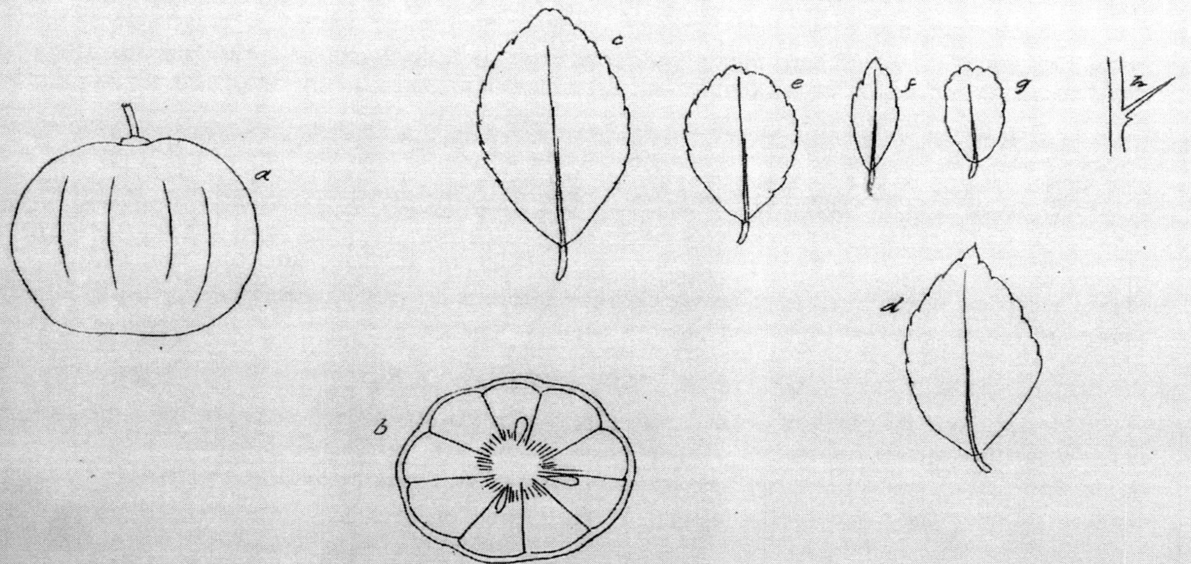

PLATE CCIX

Saddphal of Public Garden, Etawah.

a is a full-sized specimen, and *c* is a smaller one. The surface looks pasty, and is covered, at regular distances, with large foveoli-depressions, shown by the large dots at A. The intermediate spaces are filled with slightly prominent smaller oil-cells. The depressions correspond to the larger oil-cells. The *Saddphal* is pale yellow, when ripe.

b is the section of *a*. Pithy part of skin sweetish; pulp pale, with a slight tinge of orange yellow; juice scanty, with a sweetish, sub-acid flavour. It had slight tinges of orange yellow, here and there, in its pulp.

d is a rain leaf, and *e* and *f* spring leaves. All have very large crenate wings to their petioles, and are leathery. The spines are shown with the leaves. The flowers and young leaves are tinged purple.

h is a pulp carpel, with the side removed, to show the convergence of the juice-vesicles to a common centre. The seeds are also arranged round that centre. *g* are the juice-vesicles of a portion of a pulp carpel. They are pedicelled and spindle-shaped, and have very little juice. The *Saddphal* which came from Benares and Saharunpur do not differ from that of Etawah.

PLATE CCIX.

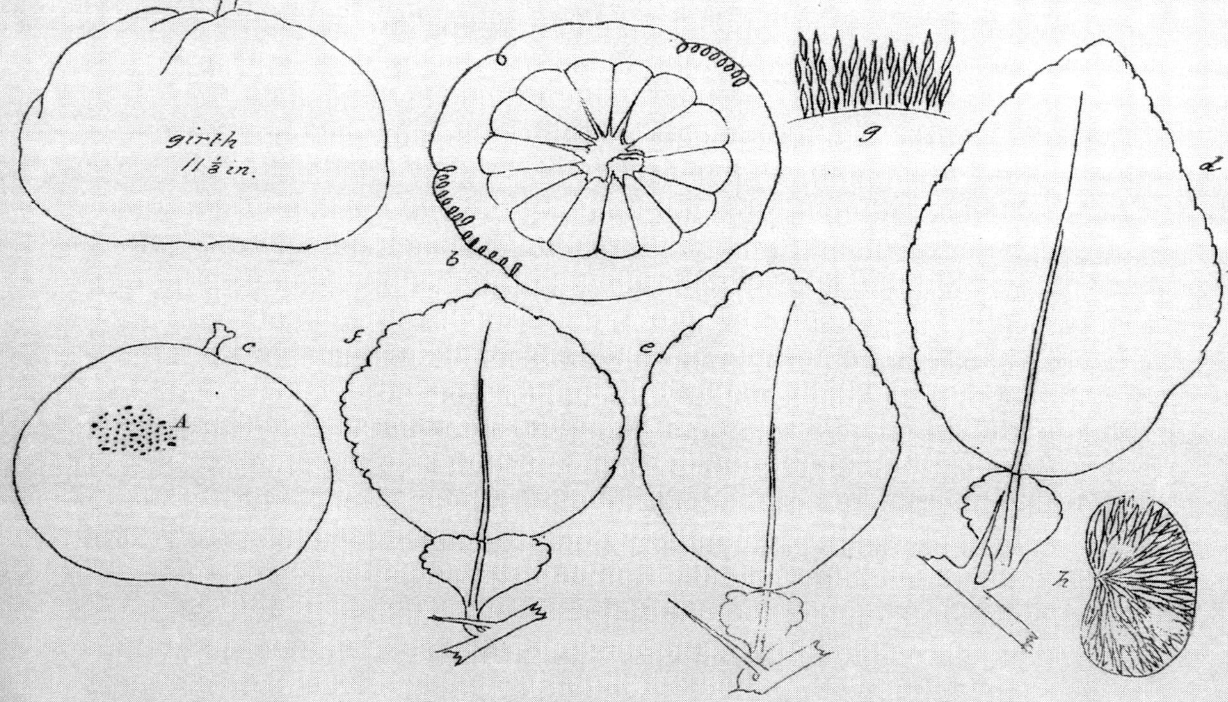

PLATE CCX.

Attàrra nimboo, obtained at one of the railway stations in the Central Provinces.

a is its shape, rugose at the apex, and gathered into folds at the base, otherwise smooth, shiny, and covered with foveoli of all sizes; colour of a clear lemon yellow; the rind has the aroma of the *Sadàphal*; pulp pale, like a lemon. The juice-vesicles are very prettily disposed in the pulp carpels, as shown at *c*. The side vesicles are all long pedicelled, and there are some also at the broad part of the carpel. Their attachments are shown at *f*, *f*. The short sessile vesicles are few, and at the corners *e*, *e*. The carpels are mostly open, and the juice-vesicles project into the hollow centre, as shown in the section *b*. The juice is abundant, and of a pure acid. The skin is comparatively thin; seeds few. Altogether this is a desirable variety.

d is the typical leaf, lanceolate, sometimes emarginate, with scarcely any scent, and with large wings to the petioles. They are leathery, and remind one of pummelo leaves.

PLATE CCX.

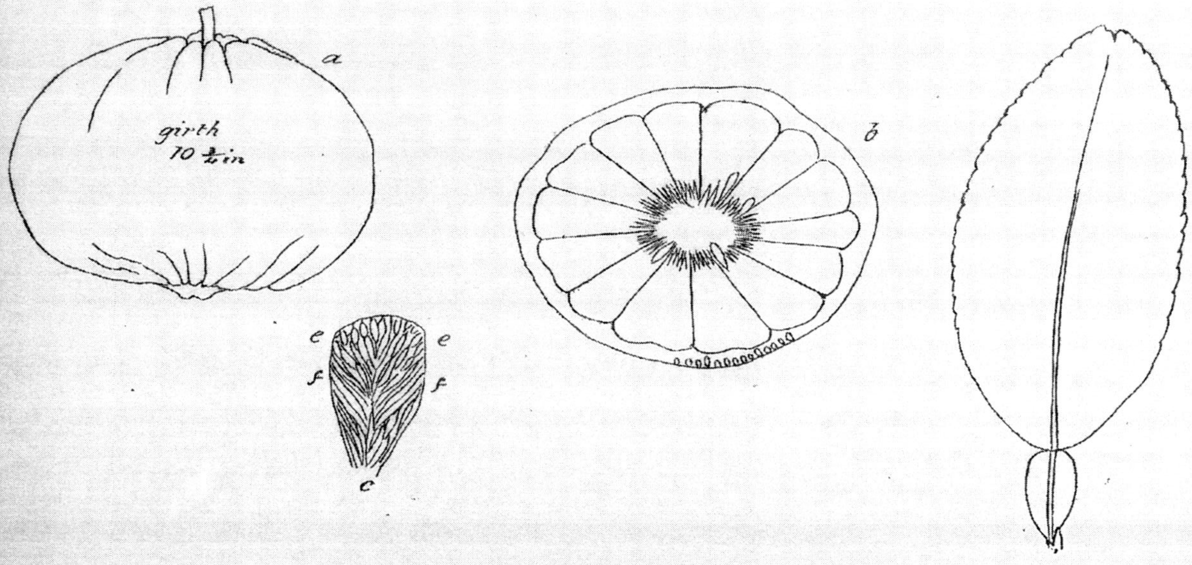

PLATE CCXI.

The *Siderun* of Kandy, Ceylon.

a, *b*, and *c* are one of its forms; lemon yellow; pitted all over with large and small depressions; rugose and furrowed at base and apex, with small warty prominences here and there. Otherwise it is fairly smooth.

b is the section of *a*. Pulp yellowish white; juice abundant and pure acid; juice-cells prettily disposed, like those of the *Attárra nimboo* (*vide* Plate CCX.). They also take root from the sides of the carpels, with short cells at the circumference. This appears allied to the *Attárra* of the Central Provinces of India. In Ceylon some pronounce the name *Sidrung*. *Rung*, I was told, in Singhalese meant *gold*. Persons who knew the language thought the name an imported word. Probably it is a modification of the English word *citron*. In the Kandy market, the sellers call this *Siderun*, and the citron proper *Nátherun*. Others, when asked, reversed the names.

PLATE CCXI.

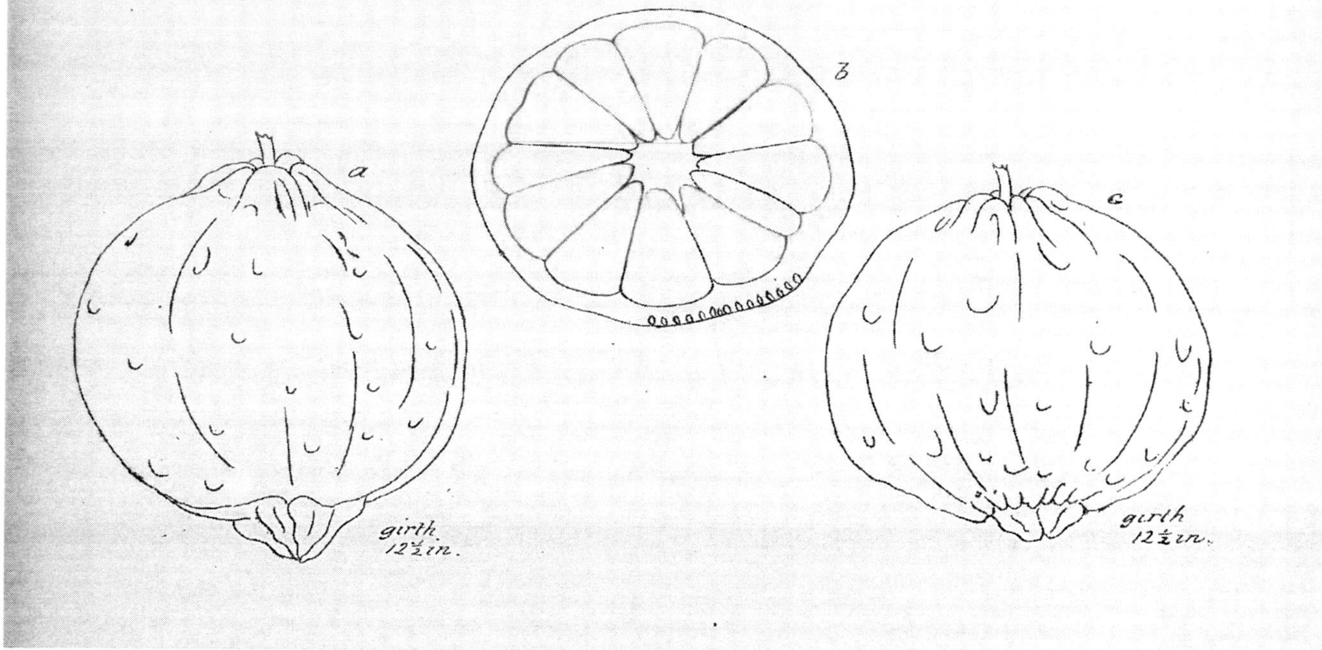

PLATE CCXII.

Another *Siderun*, more furrowed and warty than the previous one.

a shows its external appearance, more warty round the apex.

b is a rain leaf, and *c* a spring leaf. They are not flat like pummelo leaves (though, like them, they are thick and leathery), but curved and curled. They have a faint lemon scent, and the petioles are broadly margined. *d* is its spine.

The *Siderun* has a lemon flavour, both in its juice and rind.

PLATE CCXII.

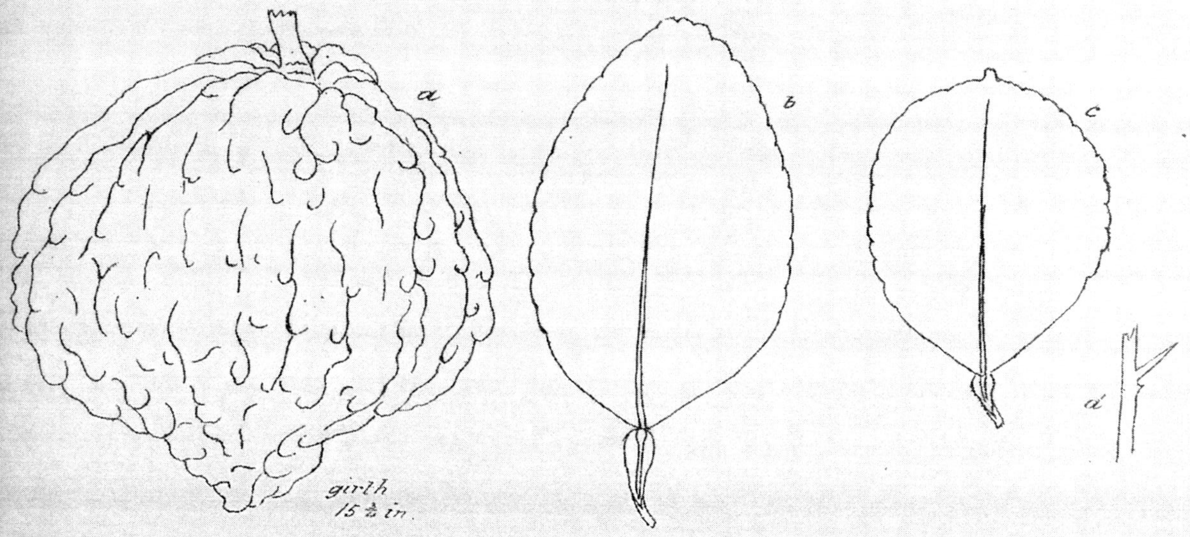

PLATE CCXIII.

This is a citrus, sent from the Botanic Garden, Saharunpur, under the name of *Amalbẹ̄d.*

a is its shape, pale lemon yellow, furrowed, and with ridged dough-like folds, converging towards both base and apex. The apex is flattened. Rind aromatic and covered with shallow foveoli.

b is its section. Pulp very pale and transparent, like the *Attárra nimboo,* with the same herring-bone disposition of its juice-vesicles; juice very abundant, and pure acid.

c is a rain leaf, with large wings to its petioles; and *d* is a spring leaf, with its petiole only broadly margined. The leaves are crenate, and have a faint lemon scent. This citrus is a good kind, and has most of the characters of the *Attárra nimboo.*

Perhaps all the *Attárra* citrus ought, more naturally, to be grouped with the *Amalbēds.*

PLATE CCXIII.

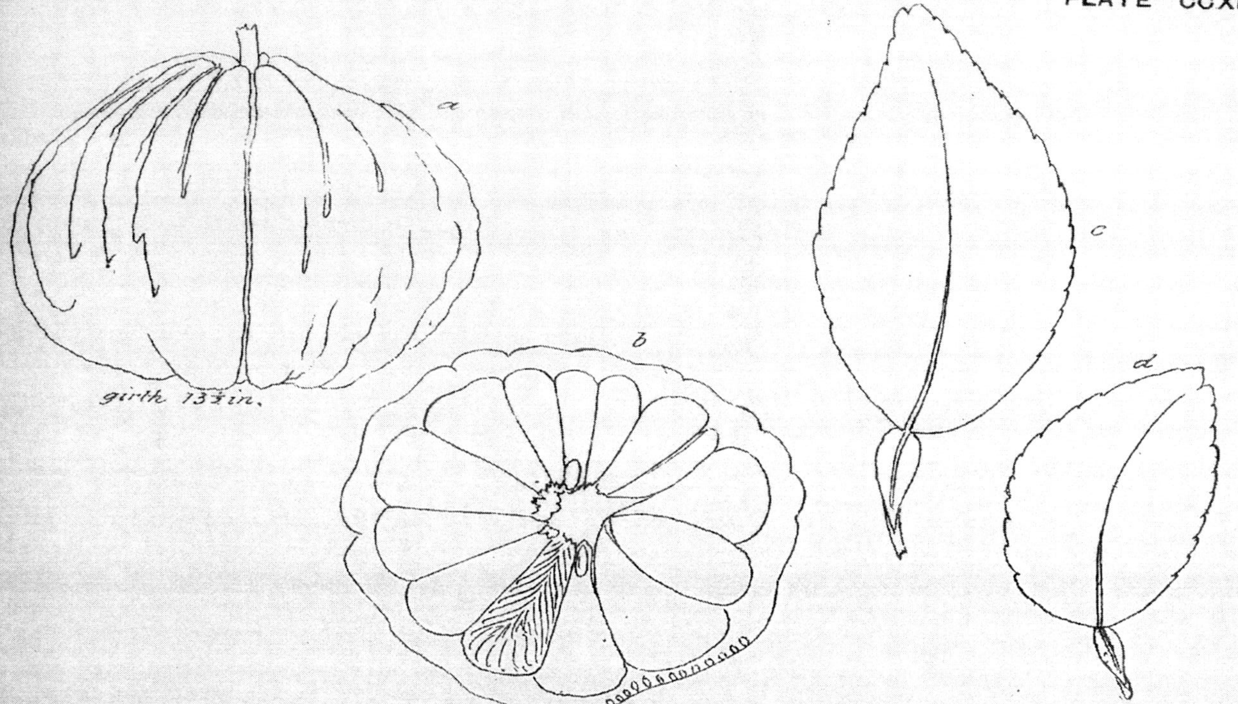

PLATE CCXIV.

This is a citrus of the *Attárra* variety, obtained from the garden of the Maharajah of Ulwar. The skin is lemon scented and lemon flavoured; the colour is lemon yellow. In section it has all the characters of an *Attárra* (see Plate CCX.). The pulp is pale and sour. The juice-vesicles have the disposition of *c* in the same plate.

b is a fully-developed rain leaf.

c and *d* are spring leaves.

e is an ordinary spine, and *f* the spine of a young luxuriant cane, with an angular, ribbed stem.

This and the following specimens were received, or met with, after the others had been arranged and numbered. They are therefore placed at the end of the group.

PLATE CCXIV

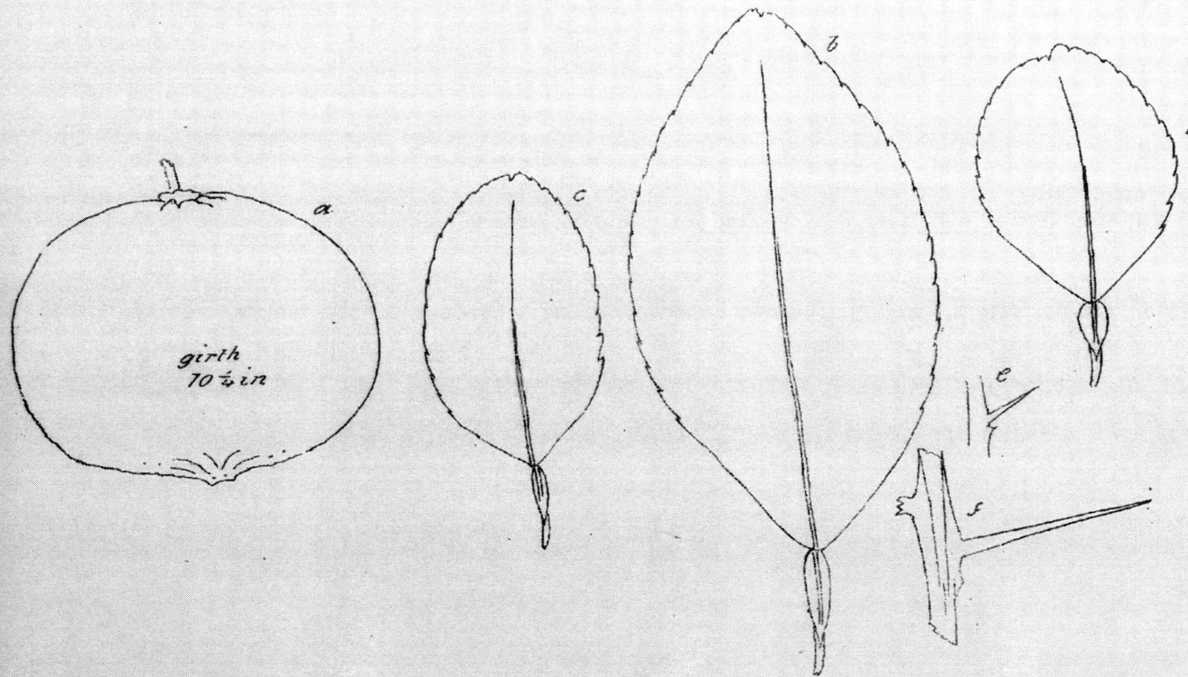

PLATE CCXV.

This is a *Bajoura* lemon, obtained from the garden of the Maharajah of Ulwar.

a and *c* show its outline. It is yellow and smooth, like a lemon, only slightly foveolate. It is scarcely distinguishable from a Malta lemon. Its mammilla is more drawn out than in the latter. It is very like the "Goosery" lemon of Mr. Stalkartt, and not impossibly may have come from Calcutta.

b is its section, showing a thin skin, though tough. The pulp is very acid, and lemon flavoured. The rind is lemon scented, and tougher than that of the Malta lemon (*vide* Plate CLXXXIII.).

c has its apex more chagrined.

d is a rain leaf, and *e* a spring leaf. They are *Bajoura*-like, and their nerves are depressed below the surface. The spines are small.

PLATE CCXV.

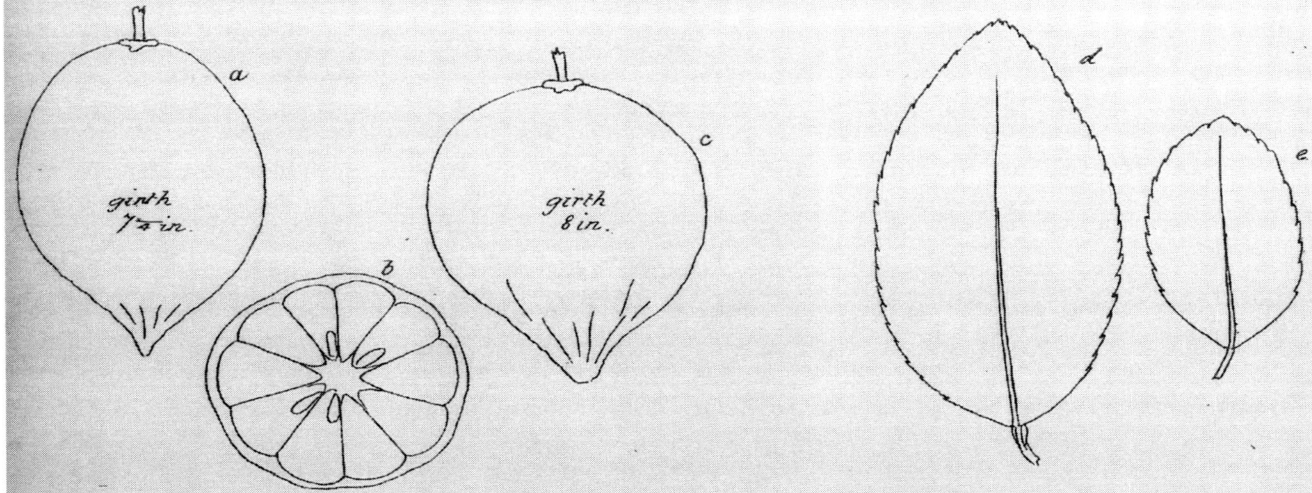

PLATE CCXVI.

This is another *Bajoura* lemon, taken from the garden of the Maharajah of Ulwar. Externally it is like an elongated Malta lemon, with a tougher skin.

b is its section, with a rather thin skin; pulp white and acid, though not sharply so; centre hollow. This specimen was seedless. Another specimen from another tree was many-seeded. It had elongated and also rounded fruits.

c is a rain leaf, and *d* a spring, well-developed, leaf. Their edges are serrated, and their petioles only ridged on the upper part. They resemble the leaves of the *Bajoura*.

Taking everything into consideration, I think that there appears little doubt that the lemon of Europe has descended from the citron proper, the *Turunj*, probably passing through the intermediate forms of the *Bajouras*. It is probable that these *Bajoura* lemons are indigenous forms, with a tough, solid skin, although comparatively thin. In India they have been probably selected further into the *Kaghzi Kalán*, and in Europe into the Malta and Sicilian lemons, which have a *softer* skin.

PLATE CCXVI.

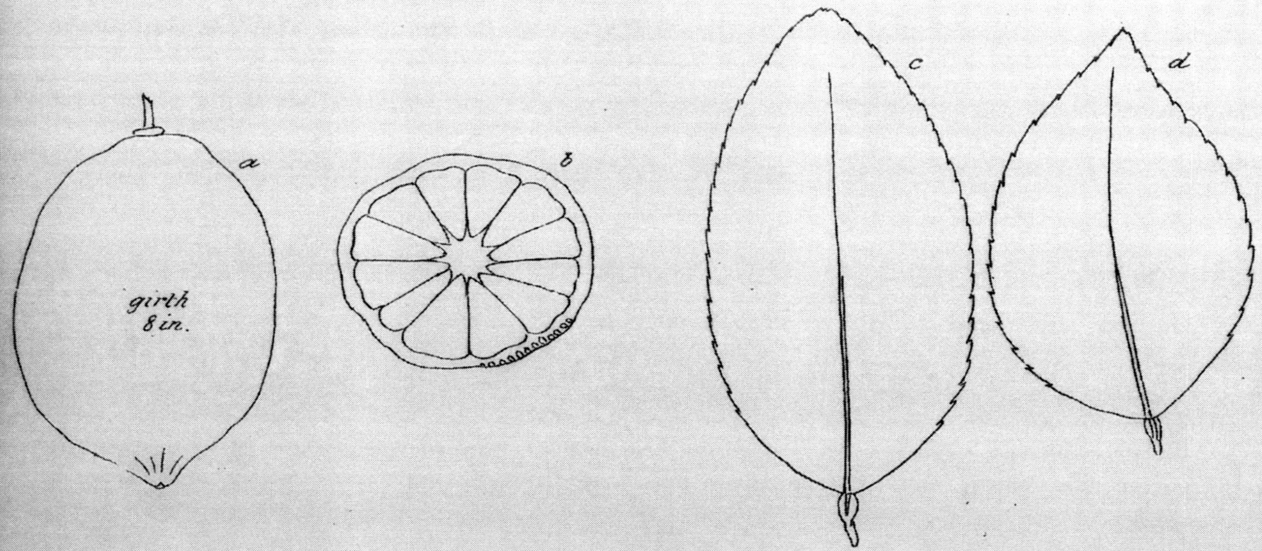

PLATE CCXVII.

a and *b* are a long lemon from Ulwar. It is like those obtained from Jhansi, at Plate CCVI. It is pale citrine, with a thicker skin, aromatic, but not of a pleasant flavour. I met with a similar long lemon in the Taj Garden. The gardener in the latter place told me that if this lemon is kept it becomes bitterish.

c is the form and size of its seed, different from that of the *Kaghzi nimboo*, or true lime.

d, *e*, and *f* are its leaves, with either a long and linear petiole, as in *e*, or with a short and winged petiole, as at *f* and *g*.

g and *h* show also other forms of petioles, from the same tree.

i is its spine.

Having had an opportunity of examining this citrus on the tree, I think I have rightly placed this and the Jhansi long citrus of Plate CCVI. and others among the *lemon* group, which, I think, is distinct from the *lime* group.

PLATE CCXVII.

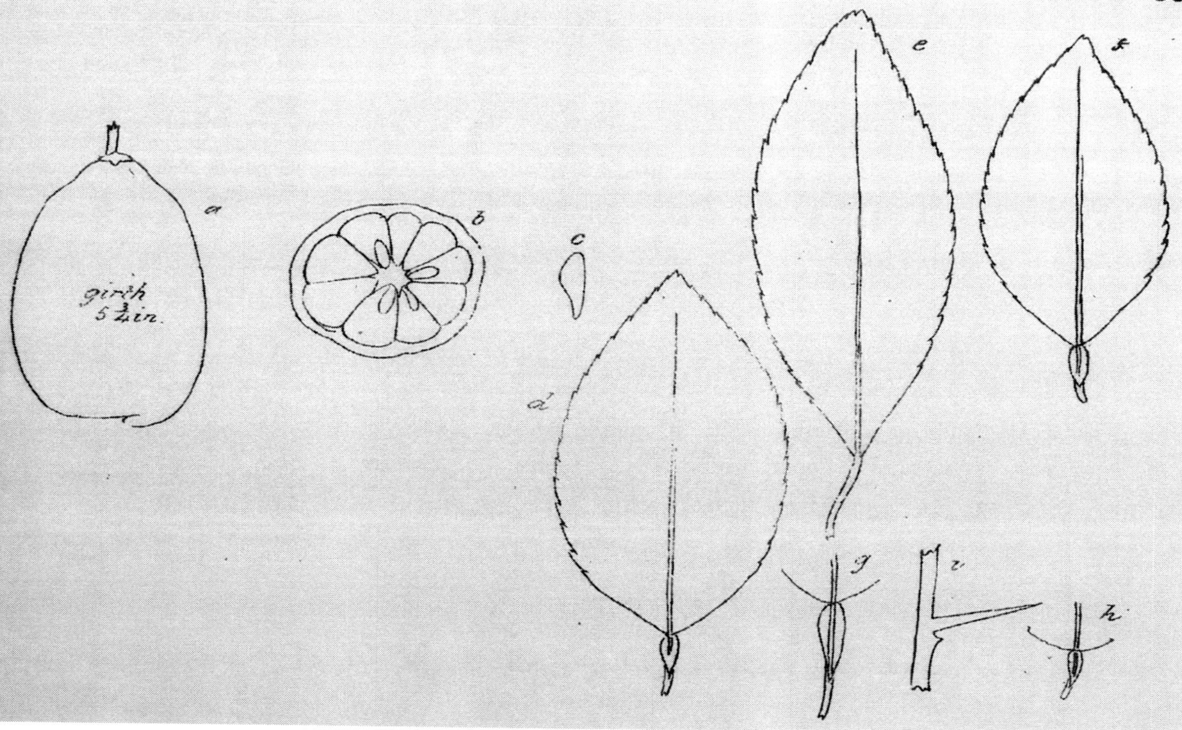

PLATE CCXVIII.

a and *b* are a specimen of the Almòra lemon sent by Mr. H. Harris. When ripe, it is deep lemon yellow, studded with large foveoli, especially on the apex half. The rind is not so aromatic as that of the Malta lemon; pulp pale, and full of sour juice. It is a desirable variety where a large quantity of juice is wanted at one time.

c and *d* are rain leaves.

e and *f*, spring leaves.

This variety is the same as the *Kumaon lemon*, only of a smaller size. The immense leaf, *c*, is probably due to the rich, moist soil of Almora.

NOTE.—All citrus trees sometimes give off long shoots from the base of the trunk. These then bear *large luxuriant leaves*.

PLATE CCXVIII.

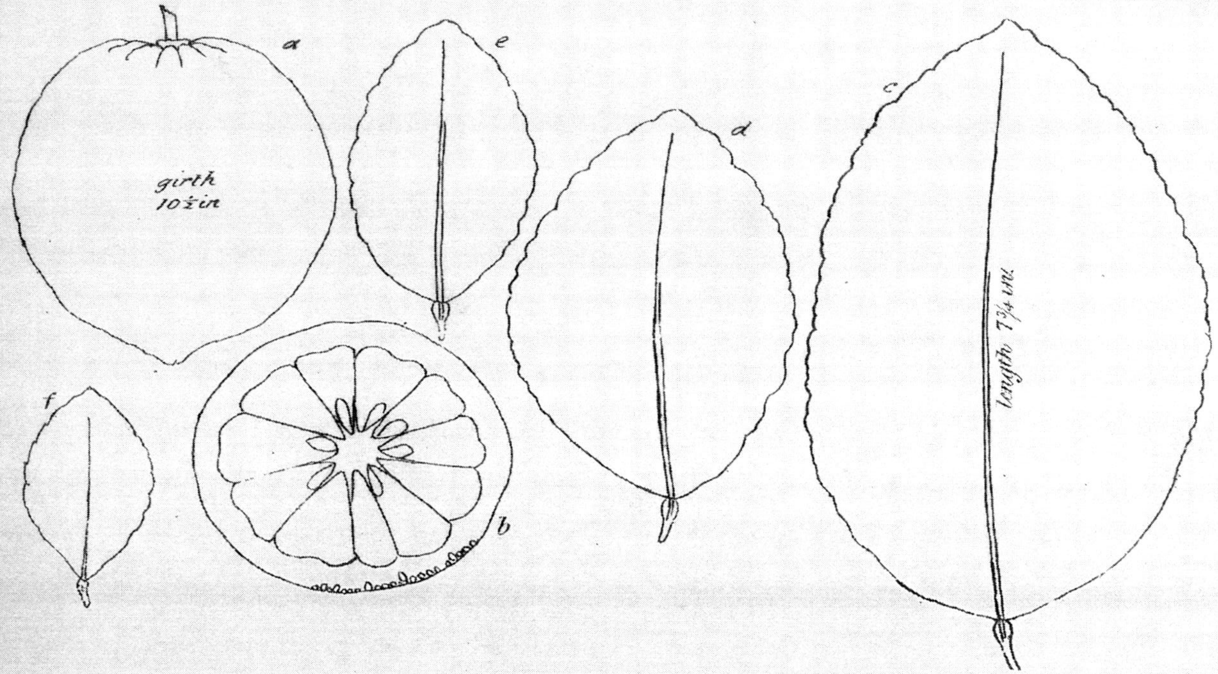

PLATE CCXIX.

This is the *Shôr*, or *Gangolée nimboo*, of Almora, sent by Mr. H. Harris. It appears a *Bajoura* lemon.

a and *b* are its outline and section. The exterior is shiny, hard, and of a pale citrine colour, slightly uneven, with rather large and distant foveoli. It is sub-warty round the apex. The skin is tough and aromatic, like that of a *Bajoura*. The pulp is pale, transparent, and sour; seeds many, with a brown pellicle under the outer shell; white, when cut.

c and *d* are typical leaves and well developed; thin, but not channelled at the ribs.

e is a spring leaf.

NOTE.—By *Bajoura* lemon I mean a transition form between the *Bajoura* and the lemon proper. I have mentioned two transition forms, viz. *lemon-citron*, that is, a citron approaching the lemon type; and *citron-lemon*, that is, a lemon having still some citron characters. I look upon the *Bajouras* as half-way forms between the citrons proper and the lemons proper; so that *Bajoura lemon* would be a still further *lemonized* form of the *Citrus medica* than the *Bajoura*.

PLATE CCXIX.

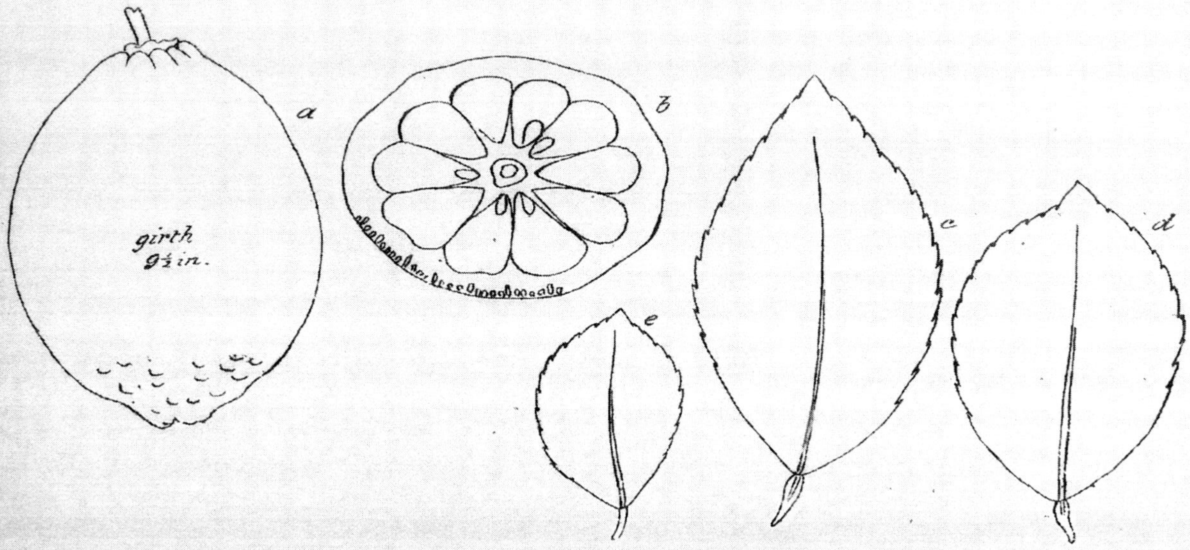

PLATE CCXX.

This plate shows specimens of a large lemon received from Pertabgurh, in Oudh; it was sent by Mr. J. A. Luffman.

b is a section of *a*. When ripe it is yellow and smooth, with scarcely any foveoli. The skin is rather thin and aromatic, the pulp pale, transparent; juice very abundant and sour; centre hollow.

c is a more elongated form of *a*.

d and *e* came from the same bunch as the other two, which contained five lemons. The pulp is pale greenish, with long and slender juice-vesicles. The juice is not *sharply* acid, and of not so pure a flavour as that of the European lemon.

All five lemons were of this shape, and all had a very small mammilla. This variety appears distinct, and not unlike the Punjab *Gulgul*, shown on Plate CLXXXVI., Fig. *f*.

PLATE CCXX.

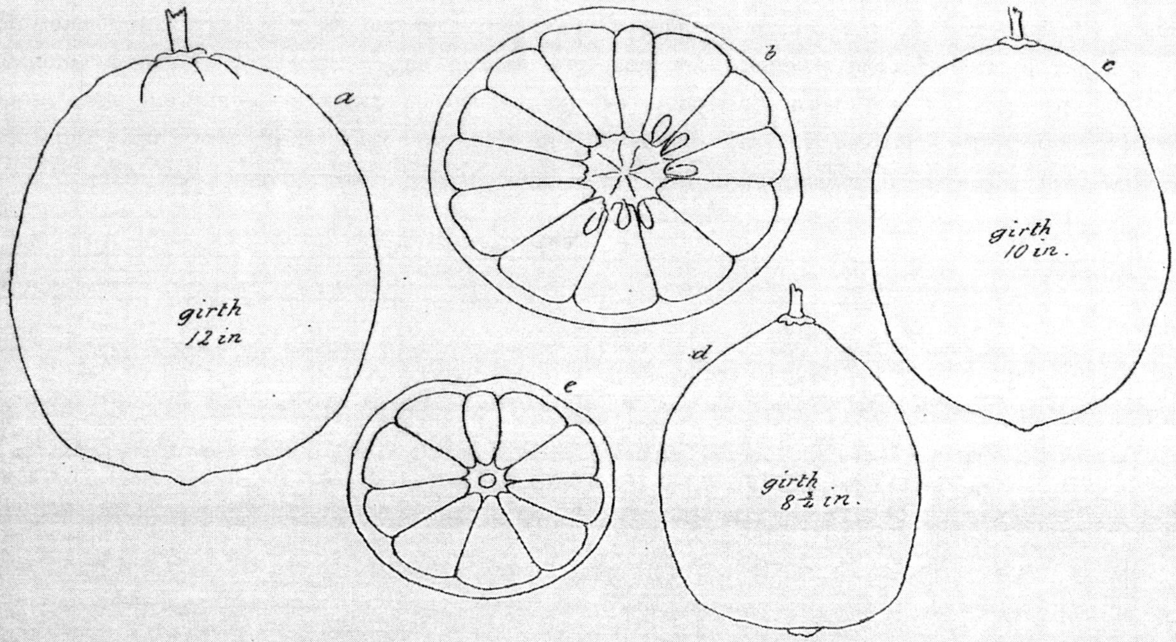

PLATE CCXXI.

These leaves are of the Pertabgurh lemon of Plate CCXX.

a and *b* are fully-developed rain leaves.

c, *d*, and *e* are spring or dry-weather leaves.

NOTE.—As stated, large leaves, such as *a*, are not uncommon on the new cane-like branches, which are given from the base of the stem, near the ground. In Europe, probably these cane-like branches would be pruned off, as detracting from the strength of the tree, without adding to the fruit. The flowers and fruit are produced from the small twigs of the previous year; therefore, in pruning, the latter should be encouraged by removing the former, which may not produce flowers till after several years. (See Chapter on "Cultivation of the Citrus.")

PLATE CCXXI.

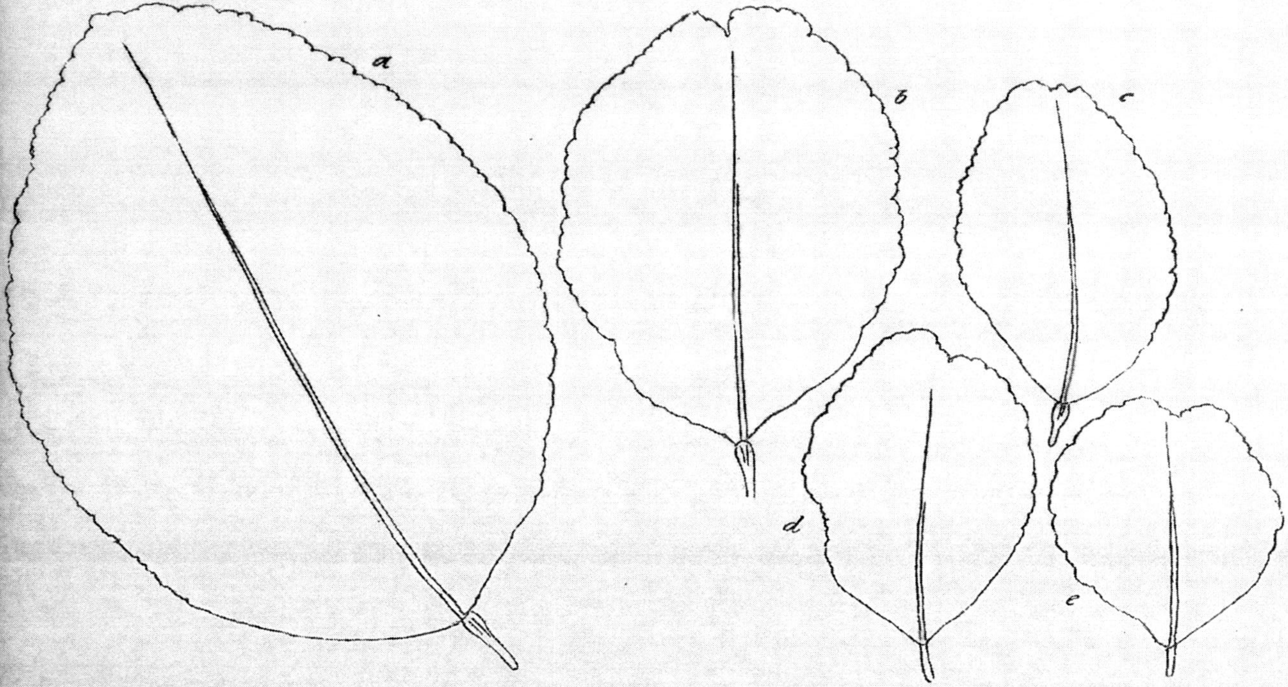

PLATE CCXXII.

a and *b* is the sweet *Gulgul* of Saharunpur. It was plucked in October, and rather unripe, and of a *dark* green colour. It grows larger by ripening. The rind is very aromatic, but has not a pleasant taste. The pulp is white, and in its unripe state dry and insipid—neither sweet nor acid—like that of the *Saddphal.* It appears a sweet or insipid *Bajoura.* I had not met with a sweet *Bajoura* before; it may have descended from the sweet *Turunj* or *Madhkakree.*

c and *d* are its typical leaves.

The essential oil of this specimen, like the "lima" of Ceylon, tinged paper permanently, of a *gamboge yellow.*

e and *f* are the *Behdri* lemon from Saharunpur, plucked also in October and unripe; when ripe, it is slightly larger. It is foveolate all over, and lemon scented. The rind and pulp are of a lemon flavour. The latter is white and acid. This specimen was seedless.

g is its well-developed typical leaf, with a wavy surface, serrated, but not prominently so, and slightly lemon scented.

h was a small and smooth leaf of the same.

NOTE.—In forwarding the specimen of Plate CLXXXVII., possibly it was mistaken for this sweet *Gulgul*, as that on Plate CLXXXVII. was *not* sweet.

PLATE CCXXII.

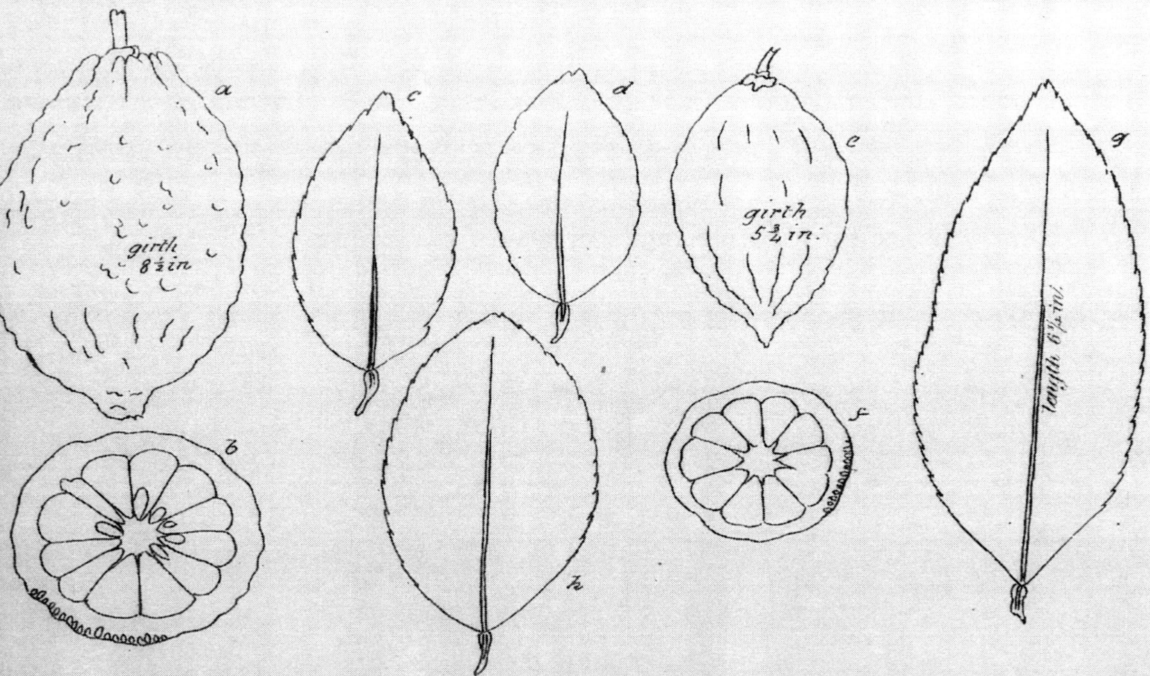

PLATE CCXIII.

a and *b* are a double lemon which I got off a tree in Etawah. It was quite seedless.

c and *d* are another double lemon, which I got at an English shop. It came from Palermo, and had seeds.

These double lemons were formed by a fusion, or fasciation of two ovaries. In *d* the centres of the two lemons are quite separate. In *b*, however, there is a tendency to fusion of the centres, in order to produce an elongated common centre.

NOTE.—It is not improbable that the large varieties of citrus may have originated either by proliferation of extra carpels between the normal ones, or, as in this case, by a *fusion of two ovaries*. I have examined three double lemons, and in no case did the rind extend *inwards* between the two lemon pulps.

With reference to double fruit, *vide* Appendix 21, on the Indian *Philippine*.

PLATE CCXXIII.

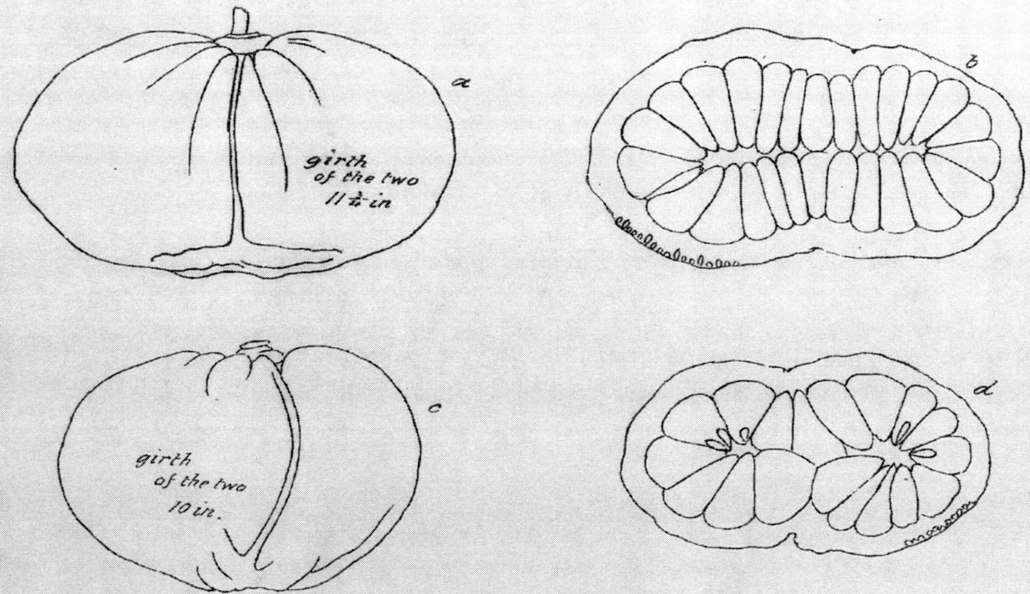

PLATE CCXXIV.

a and *b* is another double lemon, which I also got from an English shop. It also came from Palermo. I give it here, because it also shows the amalgamation of the two centres, producing *one* elongated centre. This specimen had many perfect seeds, and, therefore, this fasciation of the two ovaries might possibly be reproduced through the seeds, and by selection *fixed* into a large citrus variety, as in Plates LXXII. and LXXXIII. A double fruit would naturally take the fancy of Orientals; they have their own game of *Philippine*, and, if they obtained seeds, they would almost surely sow them, to obtain a continuance of this doubleness. I think it probable that many large kinds of citrus may have originated in this way, and by selection perfected, so as to lose all trace of their *double* origin.

c, *d*, and *e* are the leaves and spines of a wild citrus, found by Mr. Duthie, "growing in the Sarjoo Valley; elevation, 2 to 3,000 feet. It had all the appearance of wildness, there being no villages anywhere. There was a small stream, beside which it was growing, and by which the seed was most likely conveyed from some village above."—Ranikhet, 9th September, 1886. (*Vide* Webster's lemon, Plate CC.)

PLATE CCXXIV.

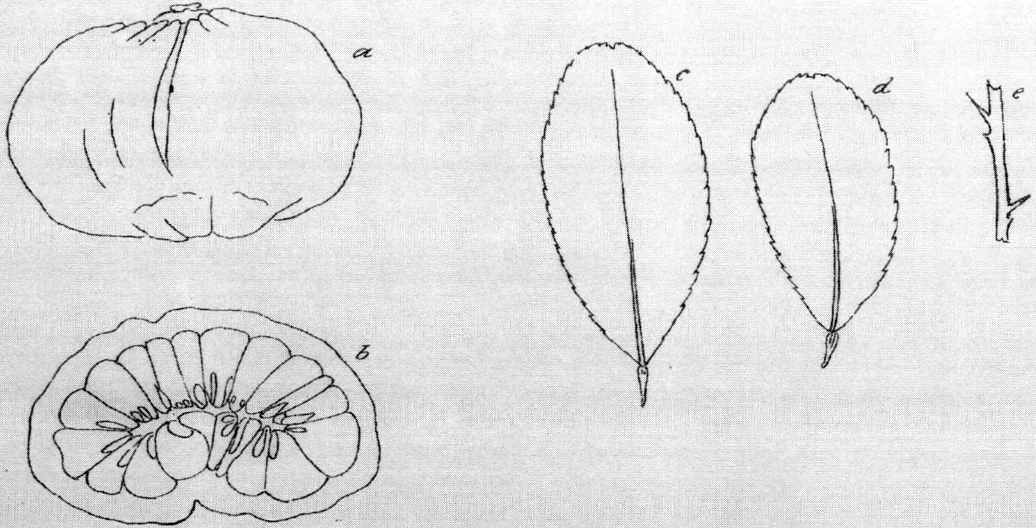

PLATE CCXXV.

Lima of Ceylon, or *Kúdalu dehi* (Leech lime or Caffre lime). This is not eaten, but is used for washing the hair, and for rubbing on the feet and legs, as an antidote against land-leeches.

a and *b* are the outline and section of the *Lima*; *c* is a smaller specimen; both were unripe, and very warty, the warts being studded with foveoli. The rind is thick, with an aromatic, resinous scent, and a bitter acrid taste. The essential oil contains a gamboge-yellow pigment, which permanently stains paper *yellow*. Pulp greenish, and juice-vesicles small; seeds greenish, when cut; pulp sour, and of a very unpleasant flavour. A riper specimen I got at Colombo had greenish pulp with small vesicles; juice very sour, with a *sui generis* aroma, not unlike that of the *Kaghzi nimboo*. The rind had a very unpleasant acrid taste and resinous scent. Dr. Trimen's foreman said it is sometimes larger than this specimen.

d and *e* are fully-developed rain leaves; dark green, thick, and leathery, with their edges slightly turned backwards; the oil-glands of the leaf-blade and petiole wings are of various sizes, as also on their edges. They have no special aroma. The petiole wings are sometimes almost as large as the leaflet, or larger, and both glabrous.

f and *g* are spring leaves. The flowers are small, *slightly* tinged red, either male or bi-sexual, and often with four petals, with either separate or partially-united stamen-filaments.

k are the spines of the lima.

h and *i* are *lime* leaves, with small petiole wings; *j* is a well-developed leaf of the Ceylon *Kaghzi nimboo*, or lime, with a large petiole, given for comparison. The small leaves of the *lima* and the large leaf of the lime have similar wings to their petioles.

PLATE CCXXV.

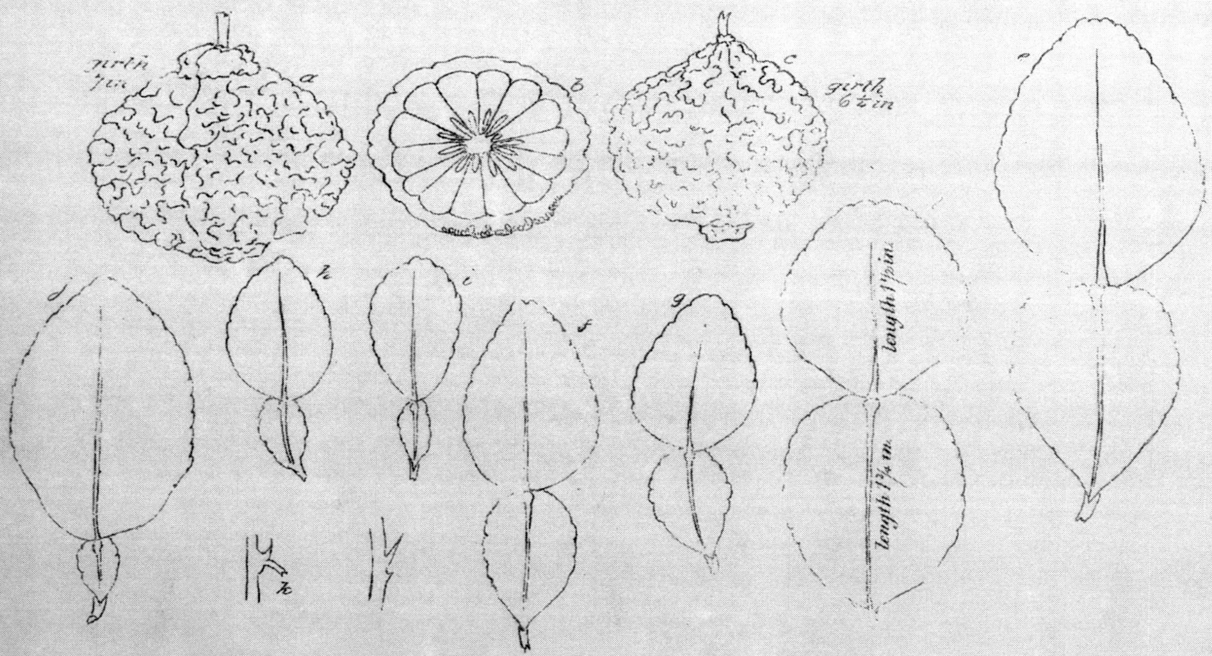

PLATE CCXXVI.

These figures are taken from the illustrations of the Flora Amboyn. of Rumphius, published in 1750.

a is *Limo ventricosus*, Vol. II., Tab. xxvi., Fig. 1. It is yellow when ripe, thick skinned, and used for washing the head; pictured by Rumphius with four petals. This corresponds with *C. Hystrix* D.C. of Kurz, Flor. of Brit. Burma. It also corresponds with the *Lima* of Ceylon; both are used for washing the head. The Cingalese, in addition, have discovered that it is useful against land-leeches, and have given it the name of *Kúdalu dèhi*. The Caffre regiments of Ceylon used it for similar purposes, and hence a third name among the English there is *Caffre Lime*.

b is *Limo agrestis*, Vol. II., Tab. xxvii. (Dutch—*Wilde pap. Leimen*) *Citrus papeda* of Miquel. Very yellow colour; pulp sour and acrid. This is evidently a close connection of *a*. It has retained its broad petiole wings, and has lost some of its warts. At the same time it is acrid like the *lima*, and pictured by Rumphius with four petals.

c is *Limo ferus*, Tab. xxviii., Vol. II., also pictured with four petals. It is another variety closely connected with *Limo ventricosus*. It retains the broad petiole wings of *Limo ventricosus*, and the fruit, though small, is still tubercled. The spines of *b* and *c* are like those of the *Kaghzi nimboo*.

d, e, f, g, and *h* are leaves from a rain-shoot of the *Kaghzi nimboo*, Etawah, given here for comparison. They have unusually large wings to their petioles.

PLATE CCXXVI.

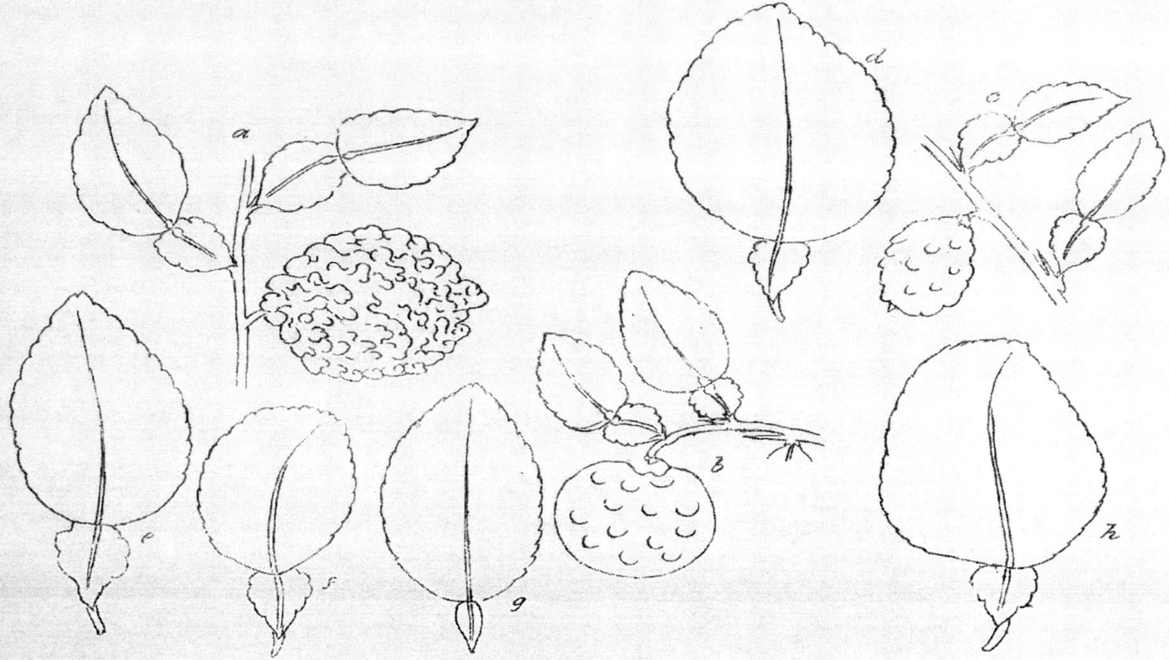

PLATE CCXXVII.

These figures are also taken from the Flora Amboyn. of Rumphius.

a would appear a smooth form of *Limo ventricosus*, but, I believe by mistake, Burmann called it *Limo ferus* (or lemon swangy), Vol. II., Tab. xxvi., Fig. 3, pictured with four petals. Here we have again the broad petiole wings of *Limo ventricosus* with an entirely smooth fruit.

b is an ovoid *Kaghzi nimboo* of India, which in no way differs from the fruit of *a*, as far as one can judge from a picture. The spines of *a* are identical with those of *b*; the latter, however, has the leaf of *e*.

c, *c* is the *Limonellus aurarius* (lemon Maas), Vol. II., Tab. xxx., pictured with four and also with five petals. This is the smallest of all citrus; not used for food, but by goldsmiths, for cleaning gold. The leaves are pictured entire, but the broad winged petiole of *a* is still maintained. I think that in some parts of India also the smallest *Kaghzi nimboo* is used by goldsmiths for the same purpose.

e and *d* are both taken from Vol. II., Tab. xxix., of Rumphius. *e* (*Limo tenuis*) is *distinctly* like an Indian *Kaghzi nimboo* in *all* its features. (*Vide* Plate CCXXVIII., Fig. *b*, and other plates, showing the small lime of India.) Rumphius says "it is thin skinned, very common, and much used." It is pictured with four petals. Loureiro, under *Citrus limonum*, says, "spinous, petioles *often linear*," and refers it to Vol. II., Tab. xxix., of Rumphius. Unfortunately this table has both *d* and *e*. *d* is distinctly a lemon (*C. medica*, *var. limonum*), and *e* is distinctly a *true lime*, which may possibly be *C. hystrix*, *var. acida*.

PLATE CCXXVII.

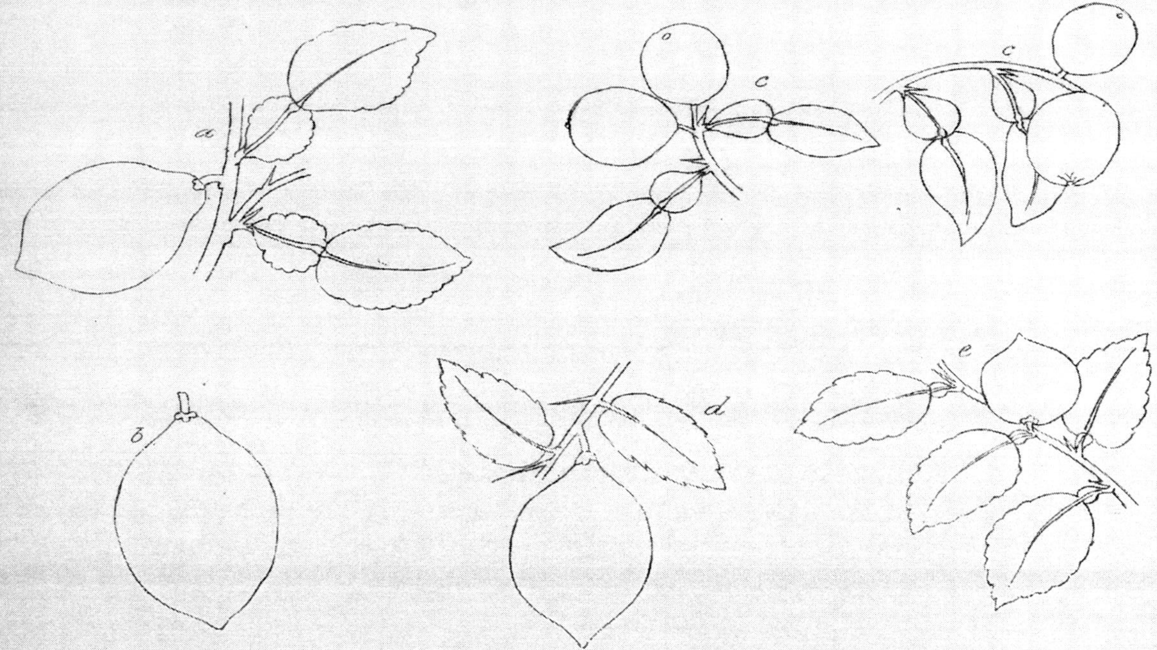

PLATE CCXXVIII.

a is the Monserrat true lime of the West Indies. It is taken from the "Botanical Magazine," Tab. 6,745, and called there *Citrus medica, var. acida,* as given in Sir J. Hooker's Flora Indica. In my opinion, it is a luxuriant variety of the *Kaghzi nimboo* (*Limo tenuis*) of Amboyn., Plate CCXXVII., Fig. *e*, and that of India Fig. *b* of this Plate.

b is the common *Kaghzi nimboo* of India, called also *dèsi,* in contradistinction to the other and larger form, the *Behàri.* It is also called *bàra màsi,* owing to its being procurable during the "twelve months" of the year.

c is section of *b*. This lime is thin skinned, with an aroma *sui generis.* The pulp is greenish, and very acid. The flowers are small, white, or *slightly* tinged purple; solitary axillary, or in cymes. The young shoots are tinged ochre colour, and the young unexpanded leaves *tomentose.* The leaves are small, rounded, oval, or lanceolate, with a distinct aroma. The spines given in *b* are typical. Fruit pale yellow, when ripe; smooth and foveolate, as shown in *b*.

d is an ovoid variety; *e* is a typical spring leaf; and *f* a well-developed rain leaf. The petiole given in *a* and *b* is usually very constant, and occurs in all the true limes I have seen.

PLATE CCXXVIII.

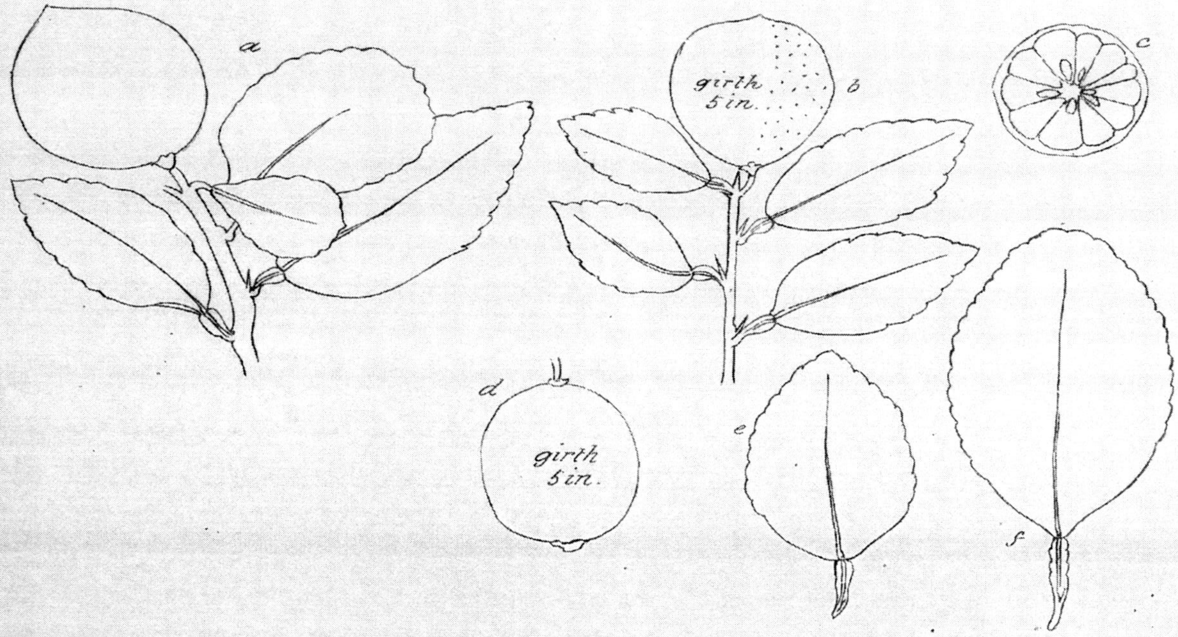

PLATE CCXXIX.

Two forms of the true lime of India (*Kaghzi nimboo*).

a, *b*, *c*, and *d* were taken from a seedling tree about four years old, and just beginning to fruit. The spines in *all young seedling* citruses are usually more developed than in older trees and those raised from buds. The wings of the petiole are here more developed.

e is a form growing in the Public Garden, Etawah. Its section *f* shows the typical skin of the *Kaghzi nimboo*. These thin-skinned limes are often slightly furrowed longitudinally, the furrows corresponding to the dissepiments of the pulp.

g is a rain leaf; *i* a spring leaf. *h* is a rounded form of leaf, which very often occurs in the true limes, and recalls the leaflet of *Lima* leaf *d*, Plate CCXXV.

j is a globose form of fruit, from a four-year-old seedling (from date of planting out the young tree, not from date of sowing the seed).

PLATE CCXXIX.

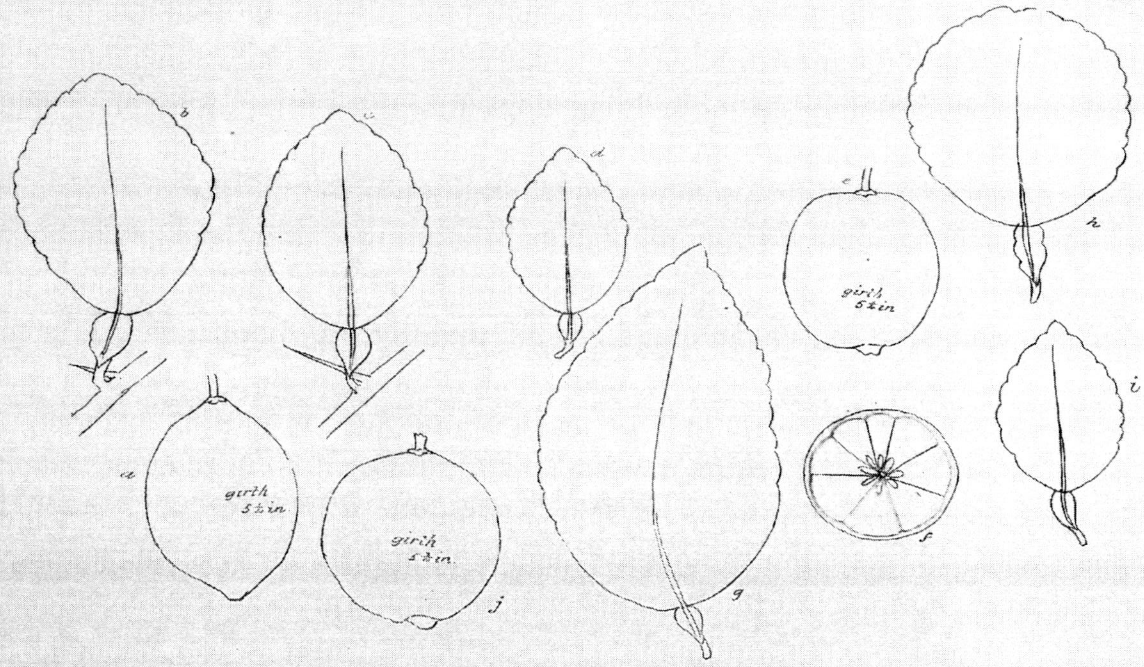

PLATE CCXXX.

Forms of true limes, found in Calcutta and Bombay.

a is the *China pâti*, or so-called China form in Bengal.

b, c, d, e, are the spring leaves which came with it. *f* its spine. Exterior smooth, pitted with concave cells; in parts they are convex. The section showed nothing new; the skin very thin; juice abundant, with a pronounced *Kaghzi* flavour.

The words *chin ka*, like *pahàri*, and *belaiti*, are often given to plants in contradistinction to *dèsi*, or common kinds. Whether, in this case, this variety had a Chinese origin, or not, I do not know.

g, h, i, and *j* is the *Dèsi pâti* of Calcutta, or the common *Kaghzi nimboo*. Pulp like that of other *Kaghzi nimboo*. The leaves and the spines *k* came with this specimen.

l, m, and *n* I purchased in the Bombay market. I was told that *l* was the *China Kaghzi*; *m* the *Kaghzi* of *Nassick*; and *n* the *Kaghzi* of *Poona*. *l* had a sour pulp, with a slightly pale orange tinge; its flavour was different from the ordinary *Kaghzi*. The other two had the *true lime* flavour. All were pale yellow and thin skinned. I did not see the leaves of any of these Bombay limes. It is doubtful whether *l* is a *true lime*. It may be something like the *udo dèhi* of Ceylon, a variety of *sour orange*. (*Vide* Plate CCXXXIII., *e*.)

PLATE CCXXX.

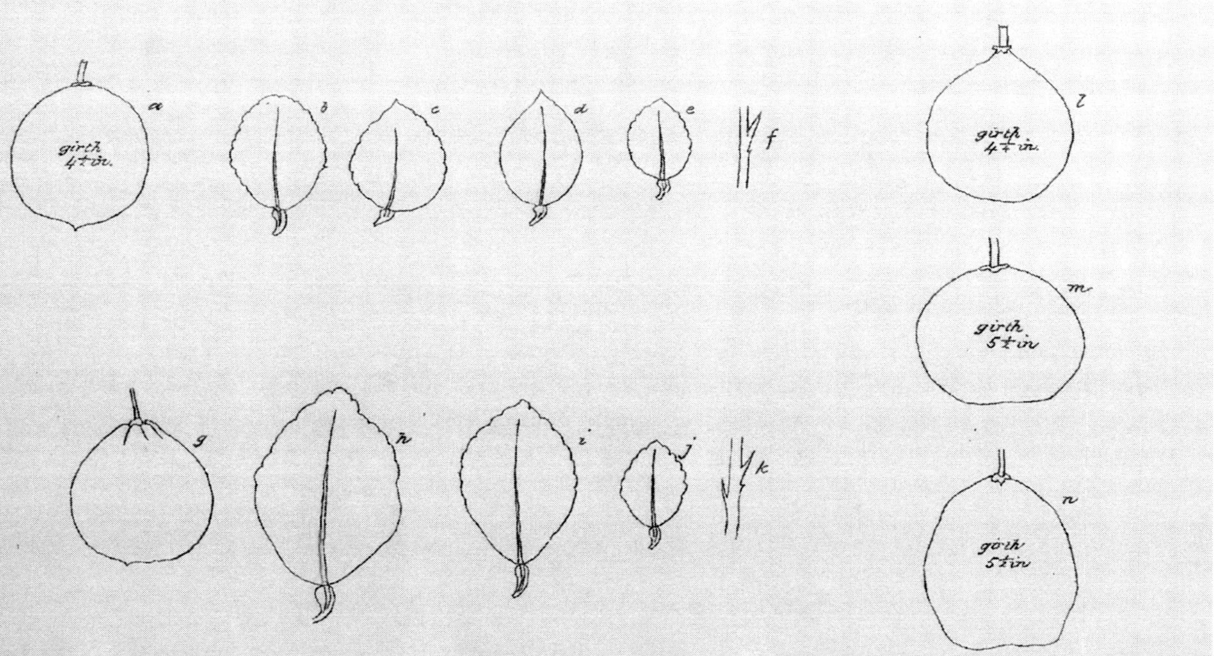

a
girth 4¼ in.
b
c
d
e
f
g
h
i
j
k
l
girth 4¾ in.
m
girth 5¼ in
n
girth 5¼ in

PLATE CCXXXI.

Ceylon limes, called there *Dèhi*.

a and *b* are the outlines and section of the lime of Kandy. This has not the papery skin of the *Kaghzi nimboo*. In India this variety would probably be called *Behàri nimboo*. It is pale yellow, and studded all over with large and small foveoli. The pulp is pale, like that of a lemon; juice very sour and abundant, and *slightly* bitter. Young unexpanded leaf buds are *tomentose*.

d and *e* are like the regular lime leaves; *j* its spine.

c is the lime of Colombo; pale yellow, pitted all over with shallow cavities. Thin skinned, though not quite *Kaghzi*; pulp pale greenish; ten carpels; juice abundant, of the flavour of *Kaghzi*; oil-cells of rind distinct; centre solid; seeds white, when cut.

f, *g*, *h*, and *i* are from a lime tree (?) I found in the *Hagkala* garden. I found none but an unripe undeveloped fruit, *h*; flowers tinged purple, four or five petals. Leaves longer than usual, with shape and scent more like those of a lemon. General aspect and spines are those of a lime.

PLATE CCXXXI.

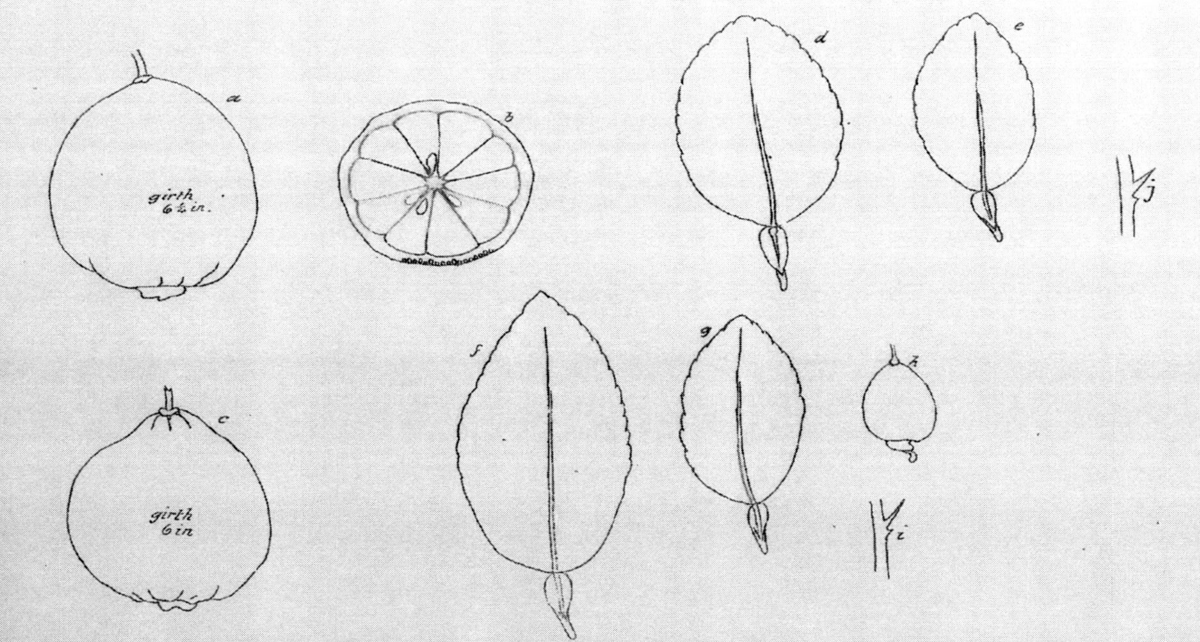

PLATE CCXXXII.

a and *b* are the *Kaghzi nimboo*, of Calcutta. This was an unripe specimen, with a thickish skin. It had foveoli, large and small, with shallow longitudinal furrows here and there. Pulp pale ; juice abundant, acid, with a fine aroma.

c, *d*, *e*, and *f* are the leaves and spine which came with it.

g is a *Kaghzi nimboo* from Bhilàwa, Auraya, Etawah District. Exterior quite smooth ; has neither elevations nor depressions ; *very* thin skinned ; aroma of the sour juice that of the true *Kaghzi*.

h, *i*, *j*, *k* are the leaves and spine of the same.

l and *m* are a lime that came from Benares, under the name of *Behari nimboo*. It appeared to be no other than an ovoid or pyriform *Kaghzi*, with pale and sour pulp.

PLATE CCXXXII.

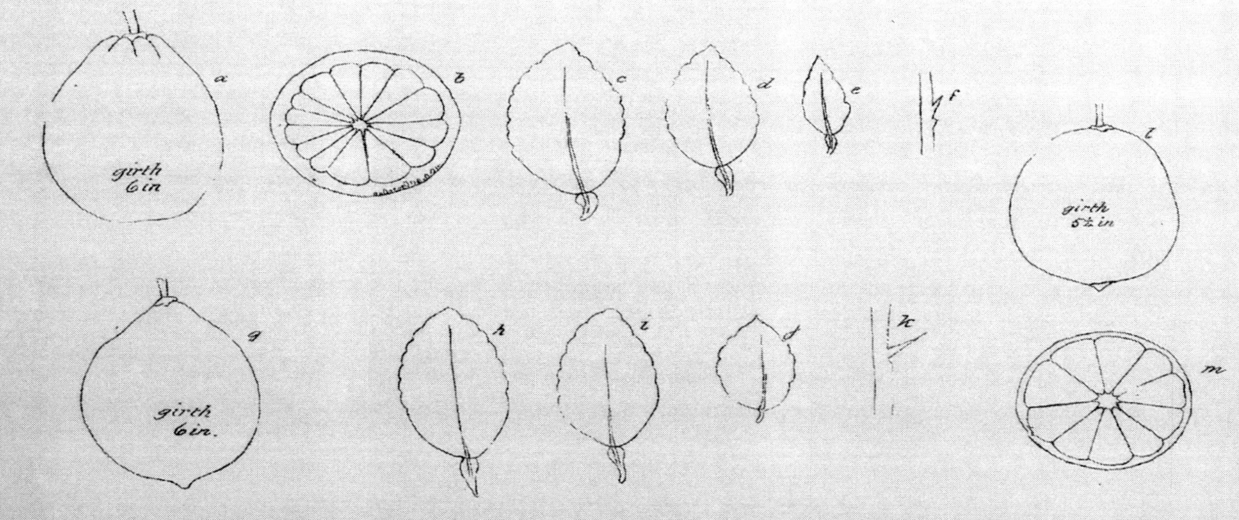

PLATE CCXXXIII.

a, *b*, *c*, *d* are leaves of the *Kaghzi nimboo*, taken from seedling plants, four or five years old. They are all dark green, and have the scent of *true lime* leaves.

e is a small citrus I obtained at the Colombo market. It was called *Oodoo Dèhi*. It is used for hair scrubbing. It has a thin skin, of a pale yellow, and smooth. The pulp had only six carpels. Its sour juice was abundant, but different in flavour from that of the ordinary true lime. The seeds were greenish when cut. Not improbably the name *Oodoo* may be a corruption of the *Usoh* of Khasia, or *Usse* of the Malay Archipelago.

PLATE CCXXXIII.

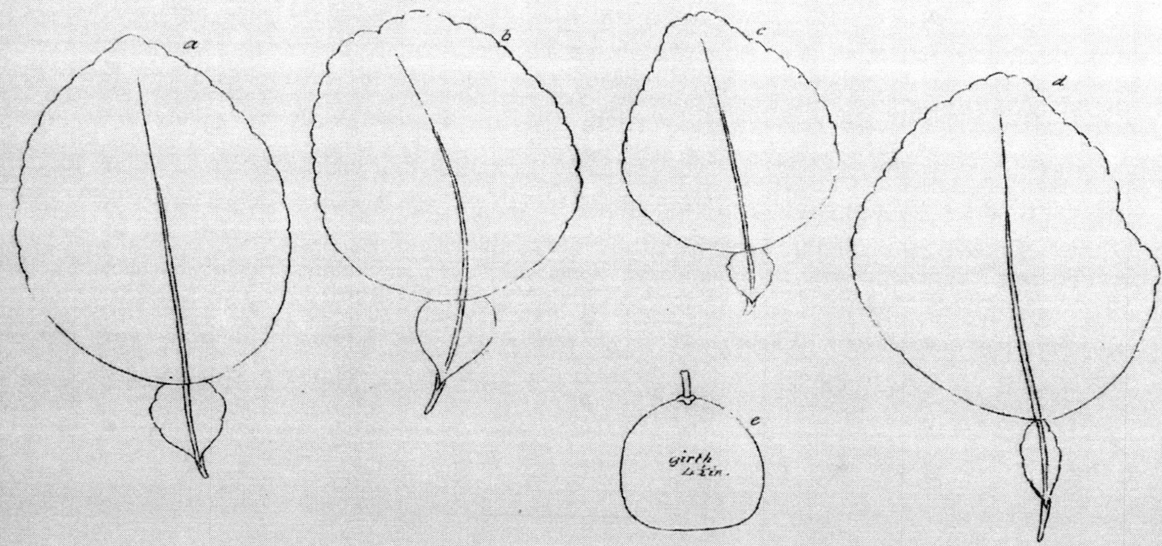

PLATE CCXXXIV.

a and *b* are the *Bor jeneru tenga* of Assam. From its leaves and size and shape of fruit, it would appear one of the *Suntara* oranges.

All the drawings of citrus from Assam were favoured me by Mr. G. E. McLeod, and are all of the size given. They give a very good idea of the oranges and lemons of that Province. He omitted, however, to give any further characters beyond what are seen in the drawings. I have, therefore, reproduced in the Appendix, No. **53**, the list of Assam citrus given by Mr. William Robinson in 1841. One of the oranges is there called *Jendru tenga*. It is probably this. Mr. McLeod adds that the *Horu generu tenga* is exactly the same, but smaller.

c and *d* are the *Júta muri* of Assam. From the petiole of its leaf it would appear a large lemon of the *Gulgul* class, or *Kumaon lemon variety*. On one side (*e*) this specimen was imperfectly developed, as was seen in its section. In *d* I have only shown the well-developed portion of the section, with its thick skin. Mr. Robinson, among the sub-acid lemons, gives *Jota mori tenga,* which, I suppose, means this variety.

PLATE CCXXXIV.

PLATE CCXXXV.

a and *b* are the *Chokla tenga* of Assam. From its leaf petioles I would say it is a lemon of the large Kumaon kind, with a thick skin. Mr. Anderson, of Sibsâgur, in his list (Appendix, No. 48, *b*), gives as No. 3 *Sdkla tenga*—a *bitter lime*—meaning, perhaps, *sour-bitter*. Mr. Robinson groups *Chakla tenga* among the sub-acid lemons, but he also gives the same name under *acid limes*. I do not think it can be a Seville, as it has no *winged* petioles, which are *large* in the Sevilles. The leaf, as shown in Mr. McLeod's drawing, is that of a lemon, or *Bajoura*.

PLATE CCXXXV.

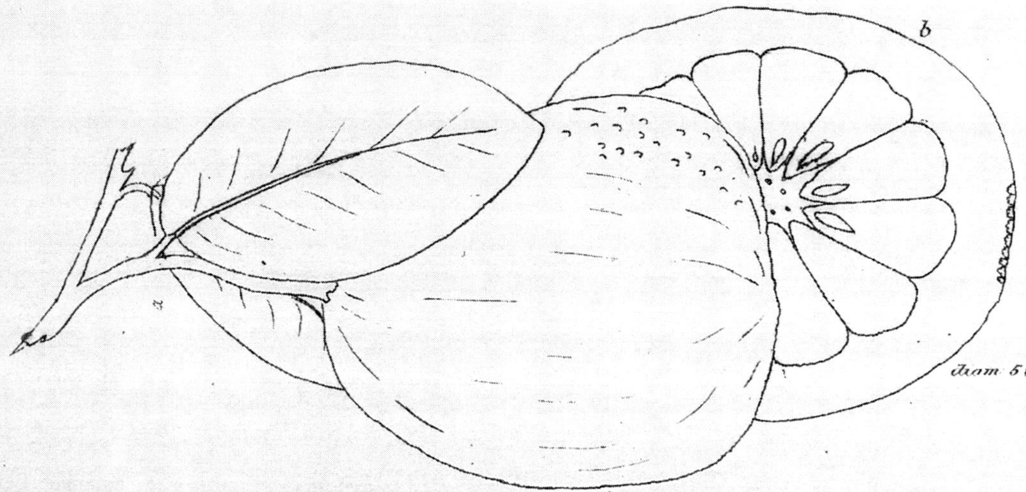

PLATE CCXXXVI.

a and *b* are the *Hùlinga muri* of Assam. Judging from its leaf, I would group it among the *Amilbêds* (which see).

Mr. Robinson, among the *sub-acid lemons*, gives *Halangá mori tenga*, which, I fancy, is the same as this.

PLATE CCXXXVI

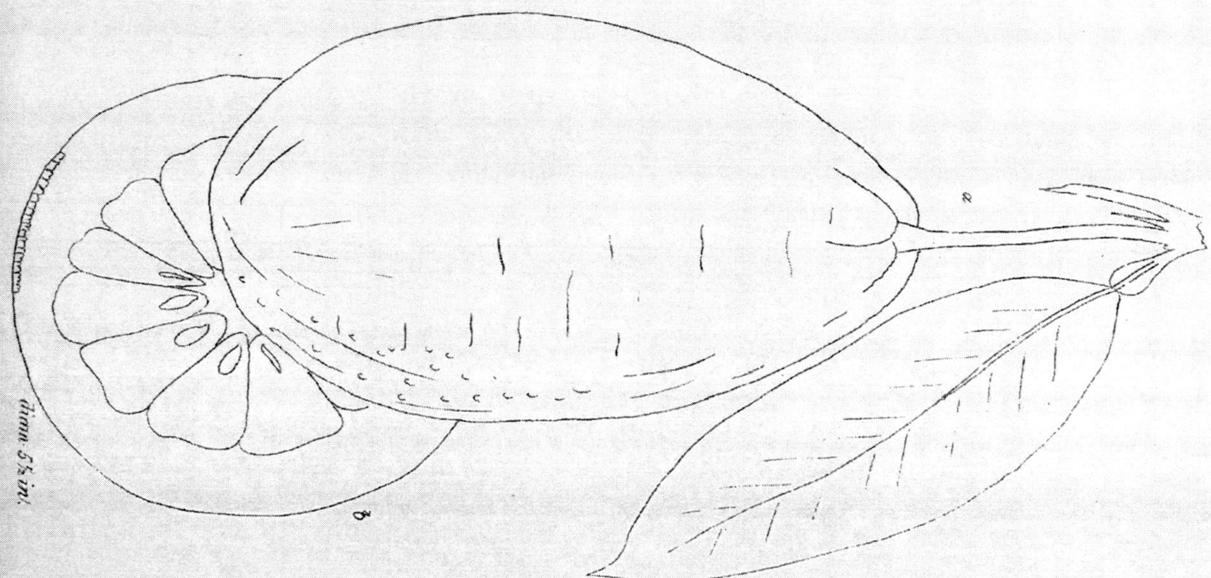

PLATE CCXXXVII.

a and *b* are the *Bor tenga* of Assam, Judging from its leaf, I would put it also among the *Amilbêds*. Mr. Anderson, in No. 4 of his list, gives *Bor tenga* as a big lime, *not a pummelo*; and Mr. Robinson, among the sub-acid lemons, gives *Bor mori tenga*. Mr. McLeod says it is *actual size*, and, therefore, might easily be mistaken for a true pummelo. It appears warty round the apex.

PLATE CCXXXVII.

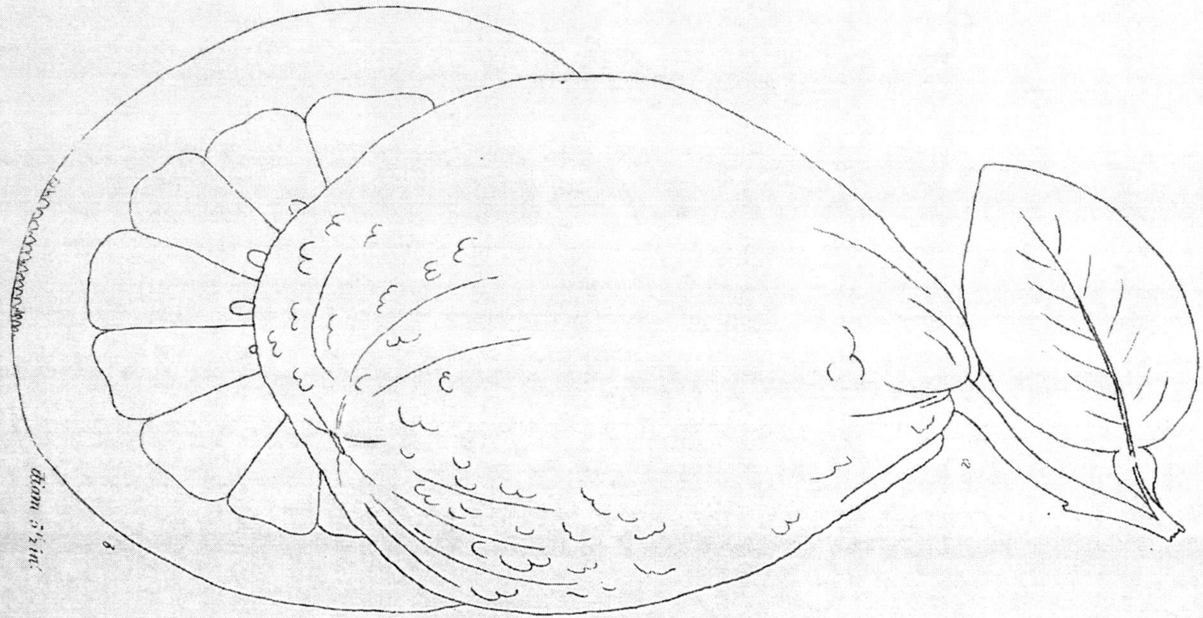

PLATE CCXXXVIII.

a and *b* are the *Rabab tenga* of Assam. Mr. McLeod adds (? Nawàb), and thinks it might possibly be a corruption of that name. Mr. Anderson gives No. 1 under the same name, but Mr. Robinson gives two kinds of shaddocks, viz., the *white—Boga robab tengá*, and the *red—Runga robab tengá*. Possibly it is one of these, but I think its petiole-wings are too small for a *true pumelo*, and would seem to belong rather to the *Ámilbêd* group. It is impossible to say whether the *Amilbêds* and the *true pumelos* have the same or different ancestors. If this were of *Batavian* origin, it would probably have retained either the Bengàli name of *Batabi tengá*, or that of *Jakatra tengá*. In upper India, however, the pumelos have, from their large size, gained different names, such as *Maha nimboo* (large nimboo) and *Gagree nimboo* (jar-like nimboo). Whether this *Rabab tengá* is one of those mentioned by Mr. Robinson as *Shaddocks*, or not, I cannot say.

PLATE CCXXXVIII.

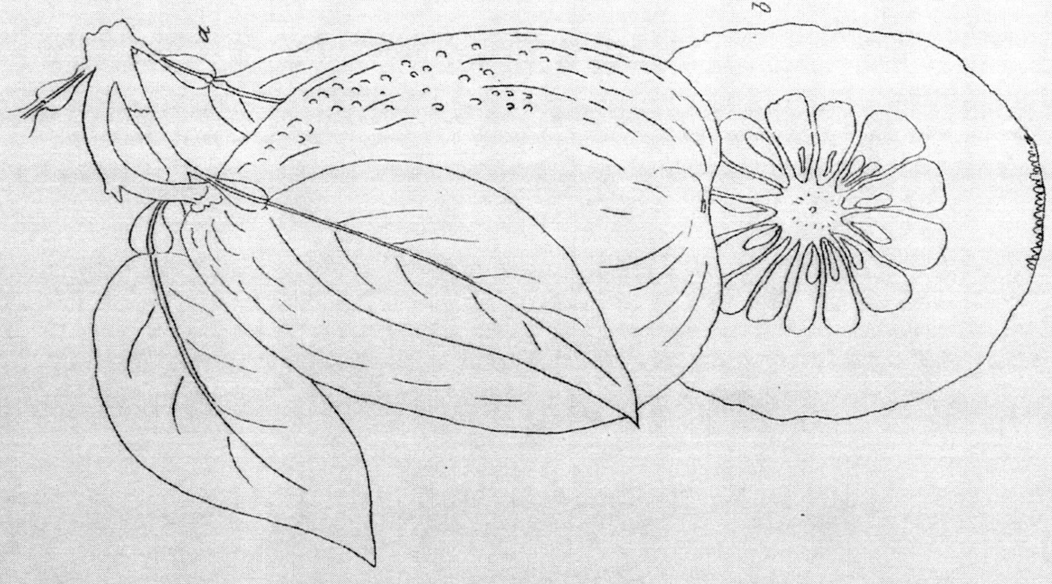

PLATE CCXXXIX.

a and *b* are the *Jora tengá* of Assam. It appears to be a true lemon of the *Nepàlee nimboo* variety. It is, however, rather thick skinned, but this may not be a typical specimen. It is No. 2 of Mr. Anderson's list. Mr. Robinson gives three varieties with this name, and *all* placed under *citrons*. Between thin-skinned citrons and thick-skinned lemons there is not, in reality, a very great difference. The drawing gives the "reduced size."

c and *d* are the *Nimboo tengá* of Assam. Judging from the shape of the leaf given in the drawing, I should say it was *not* the *true lime* (*Kághzi nimboo*) of the plains, but rather a small variety of the *Nepal lemon*. Its spines are too large and its leaves too oblong for a true lime. (*Vide* Plate CXCVII., Figs. *d* and *e*.) Mr. Robinson, among the *acid limes* of Assam, gives *Nimu tengá*, which, I suppose, means this.

PLATE CCXXXIX.

PLATE CCXL.

a and *b* are the fruit of the "Bigaradier fetifère" of Risso. They show oranges developing within oranges, and the section *b* shows a multiple fruit. At A is shown a rind carpel developed *within* the pulp carpel, and a second whorl of pulp carpels within the outer one.

c and *d* are the fruit of the "Bigaradier à fruit corniculé" of Risso. They show several carpels remaining distinct, and unamalgamated with the others, to form a uniform round fruit. The section, at *e* and *f*, shows *separate pulp* carpels, belonging to the separate rind carpels.

g is the fruit of the "Oranger à fruit cornu" of Risso. It shows a single carpel persisting in remaining separate. This horn varied in size, but *all* the oranges of that variety had it more or less developed, and every large appendage had within it a *separate* pulp carpel. Whatever may be the origin or nature of the citrus *rind*, it would appear that each pulp carpel had originally its own rind (carpel or not); that, in the process of selection and perfection, the pulp carpels remained *distinct*, while the rind coverings became amalgamated and their separate nature *obliterated*.

These figures are referred to in the Chapter on "Morphology."

PLATE CCXL.

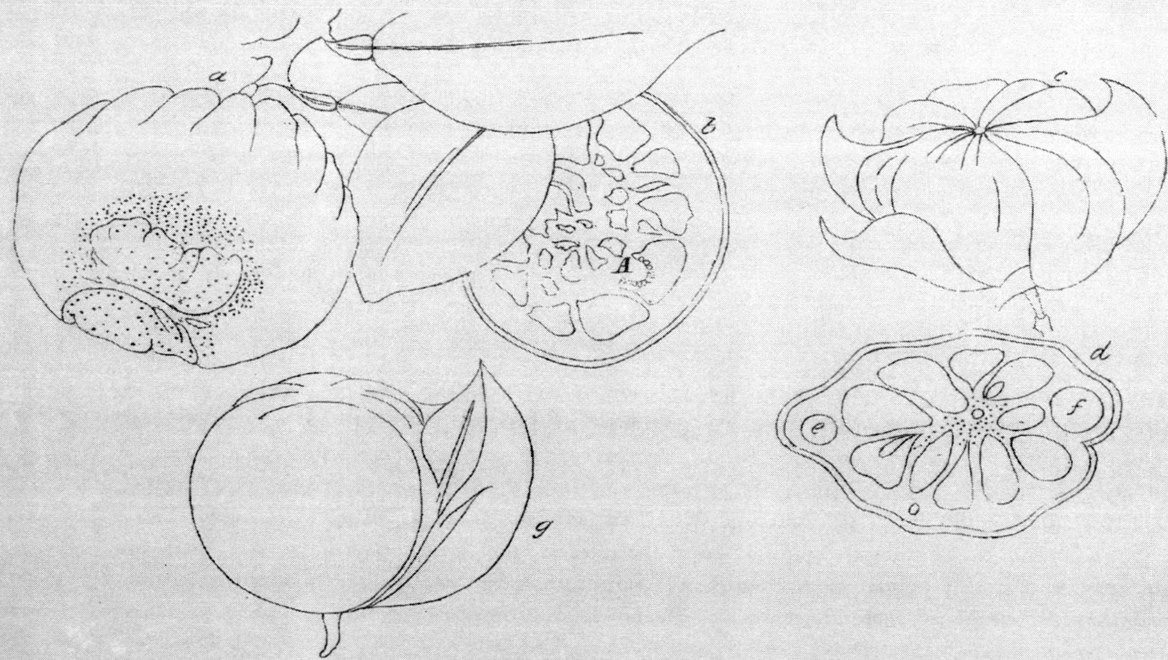

PLATE CCXLI.

a and *b* show the fruit of the "Bergamottier mellarose à fleur double" of Risso. *a* shows the rind carpels *all distinct*, and ununited at their distal ends, forming a sort of cup-rim, out of which come out numerous other carpels, belonging to inner whorls. The section *b* shows a very interesting multiplication of rind and pulp carpels. Within the outer whorl of pulp carpels there is a whorl of *rind* carpels, shown at *b'*, with their oil-cells; within these, again, is a complete whorl of smaller *pulp* carpels. The centre of the fruit is occupied by pulp carpels of various sizes. At A there is also a *rind* carpel. Innermost of all is a circle of *rind* carpels, with essential oil-cells.

c is the fruit of the "Bergamottier mellarose" of Risso, showing distinct carpels, and a second whorl of carpels at the distal end.

d is the anomalous form of orange given by Dr. Masters in his "Teratology," Fig. 32, Plate LXXIV. If I have interpreted it rightly, it consists of single carpels of the centre *leaflet* and one of the *side* leaflets of the original *trifoliate* leaf. By the dotted carpel *d'*, I have endeavoured to complete the *trifoliate* ancestral form, changed into a *tri-carpellar fruit*, with *all three carpels completely disunited* (?).

e is also taken from Dr. Masters' work, p. 303. It shows the whorl of stamens changed into carpels or pistils.

PLATE CCXLI.

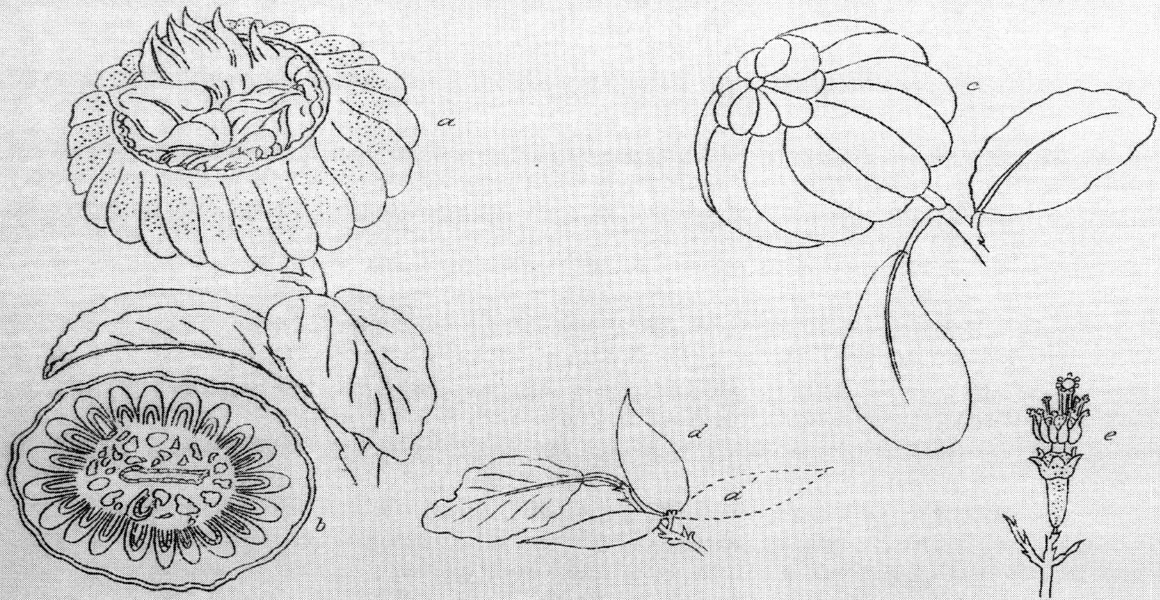

PLATE CCXLII.

a and *b* are the ovoid form of the *Bæl* fruit (*Ægle Marmelos*). Although heavy and solid, it *floats* in water. The rind is pale green, and when ripe of a yellowish brown studded with large and small oil-cells. *b* is the section, showing the isolated pulp-carpels. *c* shows a longitudinal section of one of the latter. Its interior surface is studded with open-monthed cells, which pour their gummy secretion into the interior of the carpel, and fill it, bathing the seed. The *Bæl* gum is a sticky astringent substance, soluble in water. The gum-cells are more numerous towards the circumferential side of the carpel, which is also the case with citrus juice-vesicles. I look upon these gum-sacs as the homologues of the *citrus juice-vesicles*. Their rim projects beyond the inner surface of the carpels, and a little more might make them closed sacks. All the rest of the fruit *b′ b′* is occupied by a yellow spongy substance, and which appears to be the homologue of the *white pith* which is on the inside of the organge and lemon peel.

d and *e* is a pyriform *Bæl*. I cut three *Bæl* fruits, from different trees, and in each found *eleven* pulp, or gum-carpels. This specimen had a very small mamilla, shown at *e.′* The large and small oil-cells of the rind were distinct.

f is the trifoliolate leaf of the *Bæl*. The minute unexpanded leaves are covered on both sides and edges with a short brownish *down*. This is shed by degrees, as the leaf grows. The oil-cells, of three sizes, are very distinct on the edges. Not so distinct on the othe parts of the blades. The spines are in pairs.

PLATE CCXLII.

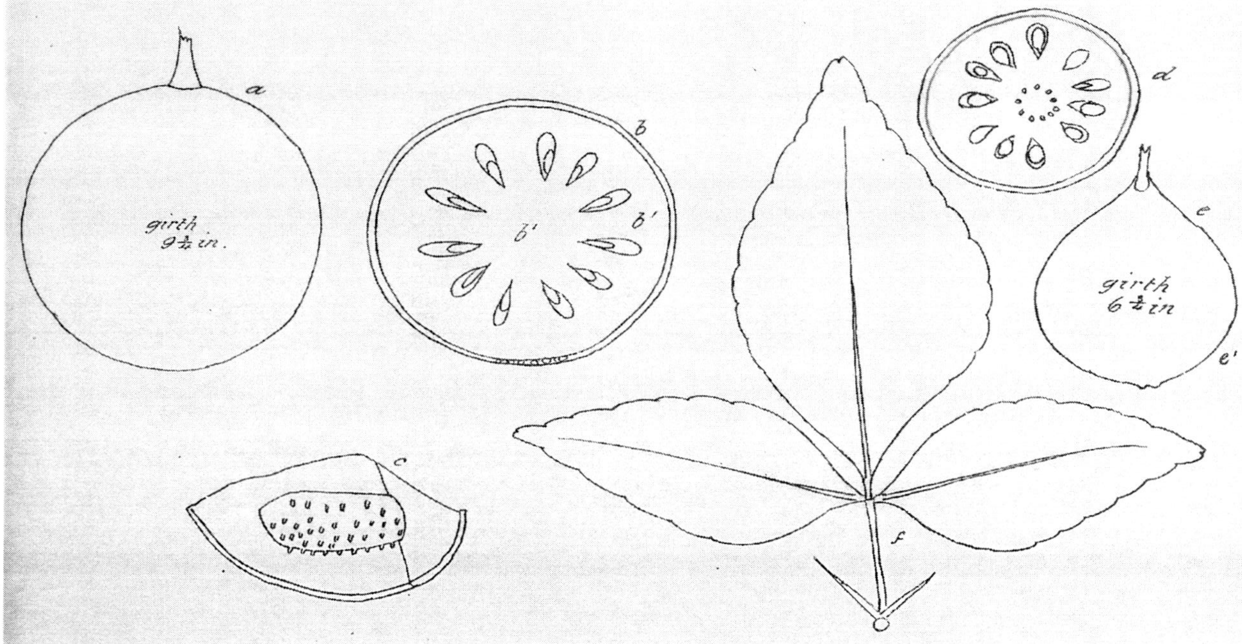

PLATE CCXLIII.

a and *b* are a large *pumelo-like* variety of *Bæl* (*Ægle Marmelos*) called *Bara Bæl*. The hard pithy substance which occupies the whole interior of the fruit, is sweetish and aromatic, of the colour of pale orange carrot. In the case of the *Bæl* fruit, this pithy matter has forced itself between the pulp carpels—squeezing and separating them, and invading also the centre of the fruit. In fact, it is the principal part of the fruit. While in the citrus, the pulp vesicles with their enclosing pod-membrane form the principal part of the fruit. By their excessive growth, they have kept the pulp carpels close together, and so have prevented the pith from invading the centre also. In the citrus, this pithy substance could only grow externally by expanding the *rind*, and so creating the thick skins of the pumelo, citron, and *Kathairee nimboo*, and others.

c shows the interior of the gum-carpel, with its gum-cells, and the seed *c'*, with its large placenta. In October this *Bæl* was pale green, and might have become larger when ripe. It was studded with oil-cells of two sizes, with intermediate white dots.

PLATE CCXLIII.

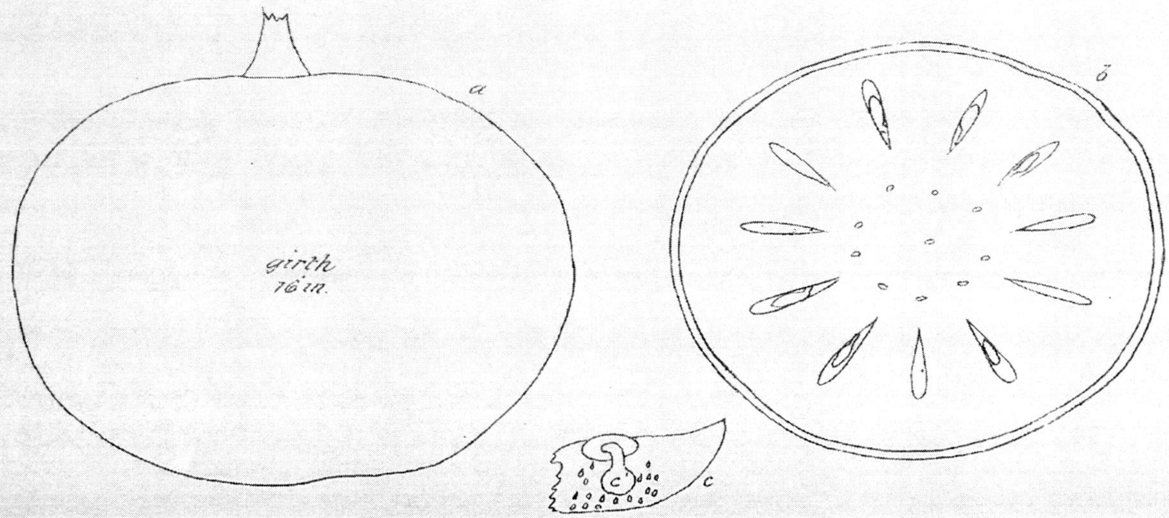

PLATE CCXLIV.

a is an ovoid fruit of the *Kaithá* (*Feronia elephantum*). It is covered with a fawn-coloured epidermis, more dense at the apex. *b* and *c* are the compound leaves of this Feronia. They are crenated as in *c*, although in *b* the crenations are not shown. The leaflets have sparse oil-cells; also in the angles, between the crenations, and on the edges of the margined petiole. Sometimes the oil-cells of the blades require a high-power glass to bring them out, while those of the edges are distinct and like minute pearls. When crushed, they have the scent of aniseed. *d* is a small trifoliolate leaf, and *e* is the spine. The older branches, in the axillæ of the spines, have small *tufty* branchlets, with five or six leaves. The fruit of the Feronia, though solid and heavy, floats in water.

f and *g* are a fruit of the Feronia of the shape of an *inverted* pear. It is covered with a furfuraceous epidermis, of an earth-colour, and easily scraped off. *g* shows the internal structure of the fruit. At *g′* are the cells of the woody rind, filled with a hard concretion. The fruit appears to consist of five large, and imperfectly closed carpels, A A. They appear to consist only of the skeletons of the carpels, that is of the feeding vessels, at the ends of many of which seed-buds are developed. B B appears to be another whorl of carpels, alternating with the first. They have their feeding vessels straight, filling the centre of the fruit with seed-buds, at the same time pushing out of the way, and curving inwards the edges of carpels A. In the section, some of the seeds are seen of full size, while others are seen in *part*, and belong to a *lower level*. As in the Ægle, the carpels of the Feronia are embedded in a dense pithy substance, homologous to the *pith* of the orange rind. It *fills* the fruit. *h* is the normal leaf of an Ægle I found at the temple of Tanjore, with very thick leaflets; so much so, that when bent, they snapped. Usually the leaves of the Ægle are very thin. The fruit of this Ægle was small and ovoid.

PLATE CCXLIV.

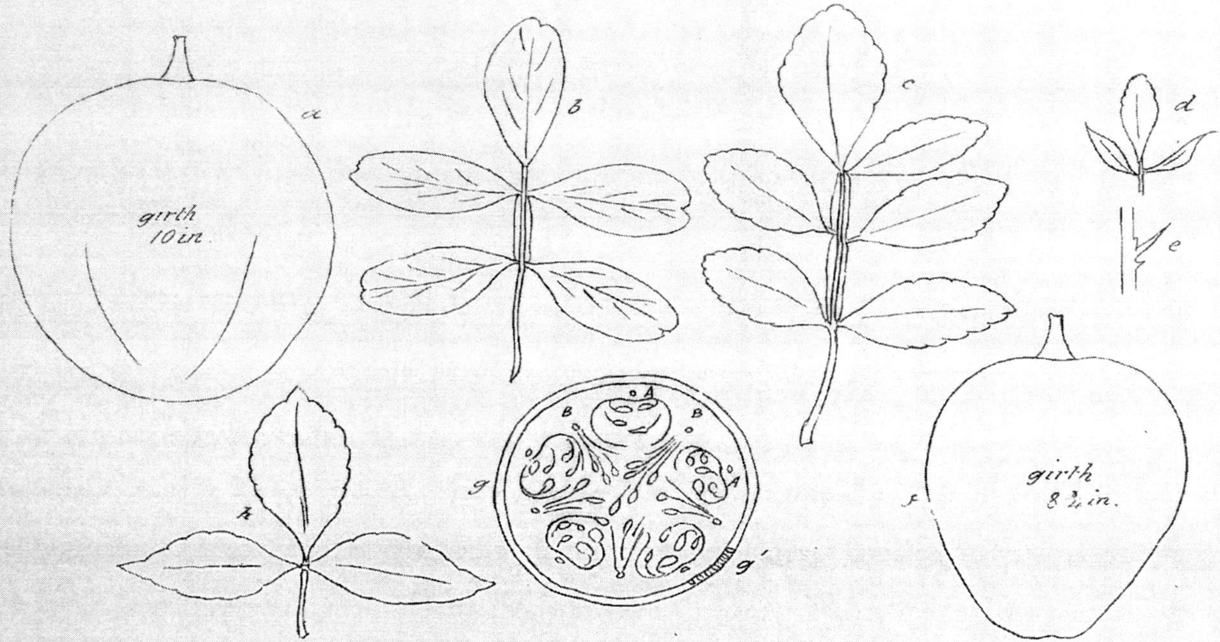

PLATE CCXLV.

a, *b*, and *c* are the compound leaves of the *Limonia acidissima*, which I got at the Saharunpore Botanic Garden.

The tree has the habit of the Feronia. The leaflets are dotted with large and small oil-cells. Their scent is almost *nil*, perhaps it distinctly recalls that of the leaves of *Feronia elephantum*. The petioles are pubescent. At the angles of the crenations there are large oil-cells, with smaller ones between them. The leaves of this Limonia might perhaps be taken to consist of a chain of winged petioles, one budding out of the tip of the other, with a pair of opposite side-buds *proliferating* from the same node, and ending in the odd leaflet, when the power of proliferation had been exhausted.

d is the Limonia fruit of the natural size. When ripe, it is purple-black. The rind is studded with oil-cells, and slightly aromatic, and bitterish, but not citrine. The pulp is *slightly* acid and bitter; I did not find it *very* acid, as its name would denote. It had one seed of the size of a Sorghum-seed.

e is its spine, with a bud at its base.

f and *g* are only diagrams, in connection with what I said in the Chapter on Morphology, and intended to illustrate a *supposed* branching of the Phyllanthus—one of the Cactaceæ.

PLATE CCXLV.

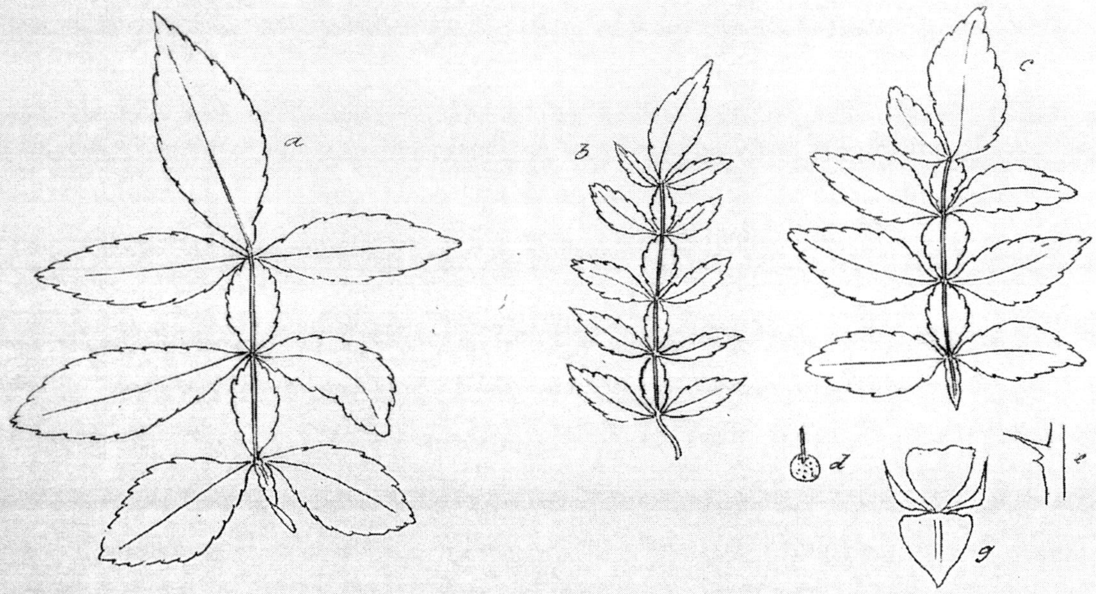

PLATE CCXLVI.

The following plates show the young seedling leaves of various kinds of citrus. The first leaves that show themselves above ground are always opposite, as shown in Plate CCLV. The second and third of these varieties came out as here shown.

a is the second leaf of the *Kumquat* (Plate XCIII., Figs. *d* and *g*), showing margins to the petiole.

b is the second leaf of the *Kathairee nimboo* (Plate XXXV.), showing a very long margined petiole, its margins being continuous with those of the blade. *b′* shows the position of the joint.

c is the second leaf of the *At' Anni* of Gonda (Plate CXII.). *d* and *e* are its third and fourth leaves. Another seedling of this variety gave a second leaf like *e*.

f is the second leaf of *Surkh nimboo* (Plate XCVI., Figs. *d* and *f*).

g is the second leaf of the *Delhi Keonla*, purchased at Bombay (Plate CXXVI., Fig. *f*).

h and *i* are third and fourth leaves of the Jhansi long lemon (Plate CCVI., Fig. *a* and *b*).

j is the third leaf of the Ceylon orange called *Punchi Jambole* (Plate LVI., Fig. *a*).

k is the second leaf of the "Lima" or *Kudalu dĕhi* of Ceylon (C. hystrix, Plate CCXXV. Fig. *a*).

l and *m* are its third and fourth leaves.

It should be noted that these leaves are taken from one particular seedling of each variety, other seedlings of the same variety might give somewhat different leaves. *The trifoliate leaves are rare.*

PLATE CCXLVI.

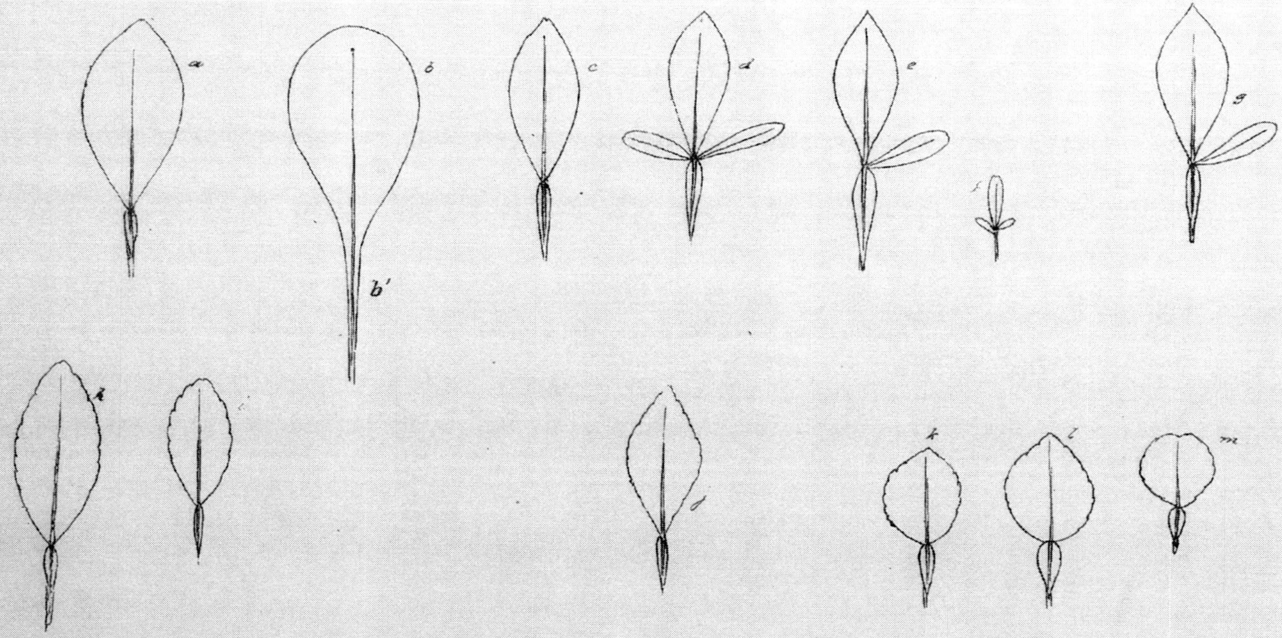

PLATE CCXLVII.

a is the third leaf of the *Kaghzi Kalàn* of Ajitmal (Plate CLXXXIX., Fig. *a*); it does not show any sign of joint between the petiole and the leaflet.

b is the third leaf of the Rangpur lime from Saharanpur (Plate CXIV., Fig. *a*).

c and *d* are the second and third leaves of the *Calamba* of Bengal (Plate CLXVI., Fig. *a*).

e is the second leaf of the Bhootan orange (Plate CVII., Fig. *a*).

f and *g* are the second and third leaves of the Nagpore *Suntara* orange (Plate CII.).

h and *i* are the second and third leaves of the *Suntola* orange of Nepal (Plate XCIX.).

j is the third leaf of the Pondicherry lemon (Plate CLXXXIV., Fig. *a*).

PLATE CCXLVII.

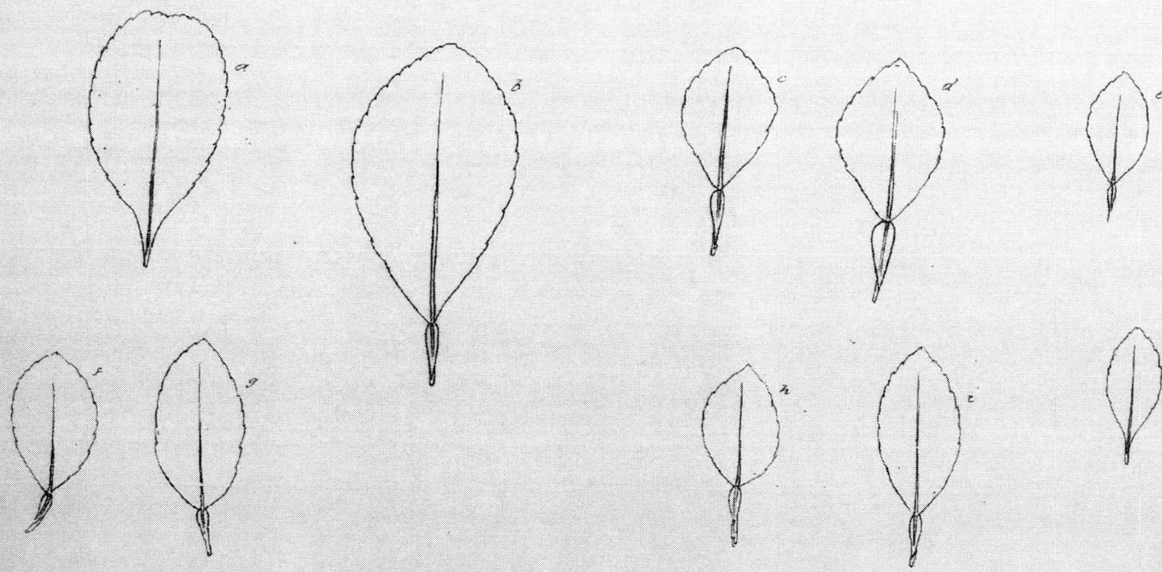

PLATE CCXLVIII.

a is the third leaf of the ovoid *Sherbetee* of Benares (Plate CXCIV., Fig. *a*).

b and *c* are the second and third leaves of Major Buller's *Kaghzi nimboo Nepalee* (Plate CXCVII., Fig. *d*). If this is a *true Kaghzi n.* its large winged petiole might strengthen the theory of the descent of the *true lime* from the C. hystrix.

d is the second leaf, and *e* and *f* the third leaves of the oblate *Nartun* of Tanjore (Plate XVIII., Fig. *f*). The pyriform *Nartun* had similar leaves.

g is the second leaf of the Bombay red pumelo. It had no sign of joint between the petiole and leaflet. Its edges seemed *entire*, but they had the unmistakable oil-cells in the places of the crenations. The oil-cells on the blade were very few and scattered.

h is the third leaf of the same pumelo. Both *g* and *h* were *glabrous*.

CCXLVIII.

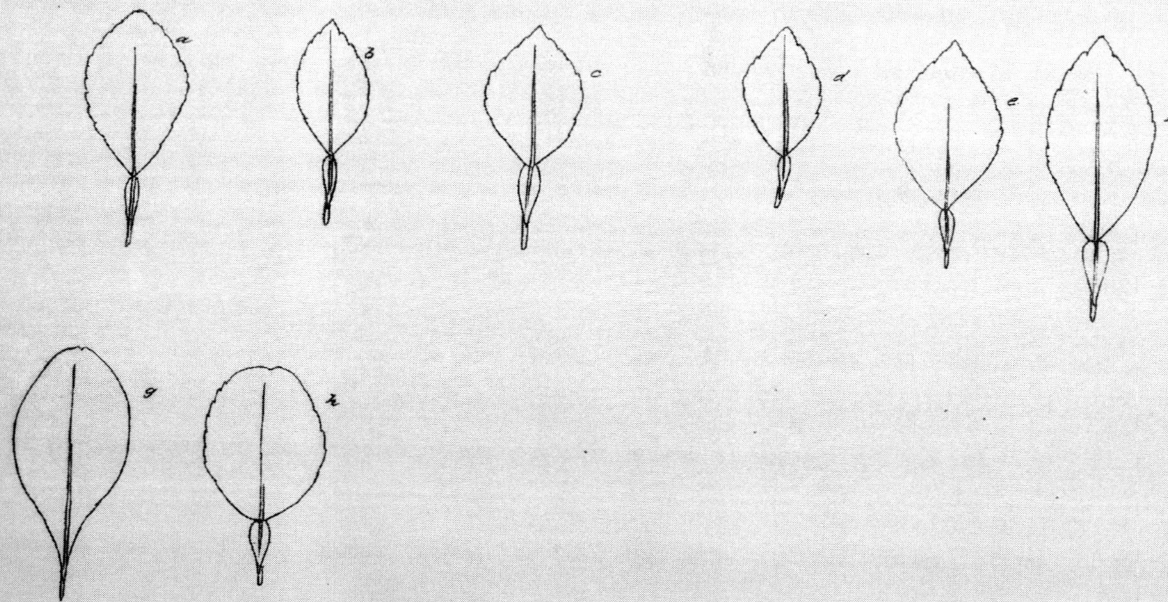

PLATE CCXLIX.

a and *b* are third and fourth leaves of Buller's large *Gungolee nimboo* (Plate CXCIX., Fig. *a*).

c is the third leaf of the ordinary round *Sherbetee nimboo* (Plate CXCI., Fig. *a*).

d is the second leaf of the *Mitha* (?) *Gulgul* of Saharanpur (Plate CLXXXVII., Fig. *a*); it has a joint at *d'*, but the edges of the petiole margin are continuous with those of the blade.

e is the third leaf of Mr. Nickel's Suez orange (Plate XLVI., Fig. *a*).

f is the third leaf of the Ceylon *Suntara* or *Konda nārun* (Plate CI., Fig. *a*).

g is the second leaf of the Lucknow *Jambiri* (Plate CXXXII., Fig. *a*).

h and *i* are the third and fourth leaves of the common *Khatta* orange (Plate XXV., Figs. *a* and *b*).

PLATE CCXLIX.

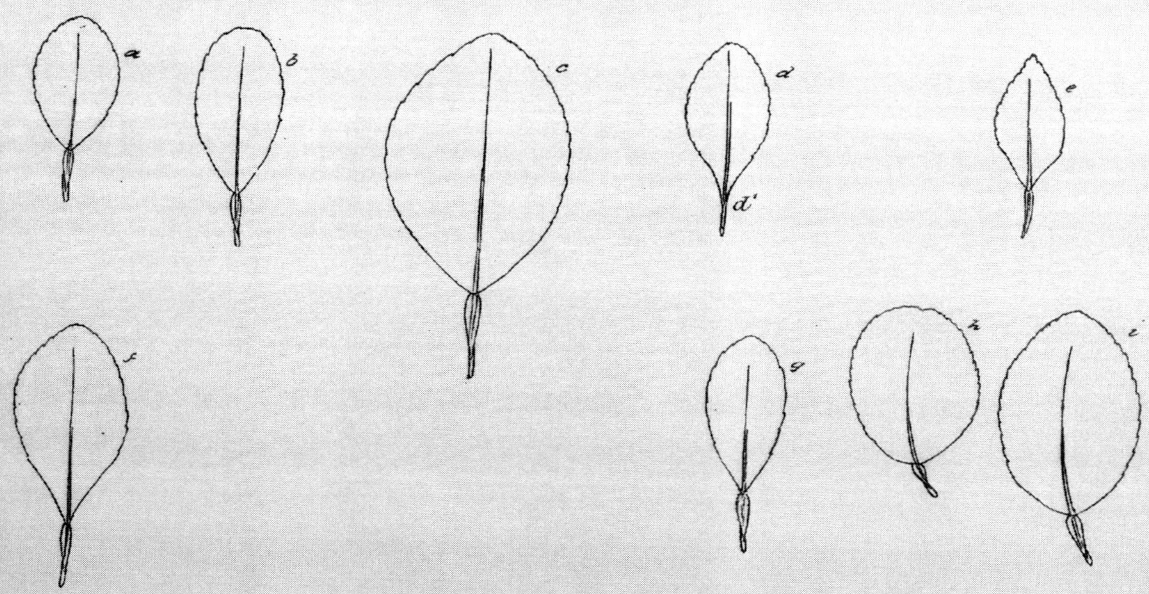

PLATE CCL.

a and *b* are the second and third leaves of the Nepal sour lemon (Plate CXCVII., Fig. *a*), with lemon-like leaves and no joints.

c and *d* are the second and third leaves of the *Desi Calamba* of Bengal (Plate LXVIII., Fig *a*), probably an *Amilbed.*

e is the second leaf of the Behàri *Nimboo,* without a joint (Plate CCII., Fig. *a*).

f is the third leaf of the Etawah *Bajoura,* with a joint (Plate CLXIII., Fig. *a*).

f′ is the third leaf of another seedling of the Etawah *Bajoura.*

g is the second leaf of the *yellow Surk nimboo.*

h is the second leaf of the Buxa small orange (Plate CVII., Fig. *a*).

i is the second leaf of the Malta Séville (Plate XI., Fig. *a*), of Lucknow.

j and *k* are the second and third leaves of the Etawah *Séville* (Plate XIV., Fig. *a*).

l and *m* are the second and third leaves of another specimen of the same Séville.

PLATE CCL.

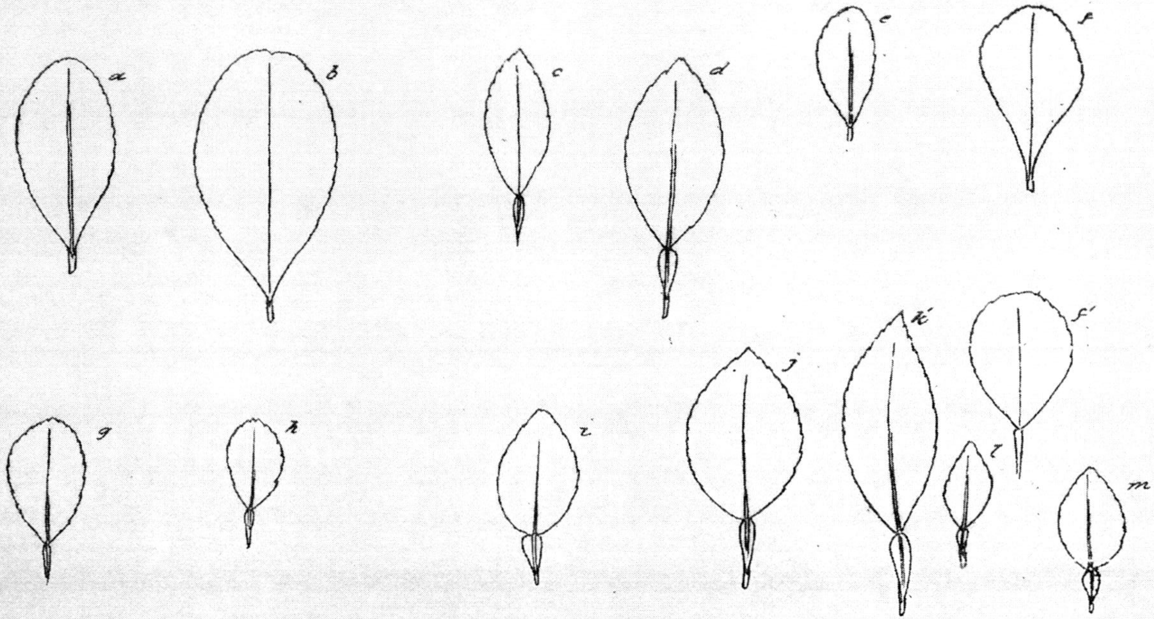

PLATE CCLI.

a and *b* are the second and third leaves of the *Gungolee nimboo* of Bulrampur (Plate CXCIX., Fig. *f*).

c and *d* are the second and third leaves of the Benares *Gulgul* (Plate CLXXXVI., Fig. *a*).

e is the second leaf of the large lemon of Kumaon, without joint (Plate CLXXXVIII., Fig. *a*).

f and *g* are the third and fourth leaves of the *Saroti nimboo* of Gonda (Plate CLXIX., Fig. *a*.) *f* is *without a joint*, and *g has* a joint.

h and *i* are the second and third leaves of the *Bándir* orange of Tanjore (Plate XLIII., Fig. *a*.)

j is the second leaf of *Qism Bajoura* of Major Buller (Plate CXCVI., Fig. *a*). Probably it is an "At' Anni."

PLATE CCLI.

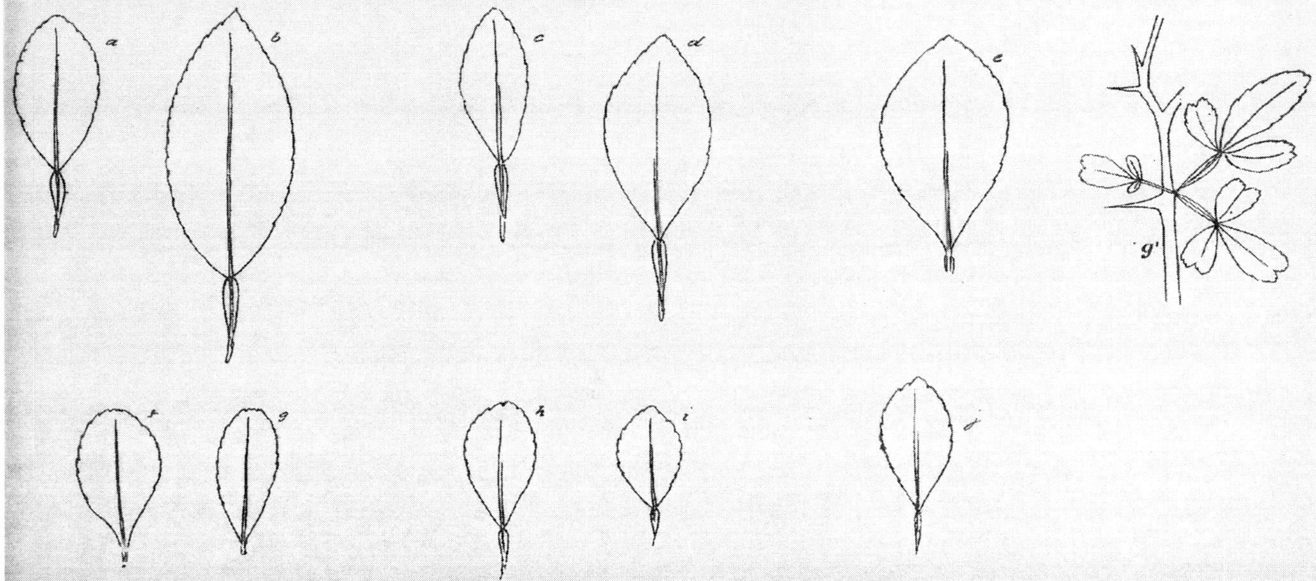

PLATE CCLII.

a is the second leaf of the Mooltan *Sherbetee*, or sweet lemon (Plate CXC., Fig. *a*).

b and *c* are the second and third leaves of the Lahore *Gulgul* (Plate XXXII.). *b* has a joint at *b'*; but the edges of the blade and petiole are continuous. *c* has also a joint at *c'*, showing a tendency to separation between the petiole wings and blade.

d and *e* are the first and third leaves of the *Aurungabad* orange (Plate CXXV., Fig. *a*).

f is the second leaf of the *Sherbetee* lemon (a *sour* citrus) of Calcutta (Plate CCVII., Figs. *i* and *j*).

g is the third leaf of the *Nepdlee nimboo* of Benares (sweet lemon) (Plate CXCII., Fig. *a*).

h is the third leaf of the *Surkh nimboo* (Plate XCVI., Figs. *d* and *e*).

PLATE CCLII.

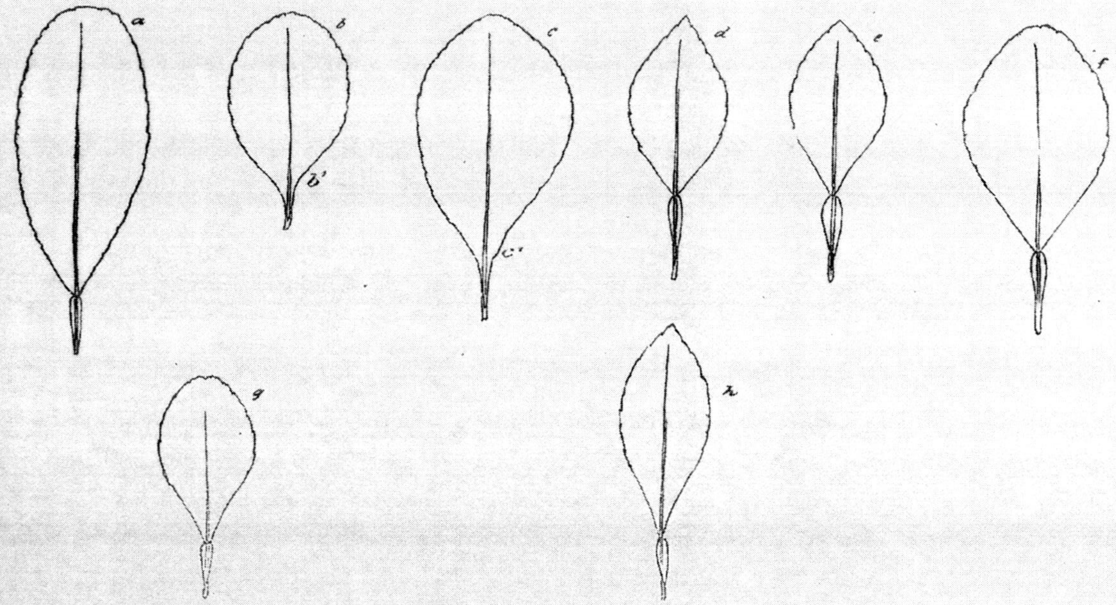

PLATE CCLIII.

a, *b*, and *c* are second, third, and fourth leaves of *Qeem* citron of Saharunpore (Plate LXIX., Figs. *a* and *b*) ; probably an *Amilbêd*.

d is the third leaf of the small *Sherbetee* of Khoorja (Plate CXC., Fig. *g*).

e and *f* are second and third leaves of the *Amilbêd* (Plate LXI., Figs. *a* and *b*).

PLATE CCLIII.

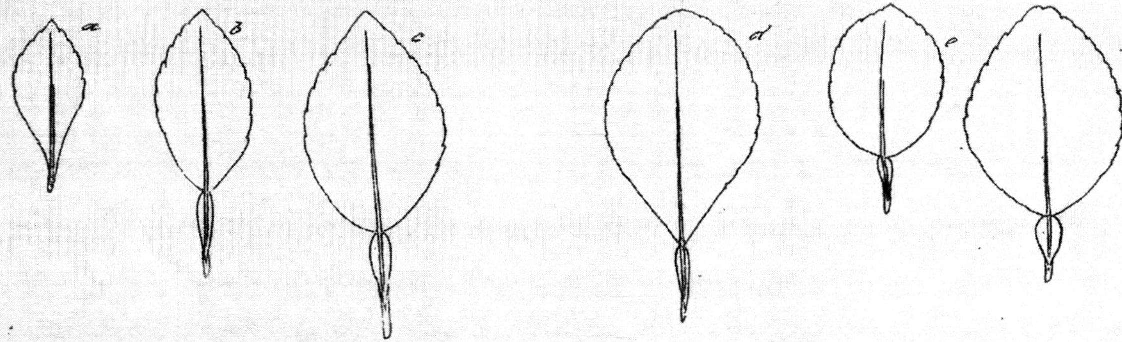

PLATE CCLIV.

a and *b* are the second and third leaves of the large *Sherbetee* lemon of **Muscat** (Plate CXCV., Fig. *c*).

c and *d* are the second and third leaves of another specimen of the same variety.

e is the third leaf of the *yellow Surkh nimboo* of Tulshipur Gonda.

f is the third leaf of the *Ocdo Déhi* of Ceylon (Plate CCXXIII., Fig. *e*).

g' are the leaves and spines of the *Citrus trifoliata*, sent from the **Botanic Garden, Saharunpore.** It has never fruited there. (*Vide* Plate CCLI., Fig. *g'*.)

PLATE CCLIV.

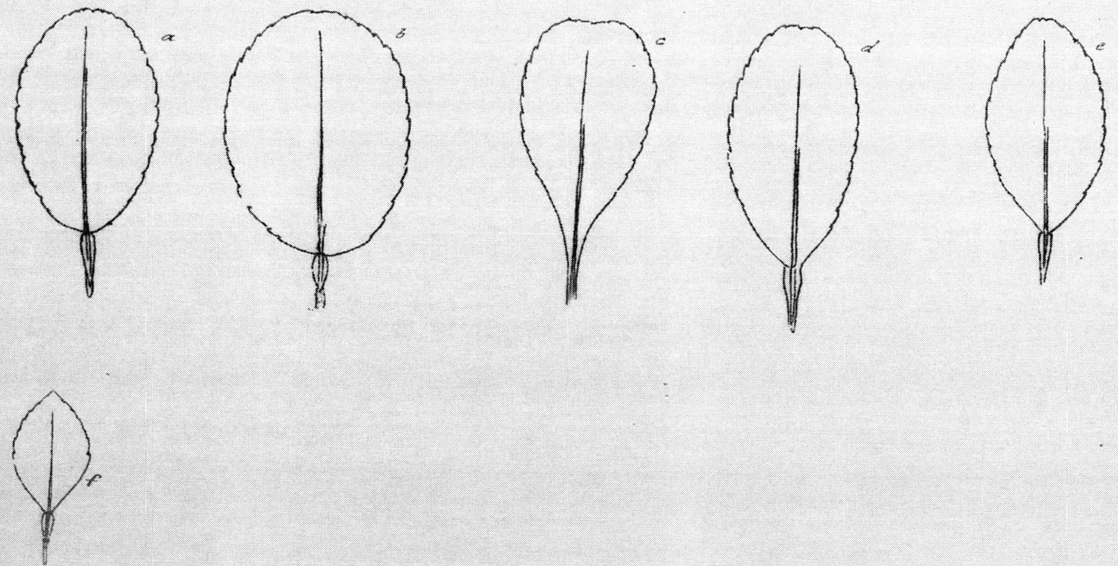

PLATE CCLV.

a shows the first pair of leaves and the second leaf of the small *Behâri Nimboo* of Lucknow (Plate CCIV.).

b shows the same in the *Sungdaraz* of Nepal (Plate CLXIV.).

c ditto of the *Turunj* of Lucknow (No. 2) (Plate CLII.).

d ditto of Etawah *Bajoura* (Plate CLXIII.).

e ditto of Big Pumelo of Etawah (Plate LXXX.).

f ditto of *Turunj* of Lucknow (No. 1) (Plate CXLIX.).

g and *h* are seedlings of the same fruit, the *Nibooá* of Nepal (Plate CLXV.).

In no case do the first pair of leaves show either margins or wings to the petiole, or *joints*, between the petiole and blade. The second leaf of all the above shows a joint, but no appendages whatever to the petiole. Might the first pair of leaves be considered the original citrus leaf, from the tip of which, by proliferation, a second leaf budded, the latter being afterwards called the *leaflet*, and the former the winged petiole? Possibly this suggestion might be hazarded, from an embryological point of view.

PLATE CCLV.

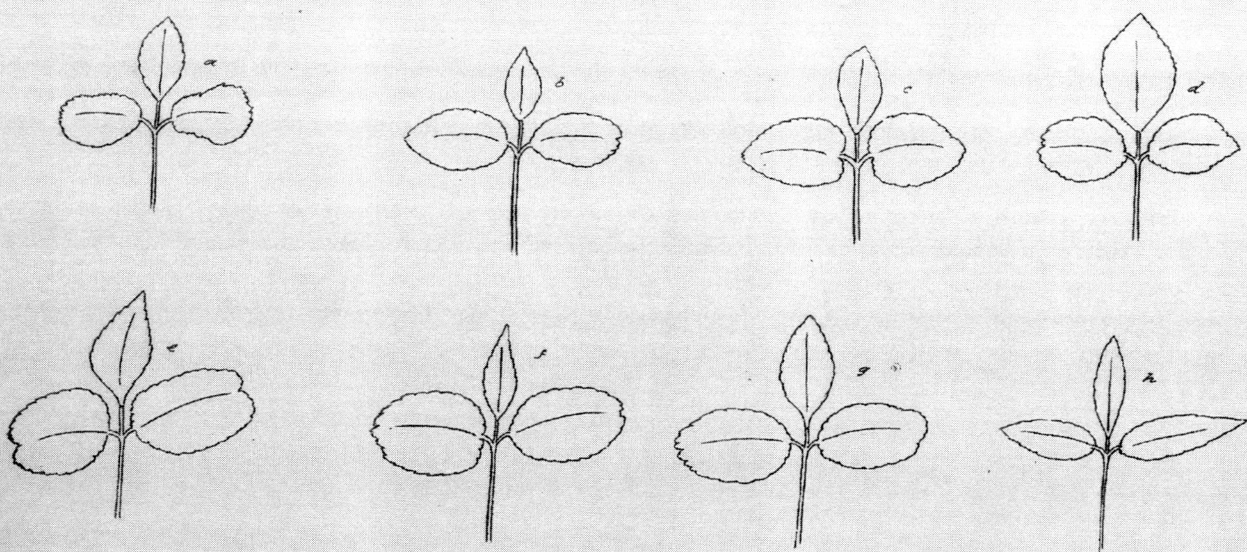

PLATE CCLVI.

This, and the following, represent some of the varieties of citrus in the Khasia Hills mentioned in Mr. G. Stevenson's letter (*vide* Appendix No. 43 *a*). These outlines are taken from coloured sketches made by Rai Jagesh Chandra Chatterjee Bahadur, subdivisional officer of Sumamgunj, and courteously forwarded by Mr. Stevenson, Deputy Commissioner of Sylhet.

a is called *Moglai* in Bengali. It has the shape and colour of the *Suntara* orange varieties.

In Khàsi, its name is *Usoh Myngor*. The *Kamalà* proper differs little from this. Mr. Stevenson says the *Moglai* has a thicker skin than the *Kamalà*.

b in the drawing is only called *orange*. It is probably the *common* orange—the *Kamalà* proper—of the Bengalis, and the *Usoh Santra*, or *Niamtra*, of the Khàsis.

PLATE CCLVI.

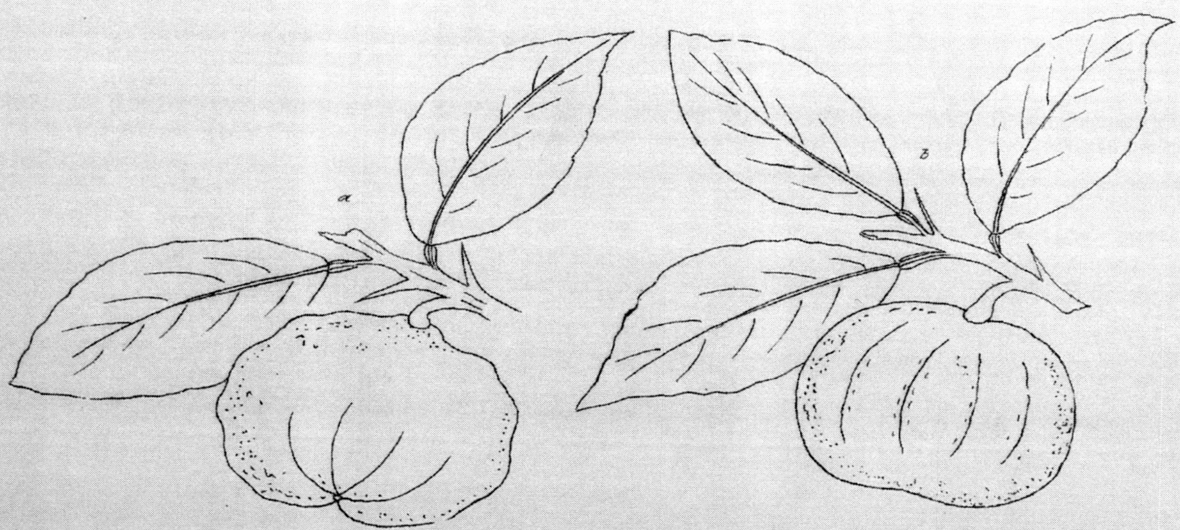

PLATE CCLVII.

a is the *Naràngi* of the Bengalis. It is coloured much redder than the foregoing, and Mr. Stevenson, in Appendix 43 (*a*), says the *Naràngi* is *sour*. Probably it corresponds to the *Keonla* of the plains.

If the *Narangi* be sour, it is not clear why its Khâsi name should be *Usoh Sim*, meaning the "Raja orange." Possibly it is only sour when *unripe*. The *Naringhi* of Upper India, although I think it of the *Keonla* type, is probably a *sweeter* variety, or one that sweetens earlier than the *Keonla* proper.

b is given as *Jhagi* in the drawing. This name is not in Mr. Stevenson's list, unless it be the one called there *Kàki*. In his list, it is said to be *sour*. Its colour is deep yellow, and may be some kind of lemon, if not the *Jhambiri* of the plains. In the drawing it looks much *chagrined*.

PLATE CCLVII.

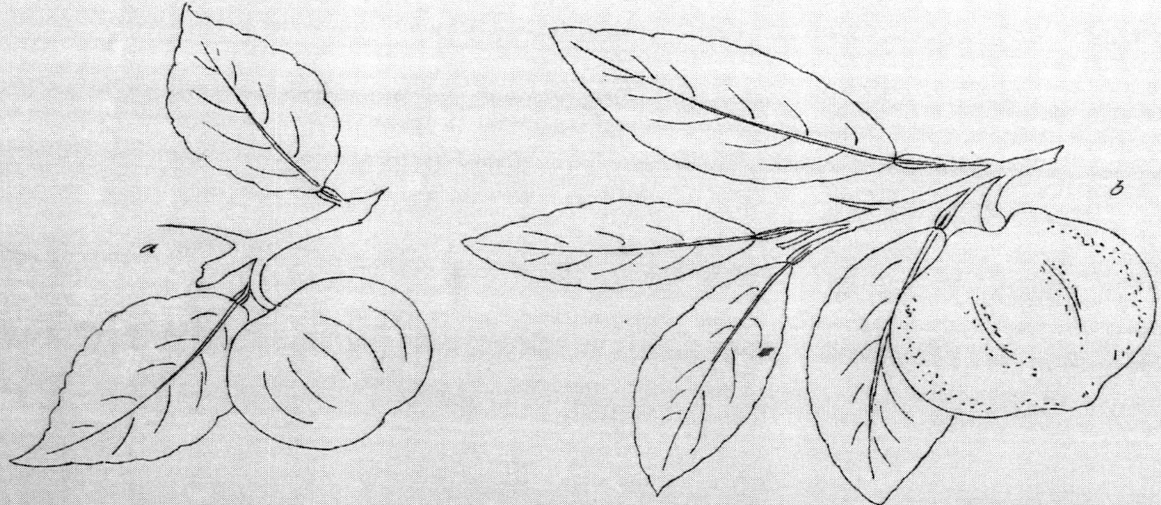

PLATE CCLVIII.

a is pictured as green, and called *Khata jamir*, the Khâsi name would be *Usoh kymphor*, and is said to be sour. It was probably taken from an unripe specimen, and its name points to its being a variety of the *Jamiri*. It is pictured as warty and much chagrined.

b is called *Satkara* and its Khâsi name is given in the list as *Usoh kuid* or *kuhit*. It is sour and eaten unripe, cooked, and used as a "chutny." It is probably one of the *Amilbêds*. It is pictured as rather warty, and chagrined, and of a lemon colour. Its leaf corresponds with the *Amilbéd* leaf.

PLATE CCLVIII.

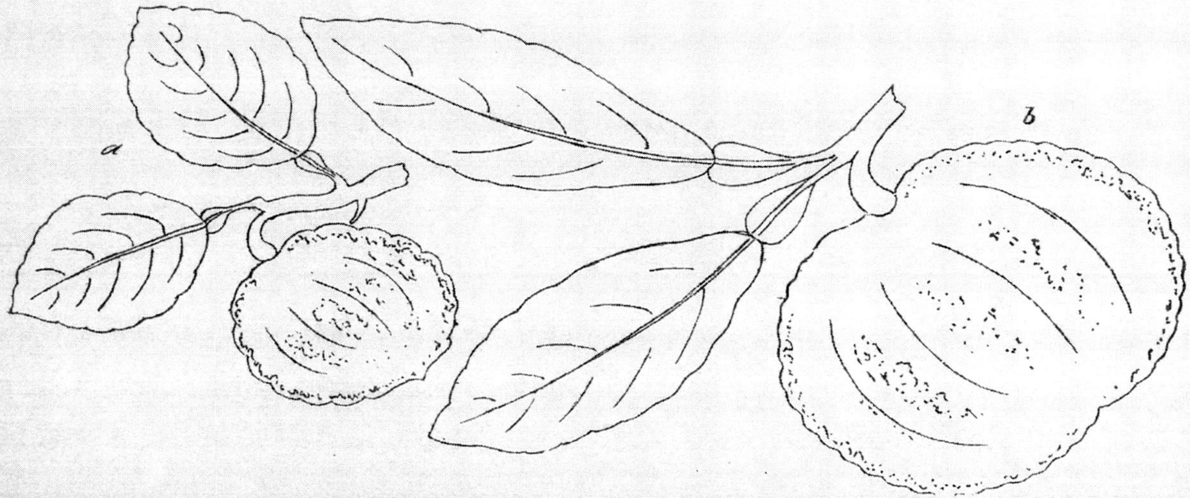

PLATE CCLIX.

These figures are taken from the monograph on the Citrus of Risso and Poiteau.

a and *b* are there called "Bigaradier bicolor." It was yellow, with green stripes, when unripe, and yellow with orange stripes, when ripe.

c and *d* are called "Bigaradier bizarrerie." The smooth parts were of an orange colour, and the warty parts of a yellow colour. They appeared a mixture of an orange and a citron in one fruit.

A seedling is also mentioned, which, on the same tree, had both *white* flowers and others *tinged purple*. Mention is also made of similar mixtures between the apple and the pear.

NOTE.—The whole subject of the hybridization of the different varieties, or species, of citrus requires to be carefully gone over by direct experiment, not only to determine certain purely scientific points, but to see whether new and useful varieties might be obtained by crossing.

N.B.—These are like the so-called *Trifacial* oranges of other writers.

PLATE CCLIX.

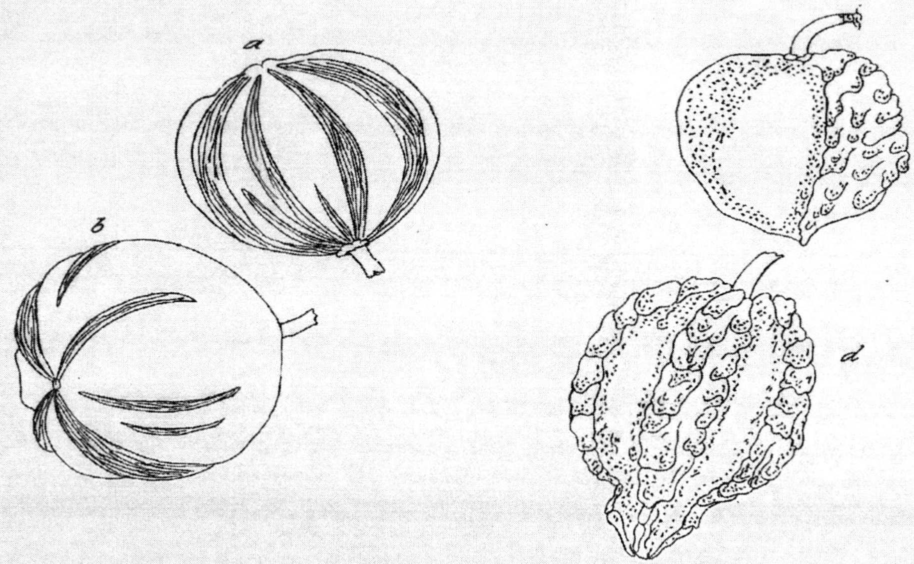